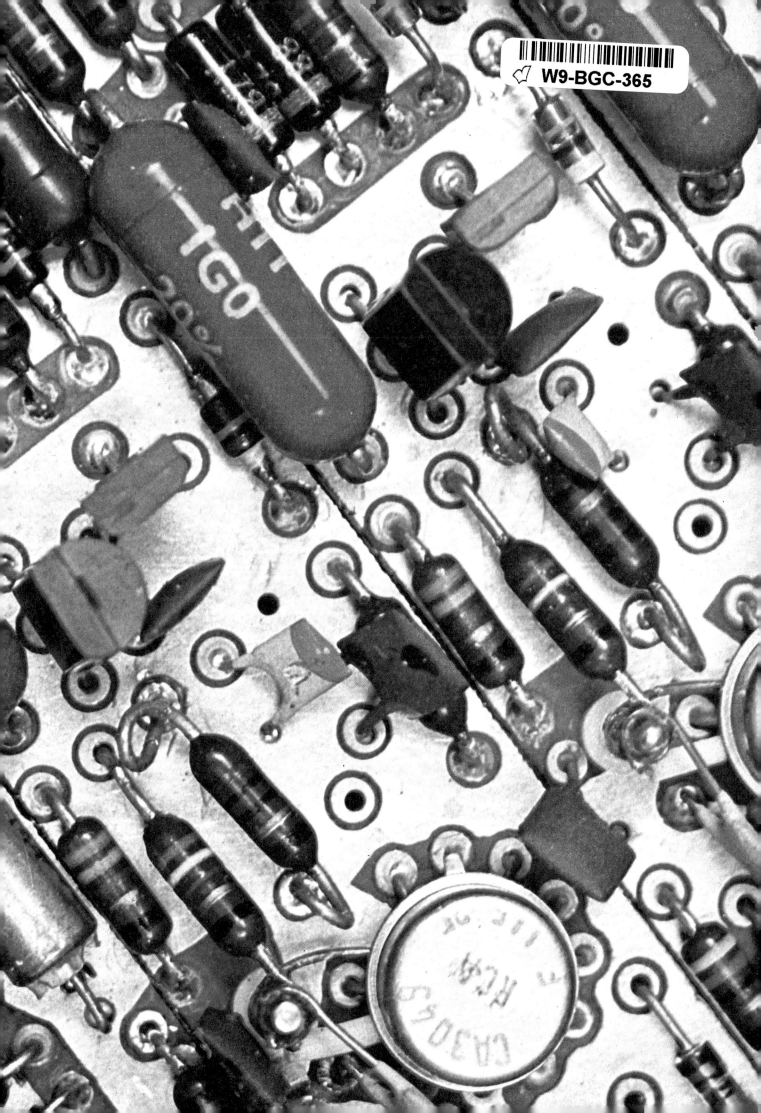

THE MIND ALIVE ENCYCLOPEDIA
TECHNOLOGY

THE MIND ALIVE ENCYCLOPEDIA
TECHNOLOGY

Marshall Cavendish London & New York

Published by Marshall Cavendish Books Limited
58 Old Compton Street, London W1V 5PA

© Marshall Cavendish Limited 1968, 1969, 1970, 1977

Printed in Great Britain by Severn Valley Press

ISBN 0 85685 299 6

This material has previously appeared in the
partwork *Mind Alive*.

Pages 2 and 3: The four-strand method of
production of continuous steel casting. This
picture was taken at Sheerness Steel Co. Ltd.
Pages 4 and 5: A typical modern 'spaghetti
junction'. This one is the Gravelly Hill
motorway interchange near Birmingham,
England. It demonstrates the association of
road building in concrete with the growth of
motor transport.
Page 6: A cross-section of a Royal Navy fleet
submarine hunter/killer. The role of this type
of boat is to seek out and destroy other
submarines and surface vessels.

Introduction

'Give me a proper fulcrum,' said an ancient scientist, 'and I will move the Earth.' There is no proper fulcrum in outer space, fortunately, or some fool would try to move the Earth, but there are not many ways we do not think of to use our technology. No sphere of human endeavour, from housework to agriculture, is untouched by applied science. In our bewildering century, some traditional areas of human interest, such as religion, are changing in character or disappearing from our daily lives. Hence insecurity: when most people lived lives which were brutish and short, most of them were content to do so, for they had not been led to expect anything else.

'How can we have any new scientific ideas or attitudes,' someone has asked, 'when 90% of all the scientists who have ever lived are still alive?' We cannot blame our scientists for the accidental explosion of technology which has taken place in the last hundred years; they were no more prepared for it than the rest of us. We can, however, try to understand the effects of science on our daily lives, and get used to the impact of it, in preparation for learning how to control it.

This book examines and explains farming, sports, housework, communications, road building—in short, virtually every area in which the human race has always been active—in terms of how it is changed by applied science. The text has been prepared by acknowledged experts in each field; the pictures and diagrams complete the revealing and stimulating effect of practical knowledge.

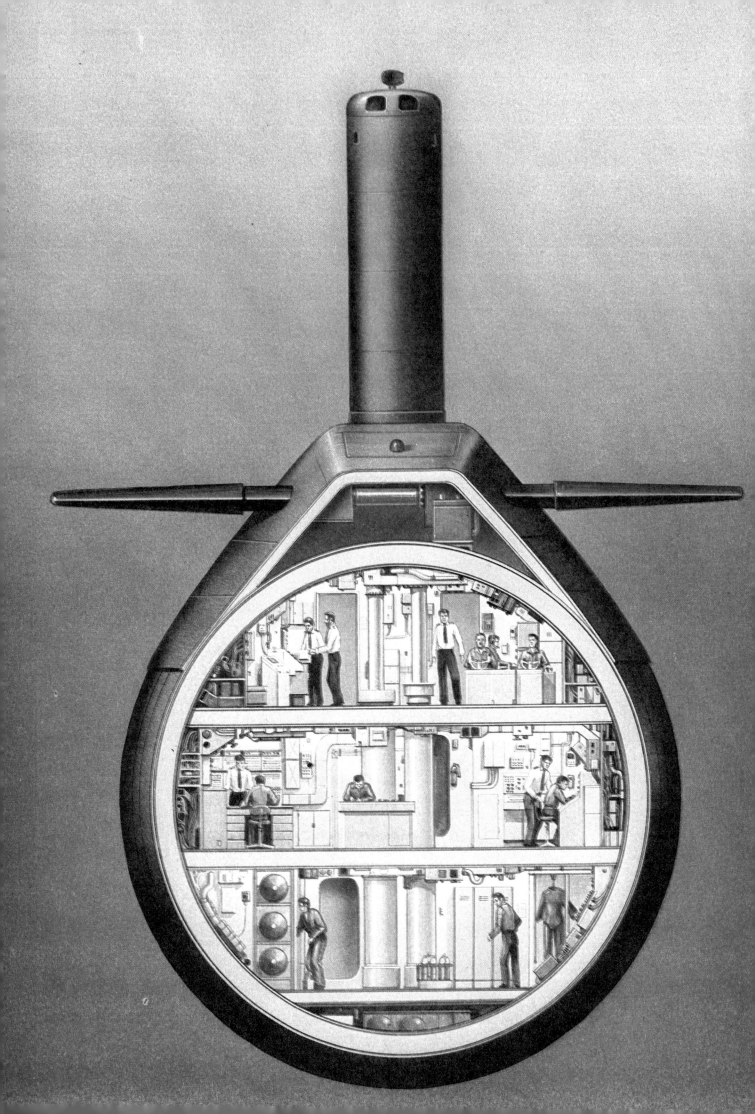

Contents

Picture Credits

Putting electrons to work

Is it possible to harness an unseen power? This article explains how electric motors, heaters, lamps and radio valves are designed to exploit typical effects of an electric current.

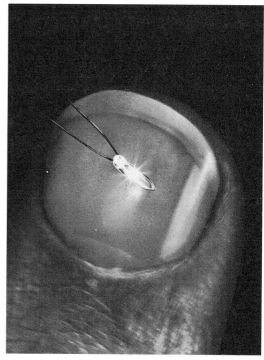

IN 1820, the Danish physicist Hans Christian Oersted discovered that an electric current flowing in a wire has associated with it a magnetic field. A pivoted magnetic needle placed near a straight wire is deflected when a current flows in the wire. If the wire is wound into a coil, each turn of wire contributes to a strong magnetic field at the centre of the coil.

This principle is used in the galvanometer, in which a magnetic needle is pivoted at the centre of a coil. Any current flowing in the wires of the coil produces a field which deflects the magnet, and the instrument may be used as a sensitive way of detecting even tiny electric currents.

If a piece of magnetic metal, such as soft iron, is placed inside a cylindrical coil of wire (called a solenoid), the magnetic field due to a current flowing in the coil magnetizes the metal. The metal behaves as a magnet as long as the current is flowing. The first electromagnets were made by an English physician, William Sturgeon (1783–1850). He bent a piece of iron into the shape of a horseshoe, insulated it, and wound a coil of copper wire round it. Such a magnet 12 inches long would lift a weight of 10 lb.

Meanwhile, in the United States, Joseph Henry (1797–1878) was also making electromagnets. He used straight pieces of iron and insulated the copper wire with strips of cotton or silk so that each magnet could have many turns of wire on top of each other. In 1832, Henry made an electromagnet weighing 60 lb that could lift a weight of nearly a ton.

The compass points south as an electric current in the wire above it deflects the needle. Michael Faraday, an English scientist, reasoned that there

But the most important applications of Oersted's discovery of electromagnetism were made by the English scientist Michael Faraday (1791–1867), who found the relation between electromagnetism and mechanical rotation, which led to the invention of the electric motor and the dynamo. Faraday reasoned that if a magnetic needle is deflected by the field near a conductor, there must be a mechanical force acting on the needle. And, more important, he also reasoned that if a mechanical force is used to move a magnet near a wire, an electric current will be generated in the wire. In other words,

was a turning force acting on the magnet. His line of thought made possible today's complex electrical industries. *Right,* a miniature lamp.

Faraday discovered that an electric current can be used to cause rotation, and that rotation can be used to generate current.

In 1821, only a year after Oersted discovered electromagnetism, Faraday performed two crucial experiments. In the first he arranged a magnet vertically in a dish of mercury with the magnet sticking through the surface. A piece of straight wire, free to pivot at its upper end, was hung with its lower end just dipping into the mercury. When Faraday applied the voltage from a cell between the wire and the mercury in the dish, the wire moved in

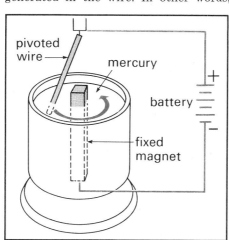

Faraday's discovery that electromagnetism could create a rotating movement led to the development of electric motors. *Above,* two forms of his

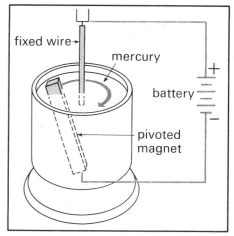

experiment. *Left,* a pivoted wire rotates around a fixed magnet. *Right,* a pivoted magnet rotates around a fixed wire carrying a current in mercury.

a circle around the magnet. That is, Faraday had made an electric current produce rotation of the wire carrying the current.

In the other experiment, Faraday arranged that the magnet was free to pivot at its lower end. The wire, dipping into the surface of the mercury, was fixed. This time, when current passed, the magnet rotated around the wire; Faraday had made an electric current produce rotation of a magnet in the field associated with the current.

Each of these devices was a crude form of electric motor. Several inventors used these principles to make motors. Some had magnets rotating in electric fields, but the best results were obtained with arrangements in which wires rotated in magnetic fields.

Electric motors and dynamos

The principle of the electric motor as it finally evolved can be understood by considering a coil of wire carrying a current and free to rotate between the poles of a magnet. As the current is switched on, the coil will rotate through half a turn and stop. But if the direction of the current in the coil is then reversed, it will rotate through a further half a turn before stopping again. If the direction of the current is again changed, the coil will move again. And so if the coil is provided with an arrangement that reverses the direction of the current every half a turn, the coil will rotate continuously.

The arrangement for automatically reversing the direction of current in the coil is called a commutator. If the coil consists of a single turn of wire, the commutator has two segments of metal on the same shaft as the coil. The segments are insulated from each other; one is connected to one end of the coil and the other segment is connected to the other end of the coil. Current is passed from a battery to the metal segments and hence to the coil through two pieces of carbon, called *brushes*. Every time the coil moves through half a turn, the direction of the current in it is automatically reversed. Large electric motors have many coils wound on the same former, and the ends of each coil are connected to a pair of segments on a multi-segment commutator.

The principle of the dynamo is exactly opposite to that of the electric motor. If the coil in the motor just described is rotated by hand, an electric current is generated in the coil. In this way, the power from any rotating machine, such as a water-wheel, a wind-driven wheel, a steam engine, a petrol engine or a turbine, can be used to turn a dynamo and generate electricity. The same machine can act as a motor or a dynamo, depending on whether it is supplied with current or with mechanical power. For example, in electric locomotives current is supplied to turn the motors which drive the wheels. But when the driver wants to stop the locomotive he switches off the current; the forward motion of the locomotive as it slows down keeps the coils in the motors turning; they act as dynamos and generate

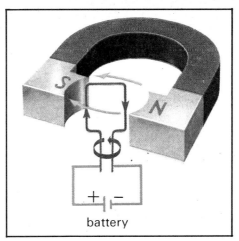
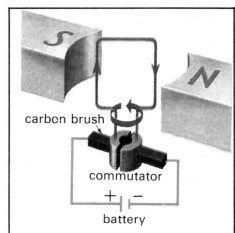
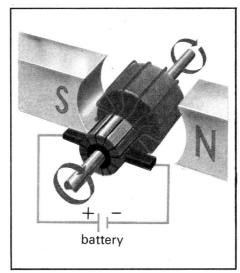
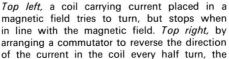

Top left, a coil carrying current placed in a magnetic field tries to turn, but stops when in line with the magnetic field. *Top right,* by arranging a commutator to reverse the direction of the current in the coil every half turn, the

coil will turn continuously. *Above left,* most electric motors have many sets of coils, each connected to a pair of segments on the commutator. *Above right,* in a dynamo, mechanical power turns the coils to generate electricity.

electricity.

The principle of the dynamo was discovered by Faraday in 1831. At first he generated short pulses of current by moving a magnet in and out of a coil. Many early dynamos made use of this idea, with moving magnets and stationary coils. Faraday also generated electricity by moving a coil in a strong magnetic field, and this is the method used in most modern dynamos which have moving coils and stationary magnets.

We now know that when an electric current flows in a metal, it is the electrons from atoms of the metal which actually carry the electricity. The movement of the electrons is accompanied by a rise in temperature of the metal. The amount of heat produced depends on the current flowing and the electrical resistance of the metal (heat equals the product of the resistance and the square of the current).

There are many practical applications of the heating effect of an electric current. Metals with a high melting-point and a high resistance, such as alloys of nickel and chromium, can be used to make the heating elements of electric fires and irons. The heat generated by the passage of the current can make these metals glow red-hot. A metal of very high melting-point, such as tungsten, can be made to glow white-hot and become *incandescent*. This

is the principle of the electric-light bulb, in which a tungsten filament is surrounded by an inert gas to prevent its oxidizing.

The first commercially successful incandescent lamp was made by the American inventor Thomas Edison (1847–1931) in 1879. His early lamps had carbon filaments, made from charred thread or paper, surrounded by a vacuum. At about the same time, Joseph Swan (1828–1914) in England also made incandescent lamps with carbon filaments, produced by charring threads of cellulose. There was for a long time a controversy about which of these men, Edison or Swan, was the first to invent the electric lamp. Their differences were settled when the two inventors combined their interests in one firm, the Edison and Swan Electric Light Company.

Fuses and arc lamps

In some applications, we make use of the heating effect of an electric current on metals of low melting-point. Most electric fuses contain a fine strand of copper wire. The wire will pass only a limited amount of current, say 5 amps. If this current is exceeded, the copper wire gets so hot it melts and the electric circuit containing it is broken. Fuses with wires that will melt at known values of current are used to protect electric circuits and appliances from overloading.

The life force of urban civilization, electric current supplies conductor rails beneath the London tube train, *top left,* and overhead wires for the British Rail locomotive at Manchester, *centre left.* In London's Piccadilly Circus, *above,* as in city centres the world over, the lights of advertising gain their characteristic glow from traces of gas left between electrodes in a tube. *Left,* the windings of a huge stator in a turbine-generator undergo inspection in Ireland.

If electricity at a sufficiently high voltage is forced through a poor conductor, the conductor will get very hot indeed. For example, a high voltage applied across a pair of carbon rods a fraction of an inch apart produces an *arc* between the rods. An arc is a continuous spark produced when air, which is a poor conductor, is forced to conduct electricity. This principle is used in arc lamps, such as those used in cinema projectors and theatre spot-lights. On a much larger scale, the same principle is used in electric arc furnaces in which the tremendous heat produced will melt iron for steelmaking or melt rock for extracting phosphorus.

If a pair of wires or plates connected to a high-voltage source of electricity are fused into a glass bulb from which most of the air has been removed, an electric current will flow between the plates (or electrodes). The electrode connected to the source of negative electricity is called the *cathode,* and the positive plate is the *anode.* An elongated bulb, with a cathode at one end and an anode at the other, is called a cathode-ray tube. When electricity is passing between the electrodes

11

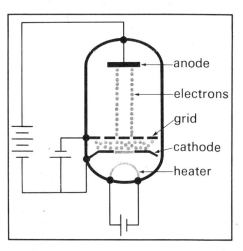

Diagram of a modern indirectly heated thermionic triode valve, *above*, shows the heater inside the cylindrical cathode. *Left*, a valve used in 1915. *Centre*, a contemporary design.

the tube may light up, the colour of the light depending on traces of gas left in the tube. For example, traces of neon gas give an orange-red light which is used in neon advertising signs. Traces of sodium in discharge tubes, as these glass tubes are called, give the characteristic yellow light that is commonly used for street lighting.

The electric current is carried along a cathode-ray tube by invisible cathode rays. In 1897, the English physicist J. J. Thomson showed that cathode rays consist of electrons. In other words, electrons move completely out of the atoms in the metal of the cathode, cross the space between the electrodes (carrying with them the electric current) and enter the atoms in the metal of the anode. The passage of the stream of electrons from cathode to anode is accompanied by a complementary passage of positive ions from anode to cathode. In the discharge tubes we described, these ions are neon ions or sodium ions.

Radio valves

Cathode-ray tubes require high voltages and pass only tiny currents. But if the metal of the cathode is heated, electrons escape from its atoms more easily; much lower voltages may be used and higher currents passed. The generation of electrons from a heated cathode is called *thermionic emission,* and it finds important application in radio valves. The number of electrons emitted depends on the material of the cathode and its temperature. Tungsten is one of the best emitters, but it needs a temperature of nearly 2,000 °C. A mixture of barium oxide and strontium oxide will emit well at about half this temperature.

The cathodes of thermionic valves may be heated in one of two ways: directly or indirectly. A directly heated cathode generally takes the form of a loop of thin tungsten wire. The cathode current passing through the loop heats it (in much the same way as an electric-fire element is heated), and clouds of electrons are emitted. An indirectly heated cathode has a separate tungsten wire filament, with its own current supply, which heats the cathode material. This is the method

which must be used when the emitter is a non-conductor of electricity, such as a mixture of strontium and barium oxides. The oxides are coated on to a metal cylinder which is connected to the source of negative electricity and heated by a filament mounted inside the cylinder. The first thermionic valve, made by Sir John Ambrose Fleming in 1904, had a directly heated cathode. It resembled an electric lamp with the filament as the cathode, and an extra plate (the anode) fused into the glass. Most modern valves have indirectly heated cathodes.

The simplest form of thermionic valve is the diode, which has only two electrodes (cathode and anode). The cathode is heated, to give thermionic emission, and the anode remains cold. When the cathode is connected to a source of negative electricity and the anode is connected to a positive source, electrons pour out of

Sir Charles Wheatstone (1802–75), English physicist and inventor, designed the 'self-exciting dynamo', *below*, to generate electricity.

the heated cathode and pass into the anode in much the same way as do the electrons in a cathode-ray tube. The diode passes electric current just like a conductor such as a piece of wire.

But if the polarities of the two electrodes in a diode are changed – that is, the cathode is connected to positive and the anode to negative – current ceases to flow through the valve. A diode will not conduct in the opposite sense because the cold anode will not emit electrons. In other words, a diode valve has the property of conducting electricity in one direction only. Most of the practical uses which have been evolved for diodes depend on this 'one-way switch' action.

Anodes and triodes

As we have just seen, a diode is like a switch: it is either 'off' or 'on', More subtle control of the electric current flowing through a valve can be obtained by introducing a third electrode between the cathode and the anode. This electrode has holes in it through which electrons can pass to the anode and is for this reason called a *grid*. Such a three-electrode valve is called a triode. If the grid of a triode is made negative with respect to the anode (though not as negative as the cathode), it will repel some of the electrons trying to pass through it. By varying the negative voltage on the grid, we can control the current passed by a triode. For this reason, the third electrode in a triode valve is also called the *control* grid.

If the voltage between the grid and the cathode varies, the current from the anode will vary in step with it. But quite small variations in the grid voltage can produce large changes in the anode current. In this way, a triode may be used to amplify small signals. And by feeding the output from the anode of one triode into the grid of another, two *stages* of amplification are achieved. In practice, circuits in radio sets and television receivers use several stages of amplification. The triode valve was invented by an American, sometimes called 'the father of radio', Lee de Forest, in 1907, who made possible its use in radio detectors, radio and telephone amplifiers, and as an oscillator.

Conductors and transistors

At temperatures near absolute zero the electrical resistance of certain metals and alloys becomes vanishingly small. In certain other substances, however, it decreases as temperature *rises*.

HIGH-SPEED ELECTRIC LOCOMOTIVES pick up their electricity from a third rail, called a conductor-rail, or from overhead wire conductors. Electricity is distributed over the country by high-level wires strung between pylons of the National Grid. And in homes, wires from the electric meter carry the supply into every room and to every appliance. The whole of the electrical industry and all applications of electricity employ metal conductors to carry current. In this article, we will look at various types of conductors and explain how they work. We shall also discuss semiconductors – substances that gave birth to transistors and all the complex electronic apparatus which employs them.

An electric current is a stream of electrons flowing in a conductor. A conductor, therefore, is any material which has a supply of 'free' electrons available to make up the current. In practice, metals are the only substances which have a plentiful supply of electrons, and most metals are good conductors. Other materials, such as wood, paper, rubber, plastics and glass, have no 'free' electrons and these materials are therefore used as electrical insulators.

Like birds in a forest

To understand why some materials have conduction electrons and some have not, and why some metals are better conductors than others, we need to know something of the structure of metals. Metals are composed of atoms, as are all other materials. And the atoms are made up of even smaller particles, such as nuclei and electrons. The atoms of a metal are held in a regular array called a *lattice*, just like the atoms in a crystal. But one or more of the electrons in each atom is less firmly bound than the others and, in an electric field, makes itself available for conduction. Remember that atoms are made up largely of empty space, and electrons are the smallest known particles. So that, although the atoms of a metal are fixed in the lattice, the electrons can easily move between them in much the same way as a bird easily flies between the trees in a forest.

Not all electrons in a metal are bound to the atoms to the same extent. The energy of an electron is a measure of how firmly it is bound to the atom. A high-energy electron can be persuaded fairly easily to leave the atom entirely. For example, heat energy supplied to the atoms of some metals in a vacuum will give them enough additional energy to 'boil' off from the surface of the metal and give rise to the phenomenon called thermionic emission.

The range of energies possessed by

Transistors the size of pencil stubs do the work of much larger valves in controlling or amplifying electric currents. But the circuit being planned above will be reproduced in even more miniature form as an 'integrated circuit' in a silicon chip less than two millimetres square.

electrons is not continuous, but consists of definite separate energy 'levels' (this is one consequence of the quantum theory of matter). For this reason, the electrons may be thought of as existing in separate energy *bands,* and two conditions are necessary for an electron to move from one band to another nearby higher band and be available for conduction. Firstly, it must be supplied with the required extra energy, which may come from light radiation, heat or electricity. And secondly, there must be room for the electron in the higher band – that is, the higher band must already be partly

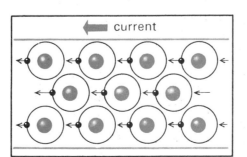

An electric current is made up of electrons on the move. Metals make good conductors because they have a plentiful supply of 'free' electrons available to move along the lattice of atoms.

empty. If the higher band is full, as it is in all materials that are electrical insulators, supplying extra energy will not promote an electron to a higher band and the material will be incapable of conducting electricity. Of course, if really enormous amounts of extra energy are applied, electrons may be forced to jump all the way into the completely empty band and made available for conduction. This is what happens at extremely high voltages and an insulator 'breaks down'.

It is interesting to notice in passing that materials which are good conductors of electricity are also good conductors of heat. On the other hand, materials which are good electrical insulators are also good thermal insulators. These facts are not surprising if we assume that a material conducts heat by means of its free electrons. Thus a metal, such as copper, conducts heat well and for the same reason that it conducts electricity. But a material such as sulphur or glass, in which all the energy bands are full, and which has no free electrons, is a bad conductor of heat and of electricity.

In all solids, the atoms are rapidly vibrating due to their thermal (heat) energy. As a metal is heated, although at first more electrons are made available for conduction, the atoms also begin to vibrate more. If we return to our analogy comparing a conducting electron moving between atoms in a metal lattice with a bird flying between trees, it is as if a high wind springs up and starts blowing the trees around. There will come a point at which the trees (atoms) are vibrating so much that the birds (electrons) begin to find it more difficult to get through the gaps. But now consider the opposite situation in which the metal is cooled down. The atoms will vibrate less and less until, at extremely low temperatures approaching absolute zero (temperatures of between about −260 and −272 °C.), the atoms will hardly vibrate at all. Under these conditions, some metals become extremely good conductors indeed and are called *superconductors*.

The temperature at which a metal becomes superconducting varies with the strength of the magnetic field in which it is placed; the stronger the magnetic field, the more the metal must be cooled before it becomes a superconductor. This fact is used in making memory elements for digital computers. Such elements, consisting of tiny coils of superconducting wire immersed in liquid helium, occupy very little space. This system has the advantage that a great number of digits can be stored in such memories and yet occupy only a small volume.

Semiconductors

One of the most useful developments of recent years, and one which incidentally helps to justify the band theory of electronic conduction, has been the discovery and exploitation of semiconductors. Some materials, such as silicon and germanium, have a band structure similar to that of an insulator with one band completely full of electrons and the next band completely empty. But the presence of small amounts of an impurity makes these basically insulating materials into good conductors, which are called *impurity semiconductors*.

There are two types of impurity semiconductors, characterized by the kind of impurity and the mechanism by which their band structure is changed into that of a conductor. Consider the element germanium. When absolutely pure, it has a completely full conduction band and so behaves as an insulator. Germanium has a chemical *valence* of four – that is, each atom has four electrons available for forming chemical bonds with other elements. For this reason, the full conduction band of germanium contains four electrons. Now imagine the effect of adding to the germanium a few 'foreign' atoms (an impurity) which each have five electrons. For example, we could add a small amount of the element arsenic, which has five valence electrons. Four of the arsenic electrons take the place of four of the germanium electrons in the conduction band. But the fifth electron cannot be accommodated (because the band is full) and must go into the next empty band. The band structure of the germanium is now changed into that typical of a conductor, with a partly filled

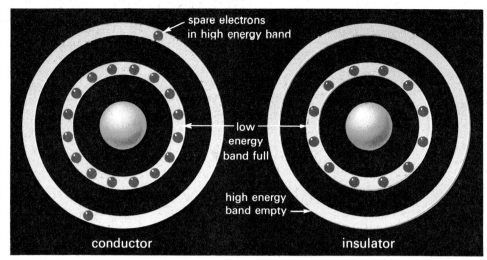

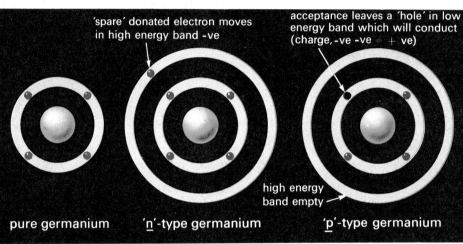

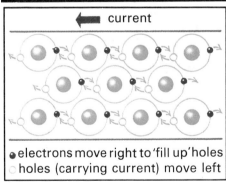

Top, in insulators, electrons completely fill the low energy bands. Conductors carry 'spares' which must move in higher energy bands. *Centre*, pure germanium insulates (it has no 'spares'). Impurities give it 'spares' or 'holes' which will conduct. *Right*, rectifiers use this principle and allow one-way flow of current only. *Above*, as on a pegboard, electrons and holes interchange.

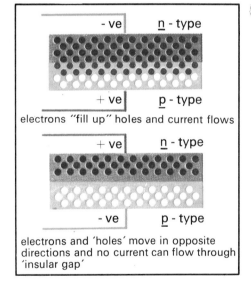

band containing electrons that are available for carrying electric current.

The arsenic in this example is called a *donor*, because it gives or donates its extra electron to the conduction band, and the semiconductor formed is called donor or *n-type* (*n* stands for negative, the charge on the donated electron). Other five-valent donor atoms include phosphorus and antimony. They may be added to silicon or germanium, giving technologists a choice of several combinations of elements for making *n*-type semiconductors.

The second type of impurity semiconductor is a little more difficult to explain. In this case, the impurity is an element with only three valence electrons (such

as boron, aluminium, gallium or indium). When an atom of, say, aluminium takes the place of an atom of germanium, it contributes only three electrons to the conduction band instead of the four formerly supplied by the germanium atom. As a result, there is a deficiency of electrons, which physicists call *holes*. A hole is an absence of an electron and, because it is mathematically a minus negative charge, can be considered as a positive charge. For this reason, semiconductors with trivalent impurity atoms are called *p*-type. The impurity is called an *acceptor* because it takes or accepts one of the germanium electrons to leave a hole in the lattice.

But how do *p*-type semiconductors con-

duct electricity? They do so by what amounts to a movement of the holes through the lattice in much the same way as electrons move through the lattice of normal conductors. One way of picturing how such a hole can move is to imagine a regular array of holes in a board, all but one of which are occupied by pegs. If we move one of the pegs next to the hole (say on the right of it) into it, the original hole will be filled and a new one left. If we move the peg on the right of the new hole into it, another new hole will appear one step further to the right. By continuing this process, moving pegs (which represent electrons) only one space at a time, the hole can be made to move across the board. In a similar way, electrons in the lattice of a *p*-type semiconductor move into the holes in one direction, causing the holes to move through the lattice in the other direction. While the conduction of electricity is still a movement of electrons, it is convenient to consider conduction in this case as being movement of the holes.

Very little of an impurity is required to change the conducting properties of silicon or germanium. One of the reasons why semiconductors have been developed only fairly recently (semiconductor action was first discovered about 30 years ago) is that techniques for producing the extremely pure materials required are themselves only recent developments. A typical impurity concentration is one part of arsenic in 10,000,000 parts of germanium.

It is interesting to note that germanium and silicon have chemical properties in between those of metals and non-metals. For this reason, some chemists call such elements *metalloids*. With a knowledge of how semiconductors work, chemists have produced compounds which behave in the same way as do silicon and germanium. By taking a three-valent element (gallium or indium) and alloying it with exactly the correct amount of a five-valent element (arsenic or antimony), they have made compounds such as gallium arsenide and indium antimonide.

The rectifier

For example, in gallium arsenide, the gallium contributes three electrons to the conduction band and arsenic contributes five. The total contribution from both atoms, eight electrons, is exactly the same as that from two atoms of germanium. But since gallium or arsenic can also be used as the impurity atoms, a slight excess of gallium makes gallium arsenide into a *p*-type semiconductor and a slight excess of arsenic makes it into an *n*-type semiconductor.

One of the earliest applications of semiconductors was in making a *rectifier*, a device that allows electric current to pass in one direction only. In alternating current, the direction of current flow changes rapidly many times a second, flowing for a fraction of the time one way and for a fraction of the time the other way. In direct current, the direction of current flow remains always the same, from positive to negative. Batteries and accumulators produce direct current (d.c.). But generators in power stations, which supply the current for the mains electricity supply to homes and factories, produce alternating current (a.c.). Any electrical apparatus that requires d.c., such as parts of a radio or television set, a computer, or many electric locomotives, must have a rectifier if it is to work off an a.c. mains supply. The rectifier passes current flowing in one direction but blocks current flowing the opposite way, so converting a.c. into d.c.

One of the most compact modern types of rectifier has a sandwich consisting of a slice of *p*-type semiconductor next to a slice of *n*-type. This arrangement is called a *p-n junction*. At the join, some of the electrons from the *n*-type will diffuse into the *p*-type and some of the holes from the *p*-type will diffuse into the *n*-type. In the middle, electrons and holes will 'cancel out' each other. Now consider connecting a battery across the junction. If the *n*-type is connected to the negative terminal of the battery and the *p*-type is connected to the positive terminal, current will flow through the semiconductor sandwich. Current flows because the battery pumps more electrons into the *n*-type which combine with more holes from the *p*-type, the current crosses the junction and emerges from the *p*-type side of the sandwich.

The transistor

But if we connect the battery the other way round (*n*-type to the positive terminal, *p*-type to the negative), no current will flow. At the junction, the electrons and holes will move in opposite directions leaving a region containing neither electrons nor holes – that is, leaving the material as an insulator.

So that when an alternating current is applied across such a *p-n* junction, the semiconductor sandwich will allow current to flow across it in one direction only. For the fraction of the a.c. cycle when the *n*-type is made electrically negative, current flows. But for the part of the a.c. cycle when the *n*-type is made positive, the current is blocked. In this way, the *p-n* junction acts as a rectifier and converts a.c. to d.c.

Perhaps the most important outcome of research into semiconductors is the *transistor,* which was invented in 1949 by two American scientists, W. Shockley and J. Bardeen. A typical transistor consists of a three-layer sandwich with a slice of *p*-type semiconductor between two slices of *n*-type. Two *p-n* junctions are formed, and the arrangement is called a junction transistor. A transistor can be made to control or amplify electric currents in much the same way as can a triode

The ability of the electrical parts in a colour television tube to conduct heavy currents without failure is tested for up to 8,000 hours on this overhead conveyor. A process known as 'spot-knocking' removes sharp points where exceptional currents may 'flash-over' causing a short-circuit.

Although the miniature dimensions of transistors have made possible the complex electronic devices and computers that now serve Man, they also make more everyday aids both cheaper and easier to use. *Above,* a tiny transistorized hearing-aid contrasts with its much larger predecessor.

valve. A triode has three electrodes: a negatively charged cathode (which must be heated to cause thermionic emission of electrons from it), a grid on to which the control current is fed, and a positively charged anode. In the transistor, the *p*-type material corresponds to the triode grid, and the *n*-types correspond to the anode and cathode.

The transistor has two great advantages over the triode. Firstly, it requires extremely little electric power to operate it. This is an important consideration both in small applications, such as a portable radio set, and in large applications, such as a radar set or a computer. Formerly, portable radios had to have batteries to supply power to heat the cathodes of its valves (the actual current consumption of the rest of a radio circuit is extremely small). Such sets had to be large

enough to accommodate a battery power supply. A transistorized portable radio needs no power supply for heating, and will run for a long time on the current from a small battery which supplies the rest of the circuit. A large apparatus, such as a computer, may contain thousands of valves which consume many watts of power.

Secondly, transistors are many times smaller than valves. A modern triode is a cylinder one inch across and about two inches long. Several thousands of these in a computer would occupy a whole room. An average-sized transistor is no longer than quarter of an inch off the end of a pencil – some are as small as a grain of rice – and thousands of them can be fitted into the space occupied by a desk. In fact, without transistors, with their small size and modest power requirements, really large computers would not be possible.

Power in a pin's head

Electronics — based on a deep understanding of the structure of matter — enables us to make circuits no bigger than a pin's head and to derive power from components smaller than the eye can see.

OF ALL the technological advances of the twentieth century the development of electronics is perhaps the most important. Not only do devices employing electronic techniques play a large part in daily life, but fundamental scientific discoveries are involved in their operation.

Radio, television, electronic computers and automatically controlled equipment are possible only through an understanding of the basic structure of matter.

Nineteenth-century physicists had begun to examine a number of phenomena related to electricity and to see the connections between them. When a voltage was applied to electrodes at either end of a tube containing gas at low pressure, a glow was observed and an electric current passed along the tube.

In 1897, J. J. Thomson was led by his experiment to put forward the view that electrical charge was transferred by the movement of *electrons*. These were tiny particles, each charged with negative electricity, and, as Rutherford showed a little later, every atom of matter was made up of a central positively charged nucleus, with electrons revolving around it. It was the passage of electrons that constituted electric current, and caused the glow in the vacuum tube.

Electrons also were identified with the 'β-rays', found to be emitted from radioactive substances.

In 1883, in the course of his work on the electric lamp, Edison had noticed that

if an electrode was placed inside one of his vacuum bulbs an electric current passed across the vacuum from the hot filament. By 1904, understanding of the nature of electricity had developed to the point where Fleming could make use of this 'Edison effect' in making the first *thermionic valve*.

Electrons did not merely remain attached to the atom. In conduction they moved from atom to atom. Under certain conditions, they were detached altogether, as in radioactive emission. A high temperature, as in Edison's filament, allowed them to be pulled away more easily.

In Fleming's 'diode', negative electrical charge, in the form of a stream of electrons moved from the 'cathode', the hot filament, to the 'anode', a metal plate when this was at a positive potential in relation to the cathode but not otherwise. This was therefore a method of 'rectifying' an alternating current, allowing the current to flow in one direction only.

The application to the development of radio was clear. Electromagnetic radiation could be made to induce an alternating current in a radio aerial. In order to allow this current to move a telegraph

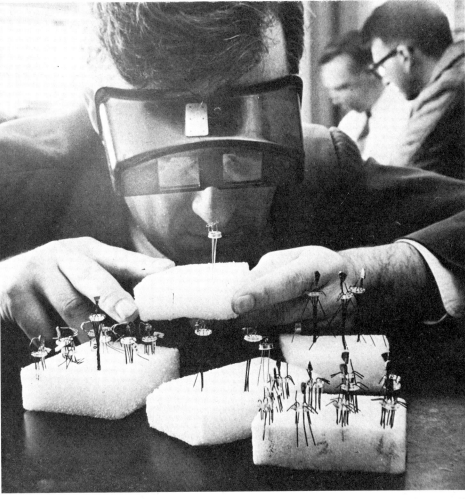

1 Automatic telephone exchanges, like this prototype undergoing tests before installation, rely heavily on electronic devices to overcome the limitations of manual and mechanical switches.
2 One of Sir Ambrose Fleming's experimental diodes. Fleming's invention, closely followed by De Forest's invention of the triode, paved the way for modern electronics.
3 An American research scientist tests different types of semi-conductors made of new heat-resistant materials. Electronics companies spend a great deal on research into new materials.

mechanism, it had to be rectified. This was already possible by means of a crystal touched by a fine wire. Owing to a peculiar property of certain crystals electrons could move out of the crystal, but not into it.

But the Fleming valve was a far more efficient rectifier than the 'cat's whisker'. Once the technique of manufacturing valves was improved, a huge industry was developed, as the radio set spread into the lives of millions of people. Filaments were made of tungsten or of barium or strontium oxide.

Another big advance was to take place in 1907. De Forest placed a metal grid between the filament and anode, producing the triode valve. A negative charge on this grid inhibited the flow of electrons to the anode. If a varying potential was applied to the grid, the degree of variation was magnified in its effect on the current flowing between the other electrodes. The triode valve was an amplifier as well as a rectifier.

By incorporating valves in circuits with resistances, electromagnetic coils, (inductances) and condensers (capacitors), devices were obtained which would resonate to oscillating currents of definite frequencies, amplify variation in their amplitudes and turn these variations into direct currents.

Later development of the valve introduced further grids, the most familiar form being the pentode, with three grids. These were usually arranged in concentric cylinders, with the cathode running along the central axis. Gas-filled tubes were also developed, in addition to the vacuum tube.

In the Fleming valve, a direct current had to be used to heat the filament. In order to run a radio set from alternating current mains valves were made in which the cathode was not itself the filament, but was heated by one, the heat being produced by alternating current.

Frequency modulation

Still more sophisticated circuits are used when the radio signal is conveyed, not by varying the amplitude of the carrier wave, but by modulating its frequency. Frequency modulation (FM) gives a far more accurate reproduction of the transmitted signal, and one less affected by 'noise'.

Since the 1950s, an entirely different type of method of constructing electronic circuits has displaced the valve. This employs the transfer resistor – for short, transistor. This uses the same principle as the cat's whisker of crystal-set days.

If certain crystalline substances have an electrical potential difference applied over a very small distance, electrons may be emitted from the crystal. This produces a semi-conductor, which will allow electricity to pass in one direction only.

Moreover, the volume of such a current is radically dependent on the potential at which the crystal is held. We thus have an analogy with the triode valve. High-frequency current will be rectified by the semi-conductor and variations in a base potential will be amplified.

Once the engineering problems of manufacturing such devices were solved, tran-

sistor circuits, far smaller, lighter and cheaper than the corresponding valve circuits, and needing less electrical power to operate, became possible.

The latest developments are integrated circuits, which are actually formed by 'growing' crystals in various chemical solutions. Tiny crystals may then embody

not only the transistors, but all the necessary connections between them.

Before the discovery of the electron, the emission in a vacuum tube from a hot filament was known as a 'cathode ray'. In a *cathode ray tube,* a beam of electrons is deflected by electrostatic or electromagnetic forces. By suitably coating one end of

1

2

the tube it is used as the anode and also made to glow at the point where the electrons hit it.

Varying the currents in electromagnetic coils deflecting the beam causes this spot to trace out corresponding shapes. The television receiver contains the most familiar form of this device, but it has many other applications in industry and in medicine, for example in radar and in electrocardiography.

We have not yet mentioned all the conditions under which electrons are emitted from matter. Television cameras are made possible by the *photo-electric effect*. When light hits certain conducting material, electrons are also thrown out.

In one of his three famous papers of 1905 (the others were on the so-called Brownian motion and on the theory of relativity) Einstein showed that whether an electron was emitted and, if so, its speed depended only on the *frequency* of the light ray, that is its colour, and not on its intensity. Only the *number* of emitted electrons varied with the intensity of light.

A television camera employs this principle by using a photo-electric cell. A ray of light is made to give rise to an electric current. This is amplified and modulates a radio wave.

In a television receiver, the signal is turned back into light on a cathode ray tube. But this is still a long way from transmitting a picture. For this, the scene must be scanned. At each instant, light is received by the photo-electric cell from one direction, one point of the scene.

This point moves across from left to right in a series of lines which cover the scene from top to bottom, as a typewriter does with letters.

At the receiver, the spot at the end of the tube is moved in a similar and synchronized manner. In this way, an entire picture is transmitted many times a second. In colour television, several such pictures must be reproduced at once, each corresponding to a different colour.

So far, we have mainly concentrated on the radio applications of electronics. In terms of the number of devices manufactured in the last 50 years, these are certainly the most important uses. But,

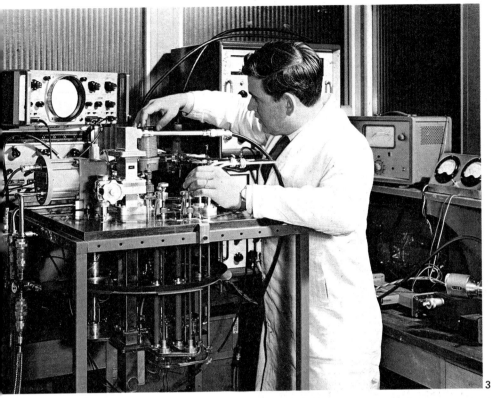

1 A special cold suit is required for testing this electronic tracking device for a space satellite. The temperature of the surface of the device is −454 °F.

2 Assembling an electron 'gun' at an electrical components factory. The 'gun' is used to provide a source of electrons for a number of electrical engineering applications.

3 An electronics development engineer tests a satellite component at a factory producing electronic devices. Stringent testing is essential for today's exacting requirements.

4 Automatic doors open as visitors to the building approach. These electronic devices are often just status symbols for large firms, but are useful in hospitals and homes for the handicapped.

5 An electron beam — the purple beam in the photograph — assists the welding of a metal work-piece in this experimental set-up in a United States aircraft company.

on the basis of the radio industry, electronics advanced in the 1920s and 1930s to a stage where other applications were possible, with still greater significance.

In transmitting messages, sounds and pictures by radio what is really happening is the transformation of information from one form to another, and the combination of different pieces of it. The variation in amplitude of a radio wave, corresponds to the kind of sound hitting the microphone in the transmitting studio. A radio receiver decodes it, transforming it back into sound.

Suppose numbers could be coded into electrical form. Could an electronic circuit be devised to combine numbers in accordance with mathematical rules? The electronic computer does just that.

Over a century ago, Charles Babbage constructed his Automatic Computing Engine. Driven by steam and clockwork, it performed addition and multiplication under instructions coded as holes in cards. The techniques then available made it impossible to take his ideas any further, and Babbage's 'engine' remained a curiosity. (It may be seen in London's Science Museum today.)

But by the Second World War, electronics made it possible to embody and develop the conceptions of Babbage. To carry out the calculations needed for the atomic bomb, John von Neumann had constructed a Mathematical Analyser, Integrator and Calculator, pronounced MANIAC.

This coded not only numbers but the 'programme' of instructions of what to do with them, in the form of electrical impulses. Since instructions were held in the same form as numbers, they could themselves be altered by other instructions, making the electronic computer a device of tremendous versatility and speed.

While they were first thought of as powerful calculators, or 'number crackers,' computers were soon seen to have wider application. Information could be sorted, analysed and combined which went beyond mere numerical data. The electronic office and the automatic factory had arrived on the scene.

In an industrial process, objects are moved from place to place, their shape changed by machining, for example, components assembled into more complex objects. Apart from the application of energy in machining, human beings are needed to decide where and when each mechanical operation should take place, correcting and halting machines when necessary.

Automatic decisions

Electronics, and in particular the computer, makes it possible for these decisions to be made automatically. For example, objects may have to be packed in boxes, 12 per box. An electronic counter, using a photo-electric cell to find out when an object passes by on the conveyor, can send a 'message' when the required number have arrived. Receiving the 'message', the packaging machine can move to the next stage of its work.

Entire plants can be run in an integrated way by such means. This is the way in which space vehicles are controlled, computers translating the requirements of the controller into the appropriate 'instructions' to the rocket apparatus.

It is in this field of automatic control, that electronics is already having its greatest effect on our lives. In the transformation of information the application of mechanical power is automatically directed.

More than one writer has asked the question, 'Can such machines take over'? After all, computers are already widely employed in the design and construction of other computers, more complex than themselves. Someone made the obvious reply to this question: 'We could always pull the plug out.'

To which a more pessimistic thinker retorted: 'Perhaps we shall find it already cemented to the wall.'

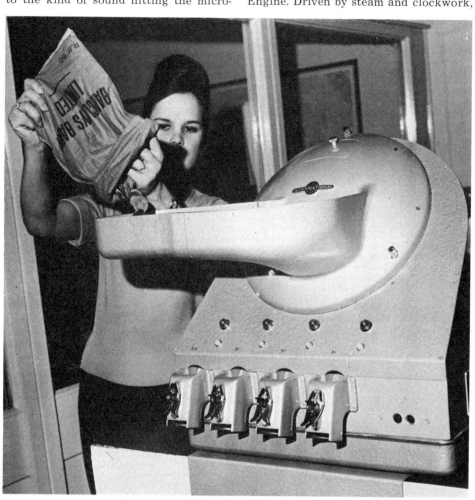

1

2

1 The bank clerk's job is greatly facilitated by this electronic coin counter, which sorts and counts miscellaneous British coinage at the Bank of England.

2 An accuracy of better than a thousandth of an inch can be obtained easily and quickly by reading off the thickness of this skin panel on an electronic thickness guage.

Open secrets in an X-ray's beam

A mysteriously fogged photographic plate was among Wilhelm Röntgen's first clues to the strange rays loose in his laboratory. Today, art, science and medicine use the name he gave them.

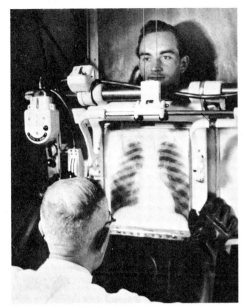  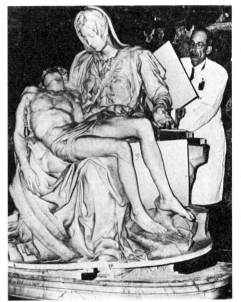

Left, perhaps the best known use of X-rays is viewing the interior of the human body. However, when X-rays were first announced, people feared their use for seeing through clothing as well. Hucksters made a fortune selling 'X-ray proof' undergarments. A lesser known use for X-rays, *right,* is checking important sculptures for tiny cracks and other dangerous flaws. The work shown here is Michelangelo's 'Pietà'. X-rays were discovered by the German physicist Wilhelm Röntgen, *centre,* in 1895. Some people still call them Röntgen rays in honour of his work.

MANY PEOPLE have at some time been X-rayed, either in hospital or at a mass X-ray unit. From X-ray pictures taken of a part of the body, doctors can detect and diagnose illness, examine bone structures, and even determine whether an unborn baby can be born naturally or requires a Caesarean birth.

But X-rays have many other important uses both in and out of medicine. For instance, hidden defects in metal structures can be detected by X-ray techniques, and the effects of crystal structures on X-rays is used to examine the forms of crystals and the arrangements of their atoms.

The discovery of X-rays in 1895 by the German physicist Wilhelm Röntgen was the result of investigations into quite different effects. Like many of his contemporaries, Röntgen was studying the newly observed cathode rays which were found to stream from the cathode of a low-pressure discharge tube when a high voltage was applied across its electrodes.

Cathode rays produce a bluish glow from the small amounts of gas or air left in the tube, and Röntgen had covered a tube with black paper to contain this light. He noticed, however, that a nearby zinc sulphide screen glowed or fluoresced when the voltage between the tube electrodes was about 10,000 volts. Also some of his photographic plates near the tube, although unexposed to light, became fogged during the experiments. Since both the tube and the plates were covered in black paper, light had certainly not caused this fogging. To trace the source of the effect, Röntgen set up near the tube a lead screen

(he had found that this prevented the new 'rays' from passing) with four holes in it. Behind the screen he put a photographic plate, and then adjusted the tube to the correct conditions.

When the photographic plate was developed, it had four spots where rays passing through the holes in the lead screen had fallen on to it. By replacing the plate in its original position and tracing lines back from the spots through the holes in the screen, Röntgen showed that the new rays came from the end of the discharge tube where the cathode rays fell. Cathode rays, when given sufficient energy by a high electric potential across the tube, had caused certain rays to be given off on striking a 'target'. Röntgen called the new rays X-rays. Today, cathode rays are known to be a stream of electrons, and, in general, any high-energy electron beam striking a metal target causes X-rays to be emitted.

Waves that could penetrate

X-rays were carefully studied to discover their nature. It was concluded that since they were unaffected by magnetic or electric fields (which a stream of charged particles such as electrons would be) and also travelled in straight lines, they must be similar in nature to light. By 1900, more evidence to support this idea had been found from diffraction patterns produced by X-rays. The form of the patterns suggested that if X-rays are waves like light, they have a much shorter wavelength. In 1912, the British physicist Sir William Henry Bragg succeeded in measuring the wavelengths of X-rays, using diffraction

patterns produced by crystals, and, as expected, the wavelengths were very short. In this way, the relationship between light and X-rays was confirmed, and X-rays were recognized as a form of electromagnetic waves, as are visible light, radio and infra-red waves.

Early X-ray tubes used cathode rays in a similar way to Röntgen's discharge tube. But they were unreliable because the low pressure in the tube was difficult to maintain at a constant level and the quality of the X-rays was unpredictable. When techniques for maintaining low pressure improved, these early tubes were replaced by the Coolidge tube. In this, the stream of electrons previously provided by the cathode rays comes from a heated tungsten filament in rather the same way as in a thermionic valve or a television tube. The electrons are then 'fired' on to a metal target, the high voltage between the filament and the target giving the electrons sufficient energy to cause X-radiation as before.

The basic properties of X-rays were observed by Röntgen: their penetrating power, their ability to cause fluorescence, and their effect on photographic plates. Later wave properties were demonstrated, including diffraction, refraction, interference, an X-ray 'photoelectric' effect, and even polarization. This confirmed the kinship of X-rays and light.

Some of these properties of X-rays are used in the X-ray spectrometer, an important instrument developed by W. H. Bragg and his son W. L. (Sir Lawrence) Bragg to measure X-ray wavelengths accurately. It is basically similar to an optical spectrometer used for measuring light wavelengths. A narrow 'beam' of X-rays is directed at an acute angle on to a crystal mounted on a turntable. The crystal diffracts the X-rays in much the same way as a diffraction grating diffracts light, and the diffracted X-rays pass towards a detecting device. This consists of a tube filled with a gas such as methyl iodide, which absorbs X-rays strongly and which becomes ionized when X-rays pass through it. The electrical charge of the gas ions is then measured using an electrometer, giving an indication of the strength of the X-rays falling on to the tube. The energy associated with a particular wavelength can be studied by moving the crystal and the detecting device to the correct positions for that wavelength.

The wavelength itself is found by calculation, using a knowledge of the crystal structure (its dimensions, atomic weight, and so on) and the angles of alignment between the crystal and the detecting device. The relationship giving the wavelength is called Bragg's Law. For this work the Braggs were awarded a Nobel prize in 1915, when W.L. Bragg was only 25.

New metal, new wavelength

Interference of X-rays can be produced by passing them through very narrow slits, and techniques using special mechanically produced diffraction gratings have been developed. By projecting the X-rays at a small angle of incidence, the grating lines appear very close together and diffraction occurs even at the very short wavelengths of X-rays. This method has given values of X-ray wavelengths which confirm Bragg's Law based on the calculated dimensions of the crystal.

Using the X-ray spectrometer, the Braggs investigated X-ray wavelengths from a tube whose target could be changed from one metal to another, and in which the voltage across the plates could be varied. For relatively low tube voltages, they found that a range or spectrum of X-ray wavelengths is produced which ends abruptly at the short wavelength end. Increasing the tube voltage moves this cut-off point to a shorter wavelength. At a certain high value of voltage, in addition to the broad X-ray spectrum the tube produces strong X-rays at definite wavelengths.

They found that changing the metal of the target from, say, copper to nickel and repeating the experiment produces another broad spectrum and again at high voltages a set of strong X-ray lines. But the lines for nickel have different wavelengths from those for copper. These strong X-ray lines are called *characteristic X-rays* because they are characteristic of the target metal.

Shortly after W.H. Bragg's observations, the origin of characteristic X-rays was linked with the production of characteristic light wavelengths by certain elements. (For example, sodium produces yellow light, neon produces red light, and so on.) From a knowledge of quantum theory these can be explained. The high-speed electrons falling on to the target have a certain energy. While this energy

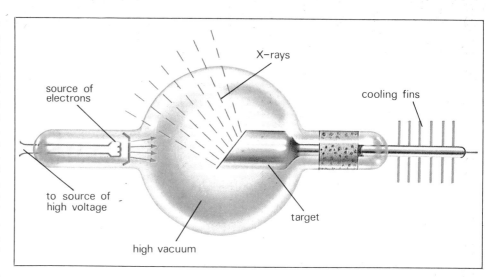

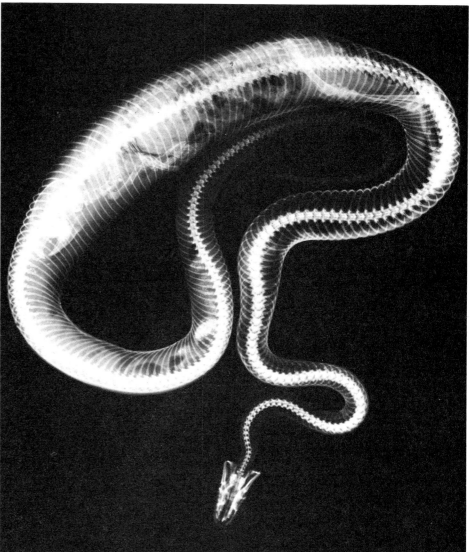

A stream of electrons 'fired' from a source of high voltage, thus carrying a large quantity of energy, strikes a metal target, *top,* and X-rays are given off. The vacuum is to prevent dissipation of the electrons' energy through collision with air molecules. This X-ray photo of a rattlesnake digesting a prairie dog, *above,* offers invaluable information to the biologist.

is relatively low (that is, at low tube voltages), the electrons collide with the heavy target atoms and are scattered about. At each collision they lose energy which is radiated in the form of X-rays.

Since they lose various amounts of energy at each collision, the X-ray wavelengths produced are many, and a broad X-ray spectrum is formed. But at a certain tube voltage, the electrons have sufficient energy to eject other electrons from the

innermost orbits of the target atoms. The spaces left by the ejected electrons are filled by electrons falling from higher orbits, each releasing a definite quantum of energy in doing so. According to quantum theory, the quantum of energy is related to the frequency of the energy released. So for a particular target atom, X-rays of definite wavelength are emitted. A different target atom has a different arrangement of orbits, and so the quanta

X-rays can probe behind the painted surface of a masterpiece to reveal important secrets. The painting of St Michael, *left,* by Piero della Francesca, now hanging in the National Gallery in London, was suspected to be part of a lost five-panel altarpiece prepared for the Church of St Agostino in Italy in the mid-1400s. An X-ray revealed a tell-tale piece of drapery in the lower right-hand corner, as in the cleaned painting, *right.* Four of the five panels have now been located, and the art world is now on the lookout for the fifth to complete the work.

of energy involved are also different, leading to characteristic X-rays of definite wavelengths.

The important investigations into the structures of crystals using X-rays were begun by M. von Laue (who in 1912 first predicted diffraction of X-rays by crystals) and continued by the Braggs. The way in which a simple crystal such as that of common salt diffracts X-rays was explained by W. H. Bragg in connection with his X-ray spectrometer. He considered that X-rays are scattered by each of the crystal atoms. In any direction, the scattered X-rays will add together only if their waves are in phase (in step). If we consider one crystal plane (in a cubic crystal there will be three sets of such planes at right angles), the scattered X-rays from that plane will be in phase for one direction only. This direction has the same relationship to the angle of incidence as do the incident and reflected light rays at a mirror. If the same effect occurs for the many crystal planes lying beneath the one considered, and if all the reflected rays are in phase, there will be a strong overall reflection in one direction only. This direction depends on the wavelength of the X-rays, the angle of incidence, and the spacing between the crystal planes, and is predicted by Bragg's Law.

If the crystal is rotated and other crystal

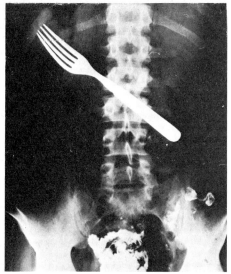

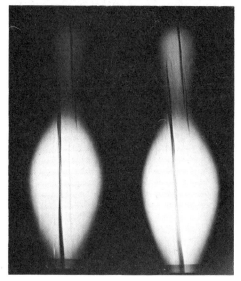

A man came to a doctor complaining of stomach pains. An X-ray, *top left,* revealed the cause. He had swallowed a fork. Bowling pins, *top right,* are regularly X-rayed to detect flaws. Brain tumours, a more serious kind of flaw, are also revealed by X-ray, with the aid of radio-isotopes, *above left.* Numerous lives have been saved in this way. Study of X-rays and other such phenomena led to the need for protection. This make-shift lead mask, *above right,* is an example of the primitive protective devices the early researchers had to fashion for themselves. It is an exhibit at the Röntgen Museum in Rem-scheid, West Germany, where Röntgen was born.

planes used, the shape and volume of the crystal can be found and the number of atoms in the crystal determined. With extremely simple crystals, the numbers of atoms can be found by calculation without using the spectrometer; but for complex crystals, this method is the basis of the most useful way of analysing them. Techniques developed by W.L. Bragg have enabled scientists to measure even the structures of organic crystals. Other important X-ray crystal studies include those of the structures of metals and new alloys, and of organic fibres.

Shadow pictures

The more familiar applications of X-rays use their penetrating properties. Unlike light, which is stopped by even a flimsy material such as paper, X-rays can penetrate quite dense materials. In passing through a material, the intensity or 'brightness' of the X-rays is progressively reduced (like light passing through cloudy water). Since different materials reduce the intensity at a different rate, X-rays passed through, say, the human body will be more strongly absorbed by bone than by the surrounding flesh. By placing a photographic plate behind the body, a 'shadow' X-ray picture may be produced. Tissues which are or have been diseased, for instance the scar tissue left in the lungs after tuberculosis, show up darker than the surrounding tissues because they

absorb slightly more X-rays. Additional techniques, such as the barium sulphate meal used for X-raying the stomach, are used to make soft tissues show up on X-ray photographs. In this example, an ulcer would absorb some of the barium sulphate and would show up strongly on the X-ray plate.

X-rays are also used in industry; for example to examine metal objects encapsulated in plastic, or to 'see' through an opaque substance as in the locating of grids in thermionic valves. Important too are X-ray techniques for detecting flaws in metals. Although a metal casting or a machined component may appear sound, it can contain an internal flaw which seriously affects its strength. If X-ray photographs could not be used, the only other ways of easily detecting the flaw would involve destroying the component. For example, hitting a small casting with a big hammer detects flaws, but it smashes the casting.

The dangers of X-irradiation to the body are now recognized, and people who work with X-ray machines are well protected by lead shielding. Until about 15 years ago, it was common to see X-ray machines in shops to aid in fitting shoes, especially for children. These machines projected X-rays up through the foot and on to a fluorescent screen. If they were used frequently, there may have been some danger, so most of them have now been withdrawn. The

effects of small doses of X-rays on tissues are negligible. But prolonged exposure can have serious consequences and ultimately destroys the tissues. Important too is the effect of X-rays on genes and chromosomes. Mutated genes can have disastrous effects if they are passed on in reproduction. For this reason, X-rays are rarely used on women in early pregnancy, although in some cases the slight risk may be justified by the essential information an X-ray examination can provide.

Medical science has turned the damaging effects of X-irradiation to good use. X-ray therapy is an important part of the treatment for malignant diseases such as cancer. Using a very carefully directed and controlled X-ray source, the affected tissues can be destroyed, and the cell-multiplying effects caused by certain kinds of cancer arrested.

The quantum explanation of the energy associated with X-rays showed that, as the wavelength of the radiation becomes shorter, so the energy becomes greater. Short wavelength X-rays therefore have more penetrating power than do longer wavelengths. Very short wavelength X-rays are very penetrating, and closely resemble their near neighbours in the electro-magnetic spectrum, gamma rays.

Gamma radiation

Gamma rays have many of the properties of X-rays (they can be diffracted by crystals, they affect photographic plates and cause feeble fluorescence, they pass through metals, and so on); their origin is different. Characteristic emission of light and X-rays is due to electrons jumping between energy levels. Gamma radiation is produced by activity originating in the nucleus of the atom. It occurs when the nucleus adjusts itself from one 'excited' state to another. It is interesting that the quantum theory again satisfactorily explains the mechanism: the nucleus can settle in only certain energy states and in moving from one state to another of lower energy, a quantum of gamma radiation is emitted. The nucleus gets into a position from which it must change in this way after the emission of a beta particle (an electron).

Gamma rays can also be responsible for the emission of X-rays. As a gamma ray leaves the nucleus, it passes through the electron orbits of the atom and may eject an electron from one of them. The conditions are then similar to those in an X-ray tube, and another electron falls into the vacant space, emitting a characteristic X-ray quantum. In this way, a radioactive material emitting gamma radiation may also produce X-rays. This phenomenon can be used for analysing mixtures of elements. If the mixture is made radioactive, its X-ray spectrum can be examined and, from the characteristic lines present, the elements in the mixture can be identified.

When X-rays were first discovered, many people were quite apprehensive. However, research has stripped them of their mystery and technology has put them to useful work. X-rays have become an important part of our daily life.

The silent echo

Once a weapon of war, radar is now used for many civil purposes as well. Fighting the locust, safer navigation, satellite tracking and even electronic walking-sticks for the blind depend on radar.

IN THE AUTUMN of 1968 a Land-Rover field car trekked across the Sahara Desert. Mounted on its roof was a small radar scanner. Inside was the radar display unit. This was not, as might be supposed, a highly secret military operation – an outpost collecting intelligence on aircraft movements. But it had a war-like intent – the war against the dreaded locust.

The expedition, led by Dr Glen Schaefer of Loughborough University, England, was undertaken on behalf of the Locust Research Centre in London. After his practical work in the desert he was able to report the feasibility of tracking locusts by radar. Large swarms of locusts, some covering an area of 20 square miles and containing possibly 100 tons in weight of insects were located and tracked at ranges of 30 miles. At night, individual migrating locusts could be detected at ranges of two miles.

The value of the experiments lay not only in being able to get early warning of large swarms of locusts and to initiate defensive action, but also to check on smaller migrations in order to control breeding. The expedition was so successful that it may result in a radar chain across locust-infected areas. This would be expensive but could prevent the loss of valuable food crops.

1 This wartime German photograph shows soldiers operating an early type of mobile radar installation. Such radars were used together with anti-aircraft batteries.
2 Radar installations frequently pick up the traces of flocks of birds. Here a radar scanner has traced a large flock of birds migrating over East Anglia.
3 The three giant 'radomes' of the Ballistic Missile Early Warning Station at Fylingdales, Yorkshire, contain powerful radar scanners to give advance warning of approaching rockets.

1

2

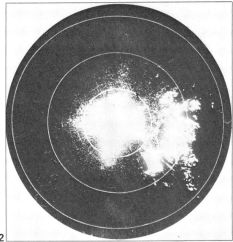

3

Radar has an interesting history. In the pre-war years of the 1930s, the only detecting devices against hostile aircraft were sound amplifiers. The most impressive of these was a 200 ft long by 25 ft high curved wall on Romney Marshes facing the Straits of Dover. The wall was shaped like a giant concave mirror to reflect sounds into microphones located at the focal point. Its object was to hear aircraft engines at great distance. But even under the most favourable conditions of wind and weather the range of detection was only 24 miles and in average conditions only half that.

Radar's birth certificate

About the same time, the techniques of generating high-powered radio waves had developed to a point at which some interest was being displayed in the possibilities of a 'death-ray' which could be directed at an aircraft to disable or destroy it. A young British Government scientist, Robert Watson-Watt, was consulted by Air Ministry officials but he declared that the idea was not feasible. But as a result of discussions he put forward to the Committee for the Scientific Survey of Air Defence, a notable memorandum, entitled 'Detection and Location of Aircraft by Radio Methods'. The date was 27 February 1935 and the memorandum was the birth certificate of radar.

If an enemy aircraft could be located in good time there was a fair possibility of destroying it by conventional ground-to-air or air-to-air gunnery. Robert Watson-Watt's thesis was that if an all-metal aircraft were to be irradiated with radio energy it would re-radiate a small amount of the energy and this could be detected. If the radio energy were transmitted in short high-powered bursts with a listening period between each burst (or pulse as it is called) then, by measuring the time interval between the outgoing pulse and the reflected signal, and knowing the speed of radio waves, it would be possible to determine the distance away, or range, of the aircraft. A further refinement would be to make the radiation highly directional so that the aircraft could be detected not only in range but also in bearing from the radar station.

Watson-Watt had been studying atmospherics – lightning discharges and their origins – and he had much practical experience in radio methods in general and in particular the use of cathode-ray tubes for visual display and for measuring devices. It was common knowledge that radio waves could be reflected. Hulsmeyer of Düsseldorf was experimenting with reflected radio waves in 1903. In 1922 Marconi noticed reflections from metallic objects some miles away when using short wavelengths. A Post Office report in 1932 referred to interference by aircraft with transmissions of very high frequency radio waves. There were surges of intensity of the signals of high nuisance value when an aircraft flew over – an effect which causes interference to television pictures.

The multi-cavity magnetron

By 1939 the approaches to Britain were already guarded by radiolocation stations, as they were then called, and a crash-programme of construction resulted in a complete chain of stations in operation by the time of the Battle of Britain.

The early stations had very large aerials quite unsuitable for mounting on aircraft and the second phase of development was to use a much shorter wavelength with small aerials. If such equipment could be built and mounted in a night fighter it could be used to close in to within gun range of an enemy bomber.

To achieve this it was necessary to develop a small but extremely powerful radio valve capable of operating on very much shorter wavelengths than hitherto. Two British physicists, J.T. Randall and H.A.H. Boot, had been working on such a device at Birmingham University. It was called the multi-cavity magnetron and had been made to work in 1939. In 1940 the British magnetron was taken to America and tested by Bell Telephone Laboratories. The Americans were duly impressed and intensive work on both sides of the Atlantic put the Allies firmly in the lead over the Germans. The term Radar was coined by the American Navy from RAdio Detection And Ranging and came into general use as a shorter and more convenient term than radiolocation.

The magnetron made the lightweight radar possible but it also did more. Because it worked at centimetric wavelengths the reflections from radar targets were much more sharply defined than when using metre wavelengths and the returned signals were also reflected from other than metal objects. By pointing the aerial systems towards the ground and using a

radar display called the Plan Position Indicator (PPI) it became possible to see a map of the ground from an aircraft even at night through heavy cloud. This type of installation was used in the pathfinder aircraft which directed heavy bombers to their targets.

The enormous development effort put into radar during the war years led directly to the electronic revolution after the war. Since the war there has been continuous development of radar for military use. The huge chains of giant radars such as the Distant Early Warning Line across the northern parts of North America and the Ballistic Missile Early Warning System with stations in Alaska, Greenland and Yorkshire are examples. Radar techniques are also used for missile guidance.

During the past 20 years radar has moved into general use in civil aviation,

1 Bats make use of the radar principle to avoid obstacles when flying in darkness. Their regular high-pitched squeaks echo from obstacles and are picked up by their sensitive ears.
2 The flight deck of the British aircraft carrier H.M.S. *Eagle* with the control tower in the background. Aircraft carriers are well equipped with powerful and versatile radar installations.

shipping, meteorology, and, to the dismay of motorists, has even evolved into a scientific method of catching offenders exceeding speed limits.

Nowadays no large civil airport is without radar for control purposes. Major airports may need several sets of equipment: for general surveillance of the skies around and another system for surveillance of the situation on the ground giving indication of aircraft positions on the runways. Yet another, known as secondary surveillance radar (SSR), detects aircraft and causes their equipment to transmit automatically the aircraft identification number, its altitude and destination or other useful information.

The aircraft itself, if it is a large passenger transport, will normally have a radar display on the flight deck with a radar scanner concealed in the nose which can scan the area ahead for bad weather conditions or be tilted downwards to show on the display tube a map of the terrain over which the aircraft is flying. Two other types of radar equipment may also be fitted. One is a radar altimeter which by directing a radar beam vertically towards the ground gives the correct altitude above ground – a superior instrument to the ordinary altimeter which shows only height above sea level – and a Doppler radar which gives true ground speed and indicates any drift from side winds. These are all valuable aids to flight safety and reduce the navigational load on the flight crew.

The *Doppler effect,* from which Doppler radar gets its name, is the change in pitch of a wave from a moving body as it passes the observer. If you stand in a railway station as an express train approaches, the sound of the train is high-pitched but as it rushes past and recedes into the distance the pitch of the sound appears to drop. Radio waves show the same effect, and by measuring the change of wavelength of the directly transmitted and reflected wavelengths it is possible to determine the velocity of the object causing the reflection. This is the principle on which police radar speed traps are based.

As with airports and aircraft so it is with shipping. There are several large harbour radar installations from which harbour masters can give advice by radio-telephone to captains on the position of their own ships in relation to others. Some ships carry as many as three separate radar installations. On ferries, for example, there could be a long-distance radar, a short-range high definition radar for inshore work and another, of similar type, fitted at the stern for use when berthing backwards.

1 The radar screens at the heart of London Airport's control tower give the flight controllers detailed information about incoming and outgoing aircraft.
2 This huge reflector at the satellite tracking station in Woomera desert, Australia, provides scientists with a means of following rockets from the moment they are launched.

A recent development in marine radar is the racon beacon. A number of these have been installed on lightships and lighthouses round the British coast. The racon is a radio transmitter/receiver working on radar wavelengths. Any ship within radar range with its radar switched on will be emitting pulses of energy. When the racon receiver detects the pulses it automatically causes the racon transmitter to send out a coded series of pulses which are picked up on the ship's radar screen giving the location and identification of the racon in relation to the ship.

Racon buoys

Because the racon sends out its own signal in reply to the ship's radar the range of the detection is much greater than would be possible with the weak radar reflection upon which the ship would normally have to rely. A coastal racon can be 'seen' on a ship's radar screen long before the outline of the coast appears. Tiny microminiature low-power racons have also been designed for mounting on navigational buoys. They can operate unattended for periods up to a

Packed with electronic equipment, the R.A.F.'s famous Shackleton aircraft is really a flying radar station. Its chief use is to track down submarines and undertake naval searches.

H.M.S. *Boxer,* heavily equipped with sensitive radar installations, searches the English Channel for the submarine H.M.S. *Affray,* lost on a diving exercise in 1951.

year and are far more effective than the common diamond-shaped radar reflectors used to help intensify an otherwise unaided radar reflection from a small bobbing object such as a buoy.

Radar principles are also used underwater but in this case ultrasonic sound waves are used instead of radio waves. The transmitter/receiver units are mounted in the hull of the vessel, the two principal uses being for measuring the depth of water below the hull and for locating fish. By directing a beam of ultrasonic waves down vertically through the water and measuring the time interval for the returned echo from the sea-bed it is possible to check the depth of water. Giant supertankers have as many as four echo-sounders mounted fore and aft and on the beams to assist navigation in shallow channels. Fish-finding equipment works in the same way, some of the more advanced installations being capable of distinguishing the echo from a single fish only a foot or two from the sea-bed. Underwater radar or, to use its correct title, sonar, is not as accurate as radar because the velocity of the ultrasonic

sound waves through the water is dependent on a number of factors such as salinity and temperature which vary from place to place.

In meteorology one of radar's most extensive uses is in wind finding. A small balloon is released and as it floats higher and higher its movements are tracked by a small radar on the ground. The balloon frequently carries a package of instruments measuring temperature, humidity and height and this information is sent back to the ground by a small radio transmitter. By using radar and an instrument package a 'picture' of the atmosphere can be obtained. Before the advent of radar it was necessary to check the flight of the balloon by optical means which meant that complete information depended on perfect visibility.

Gunn diode

The future of radar in really wide-scale use now lies in the development of low-cost solid-state semiconductor electronic devices which can generate pulses of very short wavelength. The most promising of these is the Gunn diode made from gallium arsenide, doped with impurities and excited in a strong electric field. That such a device could generate oscillations at microwave frequencies was first observed in 1963 by John Gunn, a young British physicist working at the IBM Research Centre, New York State.

Complete radar sets using the Gunn diode have been built small enough to be held in the hand. One model is held like a pistol and merely pointed at a moving object to detect its speed which is read from a calibrated scale. Weight can be as little as a couple of pounds and operation is from ordinary torch batteries.

Mini-radars of this type, if produced in sufficient quantity, could be sold for a few pounds and would have wide application as burglar alarms, for instant speed indication of moving objects, for navigation of small vessels and, with suitable audible alarms generated by the radar, as 'seeing' aids for the blind.

On the bridge of a modern trawler. Small ships are now generally equipped with compact and efficient radar and other electronic navigation equipment.

The maser and laser

Pure single frequencies of light and of radio waves beamed coherently out from a special source are the basis of the laser. This powerful tool has given rise to a new and useful technology.

WHEN THE AMERICAN ASTRONAUTS, Neil Armstrong and Buzz Aldrin, blasted off from the moon in 1969 on the start of their return journey, one of the pieces of hardware they left behind on the moon's surface was a laser reflector. Within hours of the blast-off, this reflector was used in conjunction with a powerful laser on Earth to confirm the exact spot where the moon landing was made and to measure more accurately than had hitherto been possible the distance separating Earth and moon.

And yet, ten years earlier the laser had not been invented. What, then, is a laser? How does it work? What can it do?

The word laser is an acronym made up of the initial letters of Light Amplification by Stimulated Emission of Radiation. The laser was developed directly from an earlier device, which operated on similar principles, but which amplified radiation in the lower *microwave* frequency part of the electromagnetic spectrum. This was called the maser – standing for Microwave Amplification by Stimulated Emission of Radiation.

The maser was born out of military research efforts to produce and amplify super high frequency radio signals for a superior radar.

As it turned out, the maser principle appears to have been discovered independently by American and Russian physicists in 1951. But this was only the principle. No working device then existed.

The first practical maser was conceived by a United States physicist, C. H. Townes,

in the laboratories of Columbia University, who managed to get a maser working towards the end of 1953.

The culmination of the research was a device which would produce an intense beam of microwaves (radio waves of a few centimetres wavelength) with each wave almost exactly the same size and in step with every other wave. The maser could also be used to amplify very weak radio signals and one of its first uses was as an amplifier in radio telescopes. The lasers, which soon overshadowed maser developments, produced similarly intense beams of much shorter, visible waves, all travelling parallel and in step. Thus was born a completely new type of light-producing device.

From Einstein

What was this new way of producing radiation that set research on optics humming in a way that has not occurred for 50 years? First of all, the basis of the new technology – stimulated emission of radiation – was not at all new, and had been considered by Einstein in 1917. There were also quite familiar lamps available, such as gas discharge tubes which operated on the principle. This was the production of radiation by exciting molecules of certain materials to well defined, high energy states, so that they then returned to a low energy, or ground state, giving up the energy as precise 'packets' of radiation with precise frequencies. The key to the maser and laser was to get a majority of molecules in a system into an excited state, and then to trigger off their return to the ground state together so that all the radiation produced was in step and reinforced itself to produce an intense, amplified beam of radiation.

It was possible to conceive of a device that would operate like this, because molecules of certain materials can be excited to a high energy level by absorbing the same or similar wavelength radiation that is produced in decaying to the ground state. In the case of the first maser, the material in question was ammonia gas, which would absorb microwave energy until most of the molecules were in an excited energy state and then emit a burst of microwaves at an exact frequency of approximately 1·25 cm.

Designing a set-up that would produce bursts of microwave energy called for a great deal of ingenuity, and Townes realized that just pumping radiation into ammonia gas was not good enough, as there was just as much chance that the radiation pumped in would be absorbed, as that it would trigger a molecule to return to a ground state and produce more radiation. There would be no build-up of excited molecules and sudden release of their energy radiation. The solution was to concentrate ammonia molecules into a stream, to excite them, and pass them into a small cavity with end walls that reflected microwaves. Most of the radiation emitted was reflected back and forth between the walls of the cavity, which were one half a wavelength apart, so that the waves were all in step and reinforced one another. In this way, the ammonia gas was pumped to a state where more of the molecules were in a higher energy state than in the lower one and the maser action could take place.

Townes's first maser was not used to

Lasers are proving very useful in certain types of microsurgery. One such use is to spot weld the retina of the eye back in place after it has accidentally come away.

The argon ion gas laser generates a beam of light that is extremely bright and narrow. The gas laser is being developed for deep-space communication, for television and for computers.

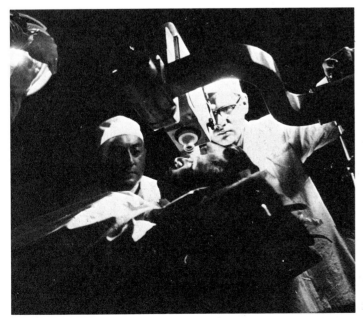

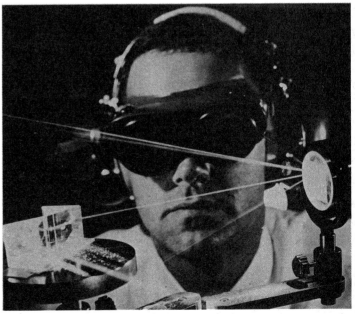

produce beams of microwave energy for very little radiation was leaking out of the end walls of the cavity. Instead it was used as an oscillator. The oscillations produced in the cavity of the ammonia-beam maser could not be tuned but had amazing stability. At its working frequency of 24,000 MHz the maser could be used as a highly accurate time-measuring device – in fact as a clock. The ammonia atomic clock, it was calculated, had an accumulated error rate of about one second in every 10,000 years which was an enormous advance on previous clocks.

When the news broke that a working maser had been achieved, interest increased to fever pitch and physicists in other laboratories started looking seriously at how to exploit the device.

Nicolaas Bloembergen, a Dutch physicist working at Harvard University, solved the problem of tuning a maser to produce different frequencies in 1956, and went on to devise a maser that would produce continuous beams of radiation rather than short bursts. The principle of this was a 'three-level' stimulation of molecules in which the radiation used for pumping would raise the molecule through the energy levels, while the energy lost by the stimulated emission would drop it through just one smaller level. This meant that pumping radiation and emitted radiation were of different wavelengths, and pumping and emission could go on simultaneously and continuously.

Working on Bloembergen's theories, a team of physicists at Bell Telephone Laboratories in America produced the first solid-state maser, an oscillator. At the Massachusetts Institute of Technology another team went one step further and produced a true amplifier of microwave signals. The maser had arrived.

The two characteristics which put the maser in a class of its own as an amplifier were its superior sensitivity and exceptionally low noise. In practice this means that if a maser is used as the first amplifying stage in a radar receiver, the radar's sensitivity, and therefore, its range, is enormously improved. As a first stage in a radio-astronomy telescope it will improve the performance at least 100 times over

1

3

1 Using lasers as death-rays has not really proved a viable proposition. However, because of their power they can be destructive, as seen when one is aimed at an ordinary light lamp.
2 The American astronauts left a laser reflector behind on the moon's surface. By aiming a laser on Earth at this reflector scientists have confirmed the position of the landing.

3 Laser beams used at the Royal Institute, London, to investigate how certain substances, such as rubber, change their molecular structure under the influence of light.
4 The coherent light from a ruby laser is so bright and piercing that it will cut through a diamond – the hardest natural material known – in a 200-millionth of a second.

other forms of amplification.

Even with the active communication satellites of the 1960s which carry their own receivers and transmitters for relaying signals, the maser amplifier is still a valuable adjunct at the ground terminal and the quality of intercontinental television transmissions would be the worse without it.

By the mid-twentieth century the physicists were already working on the possibility of applying the maser principle to even higher frequencies. Why not an optical maser? One that worked at or near the frequency of visible light?

'Mechanical men'

Again, Townes was to the fore and, together with Arthur L. Schawlow, suggested a way of achieving an optical maser, or laser as it was later to be called. Their hypothesis called for molecules that could be excited to produce visible wavelength radiations to be placed between two parallel mirrors. The material would be pumped by a flash of light, and the radiation produced by the decay of molecules to the ground state would be reflected back and forth between the mirrors, stimulating further emissions. Schawlow described the stimulated emission going on between the two mirrors in a laser cavity – 'It is as if tiny mechanical men, all wound up to a certain energy and facing along the axis of the laser were set in motion by other marchers and fell into step until they became an immense army marching in unison row upon row (the plane wave fronts) back and forth in the enclosure.' One of the mirrors in the laser would be semi-transparent so that some of the light could escape as a beam, all of it at practically the same wavelength, with all waves in step, travelling parallel, to the laser axis. This was the coherent beam of light unique to the laser.

In July 1960 at Hughes Research Laboratories in southern California, a young physicist, Theodore H. Maiman, produced the first working laser. It consisted of a ruby crystal irradiated by a xenon flash lamp. It produced a coherent light beam of deep red light such as had never been produced before.

Maiman's achievement triggered off an even greater wave of research activity. Men of vision saw the laser as the key not only to new forms of offensive and defensive weapons but also as a powerful tool which had a vast potential in peaceful applications in communications, industry, medicine and science.

Maiman's ruby laser emitted short pulses of light of exceptional brilliance, brighter than the sun, and of extreme spectral purity. It was true coherent light.

When we look around us, what we see is illuminated by incoherent light. Sunlight covers a broad frequency spectrum. It is a jumble of many frequencies of electromagnetic radiation as can be shown by passing light through a prism and seeing the individual colours (frequencies) separated out which, mixed together, make what we call 'white' light. The waves are also all out of step – they are not coordinated in phase.

Laser beams make excellent signals for transmitting television and voice. In this experiment the lower television set is laser-operated and the other conventionally.

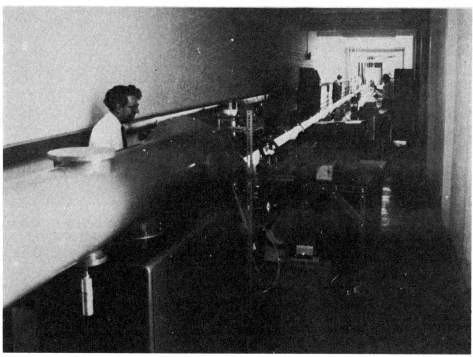

Physicists hope to use this powerful carbon-dioxide laser at the University of Essex to raise plasma to such high temperatures so as ultimately to lead to the fusion of atoms.

Laser light, on the other hand, is both coherent in frequency and in phase. Because it is coherent, it does not waste its energy by fanning out. With a suitable optical system using a 12–in. mirror, a laser beam from Earth may be only one mile wide by the time it reaches the surface of the moon. At short range the energy in the beam is so concentrated and intense that it can burn holes in steel plate. Moreover, because the laser beam is coherent, it can be modulated in a similar manner to the more familiar radio waves to carry voice, music or television signals. It has the added advantage that a single laser beam used as a communications link can carry tens of thousands of simultaneous telephone conversations or several television channels.

Maiman's ruby laser was indeed a breakthrough but it was followed by other types soon afterwards. In 1961 the gas laser was developed at Bell Laboratories by a team headed by Ali Javan. This laser used a radio frequency to excite an electrical discharge in a tube containing a helium neon gas mixture. The radio frequency excited the helium atoms, which, in turn, passed energy to the neon atoms to produce higher and lower energy levels, thus achieving the conditions for 'lasing'. Javan's gas laser was of even greater spectral purity than the ruby laser and it worked continuously, unlike the ruby laser which worked only in short pulses with an interval between each burst of energy. The radiation from Javan's gas laser was in the invisible infra-red regions.

The next development, towards the end of 1962, was the injection laser developed almost simultaneously by a number of research groups. This laser uses gallium arsenide, a semi-conductor element, which had long been observed to give an infra-red radiation when an electric current was passed through it. By increasing the current to a critical level it was discovered that laser action occurred.

Since 1962 all three types of laser have been under intensive development, and many applications have been found, but there are few of great practical significance or which promise a mass market for the laser, although one American company recently proposed a colour television system using lasers. One reason for this is that the laser is moderately expensive, but in specialized applications it is well worth the expense.

For communications on Earth the big disadvantage is our own atmosphere which, even in clear weather, can cause 'noise' on a point-to-point system through random atmospheric variations. In outer space, however, there is no such limitation and it has been theoretically calculated that with lasers of today's power a communications link over a distance of ten light years would be possible. The snag, even in space, is that the laser beam is so narrow that it is extremely difficult to aim the beam accurately at the receiving station. So far as is known every attempt by American astronauts to aim a beam from an orbiting satellite on to an Earth receiving point has failed.

No death ray

One area of development which has been under investigation is to protect the laser beam from our atmosphere by sending it along pipelines either directly or through the medium of fibre-optic paths. Although basically an expensive system it could be economically viable for very high density traffic in the tele-communication service.

In the military sphere the laser brought a great wave of optimism as a countermeasure to the intercontinental ballistic missile. Here, at last, was the death ray so popular in science-fiction. Batteries of lasers could be used to vaporize missiles before they hit the ground and enemy tanks and troops could be made to disappear in a puff of smoke. This is an extremely unlikely development.

But the laser is already in military use. Laser rangefinders are superior to either optical or radar rangefinders. A good optical rangefinder with a one metre base length is typically accurate to within ten metres at a range of 1·5 kilometres. The laser rangefinder has an accuracy of ten metres at a range of ten kilometres.

Using optical interference methods engineers can achieve a great improvement in accuracy for measuring length by using the coherent light from a laser rather than a conventional lamp. The National Physical Laboratory was among the first to use a laser in this way and using a helium neon laser achieved checking accuracies over a distance of one metre of 0·0000005 in.

The 'death-ray' concept has already found many applications in engineering where high-powered pulsed lasers can be used for microwelding or for piercing tiny holes or for cutting intricate shapes in metal up to $\frac{1}{8}$ in. thick. Another application is in surgery where the very fine laser beam can be used most effectively on the eye. Among the most successful surgical uses has been the correction of a detached retina which can be spot welded back in place with a laser beam. Other methods have been used but treatment time, for example, using an optical photo-coagulator, takes as long as a second, during which time the patient's eye might move. The laser flash lasts only about one thousandth of a second and the chances of getting the shot spot on at the first attempt are very much better.

The laser, hailed as the wonder of the age, perhaps had too much publicity at the beginning but after ten years of life it is steadily gaining acceptance as new and practical uses are found for it in the fields of communications and medicine. Clearly, it is not going to solve every problem but in suitable applications it has more than proved itself as one of the most brilliant developments of the mid-twentieth century.

Electric messengers

We are so accustomed to telephones, television, radio and other means of telecommunication that we often overlook the vast changes these devices have brought about in their short history.

THE TRANSMISSION of information over long distances is one of the aspects of technology which has transformed life in the twentieth century. Telephones and television sets have rapidly become everyday objects for millions of people. As media of communication they now almost rival direct speech and written language.

When human beings communicate in speech or writing, the information must first be transformed into sounds or written words. The recipient of the transformed message or *signal* must then 'de-code' it, turning it back into its original form.

With the discovery of electricity, it occurred to many people that an electric current could be so varied so as to convey a message. As early as 1800, such a *telegraph* system was devised.

In 1836, the American Samuel Morse invented his code of long and short pulses, 'dashes' and 'dots', to represent the alphabet in electrical currents. He later constructed machines which automatically coded and decoded such messages but it was soon found that this could be done faster and more accurately by hand. Nowadays, of course, the job is done automatically, but using perforated paper tape. The tape is punched on a *teletypewriter* and fed into the transmitter which converts it to electric pulses. At the receiving end another paper tape is produced, and a second teletypewriter turns this into printed form.

A world-wide telegraph system of cables was laid in the last century, the first transatlantic cable being begun in 1858.

The telephone

A still greater advance in communication was made in 1876. This was the invention by Alexander Graham Bell of a device to turn speech into variations in electrical currents and vice versa. Bell's *telephone*, both transmitter and receiver, consisted of a magnetic diaphragm in front of an electro-magnet. When the diaphragm was moved by sound waves, electricity was generated in the coils of the electro-magnet. Sent through the coils of a similar device, current caused the receiver's diaphragm to be attracted and repelled and thus to produce sounds imitating the transmitted message.

Later, the transmitting mechanism consisted of carbon granules, compressed more or less by a diaphragm. The resulting electrical resistance was thus altered in time with the sound waves hitting the diaphragm. A current passed through the carbon was therefore increased and decreased in a way which reproduced the sound at the receiver.

With the spread of the telephone system, *switchboards* were needed, to connect one telephone with another. These were opera-

ted by hand in accordance with verbal instructions to the operator. So fast did the system grow, that it was calculated in 1914 that several million telephone operators would soon be required in the United States.

In practice, however, this did not happen, because of the invention of automatic switching apparatus. A dialling system had already been invented in 1889. The dial produces a series of electrical impulses which operate an automatic device to connect the caller with the desired number.

Michael Faraday began his experiments with electro-magnetic radiation early in the last century, but it was not until 1888 that Hertz was able to transmit radio waves and detect them at a distance.

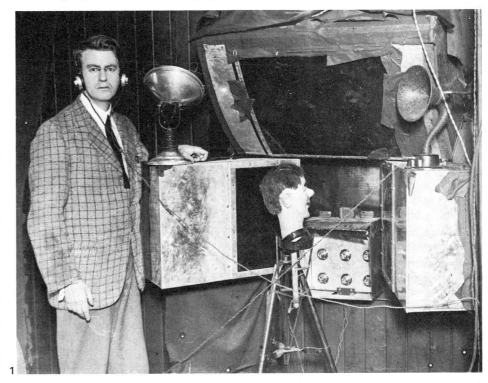

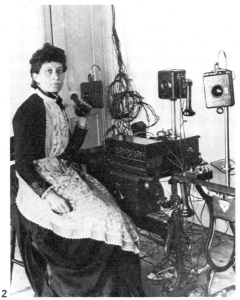

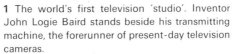

1 The world's first television 'studio'. Inventor John Logie Baird stands beside his transmitting machine, the forerunner of present-day television cameras.
2 The Croydon telephone exchange in 1884. One operator and a small amount of equipment was all that was required to service a town of more than 100,000 people.
3 Wiring up equipment for a modern telephone exchange. Large numbers of skilled workers are required to build and maintain the intricate wire mazes that form the 'guts' of the exchange.

Radio waves are produced by rapidly alternating electric currents. If they are to be received, they must be made to induce a similar, though naturally weaker, current, some distance away and cause it to actuate some mechanical movement. But to turn radio waves into mechanical (sound) energy more effectively, the alternating current in the receiving apparatus must be converted to direct, one-way, current, or *rectified* as was done in the early 'crystal sets' with a silicon crystal and a fine 'cat's whisker'.

By 1896, Marconi was able to use such means to send 'wireless' messages, and in 1901 the first radio telegraph message was sent across the Atlantic. The potential of the new medium was brought home vividly when the ship *Republic* sank in 1909, and rescue of survivors was only made possible by the wireless calls for help.

In 1904, the next big step was made towards the modern radio: Fleming invented the *thermionic valve*. By passing currents between a heated filament to a metal plate through a vacuum, Fleming obtained a method of turning high-frequency alternating current into direct current, and also of *modulating* the amplitude of alternating currents. This is because only the hot filament will emit electrons.

A microphone could thus be incorporated in the radio transmitter and a telephone receiver could be operated at the receiving end. *Radio telephony* had arrived.

The basic radio wave, at whose frequency the receiver is tuned to resonate, is called the *carrier wave*. Its amplitude varies with the sound waves hitting the microphone, waves of *audio-frequency*. More modern forms of radio transmission

employ *frequency modulation,* instead of this *amplitude* modulation. The transmitter converts sound waves into changes in the frequency of the carrier wave above and below its average level. This enables the message to be reproduced much more accurately than by the older method.

During the Second World War, the use of *semi-conductors* was developed, chemical devices which only allow electricity to pass in one direction. These were used as

rectifiers and made possible radio circuits which were smaller and eventually cheaper than those using valves.

In the early days of radio, the distance a message could be sent was thought to be limited by the curvature of the Earth. Later, however, it was discovered that this limitation could be overcome. Surrounding the Earth a layer of electrically charged particles was discovered, the Heavyside Layer. Short radio waves (i.e.,

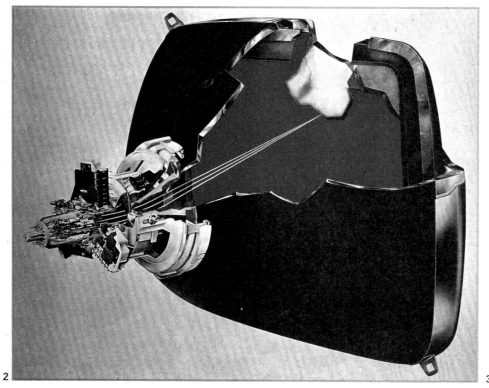

1 Inside the BBC's video-tape library. On the left is a video recorder with large reels of tape, while the operator at the console is watching taped images in colour and black and white.

2 Cutaway diagram of the interior of a colour television tube shows how the screen is struck by three electron beams which activate the three primary colours on the screen.

3 Testing the U.S. Navy's Sealab II submarine in shallow water off the coast of Californ. The diver in the background is using a television camera to monitor his colleagues' work.

those of higher frequency) were found to bounce off this layer back towards the Earth's surface. It was thus possible to receive radio transmissions 'round the corners' of the globe.

The rapid development of the radio industry in the 1920s and 1930s made possible a still more astonishing application. For some time, radio had been used to transmit pictures for newspapers. The picture is broken into small squares and the radio signal indicates how dark each square is.

Television applied this idea to 'live' pictures. A television camera 'scans' the scene to be transmitted in a series of horizontal lines. At each instant, the light from the particular point being viewed is converted into an electrical current whose level is proportional to the intensity of light, by means of a photo-electric cell. This 'message' is transmitted by radio and must be converted into a spot of light simultaneously 'scanning' the receiver's screen.

Television tubes

In the modern television tube a beam of electrons strikes the screen and produces a luminous spot. The direction of the beam is controlled electro-magnetically with great precision and moves in a way which is exactly synchronized with the camera.

Speech, music and pictures are not the only 'messages' which are nowadays transmitted by radio waves or telephonic lines. Instructions to automatic equipment, data for computers and information from remote industrial processes are all sent and received by such means.

The best known examples of these today are perhaps to be found in space vehicles. Rockets are fired far away from the Earth

1

2

3

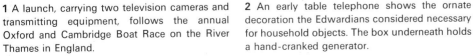

1 A launch, carrying two television cameras and transmitting equipment, follows the annual Oxford and Cambridge Boat Race on the River Thames in England.

2 An early table telephone shows the ornate decoration the Edwardians considered necessary for household objects. The box underneath holds a hand-cranked generator.

3 The television aerials at Emley Moor, Yorkshire carry the television broadcasts over the top of surrounding natural and man-made obstacles and increase the station's range.

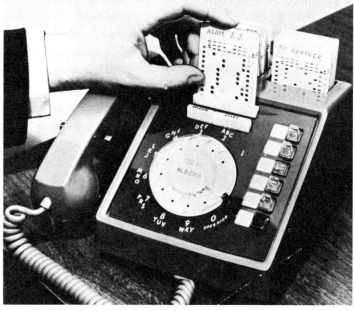

1 Alexander Graham Bell built his first telephone in 1871. The wooden framework supports an electromagnet over a drumskin with a metal vibrator attached to it.
2 On this modern telephone, by contrast, numbers in frequent use can be pre-recorded on punched cards, which are then merely inserted into a slot to give the required number automatically.
3 A picture transmitter, a regular item of equipment in newspaper offices, makes it possible to send and receive photographs instantaneously over the public telephone system.

as a result of instructions coded and sent out by radio. Not only can television pictures be received from the moon, but also information about temperature and radiation levels. Highly sophisticated equipment is needed, to convey such 'messages' with the required degree of precision and freedom from error.

On a more mundane level typesetting of newspapers is frequently carried out by machines controlled by tapes, whose instructions may be conveyed over radio and telephone links.

A completely new development in recent years has been the application of the laser beam to communication. Since the laser makes it possible to produce light waves covering extremely narrow bands of frequency, these may be used to convey messages similar to the use of radio waves. Because the frequency of light is so much greater than radio, large quantities of information may be transmitted using a single beam. The laser, as in so many other applications, may one day revolutionize telecommunications.

What do we mean here by 'quantity of information'? it may be asked. In the course of the expansion of the American telephone system, this question became very important. Hartley, Shannon and later Norbert Wiener, investigated mathematically the nature of messages in general.

Essentially, the signal conveying a message is the variation of some quantity, for example, the level of an electric current, or the amplitude of a radio wave. The amount of information conveyed in a signal was related to how far this variation was from what might be predicted. For example, a message from the North Pole: 'It is cold here!' would not appreciably increase our knowledge, while the news of a heat wave might.

Information theory

The *theory of information* enabled scientists to consider the problem of 'noise'. When a signal is transmitted, it inevitably gets distorted, mixed up with random variations which interfere with it. The decoded message at the receiver will thus be more or less different from the message originally sent off. The *capacity* of a channel of communication could be measured and the best means of sending information decided in terms of the 'signal to noise ratio'.

For example, it can be proved that frequency modulation is less affected by noise than amplitude modulation. Modern telephone systems also employ *pulse-modulation*, in which the signal consists of a series of pulses, the intervals between which may be slightly varied. This can give very small amounts of distortion even when the same channel is conveying many different messages simultaneously.

And so we see that the rise of telecommunications has given rise to entire new industries and sciences. Vast resources are devoted to improving the ways in which men can communicate ideas to each other, all over the world.

However, *what* they communicate is quite another matter.

Messages 'on the air'

The pioneers of radio and television — men like Hertz, Marconi and Baird — could scarcely have dreamed that their inventions would transform communications to the extent that they have done.

THE DATE was 12 December 1901. The location, Signal Hill, St John's, Newfoundland. Guglielmo Marconi and two assistants could hardly believe the evidence of their ears. Ever so faintly, but unmistakably, they heard on their primitive receiver *dit-dit-dit* – the letter 'S' of the Morse Code – transmitted at a pre-arranged time from Poldhu in Cornwall, some 1,700 miles to the east. The Atlantic Ocean had been bridged for the first time by wireless telegraphy!

Marconi was jubilant. He was no great scientist but he had faith in wireless communication. The best scientific opinion of the day was that transmission of signals without wires was a novelty suitable only for short ranges. Marconi had shown his critics they were wrong and by a single practical demonstration he accelerated the development of one of the most potent forces for good, and for evil, of the twentieth century.

The Atlantic had been bridged by a submerged telegraph cable as early as 1866. By the time Marconi made his historic experiment most important centres in the world were linked by the electric telegraph. But to be able to transmit information without wires over vast distances – this was really something new. It seemed as if it might prove profitable, too. To lay a transatlantic cable cost a lot of money. The cable itself cost plenty and its annual upkeep even more, spread over the years. Figures of £1 million for first cost and £100,000 a year for maintenance were quoted. In contrast a wireless transmitter would cost, perhaps, £50,000 and its maintenance only £12,000 a year.

Marconi's genius lay not in his inventive capacity but in his ability as a practical innovator. The German physicist Heinrich Hertz is credited with being the first man to demonstrate that electromagnetic waves could be generated at one point and received at another. This was in 1888 and what Hertz did supplied experimental proof of a theory propounded by James Clerk Maxwell some years earlier.

Marconi had heard of Hertz's work. So had the Russian scientist Popov and the British scientist Oliver Lodge. All three had achieved wireless transmission by 1895 but it was Marconi alone who had the vision to see the new science in practical terms.

His family had money and connections in England and in 1896 Marconi sailed from his native Italy armed with letters of introduction and unbounded enthusiasm. He was granted the first patent for telegraphic communication without wires and in the following year formed the Wireless Telegraph and Signal Company. Marconi was then only 23 years old. Three years later the company, based at Chelmsford, changed its name to Marconi's Wireless Telegraph Company.

Wealthy backers of the new company, greedy for the rich dividends that had accompanied the growth of wire telegraphy were in for a shock. Wireless was slow to catch on and no dividend was paid during the years 1897 to 1910. But if there were no dividends there was technical progress. The first wireless station in the world was set up at Alum Bay on the Isle of Wight in 1897. It handled its first paid message in 1898. In that year, too, the newfangled wireless received royal patronage with Queen Victoria using it to keep in touch with the Prince of Wales who was aboard the royal yacht. In 1899 radio signals from Chelmsford were received in Boulogne – a distance of 85 miles.

Then came the great triumph of 12 December 1901 with the Atlantic bridged for the first time. Marconi achieved this by using a very much longer wavelength than had previously been used. It had been supposed, up to that time, that wireless waves travelled only in straight lines in the same way as light. This would mean that to overcome the curvature of the Earth the transmitting and receiving aerials would need to be immensely high so that they could 'see' each other. Marconi demonstrated that long waves (he used a wavelength of 1,500 metres) must, in some way, be reflected from the sky to get round the bulge of the Earth.

The following year the theory was propounded independently by Oliver Heaviside in England and A. E. Kennelly in the United States that there was, in fact, a layer in the sky which reflected wireless waves of suitable wavelength. In 1925 Appleton was able to demonstrate experimentally that such a layer existed about 60 miles above the Earth's surface. It was also found that other layers existed at

1 Marconi (second left) and his research team outside the tower on Signal Hill, St John's, Newfoundland, where the inventor received the first successful transatlantic radio transmission.
2 Radio for traffic control. The New York policeman at the entrance to the Lincoln Tunnel reports traffic movements to central control using a miniature transmitter-receiver.
3 This tracery of aerials is part of the BBC shortwave transmitting station at Skelton, Cumberland. Its broadcasts span the world.

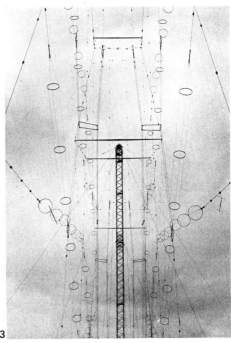

heights varying from 55 to more than 200 miles high in a belt we now call the ionosphere.

The behaviour of the ionosphere is important. It consists of positively charged ions and free electrons and is completely transparent to light and to very short wireless waves. Long waves are heavily reflected and medium waves less so. The layers and their composition vary in a complex manner according to time of day, season and the degree of radiation from the sun. The number of sun spots, for example, has an intense effect on the ionosphere. The ionosphere can be distributed so fiercely at times by abnormal solar radiation that communication is completely obliterated. At other times changes in the height of the ionized layers give rise to fading and distortion.

Despite Marconi's success with transatlantic trials he was unable to capture commercial traffic between land stations from the cable companies and he turned to the use of wireless for communication with shipping as a profitable alternative. It was here that he succeeded. By the outbreak of the First World War, wireless equipment was becoming a commonplace on ships. Its usefulness was demonstrated dramatically by the sinking of the *Titanic* in 1912. The *Carpathia* picked up the distress signals from the sinking ship and 700 lives were saved. It was shortly after this that most maritime nations passed legislation to oblige all ships over a certain tonnage to fit wireless. From this moment on the commercial success of the Marconi companies was assured.

Spark transmitters

All the early wireless installations used spark transmitters. The signals were generated by starting and stopping spark discharges with a Morse key and messages were universally sent in the dots and dashes of the Morse Code. At the receiving end the detection device was the coherer, a glass tube containing fine particles of metal which had the property of varying in electrical resistance as the spark signals were received and made it possible for them to be heard on headphones.

Ambrose Fleming, a British professor of electrical engineering, had invented the diode valve which was patented in 1904. Fleming was a consultant to Marconi and it was Marconi who held the patents. Another young engineer, Lee de Forest, was also busy experimenting in America and it was he who invented the triode valve. Both valves worked better as detection devices than the coherer. But whereas Fleming's valve was a better solution than the coherer, Lee de Forest's triode valve was superior to both in that it not only detected the weak wireless signals but also amplified them. Lee de Forest demonstrated his triode valve to an American telephone and cable company in 1912 but it was some years before production techniques had developed sufficiently to make the thermionic valve a commercial proposition.

It was the invention and subsequent development of the thermionic valve which made radio broadcasting possible. To

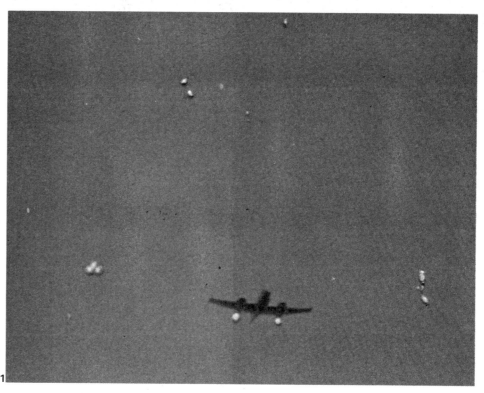

1

1 This old Gloster Meteor aircraft is about to end its life as a target for naval 'Seacat' anti-aircraft missiles. Radio-controlled pilotless 'drone' aircraft are often used for target practice in the testing and development of new types of anti-aircraft weapons.
2 Radio has obvious military applications. It provides the infantryman with a welcome direct link to his headquarters, so that he can call in air support or report incidents instantaneously. Here, an infantry radio operator on patrol in Cyprus uses a 'back-pack' transmitter.
3 Now a museum-piece, this 1938 combined radio and television receiver incorporated a seven-inch screen and cost 35 guineas. In those days, television was a novelty, almost a toy. Now it is the basis for a massive industry, and a widely used means of communication.

2

3

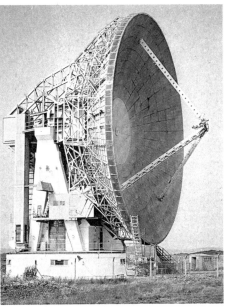

1 For many months of the year, the radio station of the Falkland Islands Dependencies Survey in Antarctica is the only link with the outside world and with the survey's outposts.
2 The reflectors at the Post Office's satellite communications centre at Goonhilly Down, Cornwall, beam vast amounts of information across the Atlantic via artificial satellites.
3 The BBC's television mast at Crystal Palace in south London towers nearly 1,000 feet over the surrounding built-up area, giving good straight-line reception for many miles around.

transmit speech or music demands a continuous wave – not the start-stop type of the spark transmitter. With the new radio valves (we shall use the more modern term 'radio' from now on) it was possible to generate continuous waves at the transmitter and to superimpose on the transmission the modulation of voice or music. At the receiving station the new valves were considerably more sensitive and were used for de-modulation to separate out the sound waves and then to amplify them to operate a loud speaker.

Regular broadcasting started in the United States from the Westinghouse station KDKA at East Pittsburgh on 21 December 1920, and two years later the British Broadcasting Company Ltd (now the British Broadcasting Corporation) was formed and the first programme was transmitted on 14 November 1922. One of the dreams of the early pioneers had been achieved.

The dream of television

But others were dreaming, too. If sounds could be transmitted through space, why not pictures? There was ample reason for believing this to be possible. Picture transmission by cable had already become an accomplished fact. Why not send pictures by radio?

John Logie Baird in Britain and C.F. Jenkins in the United States were both experimenting with television systems by 1923. In 1925, Baird demonstrated his system publicly for the first time. It was based on a principle developed by Paul Nipkow in 1884. Nipkow had evolved a method of sequentially scanning an object, his intention being to transmit pictures by cable. The scanning mechanism was a rotating disc with a series of punched holes in a spiral starting at the outer edge of the disc and progressively getting nearer the centre. If an object is viewed through the holes as the disc is slowly rotated each part of the object is seen in turn. If reflected light from the object passes through the holes and is allowed to fall on a photo-electric sensing device, a series of electric pulses, each proportional to the amount of light, can be generated. These could then be sent down a cable and used to control the brilliance of a light source at the receiving end which is viewed through the spirally set holes of a second Nipkow disc. If the two discs are in perfect synchronism a reproduction of the object can be built up at the receiver. To get a complete instantaneous picture reasonably fast the Nipkow discs must revolve at high speed. This takes advantage of the persistence of vision of the human eye

which does not notice interruptions in vision provided they are of very short duration. All television systems take advantage of this human defect.

Baird was no more a classical scientist than Marconi. He invented television first as Marconi invented radio, but neither discovered the laws of electromagnetism. But he was a keen experimenter and has his place in history as a practical man who made the system work. Nipkow had the idea but was unable to convert the electrical signals back into a picture.

The original Baird system was very crude. His disc had 30 holes in the spiral and so the picture was divided up into 30 lines – a very low standard of definition by modern standards. Nevertheless, it was a start and the British Broadcasting Corporation was first in the world with a regular television service in 1929 using the Baird system. It was transmitted on the medium-wave band on 261 metres for half-hour periods, five days a week.

Meanwhile, other workers had recalled a forecast made by A. A. Campbell Swinton in 1908 that the then newly invented cathode-ray tube might one day become a central component in the transmission of pictures. The mechanical systems involving Nipkow discs, mirror drums or other spinning scanning systems had obvious limitations. It had been mathematically calculated that for a reasonable quality picture the number of individual picture elements to be transmitted should be of the order of 100,000 repeated 20 times every second and no mechanical system could cope happily with this volume of picture information. The next leap forward would have to be an all-electronic system with no moving parts bigger than electrons.

The prime mover in developing modern television was Dr Vladimir Zworykin, a Russian who went to America after the Russian revolution. He joined Westinghouse and worked on new and more sensitive photocells for use in talking films – the talkies – which transformed the cinema industry when introduced in 1926.

By 1928 Zworykin had invented the iconoscope, the first all-electronic television camera tube with no moving parts. In 1930 he continued his work with the Radio Corporation of America which had taken over the radio and television interests of his former employers.

Since those first pioneer days television technology has moved strongly ahead to give the world colour television, and through satellites, the transmission of live pictures over vast distances.

It will be recalled that the development of long-distance radio communication depended very much on the existence of the ionosphere to reflect radio waves from the sky. It should also be recalled that while possessing this valuable property the ionosphere was, by its nature, unreliable. Because of hour to hour variations the quality of signals over long-distance paths was variable and a transmission would often be entirely lost. And because of this unreliability the new science of radio was unsuccessful in ousting the expensive but demonstrably reliable long-distance cable. Moreover, the ionosphere

Television from the moon. The United States' Surveyor VII lunar probe scoops up a sample of the moon's surface and brings it within range of the automatic television camera.

does not reflect short waves which alone can carry the wealth of information (100,000 elements 20 times a second) demanded by television.

This situation has been transformed by the communications satellite and the most promising medium of transmission is now the ultra-short wave directed in an absolutely straight line through the iono-sphere to the satellite where the signals are received, amplified and retransmitted back to Earth. The scientists have dis-covered that very short wavelengths are best after all!

The satellite communication system is now the wonder of the world. On 22 January 1969, Goonhilly 2, Britain's latest and largest space communication station was officially opened by senior representa-tives of the British Post Office and the Marconi Company. It is located, appro-priately, in Cornwall, not far from where Marconi staged his first transatlantic experiments.

But instead of only a letter 'S' of the Morse Code, Goonhilly 2 can handle 400 intercontinental telephone circuits and a television programme simultaneously. Working through the Intelsat III satellite 23,000 miles high over the Atlantic it can handle more traffic alone than all the transatlantic cables and the earlier Goon-hilly 1 station capacity added together. It will not only be used for instant com-

munication with the United States and Canada but to Africa and the Middle East as more satellites become available. More-over, its operational reliability is 99·9 per cent which means that in any one year it will never be out of service for more than a total of nine hours.

Even a visionary like Marconi would be amazed to see a single radio station cost-ing £1·5 million and with an aerial struc-ture weighing about 1,000 tons. Marconi died in Rome on 20 July 1937, but his name as the pioneer broadcaster remains a household word all over the world.

1 Sun spots, associated with intensive magnetic disturbances in the ionosphere, can cause 'fade-out' of radio and television transmission, and interfere with communications.
2 Radio-controlled boats, like this handsome model warship, give pleasure to thousands of amateurs, both children and adults. Many enthusiasts build their own models.

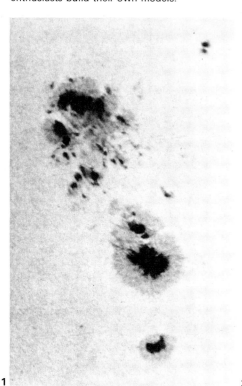

1

2

The mechanics of music

The design of musical instruments involves some basic sciences, from acoustics to electronics. The relationship of science and music has always been close, and may now involve the ubiquitous computer.

THE SOUND OF MUSIC is almost inescapable in modern living. The electronics industry has seen to that by developing new means of recording, sound reproduction, and broadcasting. The transistor and miniaturization in general have made radios and record players fully transportable, so that whether your taste is for the Beatles or Beethoven, it can be satisfied almost any time by the flick of a switch.

Most people are aware that this modern gadgetry owes its existence to the application of scientific principles, even though they may not understand them. What is less generally perceived – or even thought about – is the fact that the primary means of musical production, the instruments, can only be understood in terms of scientific principles. The disciplines involved are many and include acoustics, mechanical engineering and electronics. Basic to the whole proposition, of course, is acoustics. We are able to hear sounds because sound waves beat upon the tympanic membrane or drum of our ear. But something has to set up these sound waves in the first place. In almost all cases, then, the process begins with a vibrating source, which, moving in one direction, pushes the surrounding molecules of air before it. These molecules crowd and therefore energize the molecules of air next to them before returning to their original position, and thus a process of alternate crowding and thinning is passed through the air. These are sound waves, and this is the basic mechanism of sound production. But in the various branches of the family of instruments – percussion, wind and strings – the manner in which the sound production is carried out varies considerably.

It is useful to take percussion instruments, in particular the drums, first since

certainly these were the first musical instruments. Since in most cases they are only capable of one note, they are also the easiest to comprehend. The first drums probably consisted simply of a piece of wood placed over a hole in the ground. When beaten with the hand, a stick, or stamped with the feet, vibration was set up in the wood and this was in turn imparted to the air in the hole and the air above the wood.

A page from a medieval manuscript shows two ways of producing a musical scale. The man in the background is striking bells of graded sizes, while in the foreground water-filled glasses are struck.

The actual note produced in this way depended upon a number of variables – the size and thickness of the wood, the depth and diameter of the hole and so on. In other words the sound depended upon the frequency, that is the number of oscillations per second, of the vibrating surface. Generally speaking, the smaller the area of drum head the greater will be the frequency of vibration and hence the higher the note. Likewise the smaller the volume of air trapped inside the drum, the higher the note.

Drum design

Modern drums, seen in any beat group or dance band (snare, tom-tom, and bass) are designed to combine these factors in different proportions to make a whole range of sounds available to the drummer. The snare drum and the tom-tom, for example, may have the same area of skin (which has long since replaced wood as a vibration surface) but the snare drum is also much more shallow. It therefore has the higher pitch of the two. Incidentally it gets its distinctive sound and also its name from snares, or thongs, which are stretched across the inside diameter of the drum just below the skin. When the surface above is beaten, these rattle against it with a sound like the impact of tiny stones.

The bass drum has the largest skin surface and the largest volume of enclosed air; it therefore emits the lowest note of the three, and since it has no snares, the note is 'clean'.

There is one other factor which affects the note produced in a drum. This is the relative slackness or tightness of the skin. Once again, the tighter the skin the more rapid will be the vibrations when struck. The sound waves therefore reach the ear

Glass-harp virtuoso Bruno Hoffmann, of Stuttgart, made his harp himself. Fifty glasses were specially blown to give a four-octave range. The harp is played by rubbing the rims with damp fingers.

Jazz musician Jesse Fuller's one-man band. Apart from guitar and cymbals, he has a mouth-organ and kazoo on a harness round his neck, while his right foot operates a bass-like 'fodella'.

Two members of a steel band from Trinidad tune one of the oil-cans which serve as drums. The drums are tuned by denting the lid of the can, thus rendering it more or less taut.

in quicker succession and the received sound is higher in pitch. It was mentioned above, that most drums are capable of only one note, but it would be more accurate to say that the note *can* be changed by slackening or tightening the skin – but only with some trouble. In other words it cannot be varied at will during the performance of a piece.

However, there is one drum on which this is possible. It is called the timpani, and the player is easily able to tighten or slacken the skin by turning 'taps' around the circumference of the bowl-shaped shell.

This by no means exhausts the list of percussion instruments, but all the rest employ the same basic principle, in that surfaces – brass in the case of cymbals, wood in xylophones and maraccas – are struck directly or indirectly and therefore caused to vibrate.

Vibration is also the key to the effectiveness of the next major group of musical instruments, the strings. But these musical machines are generally much more sophisticated in a number of ways.

The guitar is probably the most widespread stringed instrument and it embodies most of the technical qualities of the stringed instruments in general. The strings are made of nylon (sometimes gut) or steel and they are stretched between two fixed points, one on the sound box and the other at the extreme end of the finger board.

When plucked with the fingers or struck with a plectrum the oscillations of the strings are transmitted to the wooden upper surface (belly) of the sound box which itself vibrates as does the air inside

1 Tunisian musicians play their plaintive, minor-key melodies on pipes and drums. These relatively primitive instruments are found in different forms all over the world.

2 Village bands, frequently with a variety of brass instruments, have long been a feature of the development of European music. Here a military band plays outside the town hall.

3 Victoria de los Angeles is one of the world's most famous operatic sopranos. The quality of a singer's voice is largely inherited, though training can improve it.

the box. The original sound of the string is therefore amplified.

Most guitars have six strings, all the same length. However, they are of different thicknesses, the thickest at the bottom, the thinnest at the top. The frequency of vibration in the thick ones is lower than in the thin; therefore the note produced is lower.

The guitar has as many notes as it has strings and even further variation is achieved by a process called stopping. This depends upon the principle that the shorter the length of a vibrating surface, the higher the note. As pointed out already, the guitar string when in its natural state is fixed at either end. If, however, a finger is pressed against the string bringing it into hard contact with the neck of the instrument, a significantly shorter length is free and the sound emitted will be raised in pitch. It is therefore possible for the instrumentalist to play complicated tunes by stopping the strings in this manner. Chords can be played by stopping two or more strings at the same time and strumming them together.

The violin family

These same principles also apply to the instruments of the violin family, except here the initial vibration of the strings is caused by friction with the strings of a bow. Stopping is again employed for melody and chord playing. But with other stringed instruments, like the piano and harp, things are done differently. Here there is a string for each note, and the range is achieved by variation in length and thickness only.

We can appreciate then that the stringed instruments are heavily dependent on applications of science other than acoustics. There is, for example, the selection of materials, wood for the main structure, nylon and metal for the strings themselves. Experiments have shown that straight-grained pine is an excellent material in which to construct the bellies of guitars, violins and so on, since it allows the transmitted vibrations to spread easily and rapidly both along and across the grain.

Again, engineering is used in the devices for tensioning the string, in the internal structure of the instruments, and in the keyboard and hammer mechanisms where there are any. The internal structure is particularly important. It must be arranged so that the relatively flimsy belly is supported against pressure of the strings, bow or hand, yet the sound is in no way muffled. In most cases the job is done by a series of transverse bars glued to the underside of the belly. They provide support but do not inhibit flexibility; on the contrary they aid the spread of the vibrations across the grain.

The wind instruments can be divided into two categories: brass, which includes trumpet, trombone, tuba and so on; and the woodwind, which includes reed instruments like clarinet, oboe and saxophone, and pipe instruments like flute and piccolo.

Without doubt the most spectacular sounding brass instrument is the trumpet. Again all depends on vibration but here it

1 Jazz immortal Dizzy Gillespie plays a bent trumpet. The horn of his instrument was swung round so that the sound would be directed into the hall rather than into the footlights.

2 A piano, showing how the strings are attached. The note given by a stretched string depends on its length and tension. Strings are short and tight for high notes, longer and looser for low notes.

43

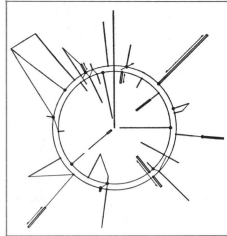

Prelude No. 7 from part II of Johann Sebastian Bach's 'Well-Tempered Clavier'. This was one of many pieces written by Bach to promote a new and more versatile system of tuning.

is the lips of the player which do the job. Very simply, he tenses them across the cup-shaped mouthpiece of his horn and blows what can only be described as a 'raspberry'. This sets a vibrating column of air echoing through the instrument to the bell, and on its journey the original noise is both modified and amplified until it emerges with the typical bright hard sound of the instrument.

Brass instruments

Just as the violinist or guitarist is able to get a wider variety of notes by shortening or lengthening his strings, the brass player can do the same by altering the length of his column of air. There are two ways in which he can do this – by means of valves as in the trumpet, French horn and tuba, or by a slide as in the trombone.

In all cases, the mechanics involved are relatively simple. In the trumpet there are three valves and attached to each is a loop of tubing. When the valve is pressed the column of air is deflected through this loop; it is therefore lengthened and the note produced is lowered. In the case of trombones it is even more simple. The slide is actually a looped sleeve which, when extended, also adds to the length of the vibrating air column. (Incidentally, similar but smaller slide mechanisms are also fitted to many brass instruments for tuning.)

The earliest form of woodwind instrument was probably the flute, which, as previously explained, has no reed. In this case the flautist produces his sound by blowing across the opening of the instrument. The air hits the far edge of this hole and forms eddies both above and below it. The result is a rapid pressure oscillation which causes the air inside to vibrate. In the simplest kinds of flute, variation of note is then achieved by opening and closing holes with the fingers, for where a hole is uncovered the column of air is allowed to escape and so is shortened. In the modern concert flute, the holes are opened and closed by a complicated system of keys.

Finally, we come to one branch of music making in which physics is most truly at home. This is, of course, electronic music, and it is a far cry from the conventional kind. The instruments involved produce vibrations which are electrical and not acoustic. They therefore cannot be heard unless passed, like radio signals, through an amplifier and loudspeaker or headphones.

The vibrations themselves can be of any desired frequency and of any harmonic content. It is possible, therefore, to imitate the sounds of most, if not all, the conventional instruments and also to produce sounds which have never been heard before. These advances in electronic music have been mostly applied to the organ. In the future it is likely that they will be used to build completely revolutionary instruments which will greatly broaden the range of tone colours and harmonies available to the composer.

Some composers have experimented using tape recorders to modify the sounds produced by instrumentalists. Karlheinz Stockhausen has written music in which the notes produced by a group of per-

Testing the thickness of a violin's sound-box. Violin-making demands exceptional skill, blending art with science to produce a full-bodied tone and an aesthetically pleasing shape.

A modern piano composition by the Japanese composer Toru Takemitsu. The composition, generated by computer, can be played as three different variations by moving the inner ring.

formers are recorded, and played back a short time later but in a greatly changed form. One performer has to 'play' the tape recorder; by moving the controls on his electronic equipment he can decide just *how* the notes are modified. As he plays the changed notes back the performers have moved on to new notes, and startling effects are produced by the combinations which arise. As the players of all the instruments (including the tape recorder) are, to a certain extent, free to choose what they will play, such pieces will never sound the same at two separate performances.

Music, of course, existed long before the Greeks attempted to explain it in terms of scientific principles. And famous violin-makers produced beautiful-sounding instruments without knowing exactly why they sounded so good. We can still enjoy music today without understanding how it works. But the alliance between physics and music is just beginning to open up a whole new world of sound which is revolutionizing the art of music.

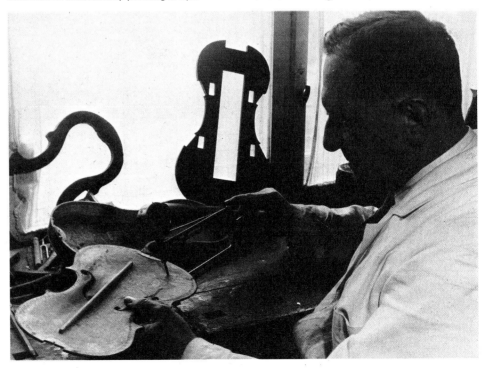

His master's voice?

One of the early commercial record companies used a label showing a dog listening to 'His Master's Voice' – recorded on wax. The problem of reproducing 'live' sound accurately is still being solved.

1

ENRICO CARUSO, the famous Italian tenor, was able to break a wine glass merely by singing a particular note. Violinists, too, have broken glasses by playing high notes. This phenomenon, which has been demonstrated many times, shows that sound has at least some of the attributes of a physical force. What we hear and understand as sound or noise in some way transfers energy, and thus must have required energy to initiate it.

If one plucks the string of a guitar, or bows the string of a violin, the string can be seen to vibrate. Plucking harder or softer produces a louder or a quieter note, and it can be seen that the distance that the string moves from its stationary position, the amplitude, is also related to the loudness or softness of the sound. In wind instruments, like the organ, the air in the pipes vibrates while a note is being produced, and the loudness of the sound is again related to the extent of the vibration.

Vibration

When an organ pipe vibrates, it sets the air molecules nearby vibrating at the same frequency. This can readily be observed by watching the motion of specks of dust near a bass organ pipe. This vibration is passed on to neighbouring molecules, so that the sound is transmitted to the listener. When these vibrations strike the ear-drums, they set them vibrating too and the listener gets the impression of sound.

The frequency of a note, played, say, on a flute, sets up in the human brain a response which indicates to the hearer the sound of a flute. The average adult can hear notes with a frequency up to about 20,000 cycles per second. At the other end of the scale, sounds with a frequency of about 20 cycles per second separate into

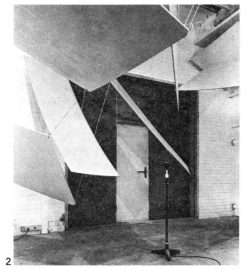

2

3

individual impulses rather than a continuous note. Thus the effective frequency range of the human ear is approximately from 20 cycles per second to 25,000 cycles per second. Measurements on the instruments of the orchestra show that the frequencies of the pure tones produced range from about 16 cycles per second to about 4,000 cycles per second.

But the pure tone produced by an instrument is only part of the story, otherwise middle C played on a trumpet would be identical with middle C played on a piano. A pure tone is normally accompanied by overtones, vibrations having a frequency which is a multiple (that is, two, three or four times) of the frequency of the fundamental tone. It is this which extends the frequency of the orchestra to the upper part of the range of the human ear.

If a guitar string is plucked, it can be found, by positioning small pieces of paper on the string, that at certain points the string does not vibrate. These stationary points are called *nodes,* and the distance between two nodes is, in fact,

1 Thomas Alva Edison invented his 'phonograph or speaking machine' in 1877. The original model recorded sound on a cylinder covered with tin foil and turned with a hand crank.
2 A reverberation chamber for testing the sound insulation of a door. The hanging baffle boards cut out echoes from the walls, enabling the sound transmitted through the door to be measured.
3 This Czech musical box, built in 1825, operates on the principle of a player piano. It has 137 organ pipes, and is equipped with 29 cylinders playing dance and opera music.
4 An early type of mechanically operated gramophone. The large horn is necessary to amplify sound produced by the motion of the stylus on the disc which carries the recording.

4

equal to the wavelength of the sound. When a string is sounding its fundamental note, these nodes are at the ends only, but when it is producing overtones, nodes will be found in other places.

Apart from frequency and loudness, other factors also influence the sound as one hears it. Everyone has heard the echo reflected off a cliff or hillside. What happens in this case is that the sound leaves the source, spreads out in all directions, and is generally heard by anyone who happens to be in the vicinity. But when the sound reaches a solid object, preferably large, hard and smooth, the sound is echoed or reflected, in roughly the same way that a ray of light is reflected by a mirror, or a ball is bounced from a wall.

Acoustic differences

Echoes also account for the difference in sound between a violin played in a cathedral and in an ordinary domestic living room. Identical notes sound entirely different, and this cannot be accounted for by frequency or overtones. In a cathedral there are a large number of hard, smooth surfaces which serve to bounce the sound back to the listener. In most buildings of this type, there is a multiple echo, which makes a single struck or plucked note appear to persist and will give a blown note from a wind instrument a fullness and swelling quality which it would lack in the open. When the echo is strong, and when the interval between sound and echo is large, however, the result is confusion between one note and its successor, so that much of the music is indistinct.

In a normal domestic lounge, reflecting surfaces which are present are usually quite close to the source, and the echo interval is so short as to be virtually unnoticeable. In addition, there are a number of objects such as carpets, curtains, cushions and people, which absorb rather than reflect the sound. There will still be a certain amount of echo, or the music would lack its lifelike quality. In concert halls, the designers aim to get the best compromise between acoustic 'deadness' – that is, no echo – and troublesome long-lasting echoes. Despite advances in acoustic design, this is still to a great degree an art as well as a science.

Loudness is another attribute of sound which must be taken into account when evaluating its quality. For scientific or engineering purposes, sound loudness is measured in terms of the amount of power which is put out by the source, or which reaches the listener. In this context, it should be remembered that the ratio of powers between a very quiet and a fortissimo passage in music may be 1,000,000, so that the scale of loudness is very large indeed. Loudness is always measured in ratios, and the standard used is a very quiet room. Everything is measured in relation to this. To avoid the use of very large ratios, and also for a number of scientific reasons, it is the logarithm of this ratio which is used. Now the logarithm of 1,000,000 is 6, and the logarithm of the ratio is a unit called a bel, and so one is able to say that the loud passage in a symphony is 6 bels louder than a

quiet passage. For many purposes, the bel is inconveniently large, and so it is subdivided into tenths, or decibels. The ratio now becomes 60 decibels or 60dB. By simple calculation, it can be shown that if one sound is twice as loud as another, then it is almost exactly 3dB louder.

It is in the light of these complex and interrelated factors, frequency, overtones, loudness and resonance, that the work of sound-recording scientists and engineers must be viewed. Sound recording is a means of holding up a mirror to the music and din of the world, in a similar manner to the recording of visual phenomena with a camera.

Sound exerts a force, or a pressure, on objects falling in its path, and it is on this note that the recording of sound depends. In the earliest mechanical recorders, a diaphragm or thin plate was placed near the source of the sound. The vibrations of the air made this diaphragm vibrate at the same frequency, and this movement was linked mechanically to a cutter which carved a groove in a moving cylinder or disc of some suitable material, usually wax. If the procedure was reversed, with a

London's Royal Festival Hall has a series of baffles in the roof to prevent too great an echo, and the position of the boxes along the side of the hall can be varied to change the acoustics.

needle moving in the precut groove and driving a diaphragm, an approximation to the original sound could be heard. Thomas Alva Edison was the first man to demonstrate that sound could be recorded in this way. But while Edison's 1877 phonograph represented a major step forward, it suffered from some appalling drawbacks. Not least of these was that the singer virtually had to stick his or her head within the recording horn, while on the other hand the volume of sound produced on playback was pitifully small. These early machines could only record a limited range of frequency, so that the high notes in a piece of music were eliminated. Because of the friction between the playing needle and the disc or cylinder, there was also a high degree of surface scratch and hiss, or noise. Add to this the fact that it was virtually impossible with handdriven machines to record and play back at the same speed and it is obvious that while the early machines were fascinating toys, they were less than satisfactory from the musical point of view.

While scientists and engineers held to mechanical methods of recording and reproducing, there was a limit to the degree of improvement which could be attained. But the invention of the thermionic valve by Fleming placed a new component in the hands of sound engineers.

The triode valve allowed electric currents to be amplified, or increased in power without introducing distortion. The microphone, which converted sound waves into electrical signals, was already in use in the telephone. Then signals taken from a microphone, and representing the sounds falling on that microphone, could be amplified by a series of valves until they were powerful enough to drive a record cutting stylus. On playback, the oscillations of a needle produced by that groove in a disc could be made to produce electrical signals, which were again amplified to activate a loudspeaker and give high volume reproduction with what was then comparatively low distortion.

The same basic principle is used today. Music is still generally recorded on flat discs, a groove being cut on the surface of the disc in accordance with the sound received by the microphone. Modern records use a new material – vinyl – which is much more durable than its predecessors, wax or shellac; emits very little scratch or hiss; will take much more detailed impressions and is virtually unbreakable, unless treated very harshly indeed.

As in so many fields, the introduction of vinyl was only one of a parallel set of improvements, each of which depended on others. To produce high-quality records it was necessary to have a cutter which

1 Echo-less rooms in which the walls are studded with baffles to absorb sound and prevent echoes are used by sound engineers to obtain special recording effects and to test equipment.
2 The acoustics of a large church like St Paul's Cathedral are mainly determined by the hard, smooth surfaces which bounce sound back at the listener, giving rise to reverberations.
3 The sound engineer's instrument panel at a recording studio enables him to control the quality of the sound recorded, to add special effects and to mix different sounds together.

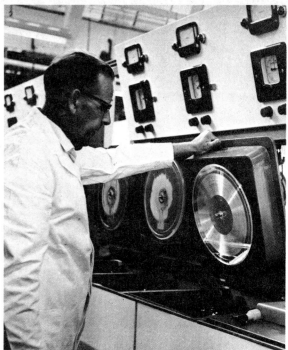

Women inspectors at a modern record factory test records taken at random from the production line. They are listening for scratches and other production faults in the records.

The master mould from which records are pressed is produced by growing nickel electrochemically on a silvered lacquer original. The nickel plate formed is an exact replica of the original disc.

would respond faithfully to the musical sounds, and on playback it was necessary to have a record player which would read out exactly the information contained on the disc, and reproduce it faithfully. If any one of these fell short, the whole effort would be wasted.

In the early days of recording it was enough to make one copy of any sound or piece of music, because the recorder was merely a toy. But with the improvement of equipment a demand was created for recorded music, and so a means had to be found of mass-producing these recordings.

Disc-cutting

The first step in making a recording is to record the relevant piece, generally on a tape recorder. This tape is then edited to remove any blemishes or accidental noises which may have strayed on to it. The next stage is disc-cutting. The disc-cutter is essentially an electronic amplifier which drives a sharp, fine-pointed cutter. This cutter is mounted above a turntable which rotates at a precisely controlled speed. The cutter itself is mounted on a threaded drive, and can be moved gradually at a predetermined rate towards the centre of the disc as the recording proceeds.

The electrical signal from the tape, is fed into the amplifier, which drives the cutter, and the combination of turntable and cutter drive produce a spiral groove running towards the centre of the disc and bearing undulations corresponding to the music. A soft material is used for this master, so that the groove can follow the sound exactly. Wax was the original material used, but it has been superseded by lacquer or plastics.

A copy of the master, a negative copy or mould, is then made. This in turn, after processing and reinforcing, is used to produce other moulds, by a two-stage

moulding process. The commercial records are made from these mould-copies. The first and second moulds, sometimes called the father and the mother, can then be stored in safety in case one of the working pressing masters is accidentally damaged.

Absolute cleanliness is essential at all stages in the making of the matrices, as a small speck of dust which sticks to a matrix will make its presence heard as an unwanted noise on the finished records. Similarly, the grinding and compounding of the vinyl material must be done with the greatest precision as a grainy material gives an unacceptable background noise. In fact the major advantage of vinyl over the acetate which was used for the older 78 r.p.m. records is this absence of surface noise.

But although records are a source of musical pleasure for many homes, it is out of the question for most people to record a family occasion on disc. In the 1940s, tape recorders became available for ordinary domestic use. These use an entirely different principle from the disc, and are almost wholly electronic apart from the driving motors. At the heart of a tape recorder are the recording and playback heads, sometimes, on less expensive machines, combined into one unit. When an electrical signal is passed from the microphone, it is amplified electronically and passed to the recording head, which is rather like a small electromagnet with a minute air gap between the poles. The fluctuating signal, or oscillations, produce a strong fluctuating magnetic field in the gap. Recording tape is a continuous narrow strip of a base material – polyvinyl acetate, polyester, or some other suitable plastic – coated on one side with a thin layer of finely-divided magnetic iron oxide. When the tape is carried at a steady speed past the recording head, the magnetic field in the vicinity of the gap magnetizes the iron oxide particles in patterns which correspond to the electrical signals.

On playback, the tape is again transported past the playback head which

'reads' these patterns from the tape. The impulses pass the amplifier and a loudspeaker, and an image of the original sound is heard. Miniaturized tape recorders developed over recent years, have made recording even more versatile than it originally was. This type of tape recorder frequently uses a cassette of tape, which can be loaded and unloaded without complications. These developments make tape recorders usable in almost every situation.

An outstanding advantage of tape recording is that the original recording can be erased at any time by subjecting the tape to a high-frequency erasing signal, and the tape can be re-used. This process can be repeated time and time again with little deterioration in the quality of the tape. In addition, the quality of sound reproduction from a well-made tape is generally considerably higher than from a gramophone record, as there is little friction to cause unwanted noise or distortion.

Permanent record

Apart from its applications in entertainment, tape recording has eased the task of people in many walks of life. The tape recorder is used by teachers for preparing lessons, businessmen for dictating letters or reports, and by journalists for recording interviews. It is used throughout science and industry for recording research data, in automatic checking procedures, and has even been used in burglar alarms.

So many of the things which we take for granted in the twentieth century depend on sound recording. It has been said that Edison did for sound what Kodak did for sight. Between them they have enabled men to put a large part of their physical world on permanent and reproducible record.

Man-made brains

The advent of the computer has changed the nature of many activities. Complicated calculations have become child's play and information handling is completely revolutionized.

SCORES OF THOUSANDS of electronic computers are now in service in the world, and the present time has rightly been dubbed the computer age. The modern computer, however, is only the latest in a long line of mechanical aids to calculation devised by mathematical Man.

The earliest aids probably resembled the abacus or counting frame. This, in its earliest form, was a tray with grooves cut to hold pebbles which later was developed into a rectangular frame supporting wires with beads threaded on them. The abacus was used all round the Mediterranean in the first millennium B C. It is known to have been used by the Aztecs and by the Chinese at the time of Confucius.

The abacus is used even today in many parts of the world and, with a skilful operator, it is still a powerful tool. In an open contest in 1946 between a Japanese abacus operator and an expert American operator using the latest electronic desk calculator, the Japanese won convincingly, using an abacus costing only a few shillings, in five types of calculations covering the basic arithmetical operations.

A big advance in calculating technique was made with the invention of the logarithm by John Napier. Napier's invention was publicly announced in a book published in 1614. His contribution made it possible to multiply and divide, the two most difficult computations, merely by adding and subtracting. And by 1621 William Oughtred, using the new principle of logarithms, had produced a working slide rule which was the precursor of the modern instrument.

The first mechanical calculator

The first truly mechanical calculator appeared in the seventeenth century. The beads of the abacus, in effect, became teeth on gear wheels. Instead of beads being moved individually by hand the teeth on the gear wheels were notched round as the calculation proceeded. Early examples of mechanical calculators built by Blaise Pascal who died in 1662 are still preserved in Paris. Leibniz, the great German mathematician, produced a machine about 1671 which could multiply as well as add and subtract. In 1810 the first commercially available mechanical calculator was developed by Charles Thomas of Colmar, Alsace, and 1,500 machines based on his design, using the Leibniz principles, were made over the next 60 years.

The distinction between a mechanical calculator and an automatic one is important. All the calculating aids so far discussed need the constant attention of an operator. He has to move beads on a frame, set dials, or punch keys for each part of the calculation. The speed of calculation is therefore determined by the rate at which the human operator can manipulate the input to the machine rather than by how fast the machine reacts internally. This was recognized by the Englishman Charles Babbage (1791–1871) who set about designing an automatic calculating machine which could conduct intricate mathematical computations without attention.

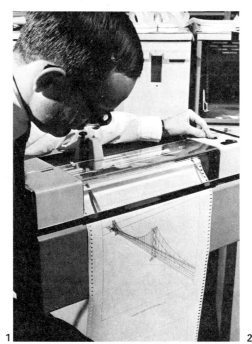

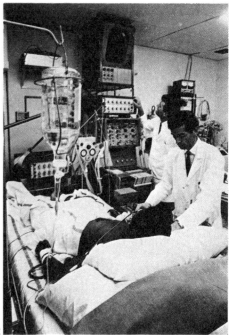

Babbage is recognized as the father of modern computing. His first computer – first in the world – was the Difference Engine, to be used for computing tables of mathematical functions. His second, the Analytical Engine, was truly universal, unlike the Difference Engine which was designed for a specific set of calculations.

1 The designer's job is made easier by computers. With appropriate information, this Elliott 900 model can produce in a few minutes designs that would otherwise have taken weeks.

2 Medical computers aid doctors to diagnose and follow the course of disease. This model automatically keeps track of heart rate, respiration and other body functions.

3 A VC 10 airliner landing in fog at London's Heathrow Airport. Computers linked to the plane's instruments keep the pilot constantly informed of his position and speed.

The Analytical Engine could be used for any type of calculation – in today's parlance it was a General Purpose Computer.

Unfortunately, neither of these machines was completed but the principles were sound. Charles Babbage had designed into his machine the five fundamental functions of a computer system, the store (or memory), arithmetic unit, control unit, input devices and output devices. His machines were a mass of gear wheels, rods and levers. The mechanical standards required to construct the machines were far too precise for the engineering methods available in the nineteenth century. Part of the Difference Engine can be seen at the Science Museum in London.

If Babbage was the father of the modern computer, Lady Lovelace (1815–52) was the mother of a necessary adjunct to it – the computer program. The computer, as we shall see, is capable only of the most elementary action without instructions. Lady Lovelace, the only child of Lord and Lady Byron, knew Babbage well and devised typical programs, some of which were very advanced. A computer program is stored in the computer and instructs it at every stage of a calculation.

Babbage's 'engines' were a concept far ahead of their time. We had to wait for the technical revolution of the twentieth century before the practical realization of the universal computer. In particular it was the rapid development of electronics that made the modern high-speed computer possible.

The breakthrough came almost simultaneously in Britain and the United States when researchers in several laboratories demonstrated working stored-program computers. The pioneer machine, developed in the United States, was ENIAC which used 18,000 electronic valves and consumed 150 kilowatts of electric power. Completed in 1946, it weighed 30 tons. Another pioneering computer was a small laboratory model designed by Professors F. C. Williams and T. Kilburn at Manchester University. This was operated successfully in June 1948. Other work was going on at London and Cambridge Universities and at the National Physical Laboratory.

Commercial machines

The early computers designed in the United States and Britain were the prototypes for commercial machines that began to appear in 1951. These machines, bearing such acronyms as EDSAC, ACE, DEUCE and LEO, had a hitherto unprecedented speed of operation and calculating power but were unreliable and consumed vast quantities of power. The invention of the point-contact transistor in 1948 and the subsequent development,

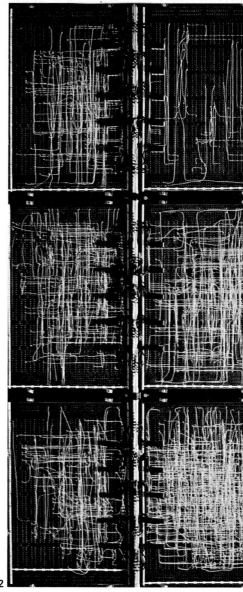

in 1957, of the planar silicon transistor transformed the situation. Computers became much smaller and faster in operation. The latest electronic development, the integrated circuit, has made computers yet smaller, faster and more powerful than those with planar transistors. These 'third-generation' machines using integrated circuits can compute at a rate of a million instructions per second.

It is important to remember that even the most modern and powerful computers cannot think. The work they do is, in fact, trivial in nature, but they do it quickly. A good computer can do simple arithmetic ten million times faster than a man, but it calculates only under orders determined by the program.

Let us look again at the five basic elements of a computer. These are: the store (or memory) unit, the arithmetic unit, the control unit, input devices, output devices.

Imagine a person sitting at a desk starting a calculation with paper and pen and a common desk calculator. The calculator is equivalent to the arithmetic unit in a computer. It performs the mathematical calculations. The person doing the calculations is equivalent to the control unit, and the pen and paper, on which are written intermediate results of the

1 The internal circuits of a large modern computer are exceptionally complex, and their manufacture involves a large amount of highly skilled labour. For this reason, computers are still very expensive.

2 The computer is formed of a number of units like this one. The maze of small wires linking various components together can be clearly seen in this view. Together, the various units compute and store information.

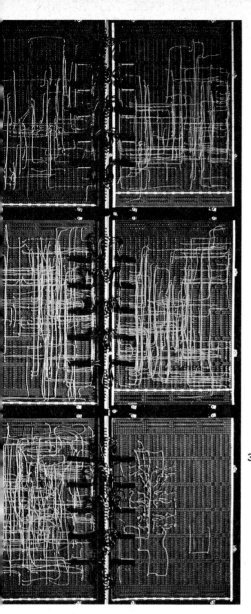

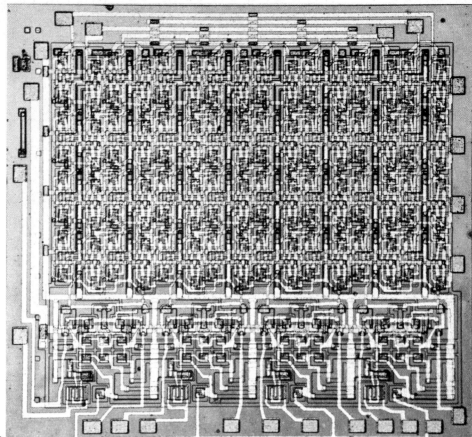

complex calculation, are equivalent to the computer store or memory unit.

Input and output devices are not necessary with a human operator because he is able to interpret directly his input data, the figures he feeds in, and the answer he needs, from the machine. The computer, however, must have input and output devices for the machine to interpret the input data in machine language and re-interpret it in understandable and usable form for the human beings at the output.

Perhaps Babbage's main failing in the design of his 'Engines' was to use the decimal notation of numbers. All modern computers use the binary system in which numbers or letters are represented by simple on-off states of electrical circuits and represent the digits 0 or 1. In the binary system, numbers are represented to the base 2 instead of to the base 10. Thus 13, which is $(8+4+1)$ or (2^3+2^2+1) becomes 1101 in binary notation. This is the simplest of all mathematical forms and the two main binary components in all digital computers are binary switching elements and binary memory elements.

A single digit in computer parlance is known as a bit and five bits commonly constitute a word. The word, then, is a set of digits of standard length, which can represent a number or an instruction to

3 The memory element of a modern computer. This tiny element contains about 650 components and measures only 0·11 in. by 0·105 in. Thousands of such elements are required for a large computer.

4 The computer as artist. A drawing executed by an IBM 7090 computer according to a program by Kunio Yamanaka. Many artists have looked towards the computer for fresh sources of inspiration and mathematical designs.

the computer. Numbers and instructions can be held in the main store and are accessible by addressing each 'pigeon hole' or register, as it is known, in the store.

Let us consider the simple operation of adding 1 and 2 in the computer. The first operation is to feed the figures into the input device where they are encoded into binary form and entered into the store. The computer must then be instructed to take them from the store, add them together in the arithmetic unit, and pass the answer back to the store. The final instruction tells the computer to pass the answer through a decoder to the output device where, for example, it might be printed out on an electric typewriter. More complex operations are simply continuous repetition, at very high speed, of the four basic arithmetical functions of addition, subtraction, multiplication and division. But at each stage the computer needs instructions from its program.

Even the fastest input/output devices of a computer installation are very slow compared with the speed of operation of the central processor. Where punched cards are used as the input the reading speed can be 1,000 cards a minute. Printed pages pouring out of a line printer at the output end appear far quicker than they can be read. Electric typewriters print far faster than a human operator could type. Even so, if a computer could be put into slow motion so that it carried out only one operation per second, the equivalent speed of a computer typewriter would be only one character per day. Modern computers are therefore designed to operate simultaneously with several input/output devices and do computation between times.

1 The minute square at the centre of this picture is an integrated circuit – a basic element of computer construction. The circuit's mounting dwarfs the circuit itself.
2 Computers are now used to predict weather. This model, at the U.S. Airforce Data Center, prints out a map of the world with tomorrow's weather indicated on it.

A significant development was the device known as the 'program-interrupt'. This device announces the arrival of important information in the input/output sections and stops the computation until the data is transferred, after which the computer carries on with its former activity. The most important modern development, however, is time-sharing, a system whereby several users can use the computer simultaneously, each working on separate problems. A large system of this type used at the Massachusetts Institute of Technology has 160 remote operating terminals of which any 30 can be in use simultaneously. What happens in this type of installation is that each user of the computer gets access to it for only a thirtieth of the time but the speed of switching from user to user is such that each individual gets the impression that he is the sole user. This is possible, of course, only because the computer works at a speed so much greater than the human mind.

Similar large installations are in operation in Britain, and the general public can get access to them through ordinary Post Office lines provided they have the necessary terminal equipment and pay

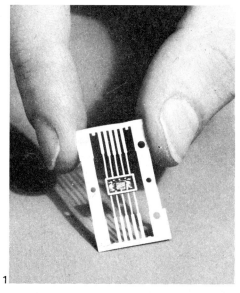

fees to the computer bureau. A number of universities have developed their own time-sharing systems (or multi-access systems, as they are sometimes called).

Time-sharing multi-access systems demand very large machines with enormous storage capacity. The Massachusetts system, for example, has stores containing a million words, 100 basic computer programs and a variety of special-purpose programs. In addition, users can insert their own private programs and one of the features is that a user can compile a program in conjunction with the computer.

Security is a major problem with computer installations of this type. Many contain vast amounts of stored information which may be quite private and confidential. Companies or individuals using the system must be guaranteed absolute privacy. One method of ensuring this is to have a secret password which alone allows access. After the initial call to the computer in which the subscriber states his name and project, the computer responds by asking for his password. If this does not correspond with the subscriber's name and project, the machine prints out a 'no access' message and denies further access.

What does a modern computer installation look like? This can be seen from the accompanying illustrations. A modern large installation, like the British ICL 1906A, has a main store with 256,000 words capacity, and the central processor chugs along happily at a million operations a second. The peripheral processor unit can sustain a total transfer rate of up to five million characters a second through the bank of additional stores, interrogating visual displays and other input devices and the banks of output devices. Among the input/output devices, the graph plotter can print out answers in graph form and the visual displays give the answers on the face of cathode ray tubes, rather like television sets, either in printed or graphical form.

Entering the computer age

In the 20 years since the high-speed electronic digital computer became a reality Man has had to learn how best to use this new and very powerful tool. In the early days, many computers were under-utilized and their full potential was not realized. Even now, we are only scratching the surface of possible computer applications. Today, there is practically no aspect of civilized life which is not at some stage under the control of a computer.

For the future we may expect that most homes will have a computer terminal just as today they have a telephone. Vast quantities of information will be stored in the computer system, which can be many miles distant. Dialling the appropriate code would enable the information required to be displayed on a TV tube. This type of transaction is known as information retrieval. But in addition to this the computer, with all its calculating power, will be available to all for working out mathematical problems.

As yet, we have only begun to penetrate into the Computer Age.

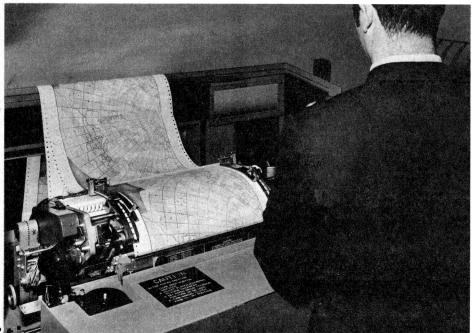

Age of automation

Man has embarked on a second industrial revolution. Not only is automation increasing the productivity of manufacturing processes, it is transforming the way of life of the industrial worker.

THE DEVELOPMENT OF HUMANITY has hinged on the continual effort to make labour more productive. From the use of tools by the most primitive men to the rise of modern industry, changes in social life have been founded on advances in technology by which the same amount of work could be done with a smaller effort.

Automation (the word, coined in 1946, is not very precise in its meaning) implies that this process is taken to the point where hardly any human intervention is required in production. The implications of such a development for the lives of men and women are incalculable.

Mechanization in its broadest sense can be traced through various stages. At its simplest, tools held in the hand replace the use of bare hands themselves. Then comes the use of an outside source of power to move the tool. The first of these machines were water or steam driven and they had to be controlled by hand.

Soon after their invention, machines such as these were being used in factories to perform complex sequences of operations, like cotton spinning or weaving. The machines were harnessed together in a rigid, inflexible system; anything interrupting the smooth working of the process – changes in raw material for example – meant that an operator was needed to intervene, adjusting the machine.

Governors

But the speed of a steam engine can be controlled by an automatic device – a *governor* – and with this a machine can be allowed to run by itself to some extent unsupervised. Invented by the Scottish engineer, James Watt, a governor basically consists of weights attached to a shaft which spins faster or slower according to the speed of the steam engine. The faster the shaft rotates the more the weights fly out from the axis, and the more they pull on a mechanism for shutting off the steam. Thus, if the engine runs too fast, the steam pressure is automatically reduced while, if it slows down, the weights fall inwards, opening the steam valve. The speed of the engine may, therefore, be *self governed*.

A self-governed steam engine is an early example of the *feed-back* principle. The governor measures engine speed and uses the measurement to correct any changes which occur. Information about the departure of the process from a pre-set state is fed back to cancel out the discrepancy.

Such processes, later called *servo-mechanisms,* are capable of replacing human control of machines. The study of their properties developed in the 1920s and 1930s.

With the rise of electronics, servo-mechanisms have really come into their own. All kinds of measurements, and

1 At a railway siding control room near Munich, Western Germany, automatic electronic controls sort wagons, apply track brakes and estimate speed and weight.
2 On the station at Ulm, southern Germany, a businessman uses a coin-operated express copying automaton. Within a few seconds it produces a good copy of any document.

observations can be translated into electrical currents. Electronic circuits then amplify and transform variations in such currents to control highly sophisticated mechanisms.

However, feed-back devices are by no means all electronic. Pneumatic and hydraulic means are also widely employed in servo-mechanisms. What is involved here is merely the form through which information is signalled back to the system being controlled.

In nature there is nothing new in the idea of feedback mechanisms. They are used all the time, unconsciously in human activity, in fact in all living processes. When a man reaches out his hand to pick up an object special sensory devices continually register the state of contraction of the muscles and control their movements to co-ordinate the picking up of the object seen by his eyes. This information is 'processed' by the brain and by the spinal cord and is fed back to the muscles controlling the hand.

The flexibility and adaptability of human activity depends on a complex hierarchy of such mechanisms. The application of similar principles to the control of machines has given Man a means of making machines carry out activities and tasks formerly thought of as essentially human. Indeed when many such mechanisms are linked together, whole industrial processes can be made to carry out production – continually checking themselves and selecting procedures required to meet various eventualities.

However, the full possibilities of developments like this could only come about because of the electronic computer. First constructed to make complex and repetitive calculations at high speed, it was realized in the 1940s that they could have much wider applications. Basically, a sequence of numbers is used as a code, and when a programme of instruction is fed in code into the machine, it is converted by the electronic circuits into a set of operations comprising numbers. One operation may mean that certain instructions are followed again and again until they have been carried out the required number of times. Then a new operation comes in and a new sequence is begun.

The *digital computer,* so called because it deals with digits or figures, is one type of computer. Essentially it is a device for storing numbers, and adding and multiplying them at high speed. It can also compare two numbers and according to whether they are equal or not, set different courses of operation in process.

Once Man recognized the versatility of the computer he began to use it to control a variety of processes, and even make decisions. True automation was now a reality. It was not merely a matter of getting a process to follow a fixed pattern and of correcting it when it departed from this set path. By transforming data on the working of the process, the computer could 'make decisions' about how it should be changed.

An oil refinery is a highly complex establishment. Complicated chemical reactions may be taking place simultaneously, and to control them at the correct pressure and temperature thousands of valves are needed at various points in the system.

Remote control

In the 1940s and 1950s refineries were built in which valves were controlled by servos to maintain pressures and temperatures at set levels. Measurements were automatically made of these levels, together with the chemical composition of materials flowing past various key points. All of this information was transmitted electrically to a central control room and changes in the working of the vast complex – including breakdowns – could thus be corrected rapidly, perhaps without the operator leaving the controls. An entire refinery of this sort can thus be controlled by a handful of men. Similar automation equipment is also widely used in the chemical processing industries.

The computer is now making even such sophisticated plants obsolete. By feeding all measurements directly into a computer, calculations can be made of how the controls may be simultaneously altered so as to produce a better result. Whereas in the non-computerized plant the operator often has to make decisions on the basis of 'hunch' or 'experience', the computer can be programmed to do the same thing but systematically.

Moreover, it is quite feasible to *programme* (instruct) the machine so that it 'learns' from its errors. It can be made to experiment with various changes, selecting the best possibilities for future action, and adapting itself to meet changes in conditions.

The chemical processing industries have been the most successful in applying concepts like these, but all sections of industry are susceptible to similar applications. The transfer machine, moving material from one stage of production to another makes it possible to integrate entire factories and consider them as a single system. All repetitive operations, so common in manufacturing industry, can, in principle, be mechanized and automatically controlled and checked. Computers can then take over the 'management' of the entire system of operations.

In the metal industry the *lathe* – the basic tool of metal-working – can be controlled by electronic devices. The piece of metal being machined is automatically moved about, while a programmed sequence of tools works on it. Measurement by optical or electrical means, may be continuously carried out, and fed back to servo-mechanisms controlling the various movements.

The entire system can be made very flexible by using a programme consisting of nothing more than holes punched in paper tape. The tape is produced by a computer, which calculates the sequence of instructions required to produce a given shape. Thus, by coding an original blueprint, the modern 'numerically controlled' machine tool can be made to carry out the necessary engineering work.

Processes like packaging, sorting or mixing are not difficult to control. Assembly of complex components is harder. Only in the last few years has any advance

1 The whole complex of a waterworks in Düsseldorf is operated, and breakdowns rectified, from this automatic control room.
2 At a modern wine-bottling factory, the bottles on a moving conveyor belt are automatically filled, corked and labelled by machine.
3 This machine tool in a British factory cuts with great accuracy patterns in steel plates to be used for shipbuilding. It is electronically controlled by a programmed computer in a nearby control booth.
4 A robot tub with trailers steers a pre-set course round a British warehouse. It stops and starts as needed for loading, and can automatically open and close doors.
5 Automatic control valves and meters operate the blending system at an oil refinery in Denmark. The rate of flow and temperatures are maintained at set levels and measurement of the chemical composition is made automatically.

been made on this front. The items to be assembled have had to be redesigned, and the relative orientation of two components being fitted together has had to be measured and programmed.

Not only manufacture may be 'automated' in this way. The 1950s saw the development of the 'electronic office'. Many clerical operations may be broken down and reorganized so that a computer can carry them out according to instructions. Many airline companies use computers to deal with seat reservations and to keep records of future flights. Cheques are sorted in some banks by automatic methods which also keep accounts and print statements.

Pay-rolls, for example, in many large enterprises are now produced by computer.

Each employee has a card, bearing coded information on his wage-rate, overtime worked, and tax code. The programme can produce the amount to be paid, allowing for such items as tax and insurance, and can also indicate how many notes and coins of different denominations are required.

The 'automation' of an office produces a phenomenon which occurs quite often in this field. Before a computer can carry out the work at present being performed by a group of clerical workers, the work they do must be looked at systematically. This process frequently brings to light routine operations whose purpose was long ago forgotten.

Pieces of information may be recorded, forms filled out, copies of documents made,

merely because 'that is how we always do it'. Only when the entire process is analysed for conversion to computer working is it discovered that a simple re-organization will make the whole operation doubly efficient.

Systems analysis, as it has come to be called, is now an essential part of automation. Because of such analysis the designs of plants and offices from the start have been affected.

The application of automation is still far behind the theory. As early as 1948, the American mathematician, Norbert Wiener published his book *Cybernetics: Communication and Control in the Animal and the Machine,* which was still about four or five years before the first computers were being produced commercially.

3

4

5

In his book Wiener introduced the basic principles of automatic control, computer control and information theory. Information regarding an error in, for example, the path of a guided missile or a human body temperature, is fed to the controlling device which acts to correct the error. He showed the relevance of these conceptions to biology, psychology and economics and pointed out their tremendous implications for social and industrial development.

Many of the possibilities he discussed are still far beyond what is technically achievable. But he was able to lay the basis for the mathematical examination of the properties of automatic devices.

Wiener and his fellow mathematician, John von Neumann, considered abstractly many of the implications of the construction of computers. For example, von Neumann asked the question: could a machine be made so complex that it could construct one more complex than itself?

He decided that there was a critical level of complexity above which this was possible. The implication of machines which programmed themselves raised the spectre of a robot conquest of the world. Someone suggested that this danger could always be countered by pulling out the plug. A pessimist answered him: by that time, you will find it has been cemented to the wall. These notions reflected the social issues raised by automation.

A great controversy began about the effect of automation on unemployment. Wiener and many others foresaw the danger of the rapid displacement of human beings by machines in a 'second industrial revolution'. At first, as automation began to affect the motor industry especially, it looked as though these dangers were immediate. Soon millions of people would be out of work.

Then, in the 1950s, the idea spread that automation, in fact, meant an increase in the demand for highly skilled manpower. All that was needed was the retraining of the former unskilled men.

Transforming industry

No investigation has supported this contention although a few specialist maintenance men are needed; electricians must be replaced by electronic engineers, for example. In any case, it is quite conceivable to carry out even these tasks automatically. Machines already exist which check their own working automatically, correcting errors and replacing faulty components when necessary.

But the bulk of production workers can and will be displaced, as automation takes over many repetitive processes. Even if its advance is slower than might have been anticipated in 1948, the automatic factory is technologically inevitable. It may well be that, when the present period of economic upheaval is considered in the future, one of the basic factors will seem to be the changes in this direction that have been occurring since the end of the Second World War.

It is sometimes said that automation is only mechanization taken a bit further. But, as always, it is this change of degree which makes the decisive difference. All the problems of transforming industry are magnified enormously by the extent and rapidity of the changes implied by the application of automatic control.

Will the spread and extension of automation mean economic ruin, as markets fail to expand, unemployment rises and productive potential soars? Or will the new machines be the servants of men, removing all drudgery and unpleasantness from the labour process?

The answers to such questions are not technical but social and political in character. One thing is certain: in the age of automation, nothing can remain the same for human life.

1 The control room of a natural gas production platform in the North Sea. The panel consists of computers, recorders, controllers and encoders which control gas flow and pressure.

2 A guard at the master control panel of an electronic system which keeps watch on factory premises. Lights warn of an emergency and information is relayed to the panel.

Watchers of the sky

Star-gazers of prehistory were primitive ancestors of the astrologers. Early beliefs and superstitions promoted study of the heavens and led to the foundation of scientific astronomy.

IT IS IMPOSSIBLE to say when the stars came to mean anything more than twinkling spots of light to our primitive ancestors. Palaeolithic hunters must have caught nocturnal animals by the light of the moon and may have learned to find their way back to their caves by the light of a familiar star. But it was not until the hunter settled down to grow food and the first farming communities came into being that Man took a more personal interest in the heavens. He could not but realize that the periods of the moon and the regular succession of the seasons must in some way be connected with what he saw in the sky.

Yet for these people who lived before the dawn of history, there was no such thing as a solar system. To them the world in which they grew their meagre crops, hunted and fished, were born and died was just a small patch of land bounded by distant hills or the line where sea and sky met. Above it all the sky formed a roof from which a mysterious yellow ball gave light and warmth by day, while at night a silvery disc shone with a paler light and tiny dots of light pierced the black sky.

Watchers of the sky

In time a few adventurous minds began to think more deeply about the daily and nightly drama of the sky: why did the moon change its shape and sometimes shine wanly by the light of day? Why did a few stars move amongst the others? Why did the sun rise in one part of the sky and set in another? Why was the light of the sun shut off by a black shadow sweeping across its surface? Why did stars suddenly shoot across the sky? All these questions tantalized our distant ancestors; and in the often fumbling search for answers lie the origins of astronomy.

So men set up primitive observatories, where without telescopes or other optical aids they watched the sky and made the first crude observations. Curiously enough, these tentative steps in astronomy were for strictly practical purposes.

By counting the days between full moons, the first calendars were compiled; and with calendars history was no longer old men's tales but became chronological records. By observing the sun's position at solstice and equinox, the changes of the seasons were understood which led to a better development of agriculture.

Most of the great civilizations of the ancient world gave star-watchers an honoured place in the social scale. In this connection it is interesting to discover that the Chinese were less advanced in astronomy than is generally supposed. There is no record of their observations earlier than the fifth century A D.

Probably the most enthusiastic star-gazers of the ancient world were the Sumerians, the Babylonians and the Egyptians. They built observatories and with their clumsy instruments managed to amass a great deal of valuable information. As long as 4,000 years ago the Babylonians were keeping records from which they could calculate the occurrence of eclipses. They had a fairly good idea of the *ecliptic,* the *zenith* and the *nadir,* and were the first to think in terms of an equator.

Once the early astronomers had established what they conceived to be the movement of the sun, moon and planets, and could predict these movements with reasonable accuracy, they were able to build up a strange hotch-potch of fact and fiction. They had no understanding of the true nature of the phenomena they observed. To them the Earth was flat, and as Man was lord of the Earth, the Earth must be the centre around which everything else revolved. The sun, moon, planets and stars were accepted exactly as they appeared to be, and their motions were equally accepted without any serious questioning of what caused these motions.

By keeping track of the sun's annual motion north and south, the astronomers of Mesopotamia correctly linked it with the progress of the seasons. Counting the days after the sun's furthest retreat towards the south, they were able to predict when the life-giving floods would sweep down the rivers. Predictions of this nature were bound to be successful because floods depend on the seasons, which in turn depend on the sun.

Even more surprising was the fact that the astronomers of 4,000 years ago had linked the moon with the tides, though the real cause of tides escaped them. All they could say with any confidence was that the tides seemed to depend on the shape of the moon at certain periods of the month.

Astronomy and religion

From these solar and lunar observations developed the religious cults of sun and moon worship. It was thus inevitable that the early astronomers began combining their studies with the functions of priests. This gave them tremendous political power, and in Babylon their importance reached such a peak that they constituted a separate and noble caste.

It was equally inevitable that the astronomer-priests should carry matters a stage further. If the sun controlled the seasons and the moon moved the oceans, was it not probable that events on Earth and the people inhabiting it were influenced by the 'wandering' stars – the visible planets Mars, Venus, Mercury, Saturn and Jupiter? In fact, might not the movements of these wandering stars make possible prediction of the future?

1 Ptolemy, the ancient Greek geographer and astronomer, used astronomical observations and results in the production of his maps, as this carving illustrates.

2 El Caracol observatory, in Mexico, was built by the Aztecs. Like many peoples, they used astronomy purely as a tool for astrological work.

Careful observation and the keeping of detailed records enabled the priest-astrologer-astronomers to fix the positions of the planets at specific times in the past and future. Their records told them where planets such as Mars or Saturn would be when a king planned to go to war. These were the war planets, and if the astrologers told their royal master that their positions were unfavourable, the campaign would be called off. Solar and lunar eclipses and the appearance of the comets were even greater portents because of their relative rarity, and it was for the astrologer to say whether these phenomena meant good or evil. The destiny of a new-born child and the success of business or matrimonial ventures depended on what the astrologers read in the sky. Astrologers were never short of clients, and prospered accordingly.

Although study of the heavenly bodies was thus made in the cause of astrology rather than for the advancement of astronomy, it would be a mistake to dismiss these early astronomers as merely practitioners of a completely pseudo science.

1 Until the Renaissance, the common view of the heavens was a sphere with the stars and planets inset as permanent objects, as in the Masoleum of Galla Placidia at Ravenna.

2–5 Ancient India was the birthplace of many astronomical and astrological techniques, and as such was rich in observatories. The periodicity of the movements of the sun, the moon and the planets led to the building of structures used in calculations and the construction of calendars. The first step was the construction of astronomical stonework whose shadows would indicate date and time. This developed into more compact and exact instruments such as those shown in the bottom two illustrations. Development along these lines is apparent in a number of different cultures. This primitive approach to the movement of the sun survives to the present day in sundials, which are now used almost exclusively for decoration rather than accurate timekeeping.

1 Comets have been regarded as objects of awe throughout history, as shown by this section of the Bayeux tapestry. They were held to portend disaster.
2 The Aztecs, who were sun worshippers, produced calendars like this which were surprisingly accurate in view of their limited equipment.

Their craft was often of direct benefit to serious astronomy. It was astrologers who measured the angle of the ecliptic, checked the relative brilliance of the stars and introduced the sine function in trigonometry. In Samarkand, astrologers built a great observatory with a quadrant having a radius of 190 feet and compiled a catalogue of over 1,000 stars.

Many astronomers were outstanding mathematicians, and it was not unusual for men whose real interest was pure astronomy to practise astrology simply as a source of income. Knowledge of the stars garnered by astrologers made possible the first tentative voyages out of sight of land. Much of the data which enabled astronomers to calculate the recurrence of comets came from astrological records.

It was the Greeks who first divorced astronomy from astrology and raised it to the level of a true science. Although the Greeks had a pantheon of gods ruling their lives, they disliked relying on the supernatural to explain natural phenomena. Above all, they were mathematicians.

Almost from the beginning of their astronomy the Greeks rejected the flat-Earth theory. They reasoned that the world must be round because ships sailed below the horizon. Also, a flat Earth was inconsistent with the Earth casting a circular shadow on the moon. On the other hand, they held firmly to the belief that the Earth was the centre of the universe and that the sun, moon and planets were smaller bodies moving around it.

Pythagoras, who lived in the sixth century B C, was the first Greek to declare that

the Earth was a sphere. As this fitted well with the Greek passion for spheres and circles, they adopted the idea to explain the movements of the sun, moon and planets. They envisaged a system in which the heavenly bodies were prevented from falling on to the Earth by invisible concentric spheres or circles that rotated and carried them around the Earth on circular courses.

Before long this theory ran into trouble since observation by improved sighting devices showed that the planets wandered about the sky and behaved in a way that no single arrangement of spheres and circles could account for.

Consequently, the spherical theory had to be bolstered by later Greek astronomers who visualized secondary spheres at-tached at varying angles to the primary ones. By this concept, a planet carried along on a secondary sphere would appear to follow a non-circular course which resembled its observed movements. Even so, two spheres per planet was not the answer to something that the mathematically minded Greeks knew to be a mathematical problem.

Eudoxus of Cnidus, who lived in the third century B C tried to solve the problem by giving each planet 27 spheres. Aristotle (384–322 B C), who was a staunch believer in the geocentric theory, gave each planet a complex arrangement of 55 spheres. Aristotle's spheres were of a pure and transparent crystal, but only a few actually carried planets. The function of the others was to adjust the bodies' movements.

Heracleides of Pontus, a pupil of Plato and a member of the Greek Academy appears to have contributed much to serious astronomy. Although most of his writings are lost and there is some controversy regarding the interpretation of the surviving fragments, it is possible that he discovered that the Earth rotated on its axis. He seems also to have solved the problem of why Venus and Mercury are sometimes further away by suggesting that they are revolved around the sun and not around the Earth. To his contemporaries this was rank heresy and raised such a storm that Heracleides abandoned astronomy.

Aristarchus of Samos was another Greek whose theories were far in advance of his day and earned him the scorn of his contemporaries. Teaching in Alexandria about 270 BC, he maintained that the sun was a motionless body in the centre of the Universe with the Earth and planets revolving around it. He also stated that the moon revolved around the Earth, and that the Earth had a double movement – rotation on its axis and rotation around the sun. Denial of the Earth's traditional position as centre of the Universe brought on him a charge of impiety, a significant forerunner of what was to happen to Copernicus 1,800 years later.

Undeterred by the tirades of his contemporaries, Aristarchus wrote a treatise *On the Size and Distance of the Sun and Moon* in which he calculated the distance of Earth from the sun to be 19 times greater than that of the Earth from the moon.

After Greek science became centred at Alexandria, a long line of brilliant astronomers produced a mass of observational and theoretical data. Hipparchus invented trigonometry and used it to measure the distance of the moon from the Earth. He first observed eclipses of the moon and noted the time lapse as the moon passed through the Earth's shadow. He then compared the apparent diameter of the moon with the diameter of the cone of shadow projected by the Earth on to the moon. Having established an approximate relationship between the apparent diameter of the moon and the diameter of the shadow cone, a trigonometrical calculation gave the distance between Earth and moon as 30 times the diameter of the Earth. Today's instruments and methods show how close Hipparchus came to the actual distance.

Ptolemy was another giant of the Alexandrian school of astronomy. He wrote a textbook called *Almagest* which, although perpetuating the geocentric theory, suggested that the planets are much closer to the Earth than are the fixed stars. He also compiled a new catalogue of 1,030 observed stars and *Geographia*, listing places on the Earth according to their latitude and longitude.

Ptolemy's *Almagest* was a brilliant exercise in attempting to prove mathematically the phenomena of astronomy as understood in his day. It is not generally acceptable in the light of modern knowledge, but it was taken as dogma until Copernicus propounded his heliocentric system some 1,800 years later.

Measuring the Earth

One of the most remarkable achievements of Greek mathematical astronomy was the measurement of the Earth's circumference by *Eratosthenes*, who learned his mathematics at Alexandria. He set up an obelisk at Alexandria and another of identical height at *Syene*, 5,000 *stadia* away. He noted that at mid-day the sun shining on the *Syene* obelisk threw no shadow, whereas at the same hour of the day the Alexandria obelisk cast a measurable shadow. He calculated the distance between the two obelisks as one-fiftieth of a circle. Multiplying the distance of 5,000 *stadia* by 50 gave the circumference of the circle as 250,000 *stadia*: in other words the circumference of the Earth. Although the exact length of the *stadium* used by Eratosthenes is uncertain, it is probable that 250,000 were approximately equal to 25,300 miles. As the circumference of the Earth at the equator is now known to be 24,901 miles, Eratosthenes' figure is a striking tribute to Greek mathematics.

Ptolemy's *Almagest* was the swan song of Greek astronomy and science in general. For a few centuries science struggled against the decadent materialism of Imperial Rome, but little original work was achieved. The Dark Ages plunged science into a morass of superstition in which astronomy became the handmaiden of astrology. Nowhere was astronomy studied any longer for its own sake. Even the great observatories in India and Arabia served astrologers rather than astronomers. Nevertheless, astrologers continued to make some contributions to astronomy. Astrologers at Baghdad observatory, founded in the eighth century, discovered lunar libration, and in the thirteenth century Arab astrologers drew up a reasonably accurate chart of the night sky. But, in general, for many years astronomy was eclipsed by the shadow of superstition and religious intolerance of scientific thought.

1 The orrery, a mechanical model of the solar system, has been used extensively from the early eighteenth century for instruction and demonstration.

2 For several centuries Greenwich, in England, was the home of modern astronomy. This old print shows the viewing room with astronomers at work.

Giant eyes on the sky

Optics has opened up new fields to the astronomer, but even the best conventional telescope has given way to the radio telescope, which can detect and examine that which the eye cannot see.

1 This replica of the original Newton reflecting telescope, at the California Institute of Technology, has a magnification of 38. It was the forerunner of modern instruments.

2 For complete accuracy, the errors in a telescope movement must be constantly checked and corrected, as shown here.

ALTHOUGH THE HUMAN EYE is a masterpiece of evolution and unrivalled for keeping its owner in visual contact with his immediate and changing surroundings, it is a poor instrument for detailed observation of the very minute or the very distant.

From the astronomer's point of view, the limitations of the human eye stem from the fact that the visible light to which it is sensitive comprises only a small segment of the electromagnetic spectrum. That is, its *resolving power*, or ability to separate close sources of light and so observe and distinguish fine details, is far too coarse for the purpose of stellar or planetary observation.

Father of the telescope

The telescope was the first instrument to transcend the limitations of Man's natural distance-vision. Some doubt exists as to who invented the telescope, but the consensus of opinion gives the credit to Hans Lippershey, a young Dutch spectacle-maker, who in about 1600 discovered by accident that when two lenses were held some distance apart, objects seen through them appeared larger and nearer to the observer. The first telescopes were simply crude spy-glasses for looking at objects on land or sea and their magnification was little more than double that of normal sight.

Then in 1609 Galilei Galileo, 'the father of modern astronomy', turned a telescope to the sky. His instrument had only 20 magnification, but it did find a chink in the blind that hitherto had hidden so much that was invisible to the unaided eye of Man.

When Galileo looked through that primitive telescope more than 350 years ago, he saw things that the astronomer-astrologers of Babylon had only dreamed might be there. He saw mountains on the moon, and found that the planet Venus had phases similar to those of the moon, proving that the planet had an orbit centred on the sun.

Despite advances in the optical telescope and the assistance it receives from the camera, this method of observation can of itself do little more than bring the stars and planets nearer and pinpoint their positions relative to the Earth. The optical telescope and the camera attached to it cannot tell the astronomer a great deal about the physical conditions of the objects observed, what they are composed of or their temperatures. Neither can the optical telescope give accurate figures relative to the distance of the observed object nor, in the case of moving objects, their speed. To obtain that kind of information, the astronomer requires a number of additional instruments, some of which function independently and some as components of the telescope.

When the eye cannot see

Another disadvantage of the optical telescope as now used in ground-based observatories is that there is a limit to the distances to which it can carry the human eye into the vastness of space. While there have been many advances in instruments and techniques in recent years, the problem of Earth's unsteady and turbulent atmosphere is one which astronomers would most like to overcome.

For years astronomers have dreamed of being able to do just that. Since 1950 tests with rockets and satellites have demonstrated the crystal clarity of space where

3 The huge radio telescope at Arecibo, Puerto Rico, uses a man-made depression in the ground as the dish. This makes the instrument extremely rigid despite its enormous size.

1

there are no atmospheric conditions to distort long-range vision. But the dream of putting an observatory in that astronomer's paradise did not become reality until 1962. Curiously enough, it was not done with a spaceship or rocket, but with a balloon – the pioneer of all aircraft.

Weighing nearly three tons, the telescope and its auxiliary equipment of cameras and other instruments was suspended from a huge nylon balloon inflated with helium gas. The whole complex was launched from the National Scientific Balloon Flight Station at Palestine, Texas, and reached an altitude of 100,000 feet, just within the fringe of the Earth's atmosphere, extending the range of astronomical visibility by several light years.

When the balloon reached its designed ceiling, technicians manning a tracking

The Vostock and subsequent satellites are valuable astronomical tools. This model of a Vostock at a Moscow exhibition shows the radio atennae and optical equipment.

The 250-foot bowl of Jodrell Bank radio telescope framed by the control-room window. This single operator can position the aerial to pick up signals from anywhere in space.

station on the ground sent radio signals which operated relays in a 'black box' on the telescope. These caused the telescope to turn round until it pointed towards the object to be observed. Other radio-controlled relays operated mechanisms to focus the lens.

Called a *stratoscope,* the space-borne telescope can be locked on to a star or planet simply by pressing a button on the ground level panel. The stratoscope's first mission was to collect information about Mars in preparation for a future landing on that planet by astronauts. It has since been used to photograph Betelgeuse, Sirius and other stars.

Each mission by the stratoscope lasts for approximately 12 hours. At the end of the mission, the ground control transmits a radio signal to release from the balloon

the L-shaped frame carrying the telescope, camera and other instruments. Another radio signal opens a parachute which brings the whole complex back to Earth. The films exposed by the cameras are then developed ready for examination by the astronomers.

Since the pioneering work by the stratoscope, several small astronomical observatories have been sent into orbit round the Earth. Unlike the balloon-borne instruments, these could not return films to Earth, but instead they have done something which no simple picture could achieve—they have built up a view of the heavens at wavelengths which can never reach Earth. Ultraviolet light and x-rays, for example, are blocked by the atmosphere, yet they carry information which is vital to astronomers.

Two Orbiting Astronomical Observatories and other x-ray satellites have scanned the skies for new sources of radiation, hitherto unsuspected. Among their discoveries, they have found evidence that the very brightest stars are even hotter than was previously known. Even more significantly, certain sources of x-rays seem likely to be caused by the enigmatic *black holes,* superdense regions in deep space.

Observing with an orbiting telescope is a comparatively easy task. For example, the UK satellite Ariel-5 carries a survey instrument designed by astronomers at Leicester. Results of the previous day's observing are telexed to them by the control centre in the USA, in good time for the scientists to reply with details of where to point the telescope for the next observing session.

As well as unmanned observatories, several US and Soviet manned missions have carried medium-sized telescopes. The

The Surveyor soft landing craft is powered by wings bearing the solar cells which derive energy from the sun. They are completely automatic and can be 'tuned' to a star.

2

3

Skylab mission resulted in a detailed survey of the Sun, for example.

During the 1980s, a very large telescope is due to be launched by the Space Shuttle, a kind of space bus. Although unmanned, the telescope will be a giant of nearly 100 inches aperture.

Not that orbiting space observatories are likely to render the ground-based telescope obsolete. It will remain for many years to come the most convenient instrument for obtaining data relative to, for example, the distance of the stars. This is measured by what is called *parallax*.

Parallax is a measure of the amount by which an object appears to move in relation to its background when an observer looks at it from two different places. A simple example of judging the parallax of something such as a vase on a table in relation to an adjacent wall, is to look at the vase first with one eye and then with the other. To judge the parallax of, say, Jupiter, the astronomer sights it at different times in a single night against the background of the stars. Due to the rotation of the Earth, his telescope has moved a few thousand miles to a new position

1

2

1 The 200-inch telescope at Mount Palomar, California, is one of the most advanced optical instruments. The versatility of the mechanical movement is almost as important as the excellence of the optics in equipment like this.
2 A *planetarium* represents star and planet motions, greatly speeded up. This instrument is at Griffith Park, Los Angeles.

relative to the stellar background at each sighting. Parallax of a star is fixed by observing it during opposite seasons of the year, so that the Earth's revolution round the sun gives a base line of 186 million miles. Theoretically, parallax could give the distance of movement of stars up to 400 light years away from the Earth. Just what that means will be appreciated when it is remembered that a light year is the distance that light, moving at a speed of 186,326 miles per second, travels in one year.

For judging the brightness of stars the astronomer uses instruments based on the properties of the photo-electric cell and other light-sensitive devices. This has resulted in stars being grouped into definite classes, each of which has the same degree of real brightness. In this way the distances of stars can be estimated by measuring their brightness one against another.

Studying the spectra

To establish the composition of celestial bodies, the astronomer uses a *diffraction grating*. This consists of a glass plate across which are closely ruled lines. When light from an observed body passes through the grating it is broken down in the same way that light is broken down by a glass prism. Since laboratory experiments have demonstrated that every element when heated emits its own characteristic line in a diffraction grating, examination of such lines enables the astronomer to establish the elements in objects light years away from the Earth.

Other instruments for analysing stellar light give reasonably accurate estimates of the speed of stars moving towards or away from the solar system. *Magnetic sensors* can measure the strength of a star's magnetic field. It is also possible to measure the speed of stellar rotation and to calculate the amount of invisible gas adrift in space between a star and Earth.

For accurate measurement of the surface temperature of bodies millions of miles away from the Earth, astronomers have developed their own special thermometers. One of these is the observatory *thermocouple,* which was invented in 1922 by the American physicist Coblentz. Light from the observed object is concentrated on to two wires of dissimilar metals which are welded together and placed in the focus of a large reflector. Filters separate the light from the infra-red rays which heat the wires of the thermocouple but to slightly different temperatures. This causes the wires to generate a minute electric current, the strength of which is an indication of the temperature of the heat source. One of the first facts established by Coblentz's thermocouple was that the temperature of the planet Mercury is 420 °C. on the side of the planet exposed to the sun, and

−220 °C. on the surface of Neptune.

An even more sensitive instrument for measuring distant heat is the *germanium bolometer* invented by Dr Low of Arizona University. The germanium crystal is enclosed in a glass tube and registers heat by contact with infra-red radiation. Electronic relays actuate a pen that traces the readings on a chart. The bolometer can detect one hundred-million-millionth of a watt. This is equivalent to sensing the heat from a lighted match at a distance of 15,000 miles.

Dr Low's first use of his bolometer was to measure the temperature of Jupiter, which proved to be higher than had been thought and gave rise to a theory that the planet may have its own heat source.

Probably the greatest advance in the development of astronomical instruments since the invention of the optical telescope is the radio telescope. Radio astronomy may be said to have begun in the 1930s when radio amateurs using new types of highly sensitive receivers repeatedly picked up weak signals which they knew could not have originated from any known transmitter on the Earth. Simultaneously, an American astronomer named Jansky was propounding a theory that there might be a radio source in the Milky Way.

The outbreak of the Second World War prevented any serious attempt to link the unknown radio signals with Jansky's theory. It was not until after the war that astronomers and radio technicians gathered sufficient evidence to prove that the transmissions were coming from objects in space. Much more was then known about nuclear energy, and it was suggested that the mystery signals were natural transmissions of stellar energy. Like everything else in the Universe, stars consist of matter, and their matter is made up of atomic particles in a constant state of movement. This movement emits radiation which travels through space in the same way that a broadcasting station transmits radio programmes.

Careful search with optical telescopes failed to find any known stars in the right position to be making the transmissions. From this fact emerged that the stellar radio does not appear to be transmitted from any star or other object that can be seen or photographed through the most powerful of optical telescopes. To find out more about the source of the transmissions, the first movable radio telescope was built in 1952 at Jodrell Bank in Cheshire. It is, in fact, a super radio-receiver with a bowl aerial that can be aimed at any point in the Universe. The aerial is 250 feet in diameter and supported between two 165-foot towers. The towers are mounted on electrically driven bogies running on a circular track so that the aerial can be positioned at any point of a circle, while the aerial itself can be raised or lowered. In this way, the aerial can be pinpointed to pick up signals from any direction in the Universe.

Computers and the sky

All movements of the aerial are remotely controlled by a single operator at a switchboard in a building which also houses instruments for measuring the strength of the signals. The information is then processed by computers and appears in the form of graphs.

The Jodrell Bank radio telescope was the largest in the world for many years, but it has now been superseded by an even bigger one at Effelsberg in West Germany, about 25 miles west of Bonn. Its diameter is 328 feet, and it was brought into use in 1971. There are radio telescopes with much bigger aerials, such as the giant 1000-foot dish at Arecibo in Puerto Rico, set in a huge natural depression, but this is limited in its view and can only scan part of the sky.

The computer has revolutionized the study and evaluation of data collected by astronomers. Modern astronomy is very much a matter of long and complicated calculations in higher mathematics. Not so very long ago this consumed an inordinate amount of the time which astronomers would have preferred to devote to direct observation. Now every important observatory has its own computer which can be programmed to work out in minutes abstruse calculations which previously took weeks or even months of tedious labour with pencil, slide rule and paper.

1 Arrays of antennae are often used rather than paraboloid dishes in radio telescopes. They can be made in larger sizes, increasing their power, but they are not so versatile.

2 *Coronographs* such as this one at Pulkovo, Russia, are used to study the sun's outer edge. In effect, it simulates the optical conditions of a solar eclipse.

Queen of the sky

For centuries men have spoken of the hunter's moon, the fisherman's moon, the harvest moon and more recently, of a bomber's moon. But they are all manifestations of the Earth's strange satellite.

1

THE APOLLO LANDINGS on the moon swept away much of the mystery and romance about our nearest neighbour in space. Before Apollo, it was possible to dream of diamond-studded caverns or vast seas of dust. Now men have been there, we gaze at the moon more dispassionately.

Even so, it ranks second only to the Sun in its importance to Earthlings— it creates the tides and brightens our nights. This may seem trifling to the city-bound, but not to country-dwellers.

Yet another distinction hedges our satellite. Altogether, astronomers have detected 31 satellites in our solar system which can be described as 'moons': Jupiter, for instance, has 12, Saturn nine and Uranus five, leaving Mars and Neptune each with two and Earth with one. But although four of this family are larger than the moon, none is as large or as massive in relation to its primary (that is, the planet round which it orbits) the Earth on which we live.

Figures emphasize this state of affairs better than any words. Earth has a mean diameter of 7,927 miles to which the moon counters with a mean diameter of 2,163 miles; again, taking the density of the Earth as 1, the density of the moon is about 0·6. Taken together, these figures mean that the Earth is slightly more than 81 times as massive as the moon, which for the solar system is a quite exceptional relationship. The next nearest partnership is between Triton (which is the heaviest

1 Photographs of the moon taken by exploratory space vehicles reveal slopes which are seldom steeper than one in two. This photograph was taken by Orbiter II, an American probe.
2 Early drawings of the moon, based on imagination rather than science, showed steep precipices and rocks showing signs of glaciation. This model, constructed by Scriven Bolton, shows the so-called Lunar Alps.

of all moons) and its primary, Neptune, which is 290 times more massive. Again, in this case, the ratio of diameters is 1:30, compared with less than 1:4 in the case of moon and Earth.

This discrepancy, in astronomical terms, is so marked that many astronomers now believe the Earth and moon to comprise a double-planet system. But they make a strange pair, for the moon's much lower density shows that it is made of lighter materials than Earth. The once-popular theory that the Moon was pulled from the forming Earth does not square with this fact. Yet there is evidence that at a much earlier stage in their evolution the moon was as close as 40,000 miles to Earth. So how was this double planet formed?

Birth of the moon

The samples brought back by Apollo astronauts can be dated by their radioactivity to show that the moon is every bit as old as the Earth and the rest of the solar system, about 4,600 million years. At that time, astronomers suggest, the solar system was chaotic, full of bodies about the size of present-day asteroids, a few tens of miles across. Some of these bodies grew in size, in the way that rolling snowballs do, to form larger proto-planets. Among these was the early Earth.

The gravitational pull of the Earth would have been sufficient to attract a family of bodies of the lighter materials, while heavier bodies would have been more difficult to retain. These bodies accumulated to form the moon.

Subsequently, the bodies still left in the solar system collided with the now solid lunar surface. The traces of this early bombardment can be seen to this day, in the pitted lunar surface. The largest bodies to fall, some 3,000 million years ago, penetrated deep enough into the surface that they caused vast lava flows—they are the dark lunar 'seas'.

The shape of the orbit

Strictly speaking, the Earth and moon both travel round a common centre of gravity, known as the *barycentre,* which is located 2,903 miles from the centre of the Earth. Our satellite, moving eastward across the heavens, completes one revolution of our planet, moving at an average speed of 2,287 miles an hour, in 27 days, 7 hours, 43 minutes and 11·5 seconds. This is known as its *sidereal period.* However, the average time from one 'new moon' to the next, which is known as 'one lunation of its synodic period', is 29 days, 12 hours, 44 minutes and 2·8 seconds. The discrepancy between the two periods is due simply to the fact that, if the Earth, moon and sun are in line at new moon, the sun will be out of line at the end of the moon's sidereal period for the very good reason that Earth will have moved during this time about one-thirteenth of its orbit round the sun. The moon therefore needs two days and five hours approximately to get in line again.

In its revolution round Earth, the distance of our satellite varies from 221,463 to 252,710 miles (centre of moon to centre of Earth). Obviously, then, it moves in an elliptical path and not in a perfect circle, and the eccentricity of the ellipse has been calculated at 0·055. If the orbits of the Earth and moon over a full year are plotted, the surprising result is that the moon's path is never convex, but always curves towards the Sun.

Various other features of the moon's movements should be mentioned. First, and most important, our satellite rotates on its axis, and its period of rotation is equal to its period of revolution round the Earth. Because it presents the same face to us all the time, many people assume that the moon does not rotate at all, but a little thought will make clear that it must. Try walking round, say, a beach ball, presenting always the same side of your body to it; if you did not rotate, each side and your back and front would face the ball for one-quarter of a revolution each.

Another important feature is that the plane of the moon's orbit is tilted to that of Earth at an angle of about 5° 9′; if the planes coincided, there would be one eclipse of the sun and one of the moon every lunar month. Third, it is worth bearing in mind that the moon's axis of rotation is not quite perpendicular to the plane of its orbit; the actual angle of tilt is 6° 41′.

Our view of the moon changes because its position relative to Earth and sun is constantly changing. We see it first as a thin crescent in the western sky after sunset. As it moves eastward, however, the size of the crescent grows until we see half of the hemisphere which is turned towards us; at this point the moon has moved one-quarter of its revolution. Continuing in its orbit, the area of illumination grows until 'full moon' when the whole daylight side of the moon is presented to us at the end of its second quarter. Our satellite now begins to wane and goes through its phases in reverse order until it comes round again to a new moon. During 24 hours, however, the moon moves about 24 times its width in an easterly direction, which means that it rises a little later in the sky each evening, until in fact Earth has turned through the distance the moon has moved eastward.

Finally, it should be mentioned here that, although the moon has one face turned to us all the time, we can in fact see about 59 per cent of its total surface area. This is due to the phenomenon known as *libration* (wobble). Our satellite in its orbit appears to swing a little from north to south and from east to west. In the first case, this is because the moon travels faster when it is nearer the Earth, so that its rate of rotation does not keep exact pace with its speed of revolution.

The visible surface

In the second case, the reason is that the moon's axis, as we have seen, is slightly inclined to the perpendicular of its orbital plane, so that we can see slightly more of its poles when the opposite pole is tilted away from Earth. Again, because we do not see the moon from a fixed position (due to the Earth's rotation) we can see a little round its western edge when it is rising and a little round its eastern edge when it is setting.

Even in a pair of binoculars or a small telescope, the moon's surface is a dramatic sight. The best time to look is when the moon is half illuminated, so that the craters and mountain chains are thrown into sharp contrast.

From Earth, one gets the impression of jagged mountains and treacherous terrain.

1 This is a model of the last stage of the Soviet cosmic rocket launched in 1959. It passed near the moon and eventually became a satellite of Earth in its exploratory journey.

2 Maps of the moon have existed for almost as long as astronomy. This particular version, incorporating twentieth-century information, was prepared in 1967 by a Soviet astronomer.

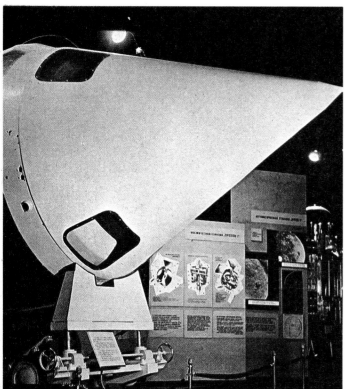

Yet as the pictures from Apollo showed, most lunar mountains are no more than gentle undulations. To someone on the surface, distance is hard to judge, because the lack of atmosphere makes distant mountains just as clear and sharp as nearby hillocks. The moon's smaller diameter brings the horizon very close.

Someone standing in the centre of one of the vast lava plains would be quite unaware of the surrounding ring of mountains, so impressive when seen from Earth. Nevertheless, some of the lunar chains rival those of Earth in their height above the surrounding plains.

The lunar environment

Although the moon is our nearest neighbour, sharing with Earth that favourable band round the Sun which receives not too much solar heat, nor yet too little, conditions on the surface of the moon are as hostile as those anywhere in space. Its lack of atmosphere means that there is no way of smoothing out temperatures between day and night, so the range is between 105°C at midday to −155°C at night. Since day and night each last

3 Colonization of the moon will depend on rendezvous between spacecraft. This picture shows a rendezvous of an Agena rocket with a Gemini XI spacecraft, which founded the technique of man and material transfers.

4 The moon and its phases determine tides, and have thus been important from the dawn of astronomy. This picture shows the moon in its last phase as only part of the illuminated surface can be seen from Earth.

5 When the Earth is interposed between the sun and the moon, the moon is in eclipse. The illustration shows the moon's surface two-thirds in the Earth's shadow.

6 An early colour picture of the moon's surface shows that grey predominates. The colour fringing is due to photographic errors. The astronauts have found that the landscape is bleak.

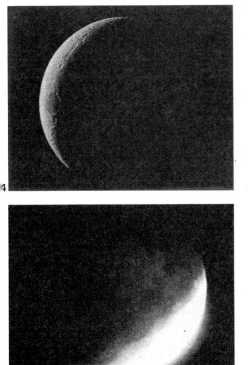

over 14 days at any particular place, there is no respite from these extremes.

What atmosphere there is has a pressure ten million million times less than that of Earth. The intense daytime heat scorches some of it off, and it is replaced at night by outgassing from the lunar surface or minor meteorite impacts.

Another feature which contributes to the lack of atmosphere is the low lunar gravity. The particles of any gas are constantly on the move, at a speed which increases with temperature. Although the temperature at the surface of Venus, for example, is much higher than that of the moon, Venus's gravitational pull is as strong as that of Earth, and it has retained a thick atmosphere. On the moon, however, the gas particles move much faster than the escape velocity and the gas is soon lost. For this reason, visionary plans to equip the moon with its own atmosphere stand little chance of success.

Danger on the moon —

An astronaut on the moon has only one sixth of his Earth weight. He can jump six times higher, and his steps take him six times farther. This has other advantages. One of the fears before the Apollo flights was that an awkward fall against a lunar rock could damage the spacesuit breathing apparatus. Although the man would have a sixth of his normal weight, his inertia would remain the same—that is, a collision would do just as much damage. In practice, however, the astronauts found that if they lost their balance, the fall took so long that they could easily walk underneath the fall, as it were, and stay upright.

What is the danger from meteorite impacts? Despite the scarred appearance of the moon's surface, major impacts

1 Hevelius's seventeenth-century map of the moon shows the major features. Minor landscape details were labelled with the names of eminent men and women.

occur very rarely. No-one has ever seen a lunar crater formed with any certainty, though one medieval report of a strange phenomenon on the moon has recently been associated with a fresh-looking crater in the right place. The evidence is thin.

Large impacts are rare, but there is a constant stream of tiny particles. These have their own effect in time, by wearing down the surface rocks. By Earth standards, this erosion takes place at a microscopic rate—of the order of 1 millimetre per million years.

The result of this constant attrition is that the lunar surface is covered by a deep layer of what is termed *regolith*—packed fine particles. As well as worn down fragments of rock, the regolith includes meteorite particles and tiny glassy beads, which caused something of a sensation when they were discovered. In fact, they were produced in basically the same way as glass on Earth—by the heating of rock—but in the case of the moon the heating was caused by large meteorite impacts, which were also responsible for spreading the tiny spheres widely across the moon's surface.

These spheres are actually responsible for the brightness of the full moon, at least in part. When the moon is full, the sun is shining almost directly on to its surface as seen from Earth. This means that there are no shadows, which adds to the surface area illuminated, but it also means that the sunlight reflects straight back from the glass spheres, in just the same way that light from a car's headlights is reflected by road-signs.

At one time, many people assumed that dust on the moon would flow, almost as if it were water. In the absence of moisture, the dust would behave like a fine dry powder and could be a trap to any spacecraft landing on it. The reason this does not happen is that the hard lunar vacuum scours all the particles clean, so that there are no contaminants to stop them sticking together. On Earth, any surface exposed

to the air rapidly accumulates a layer of oxides and other chemicals which forms an effective barrier. On the moon, however, the vacuum and bombardment by atomic particles from the Sun removes any such layer and the particles readily adhere to one another. This is why the regolith has the texture of wet sand, retaining footprints, while any stray particles quickly attach themselves to spacesuits and other exposed items.

Inside the moon

The regolith of debris has a depth of between 35 and 60 feet, and overlies a layer of shattered rock. This goes down many miles, and may be the result of the constant battering by meteorites. This gives way to a lunar crust going down some 40 miles. At this depth, the rocks change in nature, and what is known as the lunar mantle continues down for another 600 miles or so. At the centre of the moon is a partially-melted core.

All this information has been gleaned by means of the seismometers which the astronauts on the Apollo missions left to transmit information automatically. To help in this, the lunar module was sent on a collision course with the moon after the astronauts had left it. The resulting impact was picked up by the network of seismometers at varying times, depending on their distance and the nature of the intervening rocks.

The scientific results from the Apollo series were not the main reason for going to the moon: the whole effort was in reality a major morale-booster for the US population, which provided employment and entertainment for millions. There are no more plans for American moon missions. But Apollo will go down in history as a stupendous achievement.

2 Photographs of the moon reveal the craters Copernicus, Tycho and Kepler, named after great astronomers. They are distinguished by the rays which extend from them over the surface.

1

2

Out of this world

The exploration of space has been one of the most exciting developments of this century. Although it is still in its early stages, we now have some idea of what to expect on neighbouring planets.

MAN HAS EXPLORED the Earth; he has climbed to the top of Everest, plunged down to the depths of the ocean and tramped across Antarctica. He has mapped the globe not only from its surface, but also from above. Now, in the 'Space Age', he is ranging further; he has broken free from his home planet, and he has begun to invade others.

In July 1969 the first Earthmen to reach the moon – Neil Armstrong and Edwin Aldrin – stepped out on the bleak rocks of the lunar Sea of Tranquillity; but the Space Age had begun earlier, in October 1957, with the launching of Russia's pioneer artificial satellite, Sputnik I. It was the size of a football, and it carried no equipment other than a simple radio transmitter, but in little more than a decade it had been developed into complex, highly sophisticated Earth satellites. These vehicles are important in our everyday lives as well as in what we often term pure science. They have even saved lives, and they have provided invaluable information about all manner of topics.

By modern standards there is nothing difficult in launching a massive satellite carrying delicate equipment. For communications purposes, a satellite is unrivalled; in no other way would it be possible to obtain television linkage between, say, Mexico and London. Also there is the question of mapping. Photographs from satellites can cover wide areas of the Earth, and by now there is no part of the world that has not been very thoroughly surveyed. The modern geographer would feel lost without the satellite coverage.

This applies with even greater force to the geologist, who can use photographs taken from satellites in helping to decide the nature of the terrain. For instance, areas which are potentially rich in oil betray themselves when surveyed from satellites, and there can be no doubt at all that these techniques will become more and more important as time goes on.

Then, too, there is the farmer to be considered – not only the European farmer who has to deal with a few acres, but the organization which controls vast areas of vegetated land. Some plant diseases tend to spread rapidly, and in the past there have been many cases in which the trouble has not been caught at a sufficiently early stage. A photograph taken from a satellite can reveal diseased areas – in forested country, for instance – and so give an early warning which may make all the difference. These techniques are coming into ever-increasing use.

So far as the smaller farmer is concerned, there is the question of weather forecasting. Meteorology has always been regarded as an uncertain science, because

it has depended solely upon reports sent in from scattered ground stations, and in many areas of tremendous meteorological importance there are no stations. Weather satellites (pioneered in the late 1960s by the Tiros and Nimbus vehicles of the United States) can photograph whole weather systems from above, and give information about the way in which the air-masses are behaving. There has already been a significant improvement of long-range forecasting, and a complete chain of meteorological satellites in orbit round the Earth could provide a continuous stream of information.

Weather and photographic satellites have given advance warnings of the development of dangerous tropical storms, so that people living in the affected areas have been able to take suitable precautions. The saving in life is by now considerable, though it is difficult to give any hard and fast estimates. They have also helped towards a better understanding of the polar ice-fields, which are of worldwide importance. Finally, satellites have told us more about the Earth's upper air, and conditions in 'near space', than we could ever have found out in any other way. Once above the shielding layers in the atmosphere, instruments can record all the various radiations coming from beyond, and they have also been responsible for an immeasurable improvement in our knowledge of the Earth's magnetic field. The first successful American satellite, Explorer I – launched in 1958 by the team headed by Wernher von Braun –

One of the Surveyor spacecraft which made a soft landing on the moon in 1967. The information which it sent back to Earth was used in planning the manned landing of 1969.

detected the radiation belts (now called the Van Allen belts), due to particles which have been trapped by magnetic forces.

The money spent on space research has, therefore, been very far from wasted (quite apart from the various technological advances which have been applied in other fields, such as medicine and industry). In future, all really accurate maps must be based upon information sent in by satellites. And yet this is no more than a beginning; there is also the geography of other worlds.

Clearly we must begin with the moon, which is a mere quarter of a million miles from the Earth, and is much nearer than any other natural body in the sky. Lunar geography (*selenography* is more correct) began in the early seventeenth century, with the work of men such as Thomas Harriot and Galileo. Until the 1960s all lunar maps were compiled by means of observations carried out from Earth, and they were naturally limited in detail as well as accuracy. With the naked eye it is possible to make out the broad dark plains which we still call seas (*maria*) although it has been known for centuries that there is no water in them. Telescopes show vast numbers of craters, together with mountains, valleys, and minor features, such as cracks or clefts. Until 1945, the moon was very much the province of amateur astronomers, and the best available charts were made by them, but the development of rocketry altered the whole situation. The moon was no longer inaccessible; it came to be regarded as a potential colony, and every effort was made to find out as much about it as possible.

Mapping the moon

Photographic maps, compiled with the help of large telescopes, were the first step. Then, in 1959, the first rockets soared moonward, and by the mid-1960s there were sophisticated American vehicles, known as Orbiters, circling the moon in closed paths, sending back thousands upon thousands of photographs taken from low level. These pictures covered not only the areas of the moon which we can see from Earth, but also the regions never examined from our home planet because they are always turned away. It is probably true to say that moon-mapping was effectively completed by 1968 – the year in which the first men were sent to the neighbourhood of the lunar world.

The moon is a hostile place. It lacks both air and water, and it is now certain that it has never supported natural life; Armstrong and Aldrin represented the first life-forms ever known there, although the moon has possibly existed for about 4,700 million years. What was not known was

Most of outer space, such as the gaseous nebula in the constellation Serpius, would seem to be permanently beyond the reach of Man because of the enormous distances involved. **1** The Earth, seen from 100,000 miles, has already benefited from space exploration. **2** An infra-red photograph taken over the Gulf of Mexico reveals diseased trees (blue) and healthy ones (red). Such photographs can help contain diseases before they spread. Geologists and meteorologists are also aided by photographs taken from satellites. **3** Less than a century ago it was widely thought that there might be intelligent life on Mars, which never comes closer than 35 million miles to the Earth. **4** The Mariner fly-by in 1969 sent back photographs of the crater-pocked Martian surface. Now most astronomers believe that the planet is sterile; its atmosphere is probably too thin to keep out lethal radiation coming from space.

5 Venus, seen in crescent, is shrouded by a dense atmosphere that permanently hides its surface. Life, as we know it, could not exist on the planet because of its surface temperature of several hundred degrees. **6** On 16 July 1969, Apollo 11 blasted off from Cape Kennedy bearing the first men to set foot on the moon. The expense of space flight is huge; even if valuable minerals were found on the moon it would be uneconomic to send them to Earth. **7** At a quarter of a million miles from the Earth, the moon is nearer to us than any other natural body in space. Until the 1960s, lunar maps were limited in detail and accuracy because all observations were made through the distorting atmosphere of the Earth. **8** With no atmosphere or water of its own, a rugged landscape and harsh shadows, the moon is an inhospitable place. To survive there, Man would always have to live under highly artificial conditions.

An American design for a space station orbiting the Earth. Spinning at 3·5 revolutions a minute to create artificial gravity, the 715-ft-long station would be a scientific laboratory.

whether there would be any natural resources which were capable of exploitation. It was always thought that the moon and the Earth must be made up of essentially the same materials – although it is now believed that they never formed one body – but the chance of valuable substances could not be ruled out.

It now seems, however, that there is no commercial value in 'lunar mining'. The surface rocks are volcanic, and not unlike some terrestrial basalts. Specimens brought back from Apollo missions have been analysed in the laboratory and, although they are fascinating scientifically, they do not contain any exotic materials. Rubies have been found, but on a microscopic scale, and there is little chance that the moon will turn out to be a prospector's paradise. Lunar practical studies are at an early stage but there is no real reason to suppose that the specimens already brought back are at all unusual.

Travel to the moon is an expensive pastime. Weight has to be calculated very carefully; and even if valuable minerals had been found, it would be hopelessly uneconomic to try to obtain them. In the future, when nuclear rockets are developed, the situation will certainly be much easier, but it seems improbable that there will ever be large-scale transfer of materials from the moon to the Earth except for purely scientific purposes.

Neither will it ever be possible to turn the moon into a sort of second Earth. If all goes well, bases will be established well before the end of the century, possibly occupied by several hundred people, but there is not the slightest chance of hoping to solve our over-population problem. The moon has no atmosphere, and life there must always be under highly artificial conditions. It is out of the question to try to give the moon air, as has been suggested by many science-fiction writers; anything of the sort would be quite impracticable and the moon's low escape velocity (1·5 miles per second, as against 7 miles per second for the Earth) would not allow it to retain a terrestrial-type atmosphere. We must accept the moon as it is, without trying to change it.

On the other hand, a manned base will be of immense value. It will serve as a physical and chemical laboratory, a biological station, an astronomical observatory and a medical research station. The gravity is only one-sixth that of the Earth, and the moon is exposed to the various radiations from space from which the Earth is shielded by the layers in the upper air. We can obtain information which could never be gained in any other way, and every branch of research will benefit.

It has been suggested that this sort of base would be better established in space, orbiting the Earth, rather than on the moon. Opinions differ, and it is perhaps premature to come to any final conclusions but, on the whole, it seems that the lunar base is the more promising prospect.

Beyond the moon there are two planets, Venus and Mars, which are now within range of our rockets. Before the first successful planetary probes were sent up, the outlook seemed quite bright. Venus, which is about the same size as the Earth and closer to the sun, has a dense atmosphere. This hides its surface permanently so that no maps could be drawn up; but it was thought possible that its temperature might be tolerable and that there would be broad oceans. Now we know better. Several probes have flown past the planet, and three, all of Russian construction, have landed on the surface. Signals sent back during the final descent through the atmosphere of Venus have confirmed that the surface temperature is several hundred degrees, and that the chances of finding life, as we know it, must be ruled out. There can be little doubt that more vehicles will be sent to Venus in the future, but for scientific interest rather than anything else; as a colony, the 'Evening Star' holds out no promise at all. The only maps so far produced have been compiled by means of radar measures from the Earth, and all we can say is that there may be mountainous areas.

The 'canals' of Mars

Mars, however, has an atmosphere so thin that its surface can be seen clearly. There are darkish patches against the generally ochre background, and the poles are covered with white caps. Less than a century ago it was widely believed that there might well be intelligent life, and that the strange straight features commonly called 'canals' represented a planet-wide irrigation system. Unfortunately, it now seems that the atmosphere has a ground pressure of only six or seven millibars (no more than the pressure at over 120,000 ft above sea-level on Earth), that the main constituent is carbon dioxide, and that even the polar caps are made up of solid carbon dioxide rather than water ice. The chances are that the dark areas are made by shifting dust rather than vegetation, and most astronomers now tend to believe that Mars is as sterile as the moon. For one thing, the tenuous atmosphere may be hopelessly inefficient as a screen against lethal radiations coming from space.

The results from the two Viking spacecraft which landed in 1976 were sadly inconclusive. The reactions which took place could just as well have been caused by chemical means as by life. In other ways, Mars is much more like the moon than like the Earth; the chances of finding useful minerals are slight, and in any case it would be absurd to suggest bringing them home in any bulk. Mars never comes much within 35 million miles of the Earth. Again it seems that the main benefits of exploring Mars will be purely scientific, but it is not certain that they will tell us a great deal more than we learn from exploring the moon. It now seems unlikely that humans will go there much earlier than 2001. Whether it will ever be practicable, or worth while, to establish permanent colonies remains to be seen; much will depend upon whether they could be made more or less self-supporting, and on the whole this must now be regarded as dubious. In its way, Mars has turned out to be even more of a disappointment than Venus, if only because it had seemed initially to be at least reasonably welcoming.

Meanwhile, mapping the surface is in progress, and our charts of Mars are becoming steadily more reliable. The same can hardly be said of the remaining member of the group of inner planets, Mercury, which is the closest planet to the sun, and which is not much larger than the moon (its diameter is about 3,000 miles, as against 2,160 for the moon, 4,200 for Mars and 7,296 for Earth). A Mariner probe which flew past Mercury in 1974 showed a cratered surface, very similar to that of the Moon except that there are no maria or 'seas'.

In short, it is probably true to say that with our present techniques and resources we shall be unable to do more than establish limited scientific colonies on the moon and Mars. Venus is too hostile; Mercury is, in its way, just as bad; and the remaining worlds in the solar system are impossibly cold and remote. But, although relatively few Earthmen will go to other worlds, the benefits to our civilization will be incalculable. This applies even in the political field. Eventually there must be real collaboration in space and once this has been achieved, we may genuinely hope for a better understanding between nations at home.

Geography began in the very remote past. It took many centuries for men to progress from Ptolemy's rough map of the civilized world to the state of being able to chart the entire globe; but our probing out into space, beginning only in 1957, has happened in a rush. We are at an early stage and the prospects are intriguing. The geography of space may well prove to be even more fascinating than the geography of our own world.

Nine worlds in orbit

Life, warmth and energy come to us from the sun. Other planets in the solar system are in the same position. Are the sun's rays sufficient to give them the vital energy for animal life?

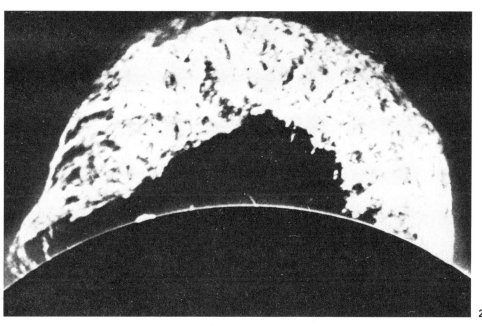

IT HAS BEEN SAID that astronomers get over the problem of trying to conceive of the inconceivable distances and forces at work in the Universe by deliberately not thinking about them at all. Radio astronomy has enabled them to detect galaxies at a distance of some 12,000 million light years (one light year being 5,878,500,500,000 miles), but they can offer little or no guidance on how the imagination can cope with such a scale.

Nor does this problem begin with distant galaxies. Our own solar system, though an insignificant feature of the Universe, is set on a scale which to human beings is stupefyingly vast. The distance from Earth to the moon is only 240,000 miles: but the solar system has a diameter at least 40,000 times greater. Alpha Centauri, the nearest star group to our sun, lies at a distance of 4·3 light years, or 25,000,000,000,000 miles.

The Milky Way galaxy, to which the solar system belongs, contains at least 100,000 million stars in a lens-shaped spiral with a diameter of 100,000 light years, with the sun some 27,000 light years from the densely packed centre. The collection of planets, moons, asteroids and comets which, together with the parent sun, comprise our particular system can thus be regarded as a closely knit heavenly family, held together by the gravitational influence of the parent.

Many attempts have been made to explain the vastness of the solar system in terms which ordinary people can understand. One of these states that, if the sun was reduced to the size of a beach ball 12 inches in diameter, then the planets could be represented as follows:

1. Mercury: a grain of mustard seed, 164 feet away;

1 Solar flares like this one observed from Boulder, Colorado, are clouds of burning hydrogen which billow hundreds of thousands of miles from the sun's surface.

2. Venus: a pea, 284 feet away;
3. Earth: a slightly larger pea, 430 feet away;
4. Mars: a currant, 654 feet away;
5. Jupiter: an orange, half a mile away;
6. Saturn: a tangerine, four-fifths of a mile away;
7. Uranus: a plum, just over a mile away;
8. Neptune: a plum, two and a half miles away; and
9. Pluto: a grain of rice at a mean distance of three miles.

On the same scale, Alpha Centauri would be 8,000 miles away.

Birth of the planets

All the planets, and the belt of asteroids lying between Mars and Jupiter, revolve round the sun in the same direction and in roughly the same plane (which is known as the *ecliptic*). However, Mercury and Pluto (respectively the nearest and furthest planets from the sun) each have highly eccentric orbits which are inclined to the plane of the ecliptic at 7° and 17° respectively. Orbital speeds of the planets also vary with the distance from the sun; a planet near the sun has to travel faster in order to remain in orbit. Thus, Mercury orbits at 107,030 mph, while Pluto can remain at its appointed distance with a speed of only 10,800 mph.

Uranus – to mention only one planet – rotates in the opposite direction to all the others because its polar axis is tilted at an angle of 97°53′ to the ecliptic; some astronomers believe this to be true also of Venus,

2 Central body in the solar system is the sun, which presents different aspects at different places. This photograph was taken from Captain Scott's base near the South Pole.

about which not very much is known for certain because of the thick layer of cloud which obscures its surface. Another curiosity is the path of Pluto, which at one point comes inside that of Neptune, though there is no danger of the planets colliding.

Among the many things still unknown about the solar system is the manner in which it was born. One theory which was very popular for a long time is that thousands of millions of years ago another sun passed within the gravitational field of our own. According to some astronomers, this resulted in a cigar shape of material being torn from the intruder. Eventually, the material condensed into 'blobs' which were the *proto-planets*. According to other astronomers, it was the intruder which tore away a portion of the sun, but the result was the same.

For various reasons, both these theories are no longer popular, having been replaced by the hypothesis that the solar system began as a huge mass of dust and gas drifting through space. Gradually, about 5,000 million years ago, the gravitational attraction between the molecules and particles in the cloud caused it to contract and, as contraction continued, the whole mass began slowly to rotate. Eventually, this took the form of a sphere rotating at a furious speed, thereby generating an enormous temperature, especially at the centre of the sphere.

At the same time, in the same way that planets bulge slightly at their equators as a result of centrifugal force, the fantastic speed of rotation of the protosphere caused

PLUTO

ASTEROIDS

CERES   JUPI

MARS   SUN

MERCURY

EARTH   VENUS

JUPITER

NEPTUNE

MERCURY   VENUS   EARTH'S   EARTH
MOON

NEREID

MARS

URANUS

MOONS OF SATURN   PLUTO

TITAN

SATURN

GANYMEDE   10

CALLISTO   EUROPA

2

4

1 Relative sizes of the planets of the sola
system. Earth is the fifth largest planet, slightl
larger than Venus, but far smaller than the fou
massive planets Jupiter, Saturn, Uranus an
Neptune. The other objects in the diagram ar
the various minor bodies in the solar system
large asteroids and moons.
2, 3, 4, 5 Eclipse of the sun, showing the pro
gressive obscuring of the sun's disc by the moon
Under these conditions it is possible to examine
the fringe of the sun (the *corona*), which is no
possible under normal circumstances.

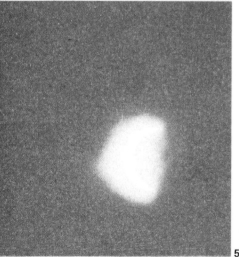

discs to form at the equator. One by one, the theory goes, these discs were thrown off into space to become the proto-planets, while the rest of the sphere became the proto-sun.

If true, the theory has one implication of enormous significance, which is that it vastly increases the probability of there being other 'families' like our own, not only in the Milky Way but in the billions of galaxies in the known Universe and beyond. Hence, it vastly increases the probability of there being life like our own elsewhere.

All life, as well as motion, in the solar system depends on the sun. Scientifically, it can be regarded as a globe of gas 865,000 miles in diameter, or as a gigantic nuclear pile with a temperature of 5,500 °C. at its surface but rising to nearly 14,000,000 °C. at its centre. Yet, astronomically speaking, the sun is only an average star as far as dimensions, brightness and tempera-

ture are concerned.

The sun, which is 330,430 times more massive than Earth, derives its energy from the enormous atomic furnace at its centre where atoms are moving so rapidly that nuclear reactions take place upon collision, converting hydrogen into helium; more than 90 per cent of the energy so generated takes place in a sphere which has only 20 per cent of the total diameter of the sun. Already, it has been carrying out this process for an estimated 5,000 million years, and it is thought to be capable of carrying on for the same length of time again before it becomes a burnt-out black cinder drifting pointlessly through the heavens.

The planets of the solar system fall conveniently into two groups: there are the inner planets, Mercury, Venus, Earth and Mars, and the outer or Jovian planets – Jupiter, Saturn, Uranus and Neptune. Pluto, which behaves more like a comet

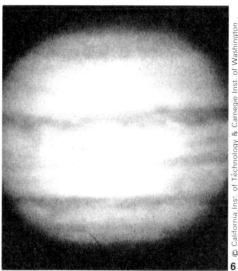

© California Inst. of Technology & Carnegie Inst. of Washington

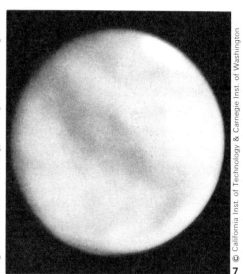

© California Inst. of Technology & Carnegie Inst. of Washington

6 Jupiter displays the characteristics of both a planet and a sun, and many astronomers believe that nuclear processes within the core maintain its surface temperature. Jupiter (Jove) gives its name to the outer planets.

7 Mars – the 'Red Planet' – appears to have both water and vegetation. It is these observations which led early astronomers to presume that life might exist on this planet.

8 The Earth photographed from space. It reflects a light on the moon rather in the way the moon lights the Earth, but six times brighter.

than a planet, seems to be the only cuckoo in the nest: it may, however, be the remains of a large Jovian planet which suffered a catastrophic nuclear explosion.

Of the inner planets, Mercury is the sunniest, being both nearest the sun and having little or no atmosphere (at least in comparison with Earth) to shield its surface. At one time, it was thought that Mercury, during its 88-day journey round the sun, presented the same face to it all the time. Astronomers, as a result, thought that the sunlit surface had a temperature of about 415 °C., while that of the hemisphere turned away from the sun was put at near absolute zero (−273 °C.).

In 1965, however, the huge radio telescope in Puerto Rico discovered that Mercury rotates every 59 days instead of every 88 days. This explained why temperature measurements of its dark side showed a comfortable 21 °C. Days and nights are long but not permanent, the sun rising at intervals of 170 days.

Other worlds

Close-up pictures of Mercury taken from a space probe show craters jumbled together. Only a careful study of them shows the difference between the surfaces of Mercury and the moon. We know rather little about conditions on Mercury, other than that it has an extremely thin atmosphere and a weak magnetic field, indicating a still partly fluid core.

Even more mysterious is Venus, the Earth's twin, whose mysteries are shrouded in a thick atmosphere containing carbon dioxide and small amounts of other gases including hydrogen, oxygen, helium, carbon monoxide and water. The dense clouds are thought to consist of droplets of sulphuric, hydrochloric and hydrofluoric acids—not an attractive prospect!

Until quite recently, the period of rotation of Venus on its axis was unknown on account of the inpenetrable clouds. From radar measures, however, it turns out to be 243 days, in an opposite sense to Earth's—that is, backwards.

The surface of Venus, when first revealed by Soviet space probes in 1975, came as something of a surprise. Instead of being gloomy and featureless, with all surface details eroded flat, it turned out to be comparatively bright and rocky. The visibility is fairly good, which suggests that the cloud layers do not extend down to the surface. The surface pressure, however, is a crushing 100 times that of Earth's atmosphere.

By contrast, the surface of Mars can be easily observed through its thin atmosphere, composed largely of nitrogen and carbon dioxide. This planet, which has half the diameter and one-ninth the mass of Earth, is generally considered to be the most likely supporter of life forms among the other planets. Such life, however, is likely to be very different from that of Earth for three main reasons: (1) the Martian atmosphere is much thinner and chemically different; (2) Mars is half as far again from the sun; (3) it has a mean density of 4 compared with Earth's 5·52, suggesting a different rock structure and core.

Even so, water vapour exists in the Martian atmosphere and liquid water may exist in relatively small amounts on and below the surface. Moreover, the planet enjoys the same axial inclination and the same rotational period as Earth, giving rise to clearly defined seasons. Snow, or frozen hoar frost, can be clearly seen at the Martian poles, and these polar caps shrink in summer just as on Earth; unlike Earth, however, atmospheric pressure on Mars is so low that the ice turns directly into water vapour. Further evidence for water is the existence of vast channels, apparently cut by flowing water at some time in the past, around the equator.

Finally, there are the two moons of Mars, Phobos and Deimos. Each of them is tiny and orbits close to the planet: in the case of Phobos, the diameter is five miles and the height of orbit only 5,800 miles, while Deimos is only three miles in diameter and orbits at a height of 15,000 miles. Recent photographs taken by space probes show that the moons, too, have cratered surfaces. Both moons are elongated, since their surface gravity is far too weak to form them into spheres.

The outer planets begin with Jupiter, though it is believed that there was once a planet orbiting between Mars and Jupiter which was shattered by the latter's gravitational field. The remains of this planet, at least part of them, are thought to be the asteroids which orbit in this band of space. Some 1,500 of these have been detected, the largest being Ceres with a diameter of 480 miles.

The Jovian planets all have a similar atmosphere, consisting of a mixture of hydrogen, helium, ammonia, methane and perhaps some water. However, hydrogen predominates because these planets are massive enough and far enough away from the sun to retain the lighter gases.

Jupiter, with a mass of more than 318 Earths and an equatorial diameter of 88,700 miles, is the greatest of the Jovian planets in all senses of the word. No one can tell yet where its solid surface begins and its atmosphere ends, but it is known to be the scene of violent storms and is a great emitter of radio waves, as befits the God of Thunder. It is also the proud possessor of a Great Red Spot in its south tropical zone which seems to be a coherent feature suspended in some form of liquid or gas. It measures some 25,000 miles in length by 8,000 miles in breadth. The planet also boasts 12 moons, and is not unlike a solar system in miniature. For all that, Jupiter's density is only 1·33 times that of water.

Planet or sun?

Many astronomers believe that Jupiter lies somewhere between a planet and a tiny sun, a body in which nuclear processes are going on but are insufficiently strong to make it luminous. Hence, it is argued, although the outer atmosphere is incredibly cold through lack of heat from the sun, its surface may receive considerable heat from the nuclear reactions at the core, and may indeed be warmer than the surface of the Earth. A similar argument applies to the rest of the family: Saturn, Uranus and Neptune.

There is little doubt that Man will soon be visiting some of the inner planets. Apart from the fact that voyages like these will constitute the greatest and most exciting challenge ever presented to the human spirit and mind, it will be also fascinating to find out how far the reality of these planets accords with what we think we know of them today.

1 Saturn boasts six satellites, four of which are clearly shown here. They supply information about the size, mass and movement of Saturn.

2 At one time total (annular) eclipses of the sun were held to be omens of disaster. Now they are observed by people all over the world, as this picture shows.

The Universe around us

The sun is only one of 100,000 million to 200,000 million stars in our galaxy. If the properties and relationships of Earth and sun are duplicated elsewhere, Man may not be alone in the Universe.

1 About 80 per cent of known galaxies are spirals. Spiral nebula Coma Berenices is seen here photographed 'edge-on' by the 200-inch Hale telescope at Mount Palomar.

2 Comets, occasionally visible from Earth, can be the most spectacular and brilliant phenomena in the sky. The comet Jurlof-Achmanof was a brief visitor in 1939.

JUST AS HYDROGEN comprises the raw material of the Universe, stars are its main product. In our own galaxy, the Milky Way, the number of stars is estimated at between 100,000 million and 200,000 million, while the number of galaxies in the detectable Universe is put at anything between 100,000 million and one million million. With figures like these, it would indeed be strange if the sun was the only star to sustain life.

Yet the sun does seem so different from the other stars in the sky that most people probably do not think of it as a star at all. We see it as a bright yellow disc and are conscious of the heat and light it provides, but only because it happens to be much nearer than any other star. The mean distance between sun and Earth is only 93 million miles, compared with 25 million million miles (4·2 light years) to the next nearest star, Proxima Centauri. Altogether, some 6,500 stars can be seen with the naked eye, and a large number of these would look very much like the sun at the same distance.

The science of astronomy abounds with unproved theories, some about when and how the stars were formed. It is believed that some stars were formed only a few million years ago, while others, including the sun, are thought to go back 5,000 million years and more. As to the manner of their birth, no theory has so far successfully challenged that called 'the nebular hypothesis', propounded by the German philosopher, Immanuel Kant, in 1755.

Kant believed that stars evolved from enormous clouds of dust and gas drifting about in space. These clouds were originally cool, but began to heat up as gravitational attraction between the particles came into play and the clouds began to condense and contract.

The planets are formed

According to Kant, the primitive cloud would begin to rotate: it grew hotter and hotter as it contracted until it began to glow like a giant proto-star. Meanwhile, the rate of spin reached a point at which centrifugal force began throwing off rings of glowing dust and gas which in time cooled and formed themselves into planets.

A similar theory was advanced independently of Kant some 40 years later by the French scientist, the Marquis de Laplace. In the opinion of Laplace, however, the cloud would be hot and rotating from the very beginning: contraction alone, he argued, could not have caused the cloud to rotate. But in any case, although it has been modified somewhat since, the nebular hypothesis is accepted in principle today.

Stars have been discovered which have more than 10,000 times the mass of the sun and more than one million times its volume. There are other stars which, in comparison with the sun, are dwarfs. Yet the remarkable fact is that more than 99 per cent of all stars in the Universe are thought to belong to the Main Sequence – that is, they can be grouped together according to their various properties to form an orderly progression from the biggest and hottest to the smallest and coolest. When this is plotted as a graph, the result is a straight diagonal line.

This progression of the stars was recognized more than 50 years ago independently by two astronomers, E. Hertzsprung and H. N. Russell. Each prepared versions of what is now known as the Hertzsprung-Russell (H-R) diagram, in which the Main Sequence stars form the straight line just mentioned. This line suggests a smooth and continuous change in the intensities of the absorption lines of the stellar spectra.

Stars in the Main Sequence have been grouped into ten main groups or classes, designated by the letters O, B, A, F, G, K, M, R, N and S with each group sub-divided by the numbers 0 to 9. The Class O stars, which are very rare, are the most massive and hottest with surface temperatures up to 90,000 °F. (50,000 °C.); the coolest and

smallest are the Class S stars whose surface temperatures can be as low as 5,400 °F. (3,000 °C.). The sun, classified as a G2, and called a yellow dwarf, has a surface temperature of about 13,500 °F. Its absolute magnitude (its luminosity at a distance of 32·6 light years) is +5, which means that at this distance it would be an inconspicuous star, just slightly more visible than the faintest stars which can be seen with the naked eye. Compare this with some of the stars in the Large Magellanic Cloud which have a magnitude of −10, and therefore shine with the light of one million suns!

The brightest stars

The simple analogy of a red-hot poker helps explain what the Main Sequence is about. If left in a fire for an adequate length of time, the tip of the poker should be white hot, perhaps even blue, whereas the further away from the tip, the duller the heat-glow. White turns to yellow, to orange and to red. Similarly with the stars: the hottest look blue to the naked eye, the coolest look red. This explains why the sun is called a yellow dwarf.

Stars in the Main Sequence are in the stable period of their existence, during which hydrogen is being converted into helium at a steady rate owing to nuclear reactions taking place at the centre. After they have consumed a certain amount of their available hydrogen (with the sun the

proportion is thought to be 12 per cent) stars expand rapidly into cool 'red giants' and leave the Main Sequence.

Ultimately, they become hot white dwarfs', stars perhaps no bigger than a planet but of incredibly high density. In the evolution towards this ultimate condition, the star may suffer a dramatic loss of mass through a 'nova' or 'supernova' explosion during which it gains a fantastic increase in brightness for a few days.

Despite immense gravitational pressures, stars keep their shape through the opposite, outgoing pressure of radiation. However, the processes of thermonuclear fusion and neutron capture gradually transform hydrogen into heavier elements, and there comes a point at which the thermonuclear reactions grow so weak that the radiation pressure surrenders to that of gravity. As already explained, the star then collapses inward, during which process the larger stars become supernovae and for a short period may shine with the light of 1,000 million stars. Less massive stars are thought to contract into superdense white dwarfs by the same process.

The remains of supernovae are among the strangest objects yet discovered. The less massive supernovae leave behind them neutron stars, in which matter is packed so tightly that the electrons and protons fuse to form neutrons. As a neutron star collapses, its rate of spin

1 This galaxy, the Whirlpool, was the first nebula to be recognized as spiral. In most telescopes it appears as a blur; the structure only shows in photographs.
2 Pleiades is a star cluster within the constellation Taurus, about 300 light years from the solar system. Nebulosity is probably caused by rarefied matter made luminous by radiation.

increases until it may be no more than a few miles across yet spinning once a second or even faster. Radio signals from these stars pulse rhythmically, hence their name of pulsars.

A more massive object may go on collapsing until its surface gravity is so high that nothing, not even light, can escape. The result is called a black hole.

The middle way

The more massive a star, the more rapidly it burns up its stock of hydrogen, hence the shorter its stay in the Main Sequence. Stars in the O class may in fact remain there only for a few million years, which is a very short time in astronomical terms and certainly not long enough for life to develop on any planets attached to such stars. By the same token, stars in the classes M to S are due to stay in the Main Sequence for a prodigious length of time – perhaps for 100,000 million years – but may not emit enough energy to start life on their satellites.

As ever, where life is concerned, the

middle way seems to be the best way. Our sun is estimated to be 5,000 million years old and to have at least another 7,000 million years to run, most of them in the Main Sequence. Similarly, it is hot, but not too hot, massive but not too massive. Thus, for various reasons to do with age, temperature and mass, it is thought that the stars most likely to support some form of life on satellite planets are those lying between F2 and M2 (inclusive) in the Main Sequence.

From star counts and classifications, it is believed that 25 per cent of all stars lie in this sector. Out of every 10,000 stars, more than 7,300 lie in the M spectral class; that is, nearly three-quarters of all the stars are small and dim. As the spectral class increases, the number of stars in each decreases: thus, of every 10,000 stars, 1,500 are in spectral class K, 730 in G, 290 in F, and so on until at O there is only one star in every 50,000.

At this point, the importance of the nebular hypothesis becomes apparent because, if true, it means that most stars – even double, treble and quadruple systems – are likely to have attendant planets. What this means in the case of the Milky Way, to name only one galaxy, has been summed up by the well-known astronomer, Isaac Asimov:

'The total number of stars in our galaxy,' he writes, 'has been estimated at 135 billion (one American billion equals 1,000 million). Therefore, the total number of stars in the range of the spectral classes F2 to M2, representing all stars that might conceivably have habitable planets, is 34 billion.

'The total number of stars in the range

© California Inst. of Technology & Carnegie Inst. of Washington

3 A seventeenth-century copper-plate engraving showing the positions of the stars and their pictorial astrological representations. The names have been adopted for the constellations.
4 The Andromeda galaxy, over two million light-years away. It can just be seen as a misty patch high in the sky on clear autumn nights.

3

4

of spectral classes F2 to K1, which can have habitable planets without special satellites (and this is the important range) is 17·5 billion. In sheer numbers, then, there is no lack of suitable stars in the galaxy.'

If we apply the Main Sequence classification to the 20 brightest stars in the sky, we find that six are too massive to be on it. These are Capella, Arcturus, Aldebaran, Pollux, Betelgeuse and Antares.

The Milky Way

Six more are of spectral class B, five of A, two of F and one (by a lucky chance, Alpha Centauri, the second nearest) of spectral class G, like our own sun. Sirius A, the brightest star in the heavens, is a white dwarf of spectral class A; at a distance of 8·7 light years, it has an apparent magnitude of −1·58, and an absolute magnitude of 1·3. Magnitude increases logarithmically, so that a star of the fourth magnitude is 2·512 times brighter than one of the fifth. However, a star of the first magnitude is 100 times brighter than one of the fifth.

But Sirius is by no means the most interesting object among the brightest stars. The second brightest, Canopus, some 650 light years away, is a fantastic body with an estimated absolute magnitude of −7·4 (one million times brighter than the sun), yet it is thought to belong to spectral class F. Canopus is not visible from all parts of the northern hemisphere. Another remarkable object is Rigel (spectral class B) with an absolute magnitude of −5·8; there is also Deneb with one of −5·2.

The sun is, of course, a modest member of the Milky Way, a star system some 80,000 light years in diameter which is often referred to simply as the galaxy. The Milky Way is actually spiral in shape, but in cross-section it looks like a disc with a central nucleus of stars (some 13,000 light years in thickness). In this nucleus, many stars are thought to be as little as one light year apart. In 1926, the galaxy was discovered to be rotating, the galactic rotation of the sun being about 200 miles a second, but speeds are higher at the centre.

The sun lies some 26,000 light years from the centre of the galaxy and just north of its central plane; at this distance, the thickness of the galaxy is only 2,000 light years. Within 22 light years of the sun, there are only 111 stars, the closest being Proxima Centauri, a very small star some 4·2 light years away. It is part of a triple star system of which Alpha Centauri (4·3 light years' distance) is a G star like the sun. Other 'near' stars include Barnard's Star (6·2 light years away), Lalande 21185 (8 light years), Wolf 359 (8·1 light years) and Sirius (8·7 light years).

According to Asimov, only 14 of the 111 nearest stars enjoy a probability greater than one in 100 of having a habitable planet (that is, a planet which is habitable from the point of view of human requirements). However, Asimov also states that 'the combined probability of the existence of at least one habitable planet in the whole volume of space out to a distance of 22 light years from the sun is about 0·43. That is to say, in gambler's parlance, the odds are about 3 to 2 against our finding even a single habitable planet in the entire list of 14 candidates.' On the other hand, we are talking about only a very tiny fraction of the stars in the Milky Way.

The probability of finding some form of life within 22 light years of the sun is, of course, vastly higher. The existence of several planets attached to nearby stars has been inferred from a study of the motions of the stars in question. In 1944, for example, the binary 61 Cygni C system showed irregularities which could be due only to the presence of a dark companion about eight times the size of Jupiter. Similar studies have shown that Barnard's

Star and Lalande 21185 A, the stars second and third closest to the sun, also have dark companions.

It is, of course, impossible to detect the existence of planets outside the solar system by optical means because the distances involved are so vast. The unit of measurement generally used in the case of stars is the parsec, which is equal to 3·26 light years. At this distance, the angle between the Earth and sun amounts to only one second of arc; and a telescope mounted in space could not detect the separation of a dim body from a bright one at an angle smaller than two seconds of arc.

Undiscovered phenomena

Space contains many strange objects, strange, anyway, in the sense that we do not yet properly understand them. There are, for instance, the quasars, phenomena many times smaller than the average galaxy but which emit more than 100 times the radio energy of a galaxy. Again there are the cepheid stars, objects which glow bright then dim at regular intervals and the pulsars which emit radio energy at regular intervals. No doubt there are other celestial phenomena awaiting discovery.

Yet when one bears in mind the distances and the forces and the time scale involved, Man has a remarkable amount of knowledge about the stars – enough anyway to be practically certain that he is not alone in the Universe. With an estimated 7,000 million stars of the same spectral type as the sun in the Milky Way alone, how can we dismiss the possibility of there being creatures similar to us sharing this corner of space? We are as we are because Earth and sun are as they are. What if their various features and their distance relationship were duplicated elsewhere in space?

1 The great nebula in Andromeda. Working with the 100-inch Mount Wilson telescope in 1925, Edwin Hubble showed a resolution of the nebula into stars. One million galaxies have been photographed at Mount Wilson. Hubble classified them according to their shape.

2 A great nebula in the constellation of the Swan consisting of clouds of rarefied gases.

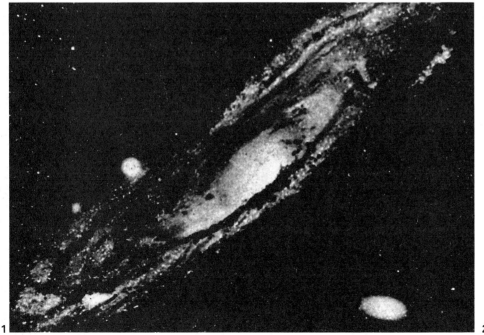

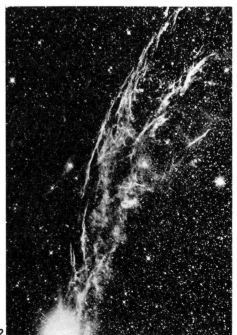

The enigmatic Cosmos

Powerful new techniques such as radio-astronomy now enable scientists to look deep into space. But many basic questions about the Universe we live in remain unsolved.

IF WE LOOK at the sky on a clear night, we can see some of the myriad bodies that make up the Universe. Astronomers, who are able to look far more closely at the heavens with the aid of telescopes than we can with the naked eye, are able to see many of the components that make it up. The objects visible from Earth are stars and galaxies. The separate stars belong to our own galaxy: the Milky Way. The galaxies are more distant and are very numerous.

The stars that make up our own Milky Way are visible as a band across the sky. The reason for this is that the Milky Way is a spiral galaxy, shaped rather like a disc, with the sun and the solar system placed towards the edge of the galaxy. While the stars appear in this way, the other galaxies are uniformly distributed, so that in whatever direction one looks one can see the same number of galaxies, provided one counts sufficient numbers. The galaxies show a tendency to occur in clusters.

The only way we have of estimating the relative distances of the galaxies we can see is to estimate how faint they look. The fainter they are, the further away they are likely to be. Estimates of the distribution of the galaxies based on faintness suggest that the Universe is uniform, that is, it is generally the same in all directions.

The uniformity of the Universe suggests that we are in fact looking at a fair sample section of the Universe, although we cannot see it all.

Speculation about the Universe has naturally occupied a great deal of human attention for many centuries. Many of the problems associated with an understanding of the Universe involved difficult concepts: the concept that space is, as Einstein maintained, 'finite but unbounded' has been one that has long puzzled laymen.

There is a second problem of this nature – namely, the Universe may be eternal, or it may have come into being thousands of millions of years ago. There is evidence to suggest that all the galaxies, and the stars and planets within them, the quasars and the supplies of interstellar gas, are in perfect balance, and may have reached this condition an infinite number of years ago. On the other hand, there is equally good reason to believe that the Universe is changing and evolving, that it is subject to cosmic laws of evolution.

For the moment at least, then, there is little we can state with certainty. The known Universe has been variously estimated to be as large as 10,000 to 12,000 million light years, while the number of galaxies has been put at anything from 3,000 million to one million million. Such discrepancies are only to be expected when we are dealing with distances far, far

beyond the range of the most powerful telescopes. Even so, the earliest discovery of galaxies beyond our own goes back 1,000 years to the time of the Arabic astronomer, Al-Sufi, who recorded Messier 31, the modern name for the spiral galaxy in Andromeda, the most distant of all the heavenly bodies visible with the naked

eye from the surface of the Earth.

In 1923, the famous American astronomer, Edwin P. Hubble, discovered six Cepheid variables (stars whose brightness fluctuates regularly and so allows them to be used as standard known light sources) in this spiral, and calculated that their distance was in the region of 750,000 light

1 A medieval view of the Universe. The print shows an explorer reaching the point at which the Earth meets the heavens. Behind the bowl of stars are the various wheels to drive the bowl.

2 Ancient Egyptian picture of the cosmos. The sky-goddess Nut arches over the reclining Earth-god Qeb. Shu, the air-god, stands between, supported by two ram-headed gods.

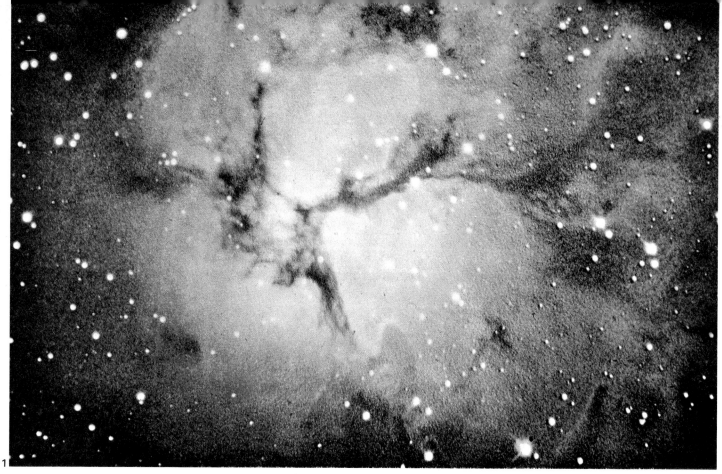

years, a staggering figure in those days; in 1952, another American astronomer, W. Baade, found that the true distance was even greater – about 2 million light years. Yet these distances are a mere fraction of those separating us from the most distant galaxies. Radio astronomers have detected objects which may be 6,000 million light years and more from the Earth (one light year being 5,878,500 million miles).

Theories of the Universe

Today, three main theories of the Universe are popular among astronomers, but while these opinions should be treated with respect, it must be emphasized that none of these theories is necessarily correct.

All these theories accept that the Universe is uniform, and that it is now expanding. In other words, the bulk of modern cosmological theory rests on the observations of astronomers that the light from distant stars is red-shifted, and that this indicates that they are moving away. Much of the theoretical work that led to the formulation of these theories was carried out by such leading mathematicians as Albert Einstein, Willem de Sitter Friedmann and Sir Arthur Eddington.

The first of the three is known as the 'steady state' or 'continuous creation' theory. Put forward in 1948 by Hermann Bondi, Thomas Gold and Fred Hoyle, all of them British astronomers, it maintains that the Universe is eternal – that is, it has always existed – and must appear to be essentially the same from whichever point of time or place it is studied. Matter, states the theory, is continuously created out of apparently nothing at the rate of 62 atoms of hydrogen per cubic inch of space every 1,000 million years. This is sufficient (and one can well believe it because there are a lot of cubic inches in

1 The Trifid mist in the galaxy Sagittarius. A mass of gas and dust 3,200 light-years away, it contains many hot newly-created stars.
2 Diagram of the 'big bang' theory of the evolution of the Universe. A dense supercondensate exploded giving rise to the Universe's expansion.

3 The 'oscillating' theory. The Universe is pulsating, expanded to a maximum and then contracting to a dense mass again.
4 Diagram of a 'steady state' universe. The Universe is expanding, but new matter (ringed) is created continuously and density maintained.

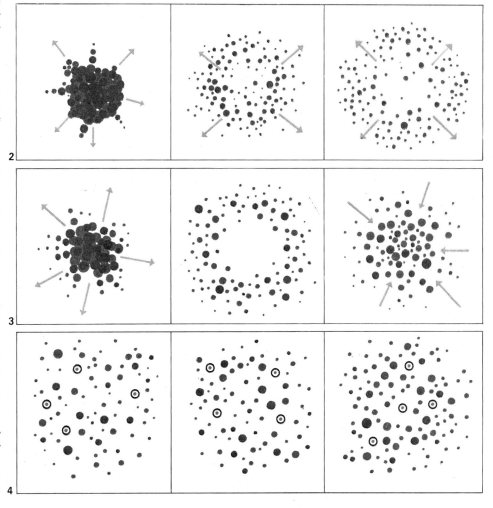

1 During the Middle Ages, astronomy declined in Europe but study of the Universe was developed in Moslem countries. Here, Persian astronomers measure the movements of heavenly bodies.

space) to form new galaxies to fill in the gaps caused by the fact that the Universe is expanding.

One major test of the steady-state theory is that because light travels at a finite speed, and because vast distances separate us even from the nearest galaxies, the light we see now from very distant galaxies was in fact emitted hundreds or even thousands of millions of years ago. Some of these observations tend to show that the Universe then was different from now thus contradicting the steady-state theory.

The second theory, and one which should appeal to all lovers of science fiction, is the 'big bang' theory, advanced in 1930 by the Belgian astronomer, Georges Lemaitre. The theory maintains that about 10,000 million years ago, all matter in the Universe was packed into one super-dense sphere – the primeval atom – so that one cubic inch of the material weighed several thousands of millions of tons. Not surprisingly, the body exploded, its various fragments becoming galaxies moving apart at fantastic speeds.

The third explanation, known as the 'oscillating' theory, was revived in 1965 by the American astronomer, Professor Allan Sandage. It is essentially a special case of the 'big bang' theory, maintaining as it does that the Universe is today 10,000 million years along the expansive stage of an 80,000 million years' cycle of expansion and contraction. Thus, the theory claims, the Universe will continue to expand for another 30,000 million years, after which the gravitational attraction between the galaxies will gradually overcome the centrifugal force of the big bang. As a result, all the galaxies will move towards each other at millions of miles per hour until finally they re-form into the primeval atom, which will again explode. In this way, the Universe is fated to undergo an infinite series of explosion-implosion cycles.

Fantastic as some of these theories may sound to the layman, it must be remembered that, to human beings, the Universe is a fantastic phenomenon. Ordinary people must have been equally perplexed when some early Greek first maintained that the Earth was round. It will be noted, however, that the steady state and the big bang theories are mutually exclusive: if one is right, the other is wrong, because the Universe cannot at one and the same time be in a steady and an unsteady state. Yet if, in a steady-state universe, galaxies are moving apart and matter is being created to fill the gaps so created, then we have the apparently contradictory notions of an eternal Universe with dynamic features. However, what appears contradictory on Earth may be perfectly valid on a cosmic scale.

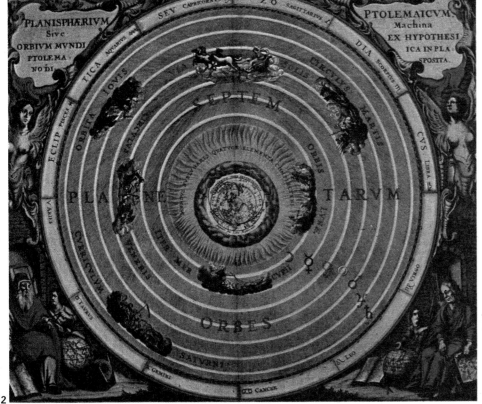

2 The solar system after Ptolemy. In this picture, the planets are orbiting the Earth. Until the sixteenth century, Earth was thought to be the centre of the Universe.

If it could be established beyond doubt that the Universe is, or is not, expanding, at least a lot of time and thought could be saved. In 1920, an American astronomer, V. M. Slipher, discovered, while working at Flagstaff in Arizona, that the light from certain distant galaxies was, in astronomical terms, 'exhibiting Doppler shifts to the red end of the spectrum'. Subsequent work by Edwin Hubble showed by 1929 that the amount of red shift was directly proportional to the distance of the galaxy concerned – in other words, the greater the shift of the light to the red end of the spectrum, the further the galaxy. It was as a result discovered (to the satisfaction of most astronomers at least) that galaxies were receding and that the more distant the galaxy, the higher its speed of recession. It has been estimated, for instance, that the pair of galaxies in Boötes, known as 3C295, are receding at over 300 million miles per hour, and are therefore assumed to be 6,000 million light years away. By such reckoning, galaxies nearing the circumference of our Universe would be receding at the speed of light.

Is the Universe expanding?

Most astronomers accept that the Universe is expanding because of the evidence of the red shift, but it is only fair to add that a number of them question not the evidence but the interpretation. Various other reasons have been put forward, but have never found wide acceptance, as explanations of the phenomenon, among them the suggestion that light on a long journey through space will be affected in an otherwise unknown way by gravity, or by electric and magnetic fields so as to exhibit a red shift. This, the so-called 'tired light' theory, is rejected by almost all astronomers because it would necessitate an entirely new physical principle which is not supported by any other evidence. Moreover, the Doppler shift has been successfully interpreted as a velocity effect in measuring the period of rotation of Jupiter which has been confirmed from

1 A modern reconstruction of Dondi's astronomical clock. The original was built in 1364. In addition to telling the time, the clock shows the positions of the sun, moon and several planets.
2 Technical experts at a flight research centre in the United States work on future space projects. The laboratory produces 'flight hardware' to protect instruments during exploratory missions. **1**

other scientific evidence.

Nothing, then, is certain yet. We can, however, claim to be much further along the path of universal understanding than the Greek cartographer, Anaximander, who 2,500 years ago held that the Universe consisted of a sphere of fire enclosing a cold, moist mass from which it was separated by a layer of mist. Eventually, Anaximander thought, the fire became the light of the stars, the mist became the atmosphere, and the cold moist mass was transformed into Mother Earth. If we laugh at this, we should bear in mind that it was not until after Columbus had discovered the New World that Copernicus, in 1512, put the sun, and not the Earth, at the centre of the solar system.

The galaxies

Only four galaxies are visible from Earth with the naked eye. These are the Milky Way, the Large and Small Magellanic Clouds which lie at a distance of about 170,000 light years, and the Andromeda Nebula at 2 million light years. The Magellanic Clouds are a different type of galaxy from the Milky Way and Andromeda: true, they probably have a basic spiral structure, but it is not nearly so prominent. Other galaxies lack an orderly structure, taking an overall elliptical form with their brightness diminishing from the centre outward.

Galaxies also tend to be found in

clusters. Those nearest the Milky Way, for example, form a small team of about 20 members, known as the 'Local Group'. They also vary considerably in size: large galaxies will have a star population ranging from about 10,000 million to more than 100,000 million. By these standards, the Milky Way (with anything between 100,000 million and 250,000 million stars) is one of the largest.

However, Andromeda, our second closest galactic neighbour, is much bigger. With a real diameter of 200,000 light years (the Milky Way's is 80,000 light years), as well as two satellite galaxies, it is undisputed king of the Local Group. It boasts all or most of the various stellar phenomena, including Cepheid stars, young stars in the nucleus, older stars in its spiral arms, compact globular clusters, novae and supernovae. By comparison, the Magellanic Clouds are small indeed, having a diameter of 25,000 light years. These include young clusters of very hot blue stars, and super stars with absolute magnitudes many times greater than the sun.

As well as moving away from its neighbours, the galaxy is rotating. In our own part of the Milky Way, the speed of rotation is about 140 miles per second, so that in its total lifetime the sun has made anything from 20 to 50 circuits; simple arithmetic will demonstrate the vastness of the scale being discussed. This rotation is not uniform like that of a wheel, but the inner parts complete a circuit much faster than the outer parts.

Important discoveries

Much of our recently added knowledge of the Universe has come from the techniques of radio astronomy, through which we can turn an ear into space where the eye cannot reach. Such techniques are, of course, based on advanced aerial systems, such as steerable paraboloids, of which the 250-foot diameter disc at Jodrell Bank and the vast moveable array of the Cambridge astronomers are examples. These, and systems based on large aerial complexes, have been responsible for a number of important discoveries, including the rotation of Mercury, the rotation in the central region of the galaxy and the identification of quasars, or quasi-stellar radio sources.

No look at the Universe, however brief, should ignore these phenomena, if only because their discovery indicates there may be many strange objects in the Universe of which we have yet no inkling. As far as can be inferred, quasars are objects possessing the same mass as galaxies, but much, much smaller in volume; hence they seem to be collapsing under intense gravitational attraction, and at the same time releasing almost inconceivable amounts of energy. It is as if they are the source of minor big bangs, generating energy the equivalent of 100 and more exploding stars.

It is easy enough to pose questions about the Universe but practically impossible to find conclusive answers. Man must be content as an insignificant spectator of the vast cosmic drama around him.

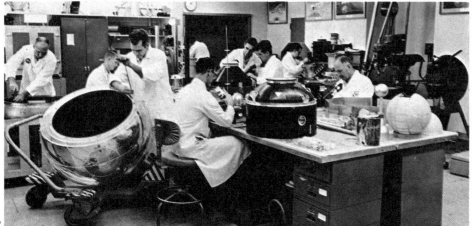

The mystery of cosmic rays

The Earth is under continual bombardment from cosmic rays coming, it is believed, from exploding stars. But how these rays obtain their phenomenal penetrating power and energy is not yet known.

IN 1893 Charles T.R. Wilson, who later became professor of natural philosophy at Cambridge and shared with Arthur Compton the Nobel Prize for physics in 1927, was studying the rings or haloes of coloured light which in hilly districts sometimes surround a shadow thrown on mist lying on slopes below the position of the person shadowed. Such haloes are caused by condensation of water vapour and Wilson wanted to find out the reason for the water vapour condensing.

He carried out a series of experiments to prove that most of the water drops were formed on dust particles in the air, but that a few of them appeared to be formed on electrified molecules, or *ions*. After further experimentation, Wilson concluded that some ions may result from some kind of radiation originating in outer space and penetrating the Earth's atmosphere. About the same time the German chemist Friedrich Giesel was carrying out experiments similar to those of Wilson and reaching the same conclusion.

No one was particularly interested in the Wilson-Giesel experiments until the beginning of the present century when physicists began turning their attention to the properties of X-rays, electrical discharges through gases, and radioactivity. The measuring and detecting instrument used in most of these studies was the gold-leaf electroscope. This consists of two tissue-thin leaves of beaten gold which, when they receive an electric charge repel each other and diverge; the degree of divergence being dependent upon the value of the charge. The electroscope was well insulated, to prevent the charge on its leaves from leaking away.

It was discovered, however, that if the electroscope was placed in the path of X-rays or radiation from a piece of radioactive material, the leaves of the instrument immediately fell together. The reason for this was that the X-rays or other radiation had ionized the air around the electroscope, so allowing the air to conduct the charge away from the leaves.

When there was no radiation to ionize the air around the electroscope, the air acted as a reasonably good insulator, but certainly not as a perfect one. No matter how carefully the leaves were insulated to prevent a charge on them from leaking away, they eventually lost their charge and came together. In other words, some invisible and unknown medium was conducting away the charges on the leaves of the electroscope.

In 1910 Victor Hess, an Austrian physicist, by going up in a balloon armed with a gold-leaf electroscope, proved beyond question that the mysterious radiation was not of terrestrial origin. The greater

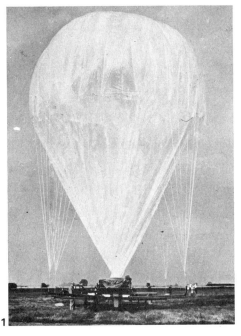

1 This balloon — when launched with its payload of instruments for measuring cosmic radiation — will travel across Britain at an altitude of 23 miles for about six hours.
2 On collision with a nucleus in a photographic emulsion, the high-energy cosmic ray particle causes it to explode into fragments. These produce a track of their own in the emulsion.

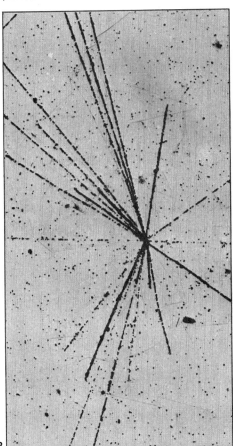

the altitude, the more quickly the gold leaves fell together, showing that radiation intensity increased with height. Subsequent experiments with balloon-borne electroscopes revealed an even more remarkable fact. Radiation intensity progressively increased up to an altitude of 15 miles, then steadily decreased between altitudes of 15 and 25 miles. Above 25 miles the radiation remained constant with altitude.

It was one thing to establish that this radiation did not originate on Earth, but it was much more difficult to establish just from where it came and what caused it. To find the answers to these questions, more and more physicists began studying the mysterious radiation. One of the outstanding of these inquirers was Robert Millikan, professor of physics at the Californian Institute of Technology and winner of the 1923 Nobel prize for physics. It was he who christened the radiation 'cosmic rays'.

By means of various detecting and measuring devices, more and more information was gathered about cosmic rays, although there still remains much to learn. It has been established that cosmic rays are continually pouring down on the Earth and we are all under constant bombardment from them. They have tremendous penetrating power, and will pass through most known materials. They are a form of energy but they behave quite unlike any other form of energy radiation.

Penetrating power

Ordinary light, for example, penetrates only a very short distance into opaque matter. X-rays and radiation generated by nuclear fission have a greater penetrating power, but even the latter can be stopped by a wall of lead and concrete. On the other hand, cosmic rays will to a considerable extent pass through a barrier of lead 6 ft thick and will penetrate to the bottom of mine shafts. Cosmic rays continue their bombardment on the tops of mountains, in the frozen regions of the Arctic and Antarctic and in the hottest parts of the tropics.

During the early period of cosmic-ray research it was thought that all cosmic radiation emanated from the sun. Since intensity of radiation varies with solar flares at least some cosmic rays must originate in the sun, but the vast bulk come from some source outside the solar system: possibly from a super-nova explosion.

Instrumentation carried into the upper atmosphere by balloons and, later by rockets and satellites has provided physicists with a mass of information relative to cosmic rays, though it has as yet failed to answer all the questions. The most important result of modern research is

that cosmic rays are particles with initial energies of anything between ten million and billions of millions of electron-volts. An electron-volt is the energy acquired by an electron when accelerated through a voltage difference of one volt. Cosmic-ray radiation energy is, therefore, infinitely greater than anything Man can produce with his most sophisticated equipment for artificially accelerating particles.

All the instruments used to detect and evaluate cosmic rays are based on the rays' ability to produce ions in the matter they penetrate or traverse. The chief instruments operating on this basis are the ionization chamber, the Geiger-Müller tube, cloud and bubble chambers and photographic emulsion.

In the ionization chamber, the current carried by the ions produced by the rays passes between two electrodes through a gas. The ionization chamber, no longer used, is not sufficiently sensitive to detect single particles of radiation. This sensitivity is accomplished by the Geiger-Müller tube. This latter instrument is a highly sophisticated version of the Geiger counter used for the detection of nuclear radiation and measuring its intensity. In the Geiger-Müller tube, single ion pairs, created in the space between a cylindrical electrode and an axial wire, trigger or release a temporary discharge. By the simultaneous employment of a battery of tubes it is possible to trace the trajectories of single cosmic-ray particles through great thicknesses of matter.

Other forms of cosmic-ray instrumentation are cloud and bubble chambers, scintillators and photographic emulsions. Cloud and bubble chambers are particu-

larly valuable in analysing the rays by making their tracks visible through droplets or bubbles formed on the ions created in gases or liquids. Scintillators make use of the light produced by the recombination of ions after the passage of the cosmic particles or by the radiation created by charged particles of high velocity. Another method to give visible proof of the existence of cosmic rays is the exposure of photographic plates coated with highly sensitive emulsion. The presence of the rays is indicated as tracks in the form of silver grains.

Counters and cloud chambers

One of the first tasks towards an understanding of cosmic rays was to establish whether radiation consisted of uncharged particles such as gamma rays, or charged particles, such as electrons and protons. It was at first thought that cosmic rays were all exceptionally energetic gamma rays of very short wave-length, but this was soon disproved. Experiments with counters and cloud chambers showed conclusively that most rays reaching the Earth's surface carried electric charges.

With the development of high-altitude instrumentation, it became possible to distinguish between two kinds of cosmic rays: primary and secondary. Primary rays are those originally coming from outer space and striking the top fringe of the Earth's atmosphere. Secondary rays are produced by the collision of primaries with the atoms in the atmosphere.

Experiments with counters and emulsions taken by rockets and satellites into the higher reaches of the atmosphere and beyond into space have shown that the

primaries consist essentially of bare nuclei of light elements, chiefly hydrogen, and, possibly, a few gamma rays of very high energy. The particles constituting primary rays are very quickly modified by collision with the atomic nuclei present in the atmosphere. The secondary cosmic rays are thus created, and these are composed of many other fundamental particles. Of these the pions (pi-mesons), muons (mu-mesons), photons (gamma rays), and negative and positive electrons are the most important.

Conversion of primary cosmic rays to secondary cosmic rays is generally initiated by a collision between a high-energy proton and the nucleus of one of the atoms constituting the atmosphere. This leads to the production of protons, neutrons and pions, and, much more rarely, some heavy elementary particles: the heavy mesons and hyperons. The pions so produced can be charged or neutral.

Secondary protons and neutrons can initiate further collisions and are then finally slowed down. The charged pions mostly decay in flight, but each produces one much with the same charge and one neutrino. The muons show little reaction with atomic nuclei, but can penetrate great thicknesses of matter. The muons eventually decay into one electron and two neutrinos.

Electrons and photons resulting from these decay processes produce new electrons and photons, and it is repetition of these processes that results in showers of cosmic rays. The intensity of cosmic radiation at sea level varies with latitude, proving beyond doubt that cosmic-ray radiation is charged. Thus rays reaching

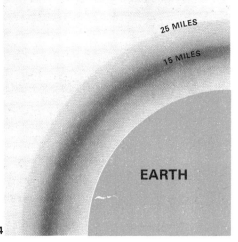

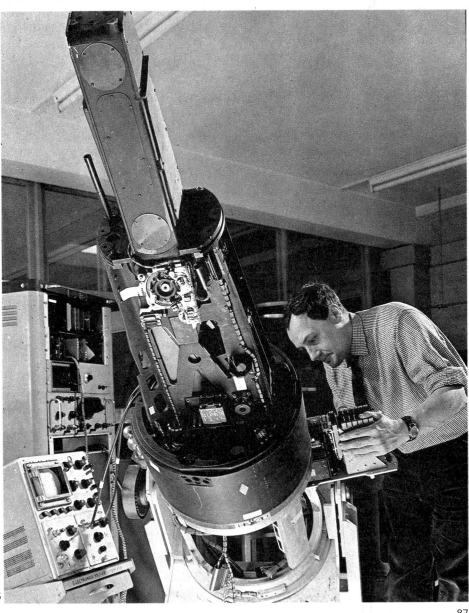

1 By measuring cosmic radiation at the Poles, physicists have discovered that the cosmic rays reaching the Earth are much more intense near the Poles than at the Equator. This deflection by the Earth's magnetic field suggests that the cosmic particles are charged.

2 Sir William Crookes (1832–1919) was the first to suggest that cathode rays were fast-moving negatively-charged particles. With his X-ray tube he performed experiments that led to the discovery of the electron.

3 The gold-leaf electroscope was one of the first instruments used to detect cosmic radiation. In 1910 Victor Hess took one up with him in a balloon and showed that the higher he went the more intense was the radiation.

4 Up until 15 miles above the Earth the radiation progressively increases, but then, from 15 to 25 miles it drops steadily. Once above 25 miles the radiation remains constant with altitude right out into space.

5 To make spectroscopic observations of the sun scientists at Britain's Culham Laboratory prepare electronic equipment that can be mounted into the cones of Skylark Rockets. The mounting is easily removable for any adjustments.

the Earth are about one-tenth more intense near the Poles than they are at and near the Equator. This suggests that the rays reaching the Earth near the Equator are deflected away by the Earth's magnetic field. From this it was deduced that as the rays could be deflected by a magnetic field, they must be moving charged particles.

The atmosphere as protection

The Earth is, in effect, a gigantic magnet and by means of its magnetic field it attracts towards it some of the cosmic-radiation particles constantly pouring through space. Primary rays usually penetrate about ten miles through the Earth's atmosphere before being turned into secondary cosmic rays. Primaries are made up of approximately 86 per cent hydrogen nuclei, 13 per cent of helium nuclei, and the remaining one per cent is made up of nuclei of heavier elements, such as calcium, iron, lithium and carbon. Most of the primary particles travel at a speed very near to that of light.

Very few primary cosmic rays penetrate through the Earth's atmosphere to reach the surface of the Earth. Nearly all of them collide with particles in the atmosphere to produce the secondary cosmic rays. Occasionally primaries generate very large showers in the atmosphere so that many millions of particles strike the ground over an area of several acres. One primary can produce a shower of secondaries which zig-zag to earth like forked lightning.

Study of the secondary particles and the curvature of their tracks as revealed by photographic plates enables their energies to be measured. The maximum energies so far registered in any atomic process are those of the primaries responsible for the very large showers of secondaries. Some of these showers have energies of billions of millions of electron-volts.

How do primaries obtain their fantastically high energies? Physicists have not yet found a conclusive solution. Some theories attribute the energy of primaries to the violent star explosions that create super-novas. Another school of thought inclines to the view that the particles' energy is built up and accelerated by their interaction with variable magnetic fields in space, in much the same way that particles are artificially accelerated on Earth by synchrotrons and other types of particle accelerators.

Because primary cosmic rays appear to arrive in equal intensity from all parts of space, it has been suggested that their trajectories undergo strong deviation in the magnetic fields of the galaxy. This has further suggested that the action of the galactic magnetic fields can trap the particles inside the galaxy for millions of years, so rendering cosmic radiation less directional and more intense.

Study of cosmic rays is helping science to make important discoveries in nuclear physics. In their experiments with synchrotrons and other accelerators, physicists are producing particles in an attempt to find out the more minute details about the structure of the nuclei of atoms. Yet with

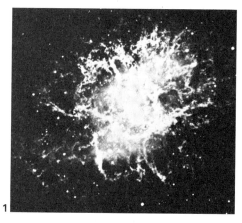

1 The Crab nebula is thought to be one of the sources of cosmic radiation. It is the remnant of a star seen to explode by ancient Chinese astronomers in 1054 A.D.
2 By setting up a series of counters, like this one in operation at a London University field station, the number of cosmic rays striking the Earth can be measured.

cosmic rays there free for the asking, physicists can penetrate far deeper than they can with particles produced in machines costing millions of pounds.

Bearing in mind the unbelievable energy in cosmic rays, it is not surprising that power engineers are tantalized by the possibility of harnessing cosmic energy. As yet, however, they have been unable to provide any practical solution.

It was during investigation into cosmic rays that radiation belts surrounding the Earth were discovered. In 1958 counters were sent up in the satellite Explorer I to measure cosmic-ray intensity and to transmit the results back to Earth. When the signals started coming in from the satellite it was found that an unexpectedly high amount of radiation was overloading the counters and jamming them.

Later satellites, carrying more sophisticated instrumentation, established that the overloading of Explorer I's counters was caused by two radiation belts surrounding the Earth and trapped in space. It was further established that the radiation belts consisted of either protons or electrons trapped in the Earth's magnetic field and spiralling around it.

Electrons, much lighter than protons, are more easily trapped and forced to spiral around the Earth in an outer belt some 12,000 miles above the surface. On the other hand, protons have a greater mass and can, therefore, penetrate deeper into the Earth's magnetic field before they, too, are trapped and forced to spiral in a lower belt about 1,000 miles above the surface. These two radiation traps are the Van Allen Belts, named after James Van Allen, the American physicist in charge of the research teams which discovered them.

The region in space influenced by the Earth's magnetic field is called the magnetosphere. A curious thing about the magnetosphere is that it is not symmetrical like the field surrounding an ordinary bar magnet on Earth. This would seem to be due to variations in the strength of the Earth's magnetic field.

A sun in the laboratory

The sun's energy results from tremendously hot gases fusing to form new elements. Scientists are now attempting to control similar reactions on Earth to give Man an unlimited source of power.

The plasma space engine has been designed for stabilizing satellites in orbit. The engine operates on batteries recharged by solar cells and uses an inert gas, such as nitrogen, as fuel.

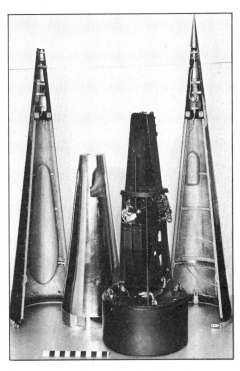

The nose cone of a rocket which is to be sent up to make measurements of the sun's corona. The cone assembly contains spectrographs and a pinhole camera to photograph soft X-ray emission.

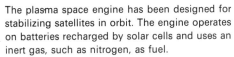

PLASMA PHYSICS is the study of ionized gases. We say that a gas has become *ionized* when one (or more) of the electrons of the atoms of molecules comprising the gas are removed leaving the atom with a net positive charge. An ionized gas, then, is made up of an equal number of positively charged gas atoms, called *ions* and *free electrons,* and in this stage it is called a *plasma.* This has also been referred to as the fourth state of matter to distinguish it from solids, liquids and gases. Although plasma physics is relatively new, plasmas are, in fact, very common in nature – the sun and all the stars are entirely composed of plasma and since the advent of artificial satellites it has been found that the Earth is immersed in an extremely weak plasma which is streaming out from the sun. Other natural plasmas are the Aurora Borealis or Northern Lights and lightning flashes; plasmas also exist inside neon and fluorescent light tubes and electric sparks and arcs. As the upper regions of the atmosphere are ionized by radiation from the sun, it is possible to transmit radio waves for much greater distances than the line of sight distance because the plasma in the upper atmosphere reflects radio waves below a certain frequency back down to Earth.

As a plasma is composed of electrically charged particles which are free to move, it behaves as an extremely good conductor of heat and electricity; a fully ionized plasma, in which nearly all the atoms are ionized is a far better conductor than silver. Another important property of plasmas is that they are strongly affected by magnetic and electric fields which enable them to be contained in the laboratory. Because of the interactions between ions and ions, and between electrons and electrons, as well as between ions and electrons, the behaviour of a plasma is much more complicated and difficult to describe mathematically than the behaviour of an ordinary gas. If the effects of magnetic and electric fields (which do not affect ordinary gas atoms) are included, the overall behaviour can be very complicated indeed. For instance, the effect of a magnetic field is to severely restrict motion across the field lines, but has little effect on particle motion along the field and the plasma is then said to be *anisotropic* (its properties are not the same in all directions).

Predicting plasma behaviour

In order to describe the behaviour of plasmas, the effect of individual ions and electrons is often ignored and it is assumed that the plasma is simply a conducting fluid like, for example, mercury, but very much less dense. This approximation works well for some plasmas and can be used to describe and predict plasma behaviour under a variety of conditions. The study of such plasmas is called *magneto-hydrodynamics,* usually abbreviated to M.H.D.

A great deal of effort has gone into what is called the *M.H.D. generator.* This is a device which would convert the energy of a very hot gas – for example the flue gases from a conventional power station or the coolant gas used in a nuclear power station – directly into electricity. The general principle on which the generator works is quite simple: the hot gas is made into a plasma by adding a small quantity of material which can be ionized by the random motion of the hot gas atoms. This plasma is then allowed to flow between the poles of a powerful magnet; that is, across a magnetic field. In doing so, the negatively and positively charged particles are deflected in opposite directions so that the plasma develops an electric potential across itself which can be picked up on special electrodes and electric current can flow in an external circuit. As electrical energy is extracted from the moving plasma, it is slowed down and the thermal energy of the hot gas can be converted directly into electricity.

Although the M.H.D. generator would have many advantages if it can be shown to be practicable, a great many, if not the majority, of the world's plasma physicists are working on an even more revolutionary form of power generation – *thermonuclear fusion.* In the 1930s, physicists solved the mystery of how the sun and the stars produced their vast amounts of energy. Their studies showed that the process responsible was the fusion of light atoms into heavier atoms and, by a complicated cycle, four hydrogen atoms

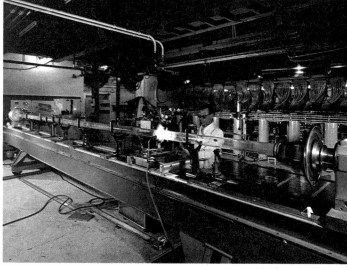

were being fused together to create helium.

During this fusion reaction, a large amount of energy is released because the mass of the final helium nucleus is less than the mass of the four hydrogen nuclei which went into its manufacture and, although the mass difference is minute, the annihilation of matter produces a tremendous amount of energy. The process is the opposite of nuclear fission in which a very heavy nucleus, such as uranium, breaks up into two or more lighter nuclei, again with a large release of energy which comes from the difference in mass between the original nuclei and the sum of the masses of the final lighter nuclei.

Destructive power

It is the fission reaction which gives the atom bomb its tremendous destructive power. The even more powerful hydrogen bomb is due to a combination of fission and fusion reactions. The temperature at the heart of a fission bomb is so high that it triggers off fusion reactions between two isotopes of hydrogen, called *deuterium* and *tritium,* resulting in an even greater release of energy than fission.

Modern nuclear power stations rely on nuclear fission and physicists have succeeded in taming the atomic bomb. What plasma physicists would like to do is to tame the hydrogen bomb. If this is possible, it would give mankind an inexhaustible source of power since the basic fuel, which is heavy hydrogen or deuterium, can be obtained cheaply from sea-water. However, the problems involved in trying to obtain a fusion reaction are very formidable indeed – physicists are attempting to create a small sun in the laboratory.

In order to get fusion reactions to take place, the nuclei must be brought very close together. This is extremely difficult since the nuclei are positively charged and therefore repel each other and try to stay apart. It is only by giving the nuclei a lot of energy and then making them collide that the electrical forces holding them apart can be overcome and fusion reactions take place.

It is possible to give energy to gas atoms by making them hot – the hotter they are the faster they travel and collisions between atoms become more energetic but, in order to obtain fusion reactions, the gas will have to be heated to the fantastically high temperature of 100 *million* degrees centigrade. How, then, can a gas at this temperature be contained when all known materials melt and vaporize at temperatures of a few *thousand* degrees centigrade? The solution lies with plasmas. Because they are composed of charged particles they interact strongly with magnetic fields so it might be possible to make a magnetic bottle to hold the very hot plasma away from any solid material walls. Plasma physicists in Britain, the U.S.S.R. and the United States, together with colleagues from other nations, have been attempting to find a good 'leak-proof' magnetic bottle since the 1940s in order to obtain thermonuclear fusion reactions in the laboratory.

In October 1969, results of some work in the U.S.S.R., on what is called the TOKAMAK experiment, have shown that thermonuclear reactions are being observed. Some of the important measure-

1 Zeta, the first major controlled fusion experiment in Britain. A current of 500,000 amps was passed through the plasma to heat it to 1,000,000 °C. in the toroidal chamber.
2 The thetatron experiment to measure the movement of plasma down a straight length of transparent silica tubing. Thetatron has now been dismantled and replaced by other experiments.
3 The plasma jet torch gives temperatures up to about 25,000 °C. by constricting an arc column in a flowing gas. In its laminar form a plasma jet can be extended up to three feet in length.

ments of the plasma were made by a visiting team of British scientists, indicating the great deal of international co-operation existing in this field. Evidence of thermonuclear reactions has also been obtained in different experiments in the United States and Britain, but the significance of the Russian result is that the reactions lasted for a relatively long time, indicating that the type of magnetic bottle being used is a fairly good one. Whether or not it is good enough remains to be seen from future experiments because, although it is a very encouraging result, the plasma density, temperature and lifetime will all have to be increased by at least ten times before the fusion reaction will be self-sustaining and capable of supplying power.

The pinch effect

The TOKAMAK is one of several experiments which rely on the *pinch effect*. This can best be described as follows. If a current is passed in the same direction down a loose bundle of straight wires, they will all attract one another to form a tight bundle due to the magnetic forces set up by the electric current – they pinch together. If instead of using wires to carry the current, a large current is passed through a tenuous plasma in a tube, then the magnetic forces set up will, if they are strong enough, squeeze the plasma into a thin thread and hold it away from the tube walls. Some of the first pinch experiments were carried out in straight tubes because they are easier to make, but they suffer from the disadvantage that the plasma is cooled by conduction to the electrodes at the ends. The simplest way of avoiding

4 Using plasma torches to clean rail of contaminants such as a thin layer of grease, British Rail hope to increase the friction between the train wheels and the track.

5 Large banks of capacitors are needed to provide sudden sharp pulses of current to energize plasma reactions. Here they are being used in a magnetic trap stability experiment.

1 A technician makes tests in a solar furnace to study the effects of high temperatures on materials. Plasma gases provide temperatures that cannot, at present, be reached by other means.

2 Technicians at the Culham Laboratory in Britain fix insulated copper foil conductors to the torus of a stellarator magnetic trap. The trap is being used to study fusion.

3 The solar corona which consists of plasma extending far out into space from the sun is seen during a total eclipse. Using special equipment the corona can now be seen at other times.

this trouble is to bend the tube round until it closes on itself to make a doughnut shape or, as it is more properly called, a *torus*. The large current required to make the plasma pinch is induced in the torus by making it the single turn secondary of a transformer. The currents required are quite large – in the range of a few thousand up to one million ampères. These large currents are not applied continuously, but electrical energy is stored in large banks of condensers which can be charged over several tens of seconds and then all the accumulated energy is rapidly discharged in a few thousandths (or in some cases a few millionths) of a second to give a large pulse of energy. Apart from pulling the plasma away from the tube walls the electric current also heats the plasma to a very high temperature. The heating mechanism is essentially the same as that of an electric fire, only on a very different scale. The element in a fire becomes hot because of its electrical resistance. Similarly, although a plasma is a very good conductor, it still has some electrical resistance. By forcing current through the plasma against this resistance, it can be raised to a very high temperature. It was soon found, however, that the pinched discharge did not remain in the middle of the tube for very long but rapidly wriggled about until it struck the tube walls. The discharge is then said to be unstable. Some of the instabilities can be overcome, or at least their effects minimized, by putting conducting walls close to, but not in contact with, the plasma and also by the addition of a magnetic field round the torus.

Perhaps the most famous and most thoroughly studied toroidal pinch was the ZETA experiment at Harwell in Britain. The torus was roughly a yard in diameter and four yards across. The plasma was heated to a temperature of five million degrees centigrade and although fusion reactions were observed, they were found not to be of true thermonuclear origin but were due to further instabilities in the

plasma.

Another scheme for confining a hot plasma in an endless tube is the *stellarator concept* which relies, not on currents carried by the plasma, but on externally produced fields. In order to hold the plasma, simple coils wound round the torus will not do, and either more complicated fields are needed or the torus with its coils has to be twisted into a figure eight. Stellarators are being studied in laboratories throughout the world in order to see whether or not they can contain hot plasmas for times of the order of one second needed for controlled fusion.

Magnetic mirrors

Although a great deal of effort is being put into the study of toroidal systems, there is an alternative form of magnetic bottle called the *magnetic mirror*. This is basically a straight tube in which the magnetic field is stronger at the ends of the tube than in the central portion. The strong field at the ends reflects most of the ions and electrons back into the central region of the tube – hence the name magnetic mirror. The magnetic mirror was found to be a good bottle for containing very low-

density plasmas, but as the plasma density was increased, the plasma started to leak out across the magnetic field due to an instability.

The plasma instability and associated loss was basically due to the fact that although the magnetic field increased at the ends of the tube, it decreased outwards along a radius and the plasma escaped to where the magnetic field was weakest. By adding extra coils the simple mirror system could be converted into what is called a magnetic *well* in which the magnetic field increases outwards in all directions from the plasma and it is unable to escape. Since magnetic mirrors are such good bottles for holding hot plasmas, there is difficulty in filling them – if the bottle is so good that plasma cannot get out, then it cannot get in either. Sophisticated filling techniques have been developed but, as yet, they are not powerful enough to overcome some very slight leakages. Because the magnetic mirror is basically a straight tube, some plasma leakage is always bound to take place through the ends because the magnetic mirrors will not reflect ions which have too high a velocity along the magnetic field. This unavoidable end-loss puts magnetic mirrors at a disadvantage with respect to the endless or toroidal systems. However, mirror systems are much simpler to build and easier to treat theoretically than toroidal systems and, in spite of their end-losses, they still stand a chance of developing into a reactor in which the end-loss problem could be turned to an advantage by directly converting the energy of the escaping hot plasma into electricity.

There are many types of bottles being used in attempts to produce and contain the equivalent of a piece of sun in the laboratory, and many techniques used by plasma physicists to examine these plasmas. Although many problems have been overcome, many remain to be solved before the energy source of the sun and stars can be used for the good of mankind.

Power within the pile

Whether in conditions of peace or war, nuclear power will clearly play an increasingly important role in our lives. What are the basic mechanisms of this potent but threatening energy source?

Small nuclear generators like this one are now widely used in remote weather and research stations and may in future provide electric power for space craft. This model weighs only 1·5 tons.

A general view of the well of the fast reactor at Dounreay nuclear power station in the north of Scotland. The tower in the centre is a machine for removing radioactive fuel elements.

These six precision-machined carbon rods form the outside of a fuel element for the Dragon Reactor at Winfrith. A uranium rod fits inside the six carbon rods, forming the element's core.

ON 2 DECEMBER 1942, a group of British and American physicists were gathered in a large shed that had been set up in the Chicago University squash court. They anxiously watched Professor Enrico Fermi operating switches and levers controlling a strange piece of equipment submerged in a pool of heavy water. The equipment consisted of uranium embedded in a big block of graphite from which projected cadmium rods. The whole was submerged in the heavy water, but the cadmium rods could be moved up and down in the graphite by linkages with the control panel. The complete apparatus was called a pile.

As the minutes ticked away on the laboratory clock, the audience became more and more tense, while Fermi calmly operated the control panel. Then at 3.25, one of the dials on the panel flickered and an instrument began ticking. Professor Fermi relaxed, turned to his audience and smiled; 'Gentlemen,' he said, 'the chain reaction is self-sustaining.' That historic statement announced the birth of the world's first nuclear reactor. It was the culmination of lines of research by physicists of all nationalities which had begun nearly 25 years before when Lord Rutherford, professor of physics at Cambridge University, had first demonstrated the possibility of obtaining energy from the spontaneous disintegration of the atom.

Fermi's demonstration set in motion the vast Manhatten Project which cost £700,000,000 and employed 500,000 people; all dedicated to the production of an atomic bomb. But his great experiment pointed to the harnessing of atomic energy for peaceful purposes as well as to a nuclear explosion designed for mass destruction.

The difference between an atomic bomb and a reactor for the generation of useful power is that in an atomic bomb the nuclear action is rapid and uncontrolled, whereas in the reactor the nuclear fission releasing atomic energy is slowed down and can be controlled to within fine limits. If neutrons were not controlled in a reactor, which is the heart of an atomic power plant, there would be a devastating explosion, just as there is when an atomic bomb is exploded.

In simple terms, a nuclear reactor is a furnace in which a nuclear fuel such as uranium is 'burned' to produce heat. The heat so produced can then be used to raise steam to drive turbo-generators. Alternatively, the heat from a reactor can be utilized to heat and so expand a gas to power a gas-turbine. The basic distinction between a conventional furnace using solid or liquid fuel, such as coal or oil, and a nuclear reactor is that the latter does not need air to 'burn' its fuel. Moreover, a few pounds of nuclear fuel in a reactor releases as much energy as would the burning of thousands of tons of coal or oil in a conventional furnace.

In 1939 the German physicist, Otto Hahn, showed that when uranium is bombarded with neutrons some of the atoms split into lighter fragments. As some of the mass of the atoms is lost during their break up, some part of each uranium atom must be converted into energy, according to Einstein's famous equation. One neutron is needed to split an atom, and even that neutron is not lost but will in turn split another uranium atom. This continuous splitting of the uranium atoms sets in motion a chain reaction.

In practice, many of the neutrons fail to split another atom, so that every time a neutron misses its target the chain reaction is weakened – if energy is to be released from nuclear fuel on a large and useful scale, there must be some means whereby the chain reaction becomes self-sustaining. In other words, the reactor must operate in such a manner that enough neutrons reach enough atomic nuclei and split them.

Chain reaction

Fermi established that slower-moving neutrons are more effective in bringing about fission (atom-splitting) than are those travelling at high speed. On the other hand, most of the neutrons released by the disintegration of an atomic nucleus are fast moving. The problem was to slow down fast neutrons to a velocity whereby they would be effective in inducing fission and so maintaining the required chain reaction.

Fermi knew from his own and other physicists' experiments, that the nuclei of graphite, a pure form of carbon, resist absorbing neutrons. In fact the nuclei rebound from the graphite just as a billiard ball rebounds from another ball after a collision. Conversely, there are certain substances which will attract nuclei and absorb them as a sponge absorbs water. By using absorbent nuclei Fermi discovered how to use the properties of different substances to maintain and control the chain reaction in much the same way that the accelerator on a car enables the driver to increase or decrease speed at will simply by pressing or depressing a pedal.

Professor Fermi's solution to the problem was relatively simple. He embedded the uranium fuel in a great mass of graphite. When fission took place the fast neutrons released by disintegration of the uranium atoms richocheted off the graphite, so slowing them down and giving them a better chance of hitting the uranium nuclei. The chain reaction thereby created was prevented from getting out of control by inserting cadmium rods into the graphite.

What happened inside Fermi's pile was that enough neutrons were slowed down to sustain the chain reaction while sufficient were absorbed by the cadmium to prevent the reaction getting out of control. If a pile were built without the cadmium rods there would be an uncontrolled fission reaction and all the energy in the uranium would be released instantly as a violent and devastating explosion. That was exactly what Fermi's pile was meant to demonstrate, and its further development was towards making a pile small enough and light enough to be carried by an aircraft; in other words, all effort was mobilized to producing a bomb.

Nevertheless, the Chicago University demonstration had proved beyond doubt the possibility of harnessing and controlling nuclear fission as a source of power for peaceful use. Although Fermi's pile was crude, its principle is the basis of the nuclear reactors now producing an appreciable amount of the electric power consumed in Britain, the United States and other countries.

Reactor design

Designing a nuclear reactor entails the solving of many difficult and complicated engineering and scientific problems. There must be an efficient source of energy; the chain reaction must be safe and controlled; the reactor must be shielded to prevent dangerous radiation from escaping; and there must be an efficient and economic method of using the nuclear energy for the production of useful power. During the past 25 years these problems have been solved in brilliant fashion and current development is primarily concerned with reducing the size and cost of reactors, adapting new fuels, and designing more efficient ways of utilizing the nuclear energy created by their fission.

Uranium is still the fuel most commonly used in reactors. Naturally occurring uranium is a mixture of various isotopes; that is, it consists of atoms of the same element but of different masses. Uranium-238 accounts for over 90 per cent of uranium in its natural state, while the lighter isotope, uranium-235, makes up less than one per cent. Only uranium-235 can create the chain reaction in a

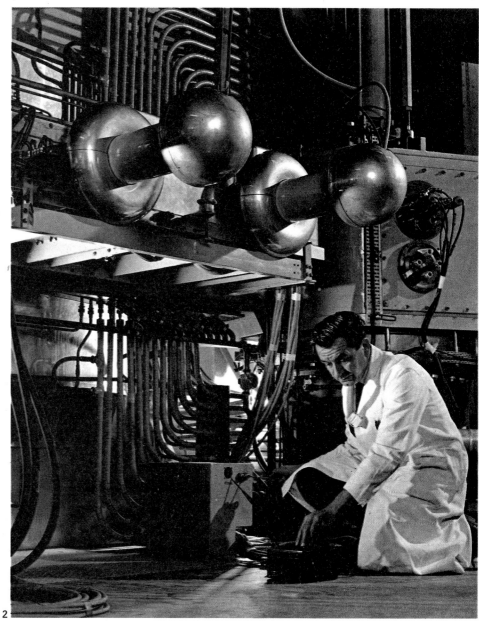

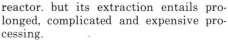

reactor. but its extraction entails prolonged, complicated and expensive processing.

Production of nuclear power would be less complicated and much cheaper if the reactor could use uranium in its natural state. The solution to this problem is to design the reactor in such manner that fission of the uranium-235 takes place and at the same time the unwanted uranium-238 is prevented from interfering with the fission process. The actual fission process is very complex, but it can be stated briefly and simply as follows.

If a piece of uranium is under bombardment by neutrons moving at different speeds, the uranium-235 will absorb the slow-moving neutrons and fission occurs, but the uranium-235 will not be affected by the fast-moving neutrons, which simply pass over it. At the same time the atoms of the uranium-238 disintegrate when bombarded by fast neutrons. Unfortunately only a few fast neutrons reach the uranium-238 so that that isotope is of little use in the pile. Moreover, the uranium-238 has the undesirable property of absorbing slower-moving neutrons without fission taking place. In other words, uranium-238 steals neutrons which otherwise would be useful in bringing about fission in uranium-235 nuclei. But it will not absorb very slow-moving neutrons.

Ideally the reactor would have only very slow neutrons moving about in the pile. The slow-moving neutrons would not be absorbed by the uranium-238 but would keep on circulating until they met uranium-235 nuclei. In practice, however, the neutrons released in the fission reaction travel at very high speeds and are absorbed by the uranium-238 nuclei and so lost to the chain reaction unless slowed down by a moderator.

A moderator is a mass of some material that has the property of slowing down fast neutrons without absorbing them. Amongst the most efficient moderators are carbon, in the form of pure graphite, and deuterium oxide or, as it is commonly called, heavy water. Whatever the moderator used it should be a material with light atoms because a light atom will take away more of the neutrons' energy than a heavy atom when neutrons collide with it. The moderator is mixed in with the uranium metal, so that any fast neutrons released by the fission of the uranium-235 or uranium-238 are slowed down by the heavier isotope and easily absorbed by the lighter one.

Selection of the current moderator ensures an adequate supply of neutrons which move at the right speed to maintain the chain reaction. It is no less important to design the pile so that neutrons are not lost through its walls. If the pile were too small, a high percentage of the neutrons would be lost. For that reason the pile must be made larger than the *critical size* (the size necessary to induce fission). Provided the pile is big enough and the right moderator is used, the reactor is said to be *critical,* and a chain reaction can be initiated and maintained.

Describing a reactor as being critical is somewhat confusing to the layman. What

1 Two artificial elements — nobelium and lawrencium — were first created in this ten-million-volt electron accelerator at Berkeley, California.
2 Very high voltages are used in this cyclotron to accelerate atomic particles to very high speeds. These high-voltage terminals are located close to the point where the high-speed particles leave the cyclotron.
3 Technicians at this atomic power station stand on a bridge over the deep water surrounding the reactor. The blue glow is given off by the water when it is bombarded with neutrons.
4 The chamber with which the English physicist, James Chadwick, discovered the neutron in 1932. The original nuclear research was done on a shoe-string, until its military uses became apparent.
5 This specially designed furnace is used for preparing uranium pellets to be used in nuclear reactors. Contamination must be carefully avoided.

it actually means is that the pile is larger than its critical size so that there are more neutrons in it than are needed to maintain a controlled reaction.

The basic design problem with all reactors is to keep the neutrons under control at all times so that the pile remains critical throughout its lifetime. One of the components that does this is the *reflector* – a shield completely surrounding the pile which reflects back to the fuel those neutrons which otherwise might leak out. As reflectors must scatter but not absorb neutrons, they are generally made from the same materials as moderators.

Reactor fuel or fissionable material is usually in the form of rods, the uranium or other fuel material being alloyed with other metals to increase its strength and heat-conductivity and to minimize corrosion. In what are classed as *homogeneous reactors,* the fuel is uniformly distributed in a fluid to form a slurry.

Because of the intense heat generated by nuclear fission, the reactor temperature must be kept under control by a substance called a *coolant.* Common coolants are carbon dioxide gas, liquid sodium, helium, certain organic liquids and even water. The coolant is pumped through the hot reactor and absorbs a large part of the heat. In power stations this heat is used to raise steam in a boiler. The steam in turn drives turbines linked to electric generators. In some power stations using gas coolants, the hot and expanding gas is used directly to drive turbo-alternators. After serving the boilers or turbines the coolant, whether gas or a liquid, passes through a system of heat exchangers and condensers which reduce its temperature so that it can be pumped back to the reactor to repeat its cooling function.

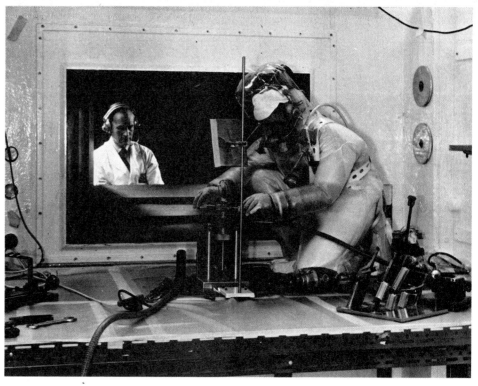

In fact, it was the necessity for a coolant that led to the development of the nuclear power station. The first reactors were built during the Second World War to make the plutonium used as the explosive in atom bombs. Plutonium is a synthetic element specially manufactured by physicists. It is capable of splitting up easily and so starting a chain reaction.

Plutonium derives from the bombardment of uranium-238 by fast-moving neutrons and is highly fissionable in a reactor using a mixture of uranium-235 and uranium-238. The fissionable material is 'burned' directly, but an even larger amount of fertile uranium can be converted into plutonium fuel. This is the principle of the *breeder reactor* which nuclear engineers believe to be the most promising type for producing atomic power in the future.

The first reactors were built only to provide the explosion element for atom bombs, and the intense heat generated was just so much waste. Heat from one of the experimental reactors built by the United Kingdom Atomic Energy Authority at Harwell had been used to warm laboratories and workshops, but as a general rule reactor heat had been wasted.

Nevertheless, engineers resent useful energy being thrown away, and after various experiments with reactors designed to produce elements for atom bomb material, it was decided to try and convert reactor heat into useful power. The result was Calder Hall in Cumberland, officially opened on 17 October 1956. Calder Hall was the world's first atomic power station. The heat from its reactors was harnessed to drive turbo-alternators which fed electric power into the United Kingdom's national electricity supply network.

Dounreay

In 1955, the United Kingdom Atomic Energy Authority began building the great liquid-cooled reactor at Dounreay, near Thurso, in Scotland. Dounreay is a breeder reactor, and like Calder Hall its chief purpose is the production of nuclear explosives but its liquid sodium and potassium coolant is used to drive turbo-generators.

Experience gained from Calder Hall and Dounreay led to the development and construction of a number of reactors in Britain designed for the production of electric power. These now contribute a substantial proportion of the United Kingdom's electricity needs for heating, light and power.

Building work in progress on an atomic power station near Naples. Such designs have to be tailored to the special requirements of stations running on atomic fuels.

Atoms for peace

Atomic energy, with a vast potential for destruction, can also be used to solve many problems in industry, medicine and engineering previously beyond the scope of conventional methods.

IN 1910 Ernest Rutherford, professor of physics at Manchester University, was conducting a series of experiments to demonstrate the radioactivity of elements and to show that certain elements which are not radioactive can be made so by bombarding them with radioactivity. Amongst Rutherford's pupils was Georg von Hevesy, a Hungarian who later won a Nobel Prize for his work on radioisotope indication.

During one of his experiments, Rutherford showed that if a speck of radioactivated lead is placed in any substance or material traces of its radioactivity persist for some considerable time. That gave the Hungarian student an idea.

Hevesy was, at that time, living in a boarding house run by a 'cheese-paring' landlady who, her boarders suspected, was using scraps of the Sunday joint left on the lodgers' plates to make the stews and pies served throughout the rest of the week. One Sunday the landlady served roast beef for dinner and Hevesy introduced a tiny speck of radioactive lead into a scrap of the meat he left on his plate. Throughout the remainder of the week Hevesy took back to the laboratory samples of all the meat dishes served up. Appropriate tests then proved beyond question that every sample was radioactive and that his landlady was indeed using scrapings from her lodgers' plates.

Trace elements

Hevesy's successful venture into scientific detection had done something more than expose a dishonest landlady: he had given the first practical demonstration of what are now called *trace elements* and suggested one of the most important of the peaceful applications of the atom. This was all the more remarkable because it was achieved long before the release of nuclear energy and the development of atomic power.

Hevesy's trace element was radium D, a radioactive form of lead. Radium is an element which in the course of time turns into another substance, lead. But throughout the centuries that the conversion takes, the lead retains some radioactivity inherited from its radium origin. Radium D is not a particularly good trace element: it is scarce, costly and poisonous. Moreover, when Hevesy used radium D to unmask the mysteries of the boarding-house dinners, very little was known about trace elements. Consequently Hevesy could not develop his meat-scrap experiments into anything of much use in everyday affairs.

Now vast quantities of trace elements or, more, correctly, *isotopes*, can be produced easily and relatively cheaply in reactors. In fact isotope production has

1 A geologist prospecting in the field can use a small but accurate spectroscope to locate the radioisotopes characteristic of the rock sample he is testing. This gives him a knowledge of the likely economic value of the rocks.
2 A gamma-radiograph, shown here testing for faults in the metal hull of a Thames tug, allows on-the-spot detection of cracks and strains in metal parts by passing radiation through them.

become a profitable side-line of nuclear fission for atomic weapons and power. Radioactive isotopes are now produced artificially by bombarding a non-radioactive element in a nuclear pile. Isotopes are produced in this way from carbon, nitrogen, iodine, sodium, phosphorus and hydrogen. Bombarding the element alters its atomic structure by adding or subtracting from it.

Whatever the element from which an isotope is derived, its presence can be detected in any substance into which it has been introduced. A quick and easy method of detection is by photography, but in liquids, and certain semi-solid substances, such as the human body, isotopes move about. In such situations they are best detected by a Geiger counter, which gives a continuous signal while it is trailing the isotope.

A radioactive material sends out a stream of fast particles which detach electrons of any material from their parent atom and so make insulating materials into temporary conductors. The isotope of any particular element emits its own kind of radiation which labels it, rather like the call-sign of a broadcasting station. Instruments can distinguish between all the different isotope call-signs and so immediately identify what kind of isotope they are tracking.

Medicine was one of the first sciences to use isotopes, which have proved to be a wonderfully versatile tool in the treatment and prevention of disease. An example is diagnosis by isotope, which depends upon the fact that the human body, like everything else in the world, is made up of various elements and compounds of elements. These atoms and molecules are in constant motion and contact with each other, and there is a continuous attraction and repulsion going on. In a healthy body, repulsion and attraction follow a pattern, but the pattern alters if some part or organ of the body is diseased or injured.

When an isotope is put into the body, either by injection or in the food, its passage through the body is trailed by the Geiger counter. If all is well, its movement registered by the counter shows no variation in its signals. On the other hand, if there is an irregular signal from the Geiger counter, the doctor knows that there must be something interrupting the healthy rhythm; perhaps a disease or an injury. Using isotopes in this way a disease can be diagnosed before the symptoms are apparent.

By injecting the isotope sodium 24 into a vein, the medical practitioner can measure with great accuracy the rate at which the blood flows through a patient's body. As the isotope travels with the bloodstream, its radiation is registered

on the Geiger counter and the speed at which the blood is flowing through the body recorded. Measuring the speed of the bloodstream with isotopes plays an important part in the prevention of blood-clot formation after an operation.

Money-savers

Isotopes are now saving industrialists and engineers huge amounts of money every year by quickly and cheaply gathering information about things which they suspect may be happening but which they cannot see.

Oil refineries use isotopes to save time and money in the operation of their pipelines, where it is the practice to pump several grades of oil through a single pipeline for filling into separate storage tanks according to quality. At one time lengthy and complicated analyzing and sampling had to be carried out on the oil to decide precisely when the change-over from one storage tank to another should be made. Now, by injecting a suitable isotope into the oil as each grade enters the pipeline, the front of each grade flowing through is effectively labelled.

1 This radio beacon on the Scottish island of Benbecula is powered by an isotope generator, which gives long periods of trouble-free electrical generating, though at a high initial cost.
2 Chromatography is used to separate radio-isotope compounds before packaging them for sale. The method uses the fact that different compounds travel at different speeds down a column of starch-gel.
3 To obtain information on kidney function, a small amount of isotope (iodine 131) is injected into the blood and detectors placed over the heart and kidneys. These measure the radio-activity in each organ.

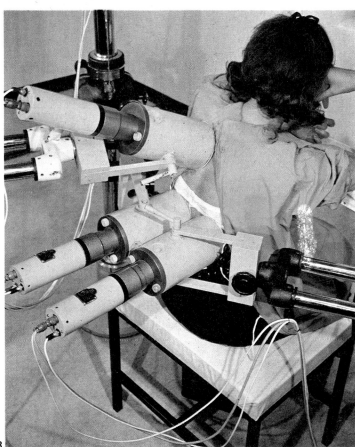

A Geiger counter at the end of the pipe-line immediately indicates when the new grade of oil arrives.

Using isotopes has solved one of the most time-wasting problems in surveying, when it is often necessary to drive mark-ing-pegs into the ground for future reference. If the survey is over farmland, the pegs must be driven several inches below ground level so as not to interfere with ploughing. When the marking-pegs are again required, considerable search and digging are needed to find them. Now surveyors fix into the top of the mark-ing-peg a disc containing an isotope. The presence of the isotope and the peg bearing it can then be detected years later by a Geiger counter – even if the peg is covered by several feet of earth or with thick vegetation.

Paper mills

Many paper mills use isotopes for the automatic testing of paper thickness during manufacture. An isotope is put into the paper pulp and the strength of the radiation received by the Geiger counter indicates the thickness of the paper during its manufacture. The paper passes over the counter which is linked through relays to a brake that automatically stops the machinery if the paper is above or below its predetermined thickness.

Another important application of iso-topes is in tracing leaks and their source. An example of this occurred at a large colliery in the north of England, where it was suspected that water might be seeping into the mine from a nearby lake. If so, expensive pumping equipment would have to be installed and extensive structural alterations made to the mine galleries. Before committing themselves to the

expense, the colliery officials threw into the lake a pound of salt containing a sodium isotope. A Geiger counter was then mounted in the mine where the seepage occurred. The counter immedi-ately picked up the isotope's call-sign, proving beyond doubt that water from the lake was filtering into the mine. When a similar problem arose in a mine close to a river, a sodium isotope and a Geiger counter proved that leaks in the roof were not from the river but due to

natural seepage. In that case the mine was able to avoid expenditure on new pumps.

Thread used in the textile industry must have a very thin but even coating of oil before it is woven into cloth. If the oil-coating is not spread evenly along the length of the thread, the fabric woven from it will be faulty and the finished cloth will look patchy when dyed. Until recently, the only method of measuring the amount of oil on the thread was to take the average coating on several

1 The 'target' end of the cyclotron at the Radio-chemical Centre, Amersham, Buckinghamshire. Materials placed at the target are converted into isotopes by bombarding with atomic particles.
2 Technicians at a glass furnace can study the convection currents inside the molten glass in the furnace by adding small amounts of radio-active glass and tracing the radioactivity.

inches of it. This rule-by-thumb method gave no guarantee that the thread was evenly coated. Now, however, a minute quantity of isotope-labelled compound called *ethylene dibromide* is added to the oil. The thread is then passed in front of a Geiger counter which registers the oil thickness on every one-hundredth of an inch of thread.

At one time it was thought that food-stuffs could be preserved indefinitely by irradiation, but practical tests proved that although irradiation was more effi-cient than refrigeration for preventing the bacterial growth that induces decay, the process destroyed flavour and nu-trient value. This type of irradiation has, however, been found highly efficient for sterilizing medical and other equipment after it has been packaged.

Bearing in mind the devastation caused by atomic explosions and despite the Test Ban Treaty, engineers have been tanta-lized by the problem of harnessing atomic

explosions for industrial blasting. The Russians are said to have developed a technique of nuclear blasting and used it for cutting channels to divert a river in Siberia. In the United States serious consideration is being given to applying nuclear explosives to irrigation and flood-control projects; for canal, harbour, road and railway construction; for surface mining and for the release of natural gases and petroleum deposits; and for the release of the Earth's internal energy. According to the United States Atomic Energy Authority, the use of nuclear explosives for blasting through rock is an economically viable proposition.

America's first practical project for of nuclear blasting is due to take place in 1970 for cutting a path through the Bristol Mountains in California to take a motorway and a railway. The path will be 300 ft wide and 300 ft deep, and will be blasted from the solid rock by 22 atomic bombs with a total explosive effect of 1·73 megatons. When plans to build a second Panama Canal mature, it is likely that the ditch will be blasted out by nuclear explosives.

Archaeology, the study of the ancient world, is linked with nuclear physics, the latest of sciences, by the technique of radioactive dating. Radioactive dating is the use of radioactive isotopes that occur naturally on the Earth to determine the period of time that has elapsed since certain events took place in the world's history. Radioactive dating is based on the fact that all radioisotopes have a characteristic decay rate, and it is believed that this rate has not changed since the formation of our planet.

Isotope dating

When atoms of a radioactive element decay, atoms of a new element are formed. Consequently, if the rate of decay (half-life) of a specific radioisotope in a given sample of rock, for example, is known, and the resulting amount of the new element can be determined, the age of the sample can be calculated.

Radioisotopes that occur naturally on the Earth and which have proved most useful in geological and archaeological dating are of three main groups: those of long half-life that have been present since the formation of the Earth; those continually produced by the decay of other radioisotopes; and those produced by reactions between cosmic rays and stable isotopes.

The first group of isotopes includes uranium 235, uranium 238, thorium 232, rubidium 87 and potassium 40. These isotopes must have half-lives of thousands of millions of years or they would have decayed away completely since the formation of the Earth. They have been successfully used in establishing rock ages ranging from thousands to millions of years.

The second group contains thorium 230 and radium. Both these are proving invaluable for dating the sediments of the ocean beds.

Carbon 14 and hydrogen 3 appear to have shorter half-lives, for they are continually being produced; a process that balances the loss by decay. Carbon 14 is the most important of the dating isotopes in the third group as it enters into the life cycle of all living matter, but this process is terminated by death. Hence the proportion of carbon 14 to ordinary carbon 12, which is a known constant for living matter, remaining in a sample is a measure of the time that has elapsed since death occurred. Carbon 14 dating can be applied to a wide variety of once living materials, including wood, cloth, parchment, glue and animal, including human, remains. Carbon 14 has made possible very accurate archaeological and geological dating of events within the past 50,000 years.

It was dating with carbon 14 that resulted in the reappraisal of the age of the human skull found at Florisbad, South Africa, in 1932. Using conventional tests, archaeologists had fixed its age at approximately 30,000 years, but carbon 14 analysis showed that the skull must be at least 41,000 years old.

Radioisotopes are used in agricultural research to study plant and animal diseases, to develop better diets for farm animals and to improve strains of food plants. If, for example, a research worker wants to study the uptake of fertilizer by a plant, he puts a small amount of an isotope in the fertilizer and traces its movement through the earth and into the plant.

Maintaining adequate supplies of fresh water for domestic and industrial use is becoming a major problem in many parts of the world. Atomic energy can play a part here, in providing energy for turning sea water into fresh water. Such plants are planned in many arid areas.

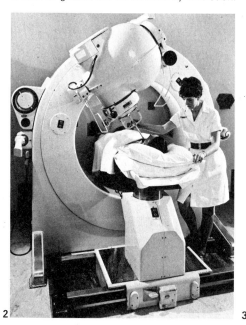

1 Another industrial application of radioactivity allows workers in this Doncaster glass factory to measure the level of molten glass in the furnace by detecting radioactivity from a source on the opposite side of the furnace.
2 Tumour growth can be arrested by irradiation.

Apparatus at a Guildford, Surrey, hospital, enables powerful radiation to focus on tissues.
3 A worker at the Radiochemical Centre takes a sample from a pile of gold grains retrieved from radon seeds. The radioactive gas decays fairly rapidly to give the precious metal.

What is engineering?

Whether building bridges, designing machines, developing new materials or constructing complex electronic devices, the engineer is a central figure in the progress of a modern industrial society.

ENGINEERS PRODUCE most of Man's material wealth, change the face of the Earth, create every new product of modern technology and increasingly make life easier, safer and more convenient.

According to one wit: 'an engineer does for twenty-five pence what any fool could do for fifty. In the same vein, an aeronautical engineer is described as 'a man who designs a part weighing eight ounces that any fool could design to weigh a pound'. Clearly, engineers have to be cost conscious, and some have to be weight conscious; almost all of them are deeply concerned with how long things will last, what they will accomplish and with what efficiency; their reliability, safety and a thousand other factors. An engineer's whole life is spent balancing conflicting factors like these, weighing one against another and coming up with the best possible answer. Each of his products is a compromise: it could always be improved if it were made more expensive; it could always be made lighter, if reliability was unimportant, and much cheaper if it did not have to last long. But what are engineers like, and what do they actually do?

Wrong notions about engineers

Most people have a hazy, and usually quite wrong, notion about engineers. It is still common to find engineers thought of as men in boiler suits or overalls, with oily hands holding a monkey wrench. Today's engineer may look like this, but only on Sunday when he (or increasingly, she) is doing jobs about the house. On Monday he puts on a smart suit, or sports jacket and flannels, and goes to work. He may go to an office that looks much like a thousand other offices except for pieces of 'iron-mongery' – pistons, turbine blades, bearings or broken pieces of metal – decorating the desks and filing cabinets. He may go to a drawing office and take his place behind a huge bench or drawing board. He may go 6,000 miles by jet to see something 'on site' or visit a customer. Wherever he goes, within five minutes of his arrival he will probably have his jacket off and be engaged in intense discussion with colleagues, customers, university professors, government officials or suppliers of material or components. Their talk would be unintelligible to most people, but out of it may come a better answer to

a problem, or a possible answer where none existed before.

And this leads to the heart of engineering. All engineers create something out of nothing. Sometimes, as with suitcases or even motor cars, the engineering design is not really a dramatic step into the unknown; the new product is technically very similar to what has been made before, and most of the effort is concerned with making it look attractive while keeping

down the production cost. But other engineers spend their whole lives pushing out the very frontiers of human achievement. Aircraft are made to carry greater loads, trains to go faster, telephone systems to handle more traffic with fewer breakdowns, newspaper presses to work faster at lower cost, home sewing machines to be more versatile yet smaller and neater than before, life-support systems to enable an astronaut or aquanaut to go where Man could not go before, and a bridge to span a great river previously thought unbridgeable. The engineer's creations are of steel, aluminium, glass, glass fibre, plastics, concrete and every other material used by Man. The engineer must have a deep knowledge of these materials and may be skilled at fashioning them; but to do so is not his job. His own tools are a drawing board and notebook, pencils and pens, slide rules, typewriter, test equipment, computer, instruments and dozens of volumes of reference books, catalogues and articles from the technical press.

The oldest category of engineer is the civil engineer. Civil engineers conceived the pyramids of Egypt, the roads of the Roman Empire and the castles and cathedrals of the medieval and Renaissance periods. Today's 'civils' design and oversee the world's motorways, hospitals, airports, harbours, power stations, factories, dams, bridges and tunnels. The civil engineer builds to last; his products will often

1 Developing a method of controlling machine tools by laser beam. Many engineers spend most of their working lives in laboratories developing new applications of technology.
2 The skeleton of the Forth Road Bridge provides a magnificent walkway for construction workers. This was the first bridge for which the suspension cables were spun on site.

outlast his own life many times over. The Egyptian engineers who designed the pyramids 5,000 and more years ago demonstrated an amazing mastery of mathematics, structural stability and precision. The task of hewing, transporting and erecting the stone blocks – in the case of the Great Pyramid, 2,300,000 blocks each weighing $2\frac{1}{2}$ tons – took 100,000 slaves 20 years, working three months each year. No civil engineer today could dream of such a labour force. He deploys machines instead of men, so that the task of constructing the Great Pyramid could now be done by 200 men working for three months in all; but they would need a lot of special equipment. Every big civil engineering job today has to be costed carefully beforehand; woe betide the engineer who tells his employers or clients a project will cost £3,500,000 and proves to have underestimated by £1,000,000! Cost and time are vital, and closely interrelated, and careful analytical techniques and computerized management are essential to control all phases of the design, building, testing and commissioning of all giant schemes in modern civil engineering.

Mechanical engineering

Perhaps the central branch of the profession is mechanical engineering, and a mechanical engineer's degree is the most common type of engineering degree. The mechanical engineer lives in a world of machines which either generate power or consume it. While the civil engineer is concerned with the stability of subsoil, the physical characteristics of rocks, wind loads on structures, the properties of concrete and the cheapest way to tunnel safely through a mountain, the mechanical engineer designs engines, gear wheels, printing presses, wine presses, laundry presses and presses that stamp out the body of a car at one blow. In 1800 the apprentice mechanical engineer soon acquired horny hands from learning how to file pieces of iron to an exact profile. Today's engineer does not make things himself but creates the concept; he does not file iron but might design a system in which a piece of iron plays a part. If he does, he will also develop the production schedule for every part, and today hand filing is obsolete, except in the 'hand finishing' of some cast or forged items made in very small numbers.

A century ago iron was the dominant material for ships, trains, rails, bridges, tunnel linings and a hundred other structures, and for the great machines and machine tools that made them. These were among the most obvious products of the Industrial Revolution, and mechanical engineers trod carefully over new ground every day, making a ship that was larger, a steam engine running faster, a boiler operating at higher pressure and a crane that would lift a greater weight than any before it. They designed conservatively, applying a 'factor of safety' (often justifiably called a 'factor of ignorance') to make everything two, five or 100 times as strong as their calculations showed it had to be. Today engineers have greater understanding of the properties of their materials

under all conditions of stress, temperature, corrosion, fatigue and other adverse influences and are able, with the help of computers, to design heavily loaded components with extreme accuracy so that they need the least amount of material, production time and labour yet will do their job reliably throughout their work-

1 Nuccio Bertone, Italian designer of the Pirana sports car, with the car and his team of craftsmen behind him. One engineer may control the work of many men.
2 Assembling valves in Mullard's Blackburn factory. Mass-production techniques and more efficient ways of producing goods are the concern of a growing number of engineers.

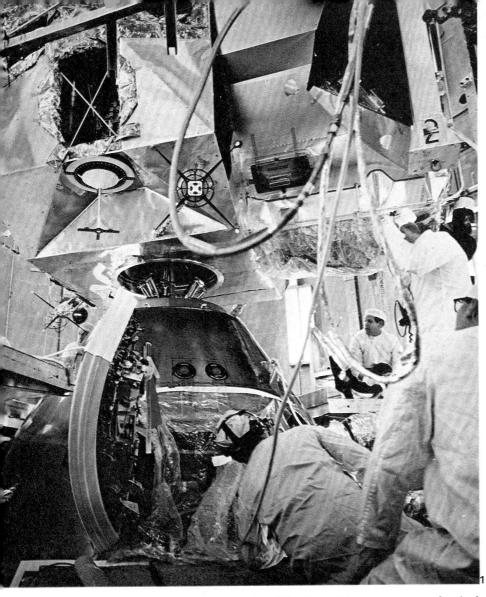

kept on punched cards or tape.

Just one example from the thousands of types of problem encountered in mechanical engineering is the design of a bearing to support a rotating shaft. A century ago the only bearing available was what today is called a plain bearing: the shaft, of iron or steel, is supported by a fixed shell of softer metal, such as brass or a special alloy of lead and bronze, with an intervening film of lubricating oil. Engineers discovered how to make the shaft ride up automatically on the oil film so that, no matter how heavily it was loaded, the fixed and moving metal surfaces could never actually touch each other. But by 1900 developments with bicycles and later the first cars had led to ball and roller bearings in which a 'cage' containing perfect metal balls or hardened rollers supported the central shaft with very little friction, thus opening the way to more efficient machines running at higher speeds. Today ball, roller and tapered roller bearings have been developed to support heavy loads at extremely high speeds with total reliability, while in recent years completely new forms of 'gas bearing' have appeared in which the shaft is supported by a thick film of air or other gas passing through under pressure. Other more efficient bearings are sure to be invented by mechanical engineers in the future.

Theory and practice

Bearing design, like the whole of engineering, requires a knowledge of the basic laws of physics, metallurgy and either hydrodynamics or aerodynamics; and the engineer must combine this theory with a hard practical appreciation of the job in hand. He designs every new type of bearing in great detail so that when the first example is made it unfailingly fulfils the performance required of it; and, if it is to be made by the million, its design must provide for the cheapest possible mass production with the fewest 'rejects'. Test bearings are made in the metals that will

ing life. Even 15 years ago mechanical engineering meant armies of designers, stressmen, calculators, analysts and mathematicians laboriously working out the correct figures and writing them in volumes of design and production books to be kept as a record. Today the computer does the arithmetic and the records are

1 Engineers wearing surgical gowns and caps swarm over the uncompleted shell of the Apollo lunar module, in which astronauts will go to the moon. Contamination of space must be avoided.
2 A Swiss watch-maker, a highly skilled engineer, at work on a watch. Many engineers work in highly specialized fields, requiring a great deal of practical experience and knowledge.
3 A young engineer in training. Engineering students are given wide practical experience in handling machinery as well as rigorous mathematical training to equip them for their work.

be used in production and also in transparent plastics or polarized glass so that the patterns of strain when in use can be rendered visible. Every eventuality must be allowed for – the need for the different parts of the bearing and its housing to expand by different amounts over the whole range of temperatures that might possibly be encountered, the probability that some bearings will at some time be overloaded or overspeeded, the pros and cons of making the whole assembly in the form of separate halves each of which could continue to run should the other half fail (to give what is called 'fail safe' design), the need to inspect and perhaps remove the installed bearing with least difficulty, the need to prevent chips or parts of a failed bearing from causing further damage – all these and many other considerations must be taken into full account and weighed against each other. And when the bearing is in production the engineer may help in preparing the technical manuals and servicing instructions, while special 'service engineers' may go out on visits to customers.

1 Many thousands of engineers work on the design side of the profession. Here a designer climbs on to the table to mark out a curve on a plan of an engineering part.
2 Super-clean conditions are essential in some types of precision engineering. In this case, the

What applies to bearings also applies to a million other engineering items. The same principles and techniques are used in every case, according to the end product that is wanted. For example, a valve controlling a Freon circuit in a home refrigerator poses few design problems apart from the fact that it must be profitably sold at a very low price; but the valve doing the same job in a manned spacecraft must never fail even under the most severe environmental conditions, and the fact that it may in consequence cost thousands of dollars is less important.

Other branches of engineering

What about the other branches of engineering? There are many hundreds, and new fields are opening up all the time as scientific discoveries find their way into useful industry. One big and long-established branch is electrical engineering, but these engineers do not merely perpetuate old designs. Far from it: every electrical engineer is engaged in making things newer and better, from exotic 'superconducting' distribution systems operat-

engineer is assembling a gyroscope at the British Aircraft Corporation factory.
3 Overhauling one of the vast turbines at London's Fulham power station. The design of these large components poses many challenges for engineers, not always solved successfully.

ing near to absolute zero temperature to designing multi-core ribbon cables suited to service in the turret of an army tank. The newer breed of electronic engineers are even more diverse, and an increasing number of them spend their time creating circuits so small that they cannot be seen except under a microscope.

There are aeronautical engineers, marine engineers, railway engineers, vehicle engineers, pneumatic and hydraulic engineers, mining engineers, acoustic engineers, and yet newer varieties. Nuclear engineers bring cheaper power, as well as many new techniques in medicine and industry. Communications engineers are improving telephones and radio and may before long give us 'picturephones' worn like a wristwatch. Environmental engineers not only ensure that modern buildings have comfortable lighting, temperature, humidity and noise level but also design equipment for people to work well at the bottom of the ocean or on the moon. Ocean engineers design equipment and develop techniques for exploring the Earth's oceans and reaping whatever harvest of marine life or minerals may be economically possible. In doing so they parallel the modern agricultural engineers whose aim is to revolutionize an ancient science and double, treble or multiply by ten the world's annual production of food for an 'exploding' population. A very new species are the medical engineers – half-electronics specialists and half-doctors. And perhaps the fastest growing family of all are those concerned with complex dynamic systems. One group of these are the computer, control and cybernetic engineers who design computers, automated measuring and control devices and all kinds of operating systems which involve 'feedback loops' which may include human beings as operators.

There are never enough engineers, except perhaps in the Soviet Union where it is one of the most exalted professions for both men and women. In Britain, as I remarked earlier, people who are not engineers tend to look down on anybody who is. But this is not the case in the United States, Germany or Japan, or in any other of the swiftly growing, technology-based nations.

1

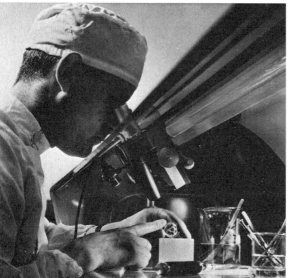
2

3

Bridging the world

Bridges and dams, pyramids and skyscrapers, tunnels and fly-overs, all are produced by the labour of construction engineers. Their proud boast that they 'shape the world' has more than a grain of truth in it.

NO ONE who has seen the Tennessee Valley irrigation scheme, the polders which the Dutch have reclaimed from the sea, the Aswan high dam on the Nile or the Simplon Tunnel under the snow-capped Alps can fail to be awestruck by the sheer scale of these projects. Beside them, the achievements of aero or electrical engineering, while still technically outstanding, pale into insignificance in terms of spectacle. The construction engineer takes over where geology left off; he uses the natural features of the Earth for the benefit of men, and he specializes in overcoming the obstacles which nature has created. If a mountain range is in the way, he will span it with roads, viaducts and causeways, or he will drive a tunnel through it; an impassable river or gorge presents little problem, as the many beautiful bridges throughout the world testify. If a city or farmland needs water, the civil engineer will construct massive dams to store it and tunnels to carry it to its destination, even though the distance involved may be hundred of miles. During the last 700 years Dutch engineers have performed what is perhaps the most remarkable construction engineering feat of all – reclaiming $1\frac{1}{2}$ million acres of land from the sea bed, more than two-fifths of their whole country.

But construction engineering, although today it uses highly advanced planning and engineering techniques, is by far the oldest branch of engineering. The pyramids, the Roman aqueducts, Stonehenge, the standing statues on Easter Island and the causeways of Mexico City are monuments to the skill and persistence of early

1 The world's largest prefabricated concrete span is the Medway Bridge, in Kent, on the M2 motorway. The 1,300-yard bridge was built by the cantilever method, and is seen nearing completion.
2 At 1,107 feet, the John Hancock Building, Chicago, is only 143 feet shorter than the Empire State building. This view shows the steel lattice which forms the building's frame.
3 A tunnelling machine in operation during the construction of London's Victoria underground railway line. Modern tunnelling machines do much of the heavy work previously done by men.

constructors. Even today, the methods which were used to build these structures are unknown to us, erected as they were in an age which lacked modern mechanical aids.

It is to the Romans, the inveterate builders of bridges and aqueducts, that we owe the invention of one of the basic materials of modern construction – concrete. Not only did the Romans use it to bind blocks of stone, but they also erected buildings entirely of concrete, an art which was lost with the decline of the empire and was not redeveloped until many centuries had passed.

Despite the variety of work undertaken in construction engineering, it depends almost entirely on two structural materials – concrete and steel. There are few structures of the twentieth century which do not employ one or other, or generally both, of these materials. In fact, one of the greatest advances in civil engineering has been the use of these materials in a composite structure known as reinforced concrete.

Concrete itself, although it is immensely strong when used as a pillar, breaks comparatively easily when subjected to a bending load. Engineers describe this by saying that concrete is strong in compression, but weak in tension. When concrete is used as a pillar to support a weight, it is in compression and serves its purpose well. If, however, a concrete beam is supported at the ends on pillars, and a load is applied to it, the beam will tend to bow downwards. The top of the beam will tend to shorten in length (it is in compression) while the bottom will tend to lengthen (it is in tension), and, unless it is particularly massive, the beam will give way. Obviously this is a severe drawback, because even when concrete is used as a vertical pillar, say in the structure of a bridge, it will still be subjected to side loads from the wind which will put it in tension. The result of this is that simple concrete structures have to be made very large to support these loads, and very often a large part of this unwanted mass is there to merely support the weight of the concrete itself.

But if the lower side of the beam could in some way be strengthened with a material which is strong in tension, this problem would be overcome. Not only could the weight of the beam be reduced, but the appearance of the structure would be slimmer and more gracious. Ordinary reinforced concrete is made by embedding steel rods in the concrete beam or slab while it is being cast. Firstly, a wooden mould, generally called shuttering, is set up. The steel rods are then placed in position and the mixture of cement, sand and stones, in the correct proportions, is poured into the mould. Various methods are used to ensure that the concrete adheres firmly to the steel, including shaping the steel surface, but more often the rods are allowed to corrode in the open air to provide the necessary grip. Since its introduction in France in the early nineteenth century, reinforced concrete has taken over many of the functions which were once the province of ordinary concrete, stone and cast iron, and has made possible structures which would at best have been uneconomic before.

However, ordinary reinforced concrete does have a number of drawbacks. The concrete surrounding the reinforcing rods contributes very little to the total strength of the beam; it does little more than enclose the reinforcement. Thus the beam will still be more massive than the load requires.

Prestressed concrete

This drawback can largely be overcome by a technique known as prestressing, which can be carried out in two ways. The first method employs steel cables in addition to the normal reinforcement. The cables are put in tension by applying a pull at both ends, and the concrete beam or slab is cast round them in the normal way. When the concrete has set, the tension is released. The forces thus set up in the cables tend to make the beam curve like a bow. When the beam is then put in position, the applied loads will merely serve to reduce this bowing effect, so that the strength of the beam under load is immense. The stresses imposed on the reinforcing cables are calculated so that they will be larger than any load which will be applied to the beam.

Another method of increasing the tensile strength of a beam is by post-tensioning. Here, the beam is cast with holes or channels passing through it. After the concrete has set, the cables, or tendons, are threaded through the channels and

are then tensioned by hydraulic jacks and anchored at the ends of the beam.

Steel is used in tensioning concrete because of its great strength under tension. It is used alone in many structures, especially bridges, but it has the great drawback that it rusts when exposed to the elements. Since this would lead to serious weakening of the structure, steel bridges, such as the Forth Bridge in Scotland and the Golden Gate Bridge in San Francisco, require an army of more maintenance men to paint them.

Apart from the materials of construction engineering, there are a number of

basic types of structure which recur again and again, particularly in bridge building. One of these, the arch, is a means by which a span made of materials such as brick and stone, with low tensional strengths, can support quite heavy loads. A load applied vertically to the top of an arch is transmitted to the stones forming it as compression loads, and the limitation on the load-carrying capacity of bridges built on this principle is usually the strength of the foundations.

For many centuries bridge and viaduct builders used the arch in all major structures. It is seen at its finest in Roman

1 The Pont du Gard at Nîmes, Provence, was built in 19 BC by Marcus Agrippa. The aqueduct carried water 155 feet above a valley to the prosperous Roman city of Nemausus.

2 Stonehenge, on bleak Salisbury Plain, Wiltshire, is one of the oldest civil engineering works in Britain – and still one of the most impressive. Some stones were brought from west Wales.

aqueducts such as the spectacular three-tiered Pont du Gard.

Although at first sight the resemblance is not obvious, the retaining walls of dams are curved for exactly the same reason as the arch is used in bridges. The mass of water pressing against the outside of the curve sets up almost purely compressive forces within the wall. When one looks around, one can see many applications of the arch principle: doorways, brick-lined railway tunnels and the vaulting of cathedrals and churches are good examples. Bridges are the most obvious examples of the construction engineer's work, and many of them are both beautiful and spectacular. Basically, there are four types which are used by the engineer according to circumstances. Termed the beam, arch, suspension and cantilever types, they can usually be easily identified although sometimes a bridge will be seen which is a hybrid, or mixture of different types.

Simplest of all is the beam, which works on the principle of a plank over a stream, surely the simplest of all bridges. For short spans this type of bridge is economical and easy to build, but where long distances are involved intermediate supports must be provided unless the beam which carries the deck (load-carrying surface) is not to be unduly heavy and

1 The Maya Pyramid and Temple of the Magician at Uxmal, Mexico, is only one of the many huge edifices built by pre-Columbian civilizations in Central America.
2 The arch of the Hoover Dam on the Boulder River on the border of Arizona and Nevada is one of the highest in the world. The pressure of the water tends to maintain the arch.

3 Wells Cathedral, Somerset. Much of the civil engineering effort of medieval builders went into the construction of religious buildings, combining function and beauty.
4 Tower Bridge has retractable leaves to allow shipping into the Pool of London. The leaves are steam operated, and give an opening 250 feet wide.

A modern cathedral under construction in Liverpool. This building makes use of prestressed concrete spars to achieve an unusual and attractive design.

expensive. Opening bridges across canals and narrow rivers are normally made on the beam principle, although a steel lattice-work forms the side of the bridge to give added stiffness.

In arch construction, before either iron or prestressed concrete were available, the bricks or stones forming the arch were built on a temporary wooden frame-work – falsework – which was removed after the keystone, the stone at the apex of the arch, was put in position. The arch then 'settled' and was ready to have the roadway built over it. This method is still used when concrete is employed, but iron, steel and prestressed concrete have made it possible to build the arch and then suspend the deck of the bridge below it. This often improves the appearance of a long bridge as well as allowing the engineer to vary the height of the deck to suit the elevation of the approach roads.

This latter type of bridge obviously does not have the load applied above the arch, but the weight of traffic is imposed from below by the cables suspending the deck. However, the stresses in the arch are the same. An excellent example of this type of bridge is the Sydney Harbour bridge in Australia, whose high, clear, wide span allows large ocean-going liners to pass underneath.

For wide spans where it is undesirable to have too many intermediate supports, cantilever or suspension bridges are usually chosen. In cantilever construction, two supporting pillars or piers are constructed in the river or ravine. These are located so that the distance between them is about half the total completed span. Construction then proceeds by building outwards in both directions from each pier. During this work, the weight of the deck on each side of the pier balances, so that only compressive loads (apart

The giant scoops of this 7,600-ton excavator can move more than 200,000 tons of earth in one day. Such machinery cheapens considerably many big construction projects.

from wind loads) are imposed on the piers.

In suspension bridges, the piers which support the structure are built a good deal higher than the final height of the deck, and again are located some way from the ends of the span. Steel cable is then suspended from the piers to anchorage points on firm ground and also between the piers, where it forms a curve known as a catenary. Round this pilot cable is spun a series of others making up an immensely strong cable with multiple strands. There are two such cables and the load-bearing deck is finally suspended beneath them by a series of vertical cables.

Building the piers for a bridge, no matter what its final form may be, is a very difficult operation in its own right. Frequently the piers have their foundations under water in the bed of a river or estuary. So that the work can be done in comparatively dry conditions, the engineers either construct a temporary

dam or sink a caisson or diving bell within which the work can be carried out.

Modern tunnelling depends to a large extent on a device invented by the great engineer Marc Isambard Brunel (1769–1849). This is a combined tunnel excavator and shield known as a drum digger, which supports the tunnel while at the same time digging out the clay or sand. It allows progressive lining of the tunnel and prevents dangerous roof falls. But while the drum digger is very useful in soft strata, when rock is encountered the tunnellers must resort to explosives. A special technique using concentric rings of explosive charges fired in sequence has simplified this difficult work, although progress is still slow.

Because of the time factor in rock tunnelling, engineers insist on a highly detailed geological survey of the proposed site before work begins. It is often possible to avoid rock by altering the course of the tunnel slightly. Whereas 40 or 50 years ago engineers would drive a tunnel under comparatively small hills, the development of really powerful earth-moving machinery in the 1950s led to another method which can be used when the depth involved is not too great and when the surface is not built on. This is the cut and cover method, which means scooping out a huge trough, lining it, putting a roof on, and replacing the soil. Modern machinery makes this an economic alternative to tunnelling in a large number of cases.

Construction and environment

A hazard which was recognized only in the late 1950s is that large structures may modify their environment to such a degree that actual damage can be caused either to the structures themselves or to existing structures in the vicinity. Good examples of this are the high winds and turbulence caused by tall buildings and the disturbance of tide patterns by man-made harbours. While the engineer may design a tall building for existing wind loads, he may find that his structure will have to deal with much greater loads caused by its very presence. Conditions like this are called 'mini-climates', and although once again computers are being used to give adequate warning of such conditions, it is still good engineering practice to over-design, just in case.

As in many other fields, the computer has transformed design procedures in construction engineering. In bridges, dams, tunnels and harbours the variables encountered are so complex that manual mathematical analysis is out of the question. Using a computer, however, it is possible to take all variables into account, with the result that structures are both stronger and much less wasteful of time and materials.

In the end, though, the success of a project comes down to the experience and skill of the man on the job, the site agent. The motto of engineers used to be: 'If it looks right it probably is right.' To this the construction engineer could add the motto of the old Roman builders: 'Build to endure.'

The road-builders

Road-building is almost as old as human society, closely linked both with conquest and trade. But the modern demand for good, fast motor-roads poses serious problems for builders and designers.

SINCE THE DAWN of recorded history the building of roads has been a prominent human activity. Necessary for trade and for the development of contact between communities, they have played a formative part in the progress of civilization.

In an age when we are accustomed to regard roads as essential for civilization, it is difficult for us to imagine a society which does not depend on roads for its transport. But primitive Man must have relied largely on tracks and blazed trails which would not now be dignified by the name of roads. The road-builder's task in those days no doubt largely comprised of blazing trails round obstacles and clearing paths which could be recognized by others. Preparation of the surface and actual road-building came later.

The societies of the Tigris and Euphrates valleys, which flourished about 3000 B C, are known to have had a widespread system of metalled roads, many of them surfaced with bitumen, a substance which has only in relatively recent times been 'rediscovered' for road surfacing in the West.

But perhaps the most tireless road-builders were the Romans, whose construction was closely tied up with the exploitation of their military conquests. Many Roman roads are still admired as notable feats of civil engineering, and in its heyday the Roman road system spanned Europe, Asia Minor and a large part of North Africa with straight, efficient, fast roads. The engineers of the Roman roads were the Legions, which frequently made use of local pressed labour to build the roads which were constructed of whatever materials were locally available. The most favoured road surface was stone flags, but where these were not available, as in forested areas, the Romans would make ingenious use of tree-trunks instead. Marshy areas presented serious problems, particularly as these were often used as hide-outs for recalcitrant tribes. In the Fens, for example, the Romans tried at first to build a road across the marshes by filling in the marsh with stones. The stones were swallowed up, but it was found that the road could still be built on the basis of tree-trunks used as a floating platform for the road surface. Remains of such roads still exist in some areas.

After the decay of the Roman Empire, road-building fell into a long period of disuse and the ancient arts were largely lost. Even during the medieval period, European states were content to rely largely on the old Roman system for their transport, and not unnaturally the system became worn through constant use. Chronicles of the period are full of complaints about the bad state of the roads, many of them little better than mud tracks, dusty in summer and impassable in winter, which served as the main highways of the country.

One of the features of the Roman roads was that they were linked to an efficient system of horse transport, served by staging stations along the route. A rider could change horses regularly along the road and arrive much faster at his destination than would otherwise be possible. This type of system was retained by the Arabs, who set up caravanserai along the main trade routes in their dominions. The medieval economy, with its self-sufficient peasant units, relied less on good roads and trade than the Romans, who were mainly concerned with speeding the flow of tribute to Rome and maintaining their grip on the scattered outposts of their empire. It was not until the beginning of the modern era, therefore, with the spread of trade and the development of mercantile relations on a scale embracing whole nations and continents that the need for

1 The art of the pavier lies in cutting the cobble-stones so that they fit together to form fan-like patterns. Although labour costs are high, the results are very durable.
2 A Roman road at Mamhilad, Monmouthshire. Even in this remote outpost of the Roman Empire, roads were carefully paved and provided with gutters for drainage.
3 The overhead section of the M4 London–South Wales motorway during construction. More than 35,000 tons of pre-stressed concrete were required to build the mile-long flyover.

good roads again became pressing and agitation about the state of the roads began to gather force.

The passing of the Turnpike Act marks the first significant step in Britain to improve the roads. The first Act of this type was passed in 1663, and its application was extended to the whole country in 1767. The levying of tolls, despite wild abuses, made it possible to find money to improve certain sections of road and led to the development of more enlightened methods of road-making. The same type of development occurred in France after the revolution, when the road system of the country, previously the product of the hated *corvée* system, of forced peasant labour, was changed radically under Napoleon, and the foundations of the present road network laid.

But the turnpike system in Britain rapidly became a medium for the worst type of abuses, and very little of the money collected from passers-by was actually applied to improving the roads. The abolition of the turnpikes, carried out progressively from the beginning of the nineteenth century, made it possible to build more convenient and less expensive roads.

Two men figure pre-eminently in the early period of modern road-building. Thomas Telford, a shepherd's son from Eskdale, Yorkshire, became a prominent road engineer after he had carried out surveying and other road-making com-

missions for the county of Shropshire. He soon became nationally known for his application of scientific principles to road construction.

An even more important influence was that of the Scot, John Loudon McAdam. McAdam was in many ways the founder of modern scientific road-making, and the first to realize that roads had to be designed so that the wear caused by the passage of vehicles would assist rather than destroy the development of the road surface. He argued that a surface composed of small stones and dust would become compacted by wheeled traffic and that the foundation of a good road should be made by exploiting the natural elasticity of the sub-soil.

Water-bound roads

McAdam's method, using crushed stones, made it possible for the first time to make roads of adequate quality fairly cheaply with local materials and labour. This type of road is known as a water-bound road, because the force holding together the surface of the road is the surface tension of water on the small stones and dust of which the road is composed.

Until the beginning of this century, when the demands of motor transport began to make themselves felt, a combination of the methods devised by Telford and McAdam was generally used in the construction of roads. Foundations would

be prepared according to the rules put forward by Telford, who favoured laying down a layer of large stones about seven inches deep and filling the spaces between them with smaller stones. Other ways of providing a foundation include the laying down of *hardcore* and the provision of a concrete slab.

Having laid the foundations, larger stones would be broken to provide a surface layer of material which would be raked together with the stone dust and watered. The cohesion provided by watering the stones provided the means that held the road together. The iron wheels used in the period would crush the broken stone still smaller and the weather could be relied on to keep the stones moist most of the year.

This method of road-building was no doubt adequate for the period and for the type of traffic which was then common, but the advent of the motor-car spelt the end of this type of road except in a few isolated country areas. Fast, wheeled traffic tends to break up the surface of such a road and to scatter the small surface stones.

The fault lay not so much with the method of construction as with the use of water to bind the road together. Other means of binding were therefore sought, and a return was made to bituminous materials which were used by the ancient Babylonians to surface their roads. By the time the question of new surfacing

1 The Kingston by-pass, a dual-carriageway development on the outskirts of London, represents a partially successful attempt to speed traffic flow into and out of the capital.

2 The asphalt lake in Trinidad, West Indies, supplies a considerable proportion of the world's asphalt requirement. Other sources are the Val de Travers, Savoy, and coal-tar residues.

3 A rock-crushing machine being operated by British army engineers in Aden, provides gravel for road-making. Historically, many roads have been built for military purposes.

4 The German autobahn system of fast motorways linking industrial and commercial centres is widely copied by other countries. Despite high initial costs, such roads cut transport overheads.

5 Laying tarmac on the road surface of the Severn Bridge, in Britain. The tarmac mixture is carefully calculated to give good conditions for car tyres to grip the road surface.

materials became a pressing necessity bitumen could be obtained in large quantities and fairly cheaply as a by-product of the refining of coal-tar. Other sources were found in various parts of the world, such as the Val de Travers in Savoy, where there are bitumen-containing rocks, and Trinidad, where there is a large natural outcrop of asphalt, a mixture of pitch and small pebbles.

Other types of surfacing were also tried, and for a time there was a fashion for wood blocks. It was found that creosoted blocks of reasonably soft wood laid in sand with the grain vertical, made a fairly durable surface for traffic. In many town centres, these wood blocks are still the basis for many of the streets, although most of them are covered with bitumen to prevent the slipping which was their main

disadvantage in wet weather.

Another type of surface which was also popular for a period was what is known as *sett paving*. This is based on the principle of the cobblestones found in many old towns, although the cobbles are far more regular and carefully shaped. Unless the setts are carefully laid, however, they become worn rather rapidly and create a noisy surface. They also tend to give a very bumpy ride when worn. On the continent of Europe, sett paving is used much more extensively than in Britain or the United States, and various forms of synthetic blocks are used. Many of the mountain passes in Switzerland and Germany are paved in this way.

One of the many objections at present to sett paving is its high initial cost. The blocks must be laid by hand, and high labour costs make this a big initial outlay, although the upkeep of sett paving, when well laid, is low.

Despite various roads of this type, the great majority of modern roads make use of bituminous materials for surfacing. They have the great advantage that they can be laid relatively easily, that they cost less than stone surfaces and that they can relatively easily be renewed when the surface becomes worn.

But bitumen or asphalt by itself is insufficient to make a road. Foundations must be laid to take the weight of the traffic and spread it as evenly as possible over the width of the road. On a well-designed road, the weight of the traffic is borne not only by the portion of the road directly underneath the wheels of the vehicle, but by a considerable part of the underlying foundations. In modern use, there are generally two types of foundation.

Hardcore is frequently used, consisting of materials such as bricks from demolished buildings, pieces of broken concrete and the like. It is generally laid over a bed of cinders or some similar material to discourage water from rising into the foundations and undermining the road. On top of the hardcore may be laid a more regular course of stones and the whole covered with a layer of asphalt or with a mixture of gravel and tar. A road of this sort must be rolled a number of times to ensure that the foundations are tightly packed and that the tarred surface is smoothly laid over them. This method is widely used for medium roads that do not have to bear continuous heavy traffic.

For roads like the motorways, more elaborate and expensive methods have to be used. The foundations may be built up of one or more layers of concrete, perhaps laid on a foundation of hardcore. The concrete will probably be reinforced with steel mesh, to provide a resilient basis for traffic flowing over it. Much of the building work on such roads is carried out with specially designed concrete-laying and tarring machinery.

The advent of this machinery has taken much of the backbreaking drudgery out of road-building. Many of the roads of the last century, and of most of this century, were built by vast gangs of labourers working with pick and shovel. Much of the work has now been mechanized and the gangs of 'navvies' replaced increasingly by massive earth-moving machinery and road-laying and rolling machines.

The growth of traffic over the past 50 years has meant that much more attention now has to be given to planning the road network as a whole than was formerly the case. Roads in the past were often laid down almost haphazardly along the lines of century-old tracks. This, perhaps, and not Chesterton's 'rolling English drunkard' was responsible for the meandering lines of many of the old roads. The tendency is now for new roads to be planned so that the traffic can travel rapidly from place to place in the greatest safety.

Road design

Modern road design has to take into account not only the need to make the roads safe but the likely pattern of future road use. Roads have to be designed with the needs of future motorists in mind. The task of the road-designer is a highly complex one, and since road-building also involves vast expenditures of public money, mistakes are hard to correct.

But the design of roads extends not only to the overall view of the needs and requirements of motorists. The road-designer must take into account also such details as the provision of a suitable surface for the high-speed motorist. A great deal of research in recent years has concentrated on making safer surfaces for tyres to grip better and to prevent skidding and 'planing' when there is water on the road. Many surfaces which are perfectly adequate for traffic moving at low or medium speeds in good weather become dangerous when used at high speed in adverse conditions.

Road signs have also to be designed so that they can easily be read, service stations sited where they will be most convenient for the driver, and many other aspects of the design have to be integrated to make a good road. The trend towards motorways, restricted to motor traffic and with fast lanes, isolated from the rest of the road system, has in many ways made this task easier, as it enables the road to be designed as a whole rather than as several separate sections.

Because roads need to cross country and to penetrate sometimes into areas of natural beauty, the road must also be carefully landscaped to conform with the lie of the land and not to obtrude on the view. This can be done, but is often relegated to a low priority.

Road-building is an important part of the modern world. Like sewers, water-supply systems and hospitals, roads are a public necessity and good roads should enhance rather than retard this need. The complex relationship between the road, the road user and the vehicle needs to be better understood if we are to have roads which will become lasting monuments to our civilization rather than merely regrettable necessities.

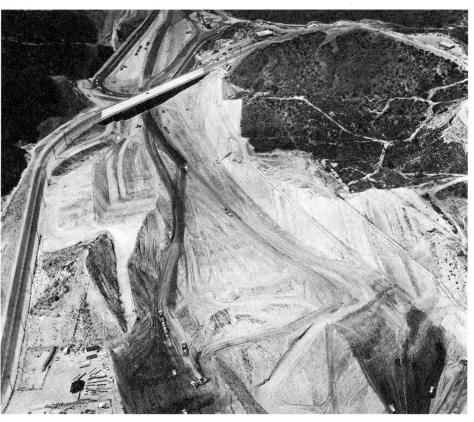

1 A huge scar on the earth marks the site of construction of California's San Diego Freeway. Road-building sometimes involves the remoulding of mountain contours.

2 Prefabricated steel sections being lowered into place on the Frankfurt–Kassel autobahn, Germany. The portable steel slabs form a serviceable surface while the road is under repair.

The car makers

The motor-car, which everyone takes so much for granted, is in reality an engineering marvel with a long history. Modern car manufacture makes use of the latest techniques of automation and mass production.

CARS HAVE DEVELOPED from carts and carriages which, through the centuries, had been drawn by animals. In Europe the horse was most common and the first cars were known as horseless carriages. What needed invention was not the carriage but the engine to drive it.

As well as being a great artist, Leonardo da Vinci (1452–1519) was also a fertile inventor and devised a self-propelling carriage driven by a large spring. This carriage could not be realized in practice at the time, but was notable for its geared mechanism which compensated for the different speeds of rotation of the driving wheels when going round curves. We now call this the differential gear.

James Watt (1736–1819) had started work on the development of high-speed steam engines by 1760 and a horseless carriage driven by a steam engine ran in 1769. The real birth date of the modern car, however, was probably 1886 when a lightweight internal combustion engine designed by Karl Benz was fitted to Daimler's first motor bicycle.

The internal combustion engine, far and away the most usual form of car propulsion today, did not have a runaway victory over other forms of propulsion until well into the twentieth century. Steam and electricity were both serious rivals. At the turn of the century an electric car held the speed record at 65·62 mph, while seven years later, in 1906, a Stanley steam car won the world speed record with a top speed of 127·38 mph, a truly remarkable achievement. Even today the internal combustion engine still has its rivals for certain applications.

With the increasing availability of engines came a long process of innovation and, with it, a continuous and accelerating process of applying new technologies and, indeed, science to the design and manufacture of cars. By 1910 Britain, France, Italy, Germany and the United States were all producing cars, and the motoring age had really begun.

In the early days car manufacturers were not interested in bodywork. The building of carriages was a craft occupation best left to craftsmen who knew their jobs. The car manufacturer made the engine and transmission and built the complete chassis on which a body, built by a specialist firm, could be fitted. Today almost all cars are of unitary construction in which the bodywork and the chassis are in one piece.

The greatest single influence on car design was mass production. In 1914 at Dearborn, Michigan, Henry Ford introduced a moving belt on which the component parts of Ford Model T chassis were assembled. Each worker had his own modest assembly job to do as the car moved slowly past. The bodies were built on another conveyor and the two major components, chassis and body, met at the gates of the factory and were joined together into a complete car. By 1915, using this original assembly technique, Ford had already completed his millionth car. Ten years later his factories were still turning out the Model T and had built up production to a rate of nearly 10,000 vehicles a day. In these ten years, however, technical developments elsewhere had overtaken the Model T and the record production run had to cease. The Model T

1 The gas-turbine car is a fairly recent innovation. The world's first, called Jet I, was built by Rover in 1950. Shown here is the later BRM-Rover mark II gas-turbine racing car.
2 The first petrol-driven motor-car. Built by Otto Benz in 1886, this chain-driven three-wheeler laid the basis for the advanced vehicles we know and use today.
3 The body deck at Ford's Highland Park factory, Detroit, in 1914. Ford's was the first motor firm in the world to make use of the conveyor-belt system for mass producing its cars.

had become a very old-fashioned motor car.

While the mass producers of the 1920s and 1930s were meeting the needs of the mass of motorists there were still plenty of creative designers who, in the smaller companies, were forcing the pace of technological advance.

The basic components of a car are its frame, either chassis and body or all-in-one, its suspension system, braking system, steering, and the engine and transmission. All have been continuously improved throughout the years but even in the case of very specialist designs, such as racing cars, every one of the basic components is subject to some compromise in design.

A decision on the positioning of the engine would appear to be quite simple to make. And, indeed, it was on the earliest cars. The obvious thing was to position the engine at the rear with a chain transmission to the rear axle. Coaches were high and there was plenty of room beneath to store the small single- or twin-cylinder low-powered unit of the day. But with the introduction of large multi-cylinder engines and a need to lower the bodywork for greater stability, a new position was needed, and ahead of the driver seemed best. Unfortunately it was not possible at the time to solve economically the mechanical problem of driving the steerable front wheels and so the drive was still taken to the rear wheels, first by long chains but soon by the Cardan shaft, named after the Italian inventor Cardano who devised it as early as the sixteenth century. This special type of shaft, with spline and universal joints, is needed because the engine has to be sprung relative to the wheels.

Rear-mounted engines

The front-mounted engine, however convenient for access and for its cooling system with the radiator facing into the wind, was not the cheapest or necessarily the best position. The rear-mounted engine was to re-enter the popularity race because it dispensed with the Cardan shaft and could be built as a unit complete with drive and rear suspension. It also allows the car a flat floor. The siting of the engine is not only a matter of economics but also affects handling of the car because of the way the weight is distributed. Ideally, the engine should be beneath the floor in a central position with drive to all four wheels. The drive would be hydraulic in which the fluid flow can be reversed to provide smooth and powerful braking.

The conventional reciprocating engine in which a piston moves up and down in a cylinder followed the pattern set by James Watt in his steam engines. The difference essentially is that in the internal combustion engine instead of steam, the fuel, in the form of an explosive mixture, is sucked into the cylinder, compressed, and then ignited, the resultant explosion forcing the piston down in the cylinder and, through the connecting rod and crankshaft, converting the linear motion of the piston into rotary motion.

Although the principle has been main-

1 Production of a modern mass-produced car involves years of planning and development before the first model rolls off the production line. Here Ford technicians examine a mock-up Capri.
2 Protecting an unfinished Ford Capri against rusting. The car body is dipped mechanically as a unit into a large vat containing a red protective paint.
3 Modern car designs undergo extensive testing under extreme conditions. Here a prototype of the Ford Capri is being rigorously tested in the arctic weather of northern Finland.
4 Part of a modern production line at the Ford factory in Halewood. This machine, called a multiwelder, joins together several sections of the cars' bodies in a single controlled operation.
5 The chassis of a battery-driven electrical car shows its attractive simplicity. Despite the obvious advantages, however, such as lack of exhaust gas, there are still development problems.

tained, modern engines are vastly different from those of the early pioneering days. Weight, for example, is important and the technologists and engineers had to devise methods of improving performance without adding to the weight of the engine. One way of doing this is to increase the speed of rotation and, whereas the early engines had running speeds as slow as 100–500 r.p.m., many of the smaller modern engines run at 5,000 r.p.m. To achieve this took the combined energies not only of general engineers but also metallurgists, chemists and other experts. New alloys had to be developed for engine parts; valve gear and carburation had to be improved; and fuels and oils of better quality had to be developed.

The reciprocating internal combustion engine will be hard to displace as the most commonly used power unit, but two challengers are already on the scene. First is an old invention called the rotary piston engine. Quite clearly it would be a big improvement if the reciprocating motion of the piston could be a rotary motion. Although the rotary principle had been used for years in pumps it was found that to reverse the process and use the force of combustion to do work demanded an unrealizable degree of hermetic sealing.

Felix Wankel, an engineer who has specialized in pressure-tight sealing, has now solved the problem and, in conjunction with the German firm N.S.U., has developed the first practical rotary piston engine. Its advantages are compactness, low weight and, because it only contains rotary parts, smoother and quieter running.

The second development is the gas-turbine engine, which has already been used in racing cars and is now finding applications in heavy goods vehicles. This engine, originally developed for use in aircraft by Frank Whittle, uses expansion

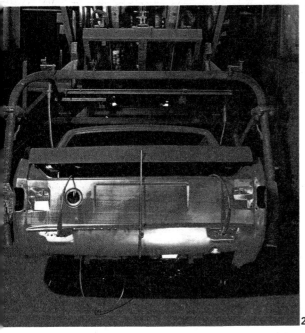

of gases caused by combustion to be expanded across a turbine to convert the chemical energy of liquid fuel into mechanical energy. It has no reciprocating parts and therefore has great smoothness of operation, but it needs an elaborate control system and is not as immediately responsive to control as piston engines.

Along with engine developments from the earliest days has been a parallel development in suspension systems and springing. Even with horse-drawn carriages it was found necessary to isolate the body from the axles carrying the wheels if frequent breakages were to be

avoided. The problem is one of absorbing road shocks, and the ideal, from the point of view of comfort, is that the vehicle body should 'float' steadily on an even keel whatever road irregularities or dynamic forces from wind, acceleration or braking encountered.

One of the great inventions was unquestionably the pneumatic tyre invented for the bicycle by John Boyd Dunlop in 1887. It is basically an air spring contained in an elastic rubber container which also constitutes the running surface. In addition to the tyre, which can only absorb minor shocks, it is necessary to have

springing and shock absorbers. Springs store shock energy when compressed and release it again in returning to their normal shape. If a car had only springs a hard shock would lead to a long-lasting vibration and give a very bouncy ride. If, however, we can make the shock energy harmless by absorbing it in some way a much smoother ride is obtained. The shock absorber takes the energy from the spring and disperses it in heat rather than back through the spring in mechanical energy.

For many years the most popular type of shock absorber has been the hydraulic type in which a piston with a number of

1 The 1969 model Brabham formula 3 car makes its debut at Brands Hatch. The two aerofoil 'wings' — one over the tail and the other over the nose — act as stabilizers to keep the car on the road at speed.
2 A Dunlop technician demonstrates the dangers of worn tyres. Despite the 800-pound load, the smooth tyre floats on the thin water film and stays still while the drum moves at 60 mph.

tiny holes in it is moved against oil pressure. To absorb a shock the oil is forced through the holes and heat, generated by molecular friction, is dissipated to the surrounding air through the metal casing of the absorber.

The first cars had very indifferent springing and shock absorption, but developments have been rapid both in materials and the way in which they have been applied. The first springs were of the leaf type and were a carry-over from the old coaching days. They are still used in some cars but have been modernized by the use of better steel. Coil springs are also extensively used as they take up little room, and torsion springs are used where there is insufficient vertical height for coils.

The feature of the hydropneumatic system is that a detector unit controls the amount of hydraulic fluid in each cylinder to keep the car, whatever the load, at a constant height above ground. The driver has a manual override and can, if he wishes, actually lift the car to give greater ground clearance, a useful facility for travel over rough terrain. If the adjustment is set for maximum ground clearance and a block is put under one side of the car and the lever is then set for the lowest level, the wheels on that side will rise off the ground automatically, thus dispensing with the need for a jack for wheel changing.

The first cars, like the carriages before them, had brake blocks which could be applied externally to the rim of the wheels. Rising speeds soon called for more efficient means of stopping quickly, and the internal expansion brake has proved the most economical and effective general solution. The brake is used to dissipate, in

the form of heat, the kinetic energy of the moving vehicle and bring it to a standstill.

The internal expanding brake came into general use in the 1920s and consists of two or sometimes three brake 'shoes' faced with a compound with good frictional properties which press outwards against the rim of a shallow drum attached to the wheel. The heat generated by friction is conducted to the air through the outer rim of the brake drum. The first brakes were operated by a cam action controlled by levers or cables. All modern systems are hydraulically operated through a small cylinder with two opposed pistons which, under hydraulic pressure, move the shoes outwards into contact with the drum.

Disc brakes are old in principle but are only now finding favour with car designers. They consist of a flat disc and the braking action is achieved by caliper pads which grip the periphery of the disc when the brake is applied. By careful design, disc brakes can be made to brake more evenly than internal expansion types, and brake 'fade' is less of a problem. Disc brakes are not very suitable for use in

parking so it is common to have internal expansion brakes at the rear and discs at the front. This is another example of compromise in car design.

Although cars have developed comparatively slowly to their present state of development over a period of some 60 years, this does not mean that intensive effort is not put into improving design. However, each new move forward becomes increasingly difficult and costly. Science has given us new materials for detailed improvement. No car is produced today, for example, without plastic fittings and some plastic furnishing. Some cars have complete bodies built from glass fibre. But while striving for perfection the designer is hampered always by the need for compromise, not least being consideration of whether it can be sold at a competitive price and if it can be mass produced efficiently.

The Ford Capri, announced a few years ago, was a typical new car with old features. The engines are common to other Ford models and so is the gearbox. The engine is forward mounted and the rear wheels are driven. Disc brakes are fitted forward and drums at the rear. And yet Ford's investment to make the car amounted to £20 million when tooling as well as research and design costs were included.

The car of the future

If there is a revolution to come in car design what may we look for? Technology has already taken care of many of the chores of driving. The automatic gear box on the more expensive models has dispensed with the need for changing gear, and power-assisted brakes and steering are already commonplace.

We may yet see a return to steam propulsion and, almost certainly, the scientists will crack the problem of electric traction, the development of which is still hampered by the weight of batteries. The fuel cell, once thought to be a good solution when fully developed, is not now thought to be suitable for private cars according to one study carried out in the United States in 1968. Instead, a high-temperature alkali-metal battery is suggested.

Whatever the shape of the car of 2000 A D and its type of propulsion, it will be a safer and better car than today's. Car design is no longer a hit and miss affair. Analogue and digital computers, wind tunnels, test tracks, finely equipped laboratories, strain-recording gear and many other aids are available to the designers at the assembly plant. The component suppliers making brakes, tyres, headlamps, carburettors, clutches and a host of other essentials which go to making up the complete car also have their individual research and development programmes. And so do the oil and petrol companies in their search for better fuels and lubricants.

If we now take our cars for granted as essential, economical and trouble-free daily work-horses we not only have to thank the manufacturers but an army of scientists and technologists who have made it all possible.

Down to the mines

Mining for coal, metals and precious stones was one of the earliest forms of large-scale industry. Although modern mines are deeper, mechanization is doing away with much of the danger and drudgery.

AMONG THE MANY endearing rags-to-riches stories, one of the most appealing is that of Dick Whittington, the poor boy who rose to fame and fortune through the ownership of a half-starved cat. The tale loses some of its charm, but in compensation becomes credible, when it is realized that the 'cat' or 'catch' refers in reality to a type of ship used to carry coal from Newcastle to London. Whittington was a forerunner of the mine-owners who made vast fortunes from coal in the eighteenth and nineteenth centuries, and even of the few miners who made fortunes in the Alaskan 'gold-rush', and who frequently lost them within months in shanty-town saloons.

But Whittington was by no means the first to benefit from mining, the extraction of useful minerals from the Earth's surface. Ancient civilizations extracted gold, silver and copper for making into decorations and utensils; precious and semi-precious stones were used both in jewellery and as items of barter long before money was in general use; and iron and bronze were used for weapons and body armour.

To most people, mining almost invariably means coal mining; the familiar picture is of dark underground tunnels with men labouring in hard and dangerous

A train of heavy trucks loaded up with ore from a chute in the Nkana copper mine near Kitwe, Zambia. The train will take the ore to the foot of the main shaft, for transport to the surface.

conditions to extract the valuable black fuel. Coal was, until comparatively recently, almost a universal fuel and it is in coal mining that almost all modern techniques of location and extraction have been developed.

It is not clear when the organized extraction of underground coal really began. By 1200 A D there were coal pits on the southern shore of the Firth of Forth, near Edinburgh, and in Northumberland. About this time, the importance of coal in trade was increasing rapidly, so that people in all parts of Europe were beginning to dig for the precious mineral, although in a haphazard way.

Early methods

Two methods of mining were in general use: digging pits or burrowing into the side of a hill in search of a seam. Of the two, the first method was the more widespread. But although these coal workings were called pits, they were in fact only relatively shallow holes in the ground. When all the coal had been extracted from the pit, the digger would move off a few yards and dig another, and so on until he reached the end of the seam or the coal became too deep for him to reach.

Much more productive was the technique of hill tunnelling. Here, diggers tunnelled into a hillside until they reached a coal seam, and then excavated horizontal branching tunnels along the coal. These coal quarries often developed into quite

complicated systems of passages in which the miners dug the coal by the light of rushes. Despite the fact that mines of this type supplied large quantities of coal as a fuel both for ironworkers and domestic hearths, their yield was severely limited by roof falls which often closed down the workings altogether.

One of the most spectacular of the early mines was that at Culross, in Fife, started by monks and referred to by them as a 'carbonarium'. Although worked by men who had nothing more than primitive wooden and cast-iron tools, this mine had many miles of galleries early in the seventeenth century. One such gallery extended for nearly half a mile out under the sea, and ended in a vertical shaft which emerged on an artificial island. Coal was brought up the shaft to this island, where it was loaded directly on to boats for transport to London and Europe.

The quarrying method used for coal in the early days of the industry was also in common use in the extraction of other minerals, notably tin and gold. In North America, gold was still being mined by this method as recently as the 1930s, although with the addition of modern aids such as pit props and infilling which reduced the risk of roof falls and allowed extraction

Washing for gold in the Australian outback. Ore placed on the chute is washed over 'riffles'. The heavy specks of gold are trapped while the lighter dirt is washed away.

to be more complete. In the seventeenth century, when the supply of minerals readily available near the surface was beginning to run out in Europe, men began to sink shafts in search of deeper deposits. This was at first merely an extension of the old pit method, except that the shafts were sunk deeper, often to a depth of several hundred feet, and the mines were equipped with windlasses for raising coal and miners.

At the bottom of the shaft, in the coal seam, digging took place in every direction, as far as it could go before the roof caved in. From their shape, these pits were known as 'bell' pits, and became common in most European countries. But although bell pits were much more productive than older systems, they were also extremely dangerous. Not only did the roof fall frequently but many miners lost their lives from fire, explosion or simply lack of air. In a coal mine, there are two main causes of explosion: methane, which is found in coal seams, and which is highly explosive when mixed with air, and coal dust, which also forms an explosive mixture with air. In addition, the deeper workings were subject to flooding, and many otherwise suitable coal seams had to be abandoned because there was no convenient method of removing the water.

The development of modern mines depended on the recognition of these problems and the devising of solutions. All deep workings are now designed to make mining as safe and as comfortable as possible, while ensuring that extraction is efficient.

A modern mine

A modern mine is designed around two shafts, known as the upcast and downcast shafts. In the sinking of a mine, work starts by digging one of these shafts towards the mineral deposit. This shaft is usually between ten and 25 feet in diameter, although some mines have elliptical shafts whose larger axis is greater than this. As the digging progresses, the shaft is lined with casing to prevent rock and earth falls and to exclude water which might seep in from the surrounding earth. Progress through the topsoil is usually fairly rapid, but when rock is encountered it used to be necessary to blast a way through, nowadays high-speed rock drills are used.

When the shaft has reached the working level, another similar shaft is sunk nearby. One of these two is termed the downcast shaft, that is, the route by which air is drawn into the workings, while the other is used for extracting stale air and gases. This upcast shaft is also the route by which the extracted mineral reaches the surface, while the downcast shaft is used for taking the miners to and from the workings. As fresh air must be circulated to all parts of the mine, the bottom of the downcast shaft is always the lowest part of any mine. Although the shafts are connected by a tunnel, this is sealed by an air-tight door, so that the air must circulate completely round the mine before being mechanically removed.

In most modern mines, roads or tunnels

1 A derelict coal mine at Tylorstown in the Rhondda Valley, Wales. Large numbers of British coal mines have been abandoned in favour of relatively few highly-mechanized pits.
2 An open-cast copper mine at Chingola, Zambia. Heavy earth-moving equipment makes it possible to extract very large amounts of ore cheaply where it occurs fairly near the surface.
3 A more primitive type of open-cast mining is seen at this West African gold mine. Gold was mined in Alaska and California by similar methods in the early days of the great gold rushes, though most surface gold is almost exhausted.

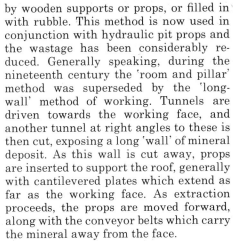

1 Another view of the Chingola open-cast copper mine. The ore in this region is so rich that it has proved economic to excavate virtually a whole mountain to extract the copper.

2 Drilling for diamonds at a mine in Uganda. The diamond-bearing rock is blasted with explosives and brought to the surface, where it is broken down and searched for the precious stones.

3 A tin dredger in operation near the Jing Jang mine at Kuala Lumpur, Malaysia. The heavy metal-bearing mud on the river bottom is a rich source of tin and of smaller amounts of antimony and other metals.

by wooden supports or props, or filled in with rubble. This method is now used in conjunction with hydraulic pit props and the wastage has been considerably reduced. Generally speaking, during the nineteenth century the 'room and pillar' method was superseded by the 'long-wall' method of working. Tunnels are driven towards the working face, and another tunnel at right angles to these is then cut, exposing a long 'wall' of mineral deposit. As this wall is cut away, props are inserted to support the roof, generally with cantilevered plates which extend as far as the working face. As extraction proceeds, the props are moved forward, along with the conveyor belts which carry the mineral away from the face.

The miner's pick is now giving way rapidly to machinery, although in Europe this has been a recent development; indeed, there was virtually no power coal cutting in Britain until after the Second World War. By contrast, in 1950, 91 per cent of all bituminous coal mined in the United States was extracted mechanically, which accounts for the enormous American output per man-shift.

Mining machines

The simplest type of mechanical aid to mining is the cutter which weakens a coal deposit by gouging out a slit at floor level. Explosives placed in this slit are used to bring the coal down, and a machine pushes the broken coal on to the conveyor belt. This method is closely analogous to the 'shot firing' technique for loosening coal deposits; although the use of explosives can be dangerous in the confines of a mine, it eliminates the need for hewing the coal with picks. Machines which are more nearly automatic in operation fall into two main types: cutters and gougers. One of the most successful of the coal cutters is the Anderson Boves trepanner. Looking rather like a giant power-driven apple-corer, it cuts deep into the coal with a rotating motion. Unlike most other mechanical cutters, it produces a high proportion of large coal, which is still demanded by many users.

Strangely, one of the latest machines to be devised for this work imitates the action of a miner with his pick. Blades resembling pick-heads are mounted on a wheel which rotates horizontally into the seam, cutting and pulling out the coal in one action. Although regarded as an entirely up-to-date machine, this cutter bears a striking resemblance to the Gillot and Copley coal cutter of the mid-nineteenth century.

Mining ploughs were developed principally in the Rühr coalfields in Germany, where the coal is soft and easily worked. These machines are very similar in action to agricultural ploughs with steel blades 'turning' the coal. Coal is brittle, and falls away in pieces, and as many of these ploughs have driving tracks which double as conveyors, the coal is automatically collected by the track and removed from the working face, as they crawl forward along the seam. Although ploughs tend to produce small coal, they are widely used because of their speed. Some will

are driven from the bottom of the shafts along the direction of the mineral-bearing stratum. These roads are in groups of three: the first is a passageway for the miners, the second is for extracting the mineral, while the third is primarily for ventilation. At an early stage in the sinking of a new mine, powerful pumps are installed to extract water from the workings, and the winding machinery at the pithead and the huge air extractor fans are erected.

Three principal methods of deep mining are in use today. By far the oldest of these is the 'room and pillar' method, in which the seam is worked in passages at right angles to each other, with the pillars between the seams being left in position to support the roof. Although a safe method, and in fact the only one which was feasible before pit-props and plates to support the roof were used, this method is very wasteful. As the demand for coal became greater, however, various methods were devised for extracting these pillars. When the 'rooms' were worked out, the pillars were then removed and replaced

remove a strip of coal a foot thick, while the faster versions skim from two to six inches in one rapid pass.

During the Second World War, when coal was in urgent demand, mining engineers reverted to a method of extraction similar to that used by early miners. Known as strip or open-cast mining, this technique involves removal of the overlying strata by mechanical diggers, extracting the coal and then replacing the top layers of soil. The coal obtained by this method is generally of poor quality since it lies fairly close to the surface but strip mining lent itself to mechanization using existing earth-moving plant. Even now when deep mines are using highly automated equipment, open-cast mining is still vastly superior in terms of yield per man.

In an age when the machine has taken over most of the dirty, arduous tasks in industry, it seems a little incongruous that men should still have to work in unpleasant and dangerous conditions deep in the Earth. What prospect is there for fully automatic mining? Equipment is already in existence which can detect coal and guide the cutters using gamma-ray detectors. The machine will then cut and load entirely automatically so that it is possible to bring coal to the surface without it being touched by hand. But development of such equipment is still in its comparatively early stages and at present the large amounts of dirt brought out with the coal make the process uneconomic. Mining by water-jet, although it has been used for many years in gold-mining, is now being adopted for extracting many minerals. Jets of high-pressure water are directed at the face, and the force breaks

the mineral down. Although the resulting mud is generally loaded on to conveyors for transport to the surface, the slurry might also be pumped to the surface. Another possibility is that the mineral can be transported using the latest fluid-bed techniques, already used for transport of solid materials on the surface.

But as the demand for solid coal as a fuel diminishes, another more interesting prospect is opened up – underground coking of the coal to produce coal gas and extract the valuable chemicals. Apart from the prospect of completely automatic mining, this process would allow the exploitation of coal deposits which would be uneconomic to work by other means. Although underground coking and gasification has been used from time to time in the United States and Europe, it is used on a large commercial scale in Russia.

Fires are started at the coal face, and a carefully controlled supply of air is pumped to the burning face, while the gas is drawn off through a second shaft.

World demand for minerals is increasing rapidly every year, and although known reserves are still substantial, there is great interest in the rich deposits which are known to exist in the Antarctic. Previously, these had been considered uneconomic because of their remote situation and the difficulties which would be experienced in exploiting them, but modern technology has made these deposits an attractive proposition to mining interests.

It has also been proposed that an incidental benefit of space exploration will be new sources of mineral wealth on the planets. Whether these will ever in fact be used is a matter of debate. Mining on Earth may have come a long way from the shallow pits of the Middle Ages, but there are few mining engineers who would suggest mining the moon before Earth techniques become fully automated.

1 The interior of a coal mine in India. Despite using a modern coal-cutting machine, the miners have neither boots nor helmets to protect them from falling rock.
2 A diver prospecting for gold in the fast-flowing Chaudiere River, northern Canada. The divers dredge gravel from the river bed and its gold content is analyzed.
3 A woman tungsten miner in Burma uses a crowbar to chip metal-rich rock from outcropping tungsten seams. Tungsten is used to make specially hard steels and in light-bulb filaments.

Energy from underground

Coal and petroleum, despite their different modes of extraction, are both fossil fuels. The by-products of these two great sources of energy are the basis for chemicals, dyestuffs and plastics.

1

2

1 Liquefied propane gas, a petroleum by-product, is used in Tokyo, Japan as fuel for taxis. The gas is considerably cheaper than petrol and is said to give longer engine life.
2 Drilling for oil on Zakynthos Island, off the coast of Greece. The oil-field on this island was known to the ancient Greeks, who used asphalt seepages to caulk their ships.

THOUSANDS OF YEARS before a drilling rig darkened the Texan sky, the infant Moses was consigned to the Nile in a basket which, so the Bible tells us, was made comparatively waterproof by caulking with bitumen, mineral oil which seeped through the sands of the Middle East. At about the same time, the natives of Glamorgan, in Wales, were incinerating their dead on pyres fuelled by coal.

From these beginnings, coal and oil have developed to become the primary fuels of civilization, and what is more, are in the twentieth century the source of an enormous range of raw materials which have changed the whole concept of chemical manufacture. It has been said that coal and oil between them provide all the materials necessary to feed, clothe and house us. Although this may, when it was said, have been slightly premature, it

is by no means the wild exaggeration which at first it appears.

Many people think that coal is formed from some type of rock, but its origins lie in the dank tropical forests of the Carboniferous Period, which ended about 270 million years ago. These were not like the present forests, but were rather huge areas covered with giant ferns and club mosses. In the tropical conditions prevailing at the time, these plants grew rapidly. They reached maturity, decayed and finally fell, to be superseded by a new generation. Over many centuries, masses of rotting vegetation, estimated to have reached heights of several hundred feet in places, built up. In time, perhaps due to volcanic action, the forests sank and the sea inundated the land. As the cycle continued, new forests arose on the sea-borne silt, and frequent repetition led to a layered structure of vegetation, silt and sometimes rock thrown up by volcanic action or earthquakes.

Over millions of years the enormous heat and pressure engendered by the overlying rock wrought a change in the masses of rotting vegetation. Like the plants of today, those strange ferns and mosses of the Carboniferous Period were composed almost entirely of carbon, hydrogen and

oxygen. Heat and pressure combined to drive off much of the hydrogen and oxygen, so that the proportion of carbon increased.

It is interesting that the deepest layers of coal, subjected as they were to the greatest pressure, and also of greater age than those above, are very rich in carbon compared with layers nearer the surface. In extreme cases, notably in Switzerland, the process has produced pure carbon in the form of graphite. But normally, the coal with the highest carbon content is anthracite, a hard, shiny, almost smokeless fuel. Anthracite contains 94 per cent carbon, but at the other end of the scale, lignite, a young brown coal, contains only about 66 per cent carbon. The youngest form, which is not really coal at all, is peat, used as a fuel in many parts of the world.

Oil formation

Similar accidents of nature brought about the formation of oil, although it is of animal as well as vegetable origin. Millions of years ago when the Earth was mainly covered by water, millions of tiny marine creatures lived and died and left their remains on the bed of the sea. Over the ages these deposits reached great depths and the accumulation, supplemented by plants washed down from the land, formed a thick slimy ooze on the sea bed. Mud brought down by river action mingled with this ooze, and the animals and plants slowly turned into oil and gas. The pressure of the seas eventually turned the mixture into oil-bearing limestone or sandstone, both of which were porous and retained the oil rather as a sponge holds water.

By a fortunate accident, many of these oil-bearing rock formations were later roofed with impervious rock layers which retained the oil. As the Earth dried out, many of these deposits were topped by land formations, but there are still a great many rich oil-fields under the bed of the sea. But whereas pressure and the passage of time has made coal almost entirely carbon, oil still retains its hydrogen and is a mixture of compounds of hydrogen and carbon.

Although oil has been under the Earth for millions of years, it was not until the nineteenth century that it was commercially exploited, much later than coal. People had gathered the oil which seeped to the surface through cracks in the rock cap and a few enterprising men went to the length of digging pits to concentrate the seepage.

In 1859 an American, Willard Drake, drilled the first oil well, which fortunately was a producer, and founded the modern oil industry. This was at Titusville in Pennsylvania, and his discovery led to a tremendous upsurge in drilling in that

The acetic acid plant at British Petroleum's Salt End, Hull, chemical factory. Acetic acid, an important constituent of a number of plastics, can be produced from petroleum.

area of the United States.

By the time Drake struck oil, the Industrial Revolution was well under way, running on coal. And coal was already being processed to yield its chemicals as well as driving the engines of industry. At a very early stage in coal-mining it was noticed that along with the coal occurred a highly explosive gas called methane, which caused a large number of deaths among miners through the use of naked lights in mines. It is by no means certain who first distilled coal to produce coal gas and use it in lighting, but it is recorded that an Englishman, George Dixon, lit one of the rooms in his house with coal gas – an experiment which came to an end with a spectacular explosion.

William Murdock, a Scottish mill-wright's son, was the first to produce gas in commercial quantities at a price less than that of candles – then the normal means of illumination. He constructed gas-making plants for sale to commercial firms, and also designed gas holders. But no history of the development of coal gas is complete without mention of Samuel Clegg, a former pupil of Dalton the famous chemist. To celebrate a visit of foreign royalty to London, he erected an 80-ft-high wooden pavilion illuminated by 10,000 gas jets. As an incidental bonus the spectators had the pleasure of seeing the whole structure burnt to the ground.

Widespread use of gas for heating and lighting depended on the availability of efficient retorts for distilling the coal, and it was in retort design that William Murdock made his greatest contribution. There are now two main types of retort, vertical and horizontal, but the latter is more useful in large plants because it can be loaded and discharged automatically

1 Aerial view of the Salt End chemical plant. Note the storage tanks for liquid and gaseous products in the background and the maze of pipes linking the various processes in the plant.
2 Drilling for natural gas in the North Sea. New areas of exploitation for oil and natural gas are constantly being opened up, though prospecting costs are very high.

by conveyors. These retorts produce gas by heating the coal in the presence of limited quantities of air. The gas is drawn off and passed through chambers which extract ammonia, coal tar, benzole and naphthalene. The residue in the retort is coke, which is itself an excellent fuel.

But the economics of the simple retort depend on a large steady market for coke. While houses were heated by open fires, the disposal of the coke was no problem, but the growth of central heating often makes these large supplies of coke an embarrassment. The coke can be converted to another gas, water gas, by passing steam and air over the red-hot coke. Water

Petroleum by-products are used in the manufacture of paints and dyes. Here distemper is being mixed with pigment in a pan mill at a paint factory in Stratford, London.

has, however, is of a lower grade than coal gas and must be mixed with methane before being fed into the mains for distribution to consumers.

Large stocks of unsaleable coke are avoided by using the Lurgi process, which has the added advantage of using low-grade coal rather than the expensive and scarce coking coals used in other processes. The plant is run at a pressure of about 25 atmospheres. Coal is heated and a mixture of oxygen and steam passed through it. The high pressure and temperature cause the formation of a mixture of carbon monoxide and methane, which is an excellent fuel. When the gas has been purified, it is ballasted (its density is adjusted) by adding nitrogen and generally some butane. The advantage of the Lurgi process is that it produces gas at high pressure so that it can be fed directly into

the main or into high-pressure storage without pumping. Of the by-products of coal distillation, coal tar is the most important from the economic point of view. Not only is it used for tarring roads, but under distillation it gives more than 200 useful chemicals. An interesting sidelight on one of these products, naphtha, is that in the early nineteenth century Charles Mackintosh used it to dissolve rubber which he then used to waterproof cloth. This was the beginning of the Mackintosh waterproof coat.

To describe the production and use of all the products of coal would take a sizeable book, but some idea of the diversity of products can be gathered from the fact that coal is the source of detergents, explosives, drugs, dyes, alcohol, paints, lubricants, motor spirit and even food. The last two are of particular interest, as many countries have no oil deposits of their own and many more countries suffer from lack of adequate food. Research into the manufacture of motor spirit started as early as 1916, but the cost was always too high in comparison with petrol produced by distillation of crude oil. In the late 1960s, however, a team of German chemists succeeded in bringing the price down almost to that of naturally produced spirit.

Food from coal

Protein research has shown that it should be possible to synthesize simple proteins from the elements in coal, and indeed this has been done. Although these do not taste like normal food, they have become a valuable animal feeding supplement, and further research should produce something which is acceptable as a supplement to the diets of the poorer countries. These proteins are also produced from oil, and since many of the oil-rich areas of the world are desperately short of food, it will be possible for the people to eat part of their crude-oil output.

But whereas there has always been a large demand for coal, when the first barrels of oil were filled there was only a tiny market. Most of the oil produced was used for caulking ships, oil lamps or for lubrication. However, during the eighteenth century many research workers investigated the possibilities of constructing an internal combustion engine, one that would dispense with the cumbersome boiler of the steam engine. Oil came to the market at just the right time, and road transport now runs almost entirely on oil products.

Oil as it comes from the well is not immediately usable, however. It is a mixture of light and heavy hydrocarbons – light oils, like petrol and paraffin; heavy oils, such as those used for lubrication, and heavy waxes. Before oil can be put to its many uses, these parts or fractions must be separated. This is done in a fractionating column, which employs the different temperatures at which these fractions

Printing inks are also by-products of oil refining. The inks have an oil base specially designed to give them the required properties of penetration and drying.

vaporize to separate them.

In the fractionating tower, the temperature is carefully controlled so that at each level, at a temperature slightly below the vaporizing temperature of each main fraction, there is a collecting tray. The hot crude-oil vapour is brought in through the bottom of the column, and the heaviest fraction condenses at the bottom. The remainder progresses upwards, as the temperature is still too hot for it to condense. But the temperature decreases further up the tower and one by one the fractions condense to liquids and are tapped off and stored. At a refinery many fractionating towers may be in use simultaneously and the crude oil is pumped in sequence through them to give complete separation.

This, however, is only one of the stages involved in oil refining, although it is the most important one. But simple fractional distillation gives an abnormally high proportion of heavy hydrocarbons – the lubricating oils and waxes – much more in fact than can be absorbed by the market. The main need is for the lighter oils for motor and aviation spirit.

The invention of the catalytic cracker (cat cracker) enabled the refineries to redress this balance between supply and demand. In a catalytic cracker, the heavy hydrocarbons are broken down by chemical action to give light hydrocarbons. In this way, the output of motor spirit per barrel of crude oil can be doubled.

During the Second World War a new industry, the petro-chemical industry, grew up on oil. Because of the war, the rubber plantations of the Far East were not available to British and American industry. As the armies needed rubber desperately for tyres and components in many pieces of equipment, scientists developed synthetic rubbers from oil. This was only a beginning, but by 1960 synthetic rubbers were being used in the majority of tyres, and the type of rubber used was adjusted to suit the tyre characteristics required.

Synthetic rubber production, however, is only a small corner in this vast industry. Like coal, oil is the starting point for an amazing variety of products, drugs, paints, explosives and plastics among them. The last is perhaps the most important of all and the development of plastic materials has transformed twentieth-century living. Although natural gas is often found in the same deposits as oil, there is also a demand for gas made from oil by a further cracking process; this is used in many countries to supplement supplies of coal gas or natural gas.

The coal and oil industries grew out of the demand of people for power – power to keep themselves warm, power to drive their transport, and power to generate electricity. But as the primary purpose of these fuels was warmth, it is interesting to note that scientists have established that the carbon dioxide produced by burning these fuels is forming a layer over the Earth and raising the atmospheric temperature slightly but steadily each year. Coal and oil are extremely versatile commodities; but it is the final comment on their utility that, even after they have been used, and the waste products have escaped from the control of Man, they should still be, accidentally, producing the end result for which they were first used.

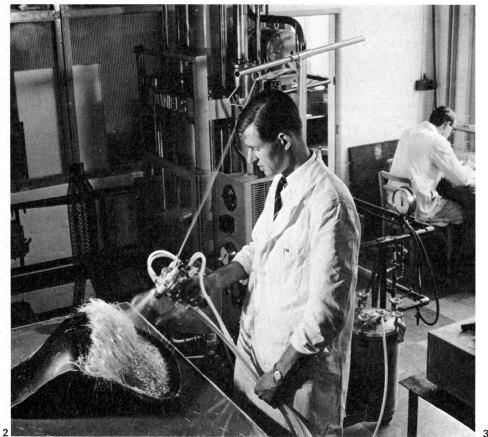

1 Naphthalene, used for moth-balls and the basis for other chemicals, is a by-product of the coking process. Here solid naphthalene, separated from oven gases, is drilled out of a tank.
2 A technician at a South Wales plastics factory produces a test moulding by spraying resin and glass fibre on to a mould. The resin, a thermoplastic, is formed from petroleum by-products.
3 Horizontal 'retorts' like these were at one time used to produce gas in Britain's major cities. A great deal of coal was used to produce coal gas for domestic and industrial use.

Inside the engine

Millions of years ago, Nature began storing energy by creating petroleum from the decaying remains of prehistoric life. Now this energy is being tapped and put to work in heat engines.

THE CAPACITY for doing work is usually called energy, and heat is a form of energy which has (like any other form of energy) the capacity of being partially transformed into useful mechanical work. This is the basis of the First Law of Thermodynamics. Since it was established, Man has consciously tried to use this knowledge to find ways of turning this capacity of heat to his advantage. An obvious way that this can be done is to build machines which can effect the transformation of heat energy into work. Machines which do this are called 'heat' or 'thermal' engines.

The Second Law of Thermodynamics says there is a definite limit to the amount of mechanical energy which can be obtained from a given amount of heat energy; within this limitation engineers have always tried to make their engines more efficient – to convert the heat generated into the maximum possible amount of mechanical work. When we say that an engine has 40 per cent thermal efficiency we mean that it converts 40 per cent of the available energy into mechanical work of one kind or another – the other 60 per cent being wasted. However, size and running costs are other practical considerations which the engineer must consider and very often they are as important, if not more so, than thermal efficiency.

Designs for efficiency

When the compression ignition engine was first introduced with a thermal efficiency approaching 40 per cent, it was said that it would displace steam plants in power stations, which then had an efficiency range of 30 per cent. But in fact this has not happened, because steam plants were found to be more reliable, more suitable for continuous working and less liable to breakdown.

While there are many different designs of heat engines, they all work on a common principle. Gas or vapour which is heated expands rapidly, and this is used to provide energy in one of several ways. In the steam engine, or the conventional internal combustion engine, the expanding gases impart motion to a movable piston, which then transfers this motion by mechanical linkages to driving wheels, airscrew, or ship's propeller. In a turbine, whether of the steam variety or fuelled by some other material such as kerosene or diesel oil, the gases, moving at high speed, convert their energy into useful mechanical work by driving what is, in effect, a sophisticated windmill. Jet engines, on the other hand, use the energy in the gas much more directly. These gases are allowed to escape at high speed through a nozzle so that they transfer energy to the vehicle (usually an aircraft) according to Newton's

The development of commercially practical steam engines transformed human society. *Top,* the elegant steamship *Britannia* here sets out on her maiden voyage from Liverpool in the year 1840. *Above,* steam locomotives opened up the American west, accelerated the Industrial Revolution and, as a result of train schedules, dramatically sharpened Man's awareness of time.

Third Law of Motion (action is equal to reaction). In these various ways the energy in the hot gas is made to do useful work.

The first practical heat engine devised was the *reciprocating steam engine,* in which a piston is pushed to and fro in an enclosed cylinder by an expansion of high-pressure steam. The steam is produced by evaporating water in a boiler heated by a fire in which any fuel may be burned.

The admission of steam to the piston cylinder is controlled by a valve which opens when the piston is at one end of its stroke, remains open for a short time to pass the required amount of steam – which starts to push the piston along – and then closes while the steam expands and pushes the piston to the other end of the cylinder. This process is then repeated, with steam now pressing against the other side of the

piston to push it back along the cylinder, while an exhaust valve opens to allow the surplus steam on the other side of the piston to escape. This cycle is known as *simple expansion* and is the most common method of driving steam locomotives.

However, in their continual quest for greater thermal efficiency, designers have sometimes made use of the exhaust steam, drawing additional work from this 'waste' which still contains a considerable amount of energy. In these engines, partly expanded steam from the high-pressure cylinder is put to work in an additional low-pressure cylinder before being allowed to escape into the air. This is known as *compound* or *double expansion.*

A further development is *triple expansion,* in which the steam passes from the high-pressure cylinder to an intermediate cylinder and thence to a low-pressure cylinder, so that minimum pressure is wasted. This system is too cumbrous and space-consuming for most locomotives, but at one time was widely used in ocean-going ships where, cost notwithstanding, it is important to obtain the maximum amount of work from each ton of fuel.

Internal combustion engines are so called because the burning or combustion takes place inside the engine – in the cylinder, unlike the steam engines, where it takes place outside the engine in the boiler which produces the steam.

All internal combustion engines work on much the same principle whether they use petrol or diesel oil. The fuel is mixed with air and is ignited in the cylinder in which there is a piston. When the mixture ignites, the expanding hot gases produce a sudden pressure in the cylinder. This pressure against the piston forces it down in the cylinder. Connecting rods attached to the piston transmit the work generated to other parts of the engine. Once again the First Law of Thermodynamics applies – heat energy is converted into mechanical work.

Most petrol engines in use today are *four stroke* – that is to say there are four strokes or phases which go to make up one work cycle.

At the *induction* stroke, the piston is drawn down in the cylinder and as the piston goes down a mixture of petrol and air is sucked in with it. This mixture consists of a mist of petrol suspended in air. It enters the cylinder through a valve called the inlet valve, which is automatically opened by the working of the engine. When the piston reaches the bottom of its stroke, it is pushed up in the cylinder by a crank to which it is attached. This is the *compression* stroke. During this stage, both inlet and exhaust valves are closed and the cylinder is tightly sealed. On its upward journey, the piston compresses the mixture into a space as much as 14 times less than it occupied before. When the piston nears the top of the cylinder, a spark is generated between the points of the spark-plug, which explodes the mixture.

Two-stroke simplicity

Because petrol or diesel oil is highly inflammable, it burns rapidly and the burning mixture heats to a high temperature and a high pressure. These gases exert great pressure on the walls of the cylinder and piston head. As the piston head is the only moving part of the cylinder, it gives way before the pressure and is pushed to the bottom of the cylinder. This is the *expansion* stroke.

The *exhaust* stroke occurs as the driving force of the explosion ends and the piston is driven upwards again by the momentum of a heavy flywheel. Meanwhile, the exhaust valve at the top of the cylinder opens and the burnt gases are swept out by the upward-moving piston. When the piston reaches the top of its stroke the exhaust valve closes and the cycle begins again.

The thermal efficiency of the internal combustion engine depends very largely

Top, automobiles have brought Man the freedom of wide-ranging mobility and the irritation of nerve-racking traffic jams. In addition, petrol engines pollute the atmosphere, so many nations are seeking to replace them with large rapid-transit systems and battery-powered mini-cars. *Above,* an artist's conception of Britain's new *Queen Elizabeth II,* a modern luxury ocean liner.

on the amount of compression given before ignition. The higher the compression, the greater the possible efficiency. This is one reason why it is uneconomical to run a large engine continuously at small loads. This does not entirely apply to the diesel engine, however, which is not throttled and which is much more economical of fuel than the petrol engine under partial loads. The fraction of the heat supplied to the engine which is converted into useful work (known as the *brake thermal efficiency*) diminishes rapidly as the load is reduced even when the indicated thermal efficiency remains the same.

The *two-stroke* engine is comparatively cheap and its structure is very simple, hence its popularity for motor cycles. It differs from other combustion engines because it needs no valves. The induction inlet and the exhaust outlet are opened and closed in sequence by the piston.

When the piston reaches the top of its upward stroke it has compressed the fuel mixture and also closed both the transfer and the exhaust port. Only the fuel inlet into the crankcase remains open and a mixture of petrol and air is sucked through it in the form of an 'atomized' mist. Immediately the explosion takes place, the piston is forced down rapidly. As it goes down it closes the inlet and exhaust ports and starts to compress the fuel-air mixture in the crankcase. Towards the end of this stroke it opens the exhaust to the suction ports to allow the exhaust gas to escape from the cylinder and a new charge of mixture to pass from the crankcase to the cylinder.

The compressed mixture enters the cylinder through the suction port, sweeping the burnt gases out through the

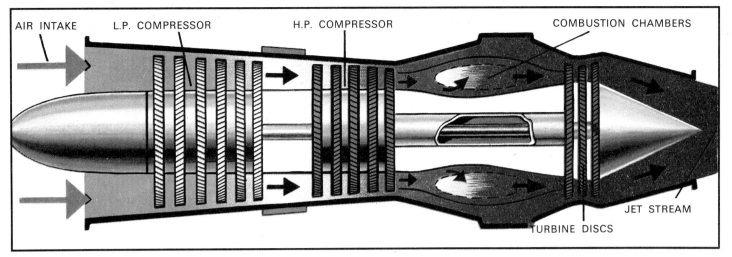

AIR INTAKE L.P. COMPRESSOR H.P. COMPRESSOR COMBUSTION CHAMBERS

JET STREAM

TURBINE DISCS

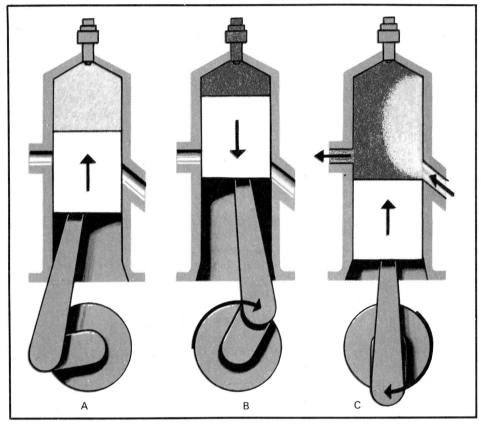

A   B   C

Above, a turbo-jet engine is little more than a hollow tube. Air taken in through the front passes through compressors, mixes with fuel in the combustion chamber, and then ignites. Propulsion is produced by the force of gases exhausted through the rear. *Left,* in a two-stroke engine, a mist of petrol mixed with air is compressed as the piston moves up in the cylinder (**A**) and ignited by a spark-plug (**B**). The piston is forced downward by expanding gas, which is exhausted out of one port as more fuel enters through the other (**C**). *Below,* two-stroke engines are most commonly found in motor cycles.

exhaust port at the same time. The piston then moves up again, closing all the ports. It compresses the mixture in the cylinder and a fresh explosion takes place.

Another type of internal combustion engine is the *diesel engine,* invented by the German Rudolf Diesel (1858–1913). It is now widely used in heavy lorries, motor ships and railway locomotives which are powered by diesel engines. The diesel engine works by burning diesel fuel oil, which is not as expensive as petrol. A diesel engine has neither carburettor nor spark-plug, but instead an injector which forces fuel oil under high pressure into the cylinder through a fine nozzle. Although the diesel engine is slower and heavier than the petrol engine, it is more economical and needs less maintenance.

At the induction phase the piston moves downwards and sucks air into the cylinder through the inlet valve. On its upward journey (the compression stroke) the piston compresses the air. This compression heats the air to temperatures as high as 1,100–1,300°F. At the injection stroke oil is injected through a nozzle into the cylinder above the piston, forming a fine mist in the hot air. Because of the very high temperature the mixture burns and the gases which are generated push the piston down. This is the expansion, or working stroke. Finally, the piston rises again and expels the burnt gases.

The gas turbine is another form of heat engine which is based on the same principle as all other heat engines, namely that when a gas (in this case air) is heated, it exerts more pressure. Gas turbines normally utilize paraffin or diesel oil, and although they often seem to be very complicated because refinements are added for greater efficiency, their operating principle is very simple.

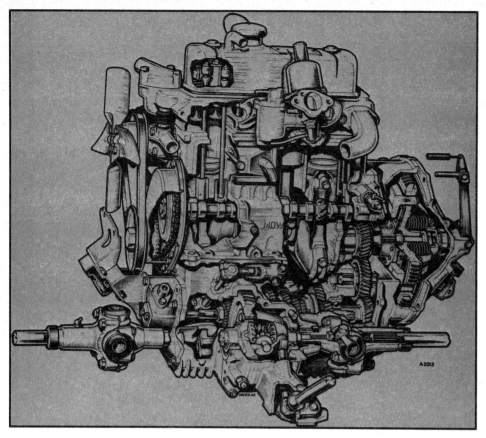

is used to work the compressor. When built on a large scale, a great volume of air is forced to the engine and as it escapes backward is concentrated as a jet which can be used to propel a vehicle – usually an aircraft. Engines of this type are called *turbo-jet* engines and can develop so much thrust that they have supersonic capabilities.

In addition to aircraft, gas turbine engines are used in hovercraft, hydrofoil marine craft and they have been used experimentally in cars. An established industrial use for the gas turbine engine is in remote-control power stations which can switch in electricity at peak times to supplement the conventional supply.

The advantage of the gas turbine engine for aircraft is that they are lighter than piston engines of equivalent horsepower and can be designed to reduce wind resistance; the fact that they usually run on paraffin also reduces the fire hazard.

One of the earliest jet engines was the *ram-jet,* which is very much like the pipe described earlier to demonstrate the principle of the gas turbine engine – indeed it has been called the 'flying stove-pipe'. A ram-jet is simply an open tube with no moving parts. As the aircraft moves forward, the air forced into one end of the tube is then mixed with fuel and ignited. The expanding gases cannot escape out at the front because more air is being 'rammed' into the tube. Thus the gases are forced out at the back and the reaction then drives the aircraft forward.

The ram-jet can be very powerful but it has one great disadvantage: it cannot work at less than about 200 miles per hour, because at speeds less than this the air in front of the plane is not scooped up fast enough to meet the demands of the igniting fuel. For this reason, planes or missiles which use a ram-jet engine must be launched with a booster before the ram-jet can be brought into action.

Strides towards perfection

Although the gases which leave a modern gas turbine engine may be forced out at speeds of more than 1,300 mph, the speed of a plane depends not only on the speed of expulsion of the exhaust gases, but also on the weight of the expelled gases. Some jet engines take advantage of this fact by injecting a mixture of water and alcohol into the combustion chamber. This injection adds weight to the exhaust gases and gives an extra thrust to the engines.

Jet engines need air to burn their fuel and for this reason will only work within the Earth's atmosphere. The *rocket* engine carries oxygen in tanks with it, so it can be used outside the atmosphere into the vacuum of space.

Designers are continually working towards the greater efficiency of heat engines and at the moment engines, such as the fuel cell, are being developed which will increase efficiencies even further. So far we are nowhere near achieving maximum thermal efficiency from our engines. Incomplete combustion, an inevitable loss of heat from the cylinders – and particularly friction losses – prevent an attainment of the theoretical maximum.

Top, to the non-mechanic, an internal combustion engine can be a frightening conglomeration of gears, wheels, cylinders and pistons. But to the mechanic, it is a masterwork, translating abstract physics into practical reality. *Above,* the world's introduction to jet-powered flight was anything but auspicious. But the V-1 flying bombs led the way to Man's adventure into space.

Basically the gas turbine engine is a piece of pipe. At one end of this pipe is a small fan which draws in air and blows it along the inside of the pipe. At the rear end, a similar fan is arranged pointing in the same direction. When the front fan is rotated, the air which is pushed into the pipe can escape only by passing the rear fan. As it escapes this air will turn the blades of the rear fan with a force which is almost equal to that used by the front fan in pushing the air into the pipe.

The flying pipe

Now imagine that in the middle part of the pipe there is a small hole through which a tiny jet of fuel is pumped. When the jet is lit, the flame heats the air inside the pipe and in consequence the air expands. To escape from the pipe this larger volume of air must flow past the rear fan more quickly than the smaller volume of cold air and thus the blades of the rear fan are turned more rapidly. Work which the rear fan can do exceeds that needed to

turn the front fan, and if the two fans are mounted on a single shaft, the power obtained from the rear fan is enough to turn the front fan, yet leaves sufficient power in the shaft to provide energy for some form of work.

In practical applications the front fan is replaced by a compressor. This is simply a more complex type of fan which usually consists of several different sets of blades designed to draw great quantities of air into the engine. The air passes into the combustion chamber where it is heated by a flame of paraffin or diesel oil. It increases in volume and escapes past the *turbine,* the rear fan turning at a tremendous speed. The turbine turns the compressor which as a result draws in more air.

In some gas turbine engines the power in the shaft is used by means of a series of gears to drive a conventional propeller. Such engines are called *turbo-prop* engines and have use in aeroplanes. In others, however, almost all the power in the shaft

The steam age

Many people do not realize that despite the advance of the internal-combustion engine, steam power continues to play a prominent part in the production of electricity and even in nuclear submarines.

AS THE FIRST of Man's many forms of mechanical power, steam is today commonly regarded as archaic. We even use the adjective in derision to mean something crude or outdated. Although it is no longer widely used by railways, steam propulsion has never ceased to be a dynamic technology. Steam power generates almost all the electricity used in Britain; it is a highly competitive method of driving large ships and is the almost universal method of using the heat from nuclear reactors. Steam is immensely important in many branches of industry in 'process plant' in which some form of physical or chemical reaction is involved. This wide use is all based on the fortunate fact that on Earth we have an abundant supply of water, a relatively dense liquid that is non-poisonous, cheap, easily pumped through pipes and valves and that can absorb a great deal of heat energy in being converted to vapour at high pressure.

The inventors of the first steam engines at the start of the eighteenth century were mocked and abused when they tried to make steam do the work previously done only by muscles. A century later those who tried to put steam engines to work driving carriages, trains and ships were

also treated as madmen. Most of their critics tended to equate steam power with the fires of Hell, and complex and ingenious arguments were often put forward to show that such fearsome engines would pollute the air, poison humanity physically and morally and destroy the wholesome agriculture by which nations lived.

The first steam engines also had to contend with the powerful influence of Aristotle who had decreed that 'Nature abhors a vacuum'. This was because the

only way Man knew how to use steam before about the year 1725 was to admit steam to a cylinder closed by a piston and then condense the steam back to water (for example, by pouring cold water on the cylinder). The cylinder full of steam would rapidly return to a volume of water about 1/1300th as great and the pressure of the atmosphere acting on the piston would then drive the piston down to fill up the volume previously occupied by the steam. Denis Papin, a Huguenot refugee from

1 This watercolour by Rowlandson shows one of the first steam trains on a demonstration track near Euston Square, London. It was built in the early nineteenth century by Richard Trevithick.
2 James Watt's first steam engine revolutionized the use of steam power. By adding a condenser to the cylinder containing the steam, Watt was able to prevent waste of heat in the engine's cycle.
3 Early steam carriages, such as this 1860 model, were extremely clumsy, very slow, and had to stop at regular intervals to get up steam. There is renewed interest today in steam power for cars.

Blois working in Germany, built various model engines on this principle from 1690 on; and the Englishman Thomas Savery devised a water pump he called 'the miner's friend' which had the same action. The strange name was given because all these early steam engines were constructed to pump water out of mines.

These early steam engines were often called 'fire engines', and it was not uncommon for preachers to pray for the souls of the misguided men who sought to raise water with the power of fire. The engines were extremely inefficient machines, because the cylinder was heated by the steam one moment and then deliberately cooled down by cold water the next, so that rather more than 99 per cent of the heat from the original fire was wasted. The man who first saw the cause of the inefficiency and did something about it was the poor Scots laboratory instrument maker James Watt. Legend has it that he was first set thinking about steam by wondering what power lifted the lid of his grandmother's kettle as it boiled away on the fire. He made a thorough study of the properties of water and steam, calculating the temperatures, pressures and quantities of heat needed to boil given masses of water at different pressures and the quantities of cold water needed to condense a given volume of steam. In 1763 the University of Glasgow, where he worked, asked him whether he could make the university's Newcomen engine work better.

Increased efficiency

Watt realized that the inefficiency lay in wasted heat in cooling the cylinder and then heating it again. He made a working model of the first engine ever to have a condenser, a separate vessel in which the steam is turned back to water while keeping the cylinder itself as hot as the steam from the boiler. It was obvious to Watt that he now held the key to steam engines far more efficient than any built before; he then set about writing a patent for his method of 'lessening the consumption of steam, and consequently fuel, in fire engines ...'

Unlike so many others, Watt happened to find a way to turn his ideas into reality. He had once met Matthew Boulton, the young owner of the great engineering works at Soho, Birmingham. Boulton was one of the few men at that time with the talent and money to back Watt, and soon the firm of Boulton and Watt was established. The ironmaster John Wilkinson devised a way of casting then accurately boring large cylinders six feet in diameter that 'did not depart from absolute truth in the worst part more than a thin sixpence', and in 1774 the first of the new engines was on test. It soon proved its power and efficiency and orders came thick and fast. At first most were required by British mines and factories, but gradually the fame of the new steam engines spread overseas and by 1800 Boulton and Watt had delivered 500 engines – a figure that grew to 10,000 sold in Britain alone by 1824. Watt incidentally, spent months in courts of law, trying to protect his firm

against unscrupulous rivals who stole his ideas as soon as they were seen to work.

The steam engine swept through industry, replacing the waterwheel that stopped during a dry summer, the windmill that worked when the wind blew strongly enough, the treadmill that worked when unfortunate beings were forced to turn it, and the power of the ill-used beast of burden or labourer. Steam power helped Britain to become the 'workshop of the world'.

One of the first to utilize steam for transport was a French artillery officer, Nicolas Joseph Cugnot, who in 1769 pro-pelled himself about Paris in a steam tractor – until he ran into a wall. Then in 1801 Richard Trevithick, helped by Watt's assistant William Murdoch, completed a more practical steam carriage and ran it up to Camborne Beacon summit with seven or eight men hanging on to it. Three years later he won a £500 wager by making a steam locomotive move a load of ten tons; in fact it pulled a train laden with this weight of iron as well as 70 passengers. By 1808 he had run a train at the amazing speed of 20 mph.

There was no great success in making a railway for public service until 27 Septem-

1 Diagram of a gas-cooled nuclear reactor. The hot gases from the reactor are made to turn water into high-pressure steam in a heat exchanger. The steam can then be used to drive turbines.

2 The *Flying Scotsman,* perhaps the world's most famous steam engine, on its last run out of King's Cross Station. British Rail have now abandoned steam in favour of diesel and electric power.

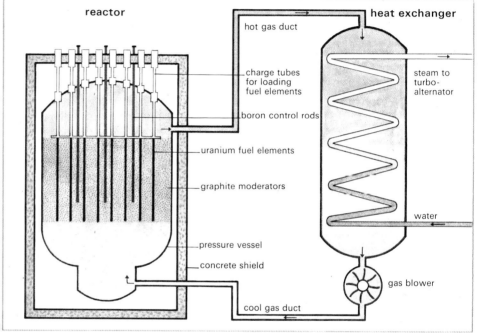

1 The Burrell traction engine *Princess Royal* on display at the annual traction engine rally near Cambridge. Steam engines of this type are still used on fairgrounds, and also as steam-rollers.
2 The heyday of the Mississippi steam-boats was the end of the nineteenth century. But a few examples of these large paddle-steamers survive, like Cincinnati's *Delta Queen*.

3 Nowadays, the steam engine is often regarded as a toy. This simple engine demonstrates clearly the principles involved in much more complex and larger steam engines.
4 The nuclear submarine H.M.S. *Dreadnought* moored in Portsmouth Harbour. Like other nuclear submarines, *Dreadnought* uses steam power to propel the turbines which drive her propellers.

ber 1825, when the Stockton to Darlington Railway opened. The line was built by the son of a poor mineworker who taught himself to write when he was 19: his name was George Stephenson. The first train was made up of 34 trucks carrying old mail coach bodies. The first six were laden with coal and flour; the next was occupied by the directors of the new railway company; 21 coaches of guests came next (there were almost 450 of them); and at the rear were another six coaches full of coal. The ten-mile trip took just over an hour.

The idea of the railway could at last be seen to work, but when the much larger cities of Liverpool and Manchester tried to join each other by rail there were riots, protests of all kinds and endless obstruction in Parliament. It took nine years for the opposition from landowners

and the road carriage owners to be overcome; then Stephenson built a masterpiece of engineering called *Rocket* to haul trains on the 30-mile route. *Rocket* was a great advance on earlier steam engines and it drew passengers at 26 mph and ran light at 35 mph. To the amazement of the onlookers, Stephenson's lungs were not sucked inside out, nor did the devil make off with him. As early as 1843 the British rail companies were carrying more than 18,000,000 passengers a year – as many as the rest of the world combined.

In contrast steam never really gained a foothold on the roads. Although by 1810 at least a dozen steam coaches had run successfully, all attempts to use them commercially from 1831 to 1860 were handicapped by the terrible roads. These crumbled under the weight of the smoky monsters, and the tollkeepers, seeing this,

slapped on crippling charges which can still be read on the old toll boards preserved in many British museums. While an ordinary coach might have to pay a toll of a shilling, a steam driven 'horseless carriage' might be levied five shillings *per wheel*. So, even though steam driven lorries and cars were occasionally built they never caught on.

At sea, after a few halting attempts in the eighteenth century, the steamship became the normal method of marine propulsion. At first steamships were thought to have little advantage over sail apart from the fact that they could sail up a river without having to tack from side to side; and, in any case, they always retained their full rig of sails. But by 1860 bold designers began to leave the sails off, and improved steam engines driving better paddle wheels or screw propellers enabled ships to run a greater distance in a day than even the best sailing ships, and to do so with far more certainty. All the first steamships had what are known as reciprocating engines, the only type of steam engine then being built, in which the steam drives pistons up and down in their cylinders and thus, via connecting rods, turns a crankshaft round

1 Early motor vessels, like Bell's *Comet* in this photograph, had steam engines but also retained their sails. This ship is driven by paddle wheels on either side of the hull.

2 The British destroyer H.M.S. *Viper*, seen here during trials in 1900, reached a speed of 37 knots with its revolutionary turbine engine. This was far faster than any previous naval vessel.

and round. But in 1884 Sir Charles Parsons made his first steam turbine and it is the turbine, in which the steam acts directly on blades on a spinning shaft, that has today become the most important type of steam engine.

Although it is one of the most modern types of engine the steam turbine is also perhaps the most ancient, because Hero (or Heron) of Alexandria made a toy steam turbine in about 100 A D. But Parsons triggered off the modern steam turbine, and he put it in the public eye by fitting turbine engines into a small boat he called *Turbinia* which was so successful that the Admiralty ordered Parsons to make a turbine-engined destroyer, and the resulting vessel, H.M.S. *Viper*, did 37 knots – far faster than any previous naval ship in the world.

Steam turbines

Today the steam turbine is the main means of driving the largest ships and much of the world's electricity generating plant. Modern turbines work just like those installed in *Turbinia* except that they are much larger and use steam of a very different quality. The basic aim in any steam engine is to take as much as possible of the original heat – liberated by burning coal or oil, for example – in order to put it to work heating the water and turning it into steam with as little wastage as possible. Just how successful the engineer is in doing this has always depended on the materials available, how

much money can be spent on designing and building the plant and how safe it should be in use.

A century ago it was considered daring to make a boiler deliver steam at 40 lb pressure per sq. in. The *Britannic* and *Titanic,* huge passenger liners built just before 1914, had piston engines taking steam at 215 lb per sq. in. pressure while the world record 50 megawatt electricity generating plant installed in Chicago in 1928 pushed the pressure up to 600 lb. Soon after the Second World War the standard generating set in British power stations was rated at 200 megawatts and was driven by steam at over 1,000 lb. per sq. in., while today we use 500 and 660 megawatt sets (each capable of supplying a million people with all their domestic electricity) driven by steam at 2,350 lb pressure per sq. in.

The increase in pressure is not merely beneficial in itself but comes coupled with higher temperature, just as it does in domestic pressure cookers. At ordinary atmospheric pressure water boils at 212°F., and on a high mountain it may boil at a temperature of no more than 180° or even 170°. But at 1,000 lb per sq. in. the temperature exceeds 1,000 °F. The boilers that generate such steam in modern power stations are as big as the largest 30-storey office blocks. They burn pulverized coal or oil with flames 100 feet long and the steam is generated in hundreds of miles of special stainless-steel pipe. The steam is then admitted to the blades of the high-pressure

turbine. The steam expands through dozens of rows of whirling blades, each row larger than the last.

Not only is a steam turbine plant of this type extremely efficient, with an overall 'thermal efficiency' of about 40 per cent compared with a thermal efficiency of 1 to 2 per cent for the steam locomotives and steam engines of a century ago, but it is designed to run continuously for many years. The first turbine built by Parsons in 1884 would have needed 22 lb of coal burned in the boiler for each unit of electricity it could generate. By 1900 the earliest big steam turbines actually put to use in generating electricity had reduced the figure to about 3 lb. In 1969, despite a general worsening in the quality of coal, the giant 500 megawatt installations generate a unit of electricity for not much more than half a pound of coal burned.

Now these machines are in competition with nuclear power, where the amount of nuclear fuel burned in making a unit of electricity is millions of times smaller. A nuclear reactor is simply a vast generator of heat. Unlike the traditional boiler it does not have to be fed with huge quantities of coal or oil but will run at high power for years on a single charge of fissile material. It contains no moving parts, apart from a cloud of neutrons which are the actual carriers of the energy from the heart of each atom. Once the reactor has been made 'critical' it will continue to generate heat until a material that absorbs neutrons is inserted to slow down the reaction. If no means were provided to withdraw the heat, the reactor would get hotter and hotter and eventually melt. In practice the reactor is made to behave as a furnace heating a steam boiler. In most British reactors the heat is taken out by carbon dioxide gas, which is pumped round and round a sealed circuit, giving up some of its heat to the water boiler on each circuit. In America's nuclear power stations the water is usually passed right through the reactor according to two methods, the 'pressurized water reactor'.(PWR) or the 'boiling water reactor' (BWR). In either case, the nuclear power is turned into steam power, and it is a steam turbine that drives the electric generator.

Nuclear ships

Nuclear ships, nearly all of which so far are naval vessels, are thus all 'steam driven'. In this case it is important to make the propulsion machinery compact as well as absolutely reliable and efficient. All the latest and largest submarines have steam turbine propulsion with the heat provided by a nuclear reactor, and in this case there is the added need not to contaminate the atmosphere.

Finally, many designers in the United States have since 1960 been trying to decide what sort of machinery will be needed in future space stations to generate electricity and serve other functions. There is no doubt the most efficient arrangements use rotating machines of various kinds driven by a form of steam power. Their steam will probably be vapour produced by molten metals.

Quinqueremes and Queens

From the crude rafts of early Man to the quinqueremes of Mediterranean traders, through steamships to modern Cunard Queens, the history of shipping is a dramatic story of struggle with nature.

THE SHIP has had a profound effect on the progress and spread of civilization. 'Trade follows the flag', said the comfortable Victorians – and of course the ship carried both to all corners of the Earth. Because of their importance, ships have received a great deal of attention from inventors: in ship design and building, science has been put hard to work.

The modern ship has evolved from the very much simpler craft of ancient times – craft like the canoe, raft and coracle. But Man first ventured on the water in something much simpler even than these. He must have noted that trees or branches which fell into water floated and consequently reasoned that these would probably bear his weight as well. Here lies the first scientific principle of the ship. Although the early sailors did not know it, they were demonstrating Archimedes' principle – that an object will float if it displaces a weight of water the same as or greater than its own – many hundreds of years before it was formulated by the great Greek engineer. They also discovered that collections of fallen branches made a more stable floating platform and that large logs could be hollowed out to form dug-outs.

We have more information about the early ships of Egypt than any others. There were papyrus reeds in plenty, and the

1

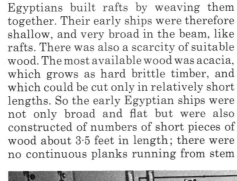

2

1 Clay model of an ancient Greek ship, found at Mochles, Crete. The high prow and stern and the typical curve of both ends are well shown.
2 The *Great Eastern*, built in Britain in the 1850s, had paddle-wheels, propellers and sails. For 40 years she remained the largest ship ever built.
3 Henri Beaudout, Gaston Vanackere and Marc Modena took 88 days to reach Falmouth from Nova Scotia on this primitive raft in 1956.
4 The control room of one of the first nuclear-powered merchant vessels. The N.S. *Savannah* can go round the world without refuelling.

Egyptians built rafts by weaving them together. Their early ships were therefore shallow, and very broad in the beam, like rafts. There was also a scarcity of suitable wood. The most available wood was acacia, which grows as hard brittle timber, and which could be cut only in relatively short lengths. So the early Egyptian ships were not only broad and flat but were also constructed of numbers of short pieces of wood about 3·5 feet in length; there were no continuous planks running from stem to stern of the vessel.

The Greek historian, Herodotus, tells us that these pieces were put together like bricks and then dowelled or dovetailed. The 'bricks' were clamped together by long gunwales which often swept upwards and backwards at the bow to form a spring and gave added resilience to the structure. The spring often terminated in a carved figurehead; a characteristic feature of the pharaohs' ships.

The Egyptian vessels had no keel – they

3

4

depended on their great beam for stability and this, added to the shortness of the hull components, brought problems of longitudinal strength. The second characteristic of their ships was a long truss which was placed overhead and stretched the length of the ship. It was of course secured at the bow and the stern to provide the needed stiffening.

Propulsion for these unwieldy vessels was usually by oars. Square sails were nevertheless developed and these were used to supplement the oar power when the wind was suitable. Here, 'square' does not refer to the shape of the sails but to the fact that they were set across the centre line of the boat from left to right. The sails were therefore suitable only for running before the wind.

Biremes, triremes, quinqueremes

The Minoans of Crete who dominated the sea trade of the Eastern Mediterranean at an early period, developed their ships from a different tradition. Crete was extensively covered with huge cypress forests, some of which grew very tall. The very early Cretans therefore adopted the dug-out as a means of travel and, about 2000 BC, discovered that they could make this type of craft even more effective by building up the sides with planks.

Cretan ships were lighter in relation to capacity than the Egyptian vessels and the fact that the heavy dug-out section was situated at the bottom of the hull meant that stability could be maintained without resorting to great width in the beam. In fact the concept of the keel developed from this stabilizing dug-out section. The Cretan ships, and those of the Greeks and Romans, were faster as well as being narrower, than the Egyptian vessels.

The main worry of the Cretan shipbuilders was to make the built-up planking watertight where it joined at stem and stern. They overcame this problem by setting the stem and stern posts back from the ends of the keel or dug-out section. Such an arrangement meant that the projecting keel took the major force of the water rather than the planking joint at the post. The resulting two-pronged bow is called a *bifid bow*.

The Phoenicians ousted the Cretans as the dominant sea power. Like the Romans they travelled as far as Britain, but it has also been suggested that they may have been the sailors employed by King Necho of Egypt in 600 BC to circumnavigate Africa, a marathon journey which took three years. The early Phoenician ships had straight keels and high end posts; they were lightly built for speed and were perhaps the first ships to have two banks of oars on either side (this kind of ship was called the *bireme* – later Grecian and Roman versions had three banks and were called *triremes*; there were even five-banked ships – the *quinqueremes*). The Phoenicians may also have built upon the bifid constructional ideas of the Cretans and developed the bow ram for their fighting ships.

In more northern latitudes ships appear to have developed more recently than in the Mediterranean, yet in some ways they seem to have evolved in a similar manner. The Norsemen did, however, pioneer a totally new method of boat construction in which the planks used to build up the dug-out were not laid edge to edge as in the Mediterranean ships, but overlapped. Boats constructed in this way are said to be *clinker-built* (the edge-to-edge method is called *carvel* construction) and such partial lamination provides extra strength and watertightness.

Steering in the Viking ships, and indeed all the early ships so far mentioned, was by one or two oars at the stern.

In these early ships can be seen a number of scientific principles put to work. First, there is the exploitation of buoyancy as described in Archimedes' principle. Then, with the development of the pointed bow and sleeker lines to the hull, we see early application of hydrodynamic ideas. Oars are simple mechanical levers, and the development of the keel shows that shipbuilders early understood that the lower the centre of gravity in a vessel the more stable it is likely to be.

Most of these considerations have remained important to the shipbuilder right up to the present day in constructing conventional craft. Others have, of course, disappeared from the scene with the arrival of new materials – like iron, steel and glass fibre – and new methods of propulsion.

As ships became steadily bigger, they became more and more difficult to move by means of oars. The early sailors had a ready-made answer to their problem in the sail, but for a considerable time they could only see one aspect of its usefulness – for catching winds blowing from astern. The sail to them was nothing more than an auxiliary propulsion system.

The Vikings developed a system by which their ships were able to sail close to the wind. They turned their square sails edge-on to the approaching wind, so that in effect they ran 'fore-and-aft'. The pressure of the wind caused the fabric of the sail to form an aerofoil section; the sail adopted the curved shape similar to the upper surface of an aeroplane wing. An aeroplane is able to fly because the air has to flow faster over the upper surface than the lower one. Because of this, a partial vacuum is formed above the wing which, together with the higher pressure under the wing, tends to lift it upwards. The same

1 The *Queen Elizabeth 2* during construction at John Brown's shipyards on Clydeside. The internal structure of the massive hull with its honeycomb of rooms is taking shape.
2 Tugs towing *Queen Elizabeth 2* down the Clyde after launching. The superstructure – the funnel and deck fittings – has still to be finished and there is still unfinished work below decks.
3 The liner *Queen Elizabeth 2* undertaking her first trials on the Firth of Clyde. Her trials were marred by problems with the complex turbines which drive her huge screws.

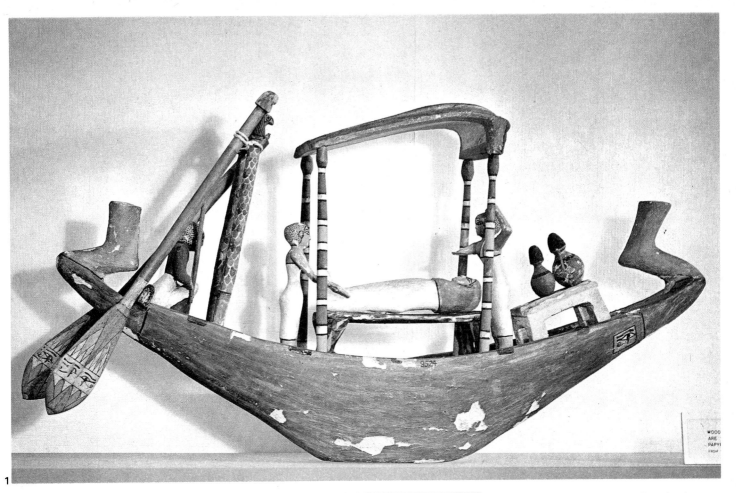

1 Wooden model of an ancient Egyptian funerary boat, found at Thebes. The shape of the ship, with its two pointed ends rising out of the water, is derived from boats made of papyrus reeds.

2 The *Cutty Sark,* probably the most famous of all sailing ships. This beautiful clipper was used for many years on the eastern run, bringing tea to London from China.

is true of the aerofoiled sail except that the force is horizontal.

The exploitation of this aerodynamic principle – whether it came by accident or design – opened the way for the age of sail. The next step was the invention of the truly fore-and-aft sail, that is one which is permanently set more or less along the centre line of the vessel. It is thought to have been invented in the eastern Mediterranean or the Indian Ocean.

Sail shapes

Various shapes of sail were then developed to perform in different fore-and-aft conditions. For example, where the vessel was required to do a great deal of its work close to the wind the sails were often triangular; where some of the trip at least was to be accomplished by exploiting strong following winds the sail remained four-sided so that it would catch the maximum amount of wind when pushed out over the *beam,* or side of the vessel.

The fighting ships of Sir Francis Drake, the Spanish galleons and the mighty clippers, used both triangular fore-and-aft and four-sided 'square' sails in various combinations for greater flexibility of operation. Others, like the many-masted trading schooners of the United States' eastern seaboard, used only the fore-and-

The four-masted barque *Lawhill,* built in 1892 for the Far Eastern case-oil trade. A number of windjammers were still in use on the Borneo run until well into the 1920s.

A modern oil tanker, the *Esso Bernicia.* Built in 1968 at Kiel, Germany, she is more than 1,000 feet long and has a dead weight of 190,600 tons. The crew's quarters in the stern are fully air conditioned.

aft kind, all of which were triangular.

Sail remained in the ascendancy for many hundreds of years and the designers concentrated on improving the hull shapes of their craft so that while they carried the maximum amount of payload they were also speedy and stable. They also used iron, copper, bronze and steel to clothe the wood; the first completely iron ships were built early in the nineteenth century. But nothing they did could really make up for the fact that the sailing ship was at the mercy of the wind.

Steamships

The advent of the steam engine in the early eighteenth century sounded the death knell of the sailing vessel. Steam soon became a reasonably efficient means of moving a ship through water. The steam engine became more refined, and eventually the steam turbine began to replace it.

Concurrently with the appearance of the steam turbine (Sir Charles Parsons patented the first in 1884), the internal combustion engine began to show its promise. The version which has been most widely used is that invented by Rudolf Diesel in 1892 and which bears his name – as does the fuel which it uses. Unlike the petrol engine this needs no spark to ignite the mixture of air and fuel in the cylinder. Instead, the diesel engine draws in air on the down-stroke of its piston. On the up-stroke, the air is compressed and its temperature is raised sufficiently to spark the injection of diesel fuel and so provide the necessary internal combustion.

But the power story does not end here. The Americans, Russians and Japanese are harnessing the nuclear reactor for propelling ships.

The early steamers used the power of their engines for propulsion by mechanical extensions of the oar concept. The closest to the original was the American John Fitch's *Experiment* which employed the power of the steam engine to work what have been called 'duck leg' paddles. Simply,

these were no more than three vertical oars set at the stern of the vessel. They were plunged into the water in rotation and then 'pulled' by the power of the engines.

More usually, however, the early steamboats were propelled by paddles arranged around a wheel. These wheels were set either at the stern as in the famous Mississippi riverboats, or on either side of the hull – as in the *Great Western* which from 1837 did 12 years on the trans-Atlantic run.

But none of these ideas was as effective as the propeller screw. The latter works like the windmill; the angled blades of the propeller press the water backwards away from the ship and consequently force the ship itself forwards. Of course, the paddle produces the same effect, but the important difference is that the three or four blades of the screw are all totally immersed in the water and thus are all doing useful work for the ship as long as the propeller is turning. The major part of the paddle wheel, however, is out of the water during any given revolution. During this time the 'dry' paddles are nothing but passengers.

In 1839 the efficiency of the screw principle was demonstrated by the small British steamer, *Archimedes*. Today, without exception, the major vessels which go down the slipways of the world are screw-driven.

Most modern conventional ships then are powered either by steam turbines or diesel motors; they are propelled by screws; they are constructed of steel. In addition, the marine architect has brought to a fine art the design of hull shape for effective travel through the water. But already there has been a new synthesis of the principles of flight and traditional ship design. It is to be seen in the emergence of the hydrofoil and the hovercraft.

In the first case, the ship does become a kind of aircraft. It rides over the surface of the water on stilts which terminate in ski-like foils. These work in water just like the wings of an aeroplane in air; they provide sufficient lift to raise the main body of the ship above the surface. The drag of the hull in the water disappears, and hydrofoils are therefore capable of very high speeds (up to 70 knots).

The hovercraft sucks air in through a giant fan on its upper side and pumps it out beneath the flattened hull. Flexible skirts contain this expelled air so that the hovercraft rides on a cushion of air over almost any surface. It is propelled by aero-engines mounted on the deck, and is in effect a very low-altitude vertical-take-off aircraft.

Container vessels

In the realm of the cargo vessel, important work has been done on the development of the container ship. In its most sophisticated form, this consists of three sections: a bow, a stern, and a central portion for cargo. The three are detachable and engines and steering equipment are situated either in the bow or stern. These are used to bring the full container into port, whereupon they are unbolted and reaffixed to another cargo section which has already been loaded – so that the cycle can begin again. Turn-round time is dramatically cut.

At the same time, oil tankers are becoming ever larger, and their length puts great strain on the middle of the hull in heavy seas. To overcome this, designers are looking at the possibility of hinged vessels, which 'give' to the violence of the waters.

The submarine may soon take the tanker's place as a cargo-carrying vessel. The important principle is that varying buoyancy enables it to sink or rise. But problems of water pressure must also be met and these, with the necessity of cheap and simple life-support systems, make submarines a complicated matter for the designers.

While the application of science to seafaring has taken Man to all corners of the globe, a great deal of work remains to be done. Probably the principal effort will now be directed at exploiting the possibilities of undersea transport. But for surface shipping there remains a vast potential, only now being fully tapped with the development of container ships.

A breath of 'fresh air'

Man lives more and more in artificial environments – in outer space, under the sea, in large office blocks. To survive he must be supplied with clean air, warmth, pressure and humidity.

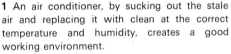

1 An air conditioner, by sucking out the stale air and replacing it with clean at the correct temperature and humidity, creates a good working environment.

2 Prefabricated buildings erected in tunnels bored out of snow provide American servicemen with a cosy refuge from the bitter winds and cold of Greenland's Arctic wastes.

TO STAY ALIVE, in addition to food and drink, Man needs a suitable environment. His natural environment consists essentially of a breathable atmosphere of gases in certain proportions and a climate which is neither too hot nor too cold. Suitable clothing plus artificial heating enables Man to survive extremes of terrestrial climatic temperatures, but he cannot survive for long in an atmosphere lacking the correct proportions of oxygen and other gases.

The atmosphere in a healthy environment, as well as being neither too dry or moist nor too hot or cold, must not be heavily polluted from extraneous sources. The air we breathe at the surface of the Earth and for a few thousand feet above it provides an adequate atmosphere, although a completely unpolluted atmosphere can now rarely be found. Despite the provisions of clean-air regulations and the enforcement of smokeless zones, the atmosphere in cities and urban areas is heavily polluted by carbon monoxide from motor vehicles and chemical and other fumes released from factory chimneys.

In large buildings, such as hotels, office blocks, cinemas, theatres and factories where large numbers of people congregate, the atmosphere becomes germ and bacteria ridden as the air is breathed in and out. In food processing plants a fresh atmosphere free of bacteria and unwanted odours is essential to hygiene. On the other hand certain industries require a damp and humid atmosphere for the successful processing of their products. One of these is cotton-spinning, where an excessively dry atmosphere causes the thread to become so dry that it snaps in the spinning machines. The damp atmosphere of Lancashire was one of the reasons for that county becoming the centre of England's cotton industry. Some industries, such as those making delicate instruments and precision machines, need an atmosphere that is neither too damp nor too warm, to avoid the corrosion or alteration in size of small metal parts.

But the most serious of all pollutants of the atmosphere is dust. Ever since the world solidified out of its original cosmic gases and diffused materials, dust has been suspended in varying degrees in its atmosphere. It is these minute particles of dust that help create fog and smog in and around large cities and industrial complexes. Even in rural districts far removed from urban centres, the air carries an alarmingly high percentage of dust which pollutes the air we breathe and contaminates the food we eat.

Without dust, however microscopic in quantity, the atmosphere would be hygienically clean, for dust distributes bacteria and other impurities in the atmosphere. Nevertheless, by using sterilizing sprays, the atmosphere can be rendered clean and bacterially sterile.

One way of providing a reasonably clean and unpolluted atmosphere in buildings and other enclosed spaces is through air conditioning. Basically, air conditioning consists of withdrawing air from an inhabited space, cleaning and purifying it, as well as bringing it to the correct temperature and humidity before it is returned to the space from which it was withdrawn.

The kind of air conditioning required can be varied. The equipment ranges from small, portable units for cleaning the air in a single room or a car to the huge plants that clean the air circulating throughout a building of many storeys. There are also the medium-size air-conditioning plants to maintain a normal and wholesome atmosphere in the pressurized cabins of airliners, within the hulls of submarines, and in the coaches of long-distance railway trains and road coaches.

A complete air-conditioning plant needs a mechanical ventilator, a filter and a unit to add or to remove heat and moisture. The temperature is regulated by thermostatically controlled heating or cooling units or by a combination of both. Heat is generated in the conditioned air either by the combustion of fuels or by electrical-resistance elements. Evaporative and refrigerative units are used for cooling. While refrigeration indirectly produces cooling by the air being in contact with a cold fluid, in the evaporation unit, as moisture evaporates into the air, it both cools and humidifies it. The hotter the air the more water vaporizes and the cooler the air becomes.

The moisture can be taken out of the air by condensing it over a cold surface or by passing the air over a desiccant which draws out the moisture. The quality of the air is regulated by forcing the air through filters to remove suspended particles. Although the air circulates naturally through any area, it is usually helped on its way by a mechanical pump. Extractor fans draw off the old air through ducts to a filter where dust and other solid impurities are removed. The air can be filtered in various ways. One depends upon changing the velocity at which the air is drawn through the ducts. Thus air may be drawn through the collecting ducts at a velocity of 4,000 ft per minute to be discharged into a chamber through an expanded duct which reduces the air speed to 40 ft per minute. Because the air is now travelling more slowly, the relatively heavy and solid impurities fall out and deposit on the bottom of the collecting chamber. A series of baffles prevents the currents or eddies induced by the moving air from sucking the deposited solids back into the slowly moving air stream.

Silent filters

Another type of filter incorporates an electrically or mechanically driven centrifuge, through which the air passes, and which forces all solid contents outwards. Air-conditioning engineers prefer to use non-mechanical filters as they contain no moving parts and are, therefore, less liable to deterioration or to be noisy. A simple filter of this type consists of a textile material stretched on a frame across the duct through which the stale air is passing. Filters of this kind collect a high percentage of solids but they are difficult to clean.

One of the most efficient of non-mechanical air-conditioning filters consists of a number of small cylinders placed side by side across the airflow to provide a honeycomb. The surfaces of the cylinders are coated with a viscous oil over which the air flows freely but to which its solid content clings. The oily surfaces of the cylinders become increasingly rougher with the deposition of the solids, but this merely increases the filter's efficiency in extracting solids from the air. When the solid depositions become so thick as to impede free flow of the air, the filters are easily cleaned by washing in hot soda-water and renewing the oil films.

After filtering, the air passes through a chamber where it is washed and its temperature raised or lowered by fine sprays of water. This dual function is possible because the temperature of air depends upon its water content and air's humidity can be increased or decreased by spraying water into it.

When the air being conditioned has a low solid content, filtering can be combined with washing and temperature and humidity adjustment. The water sprays are installed in front of the air inlet so that the

138

1 Men in a submarine may spend many hours submerged. Because they are breathing in a closed system the air must be constantly filtered and the exhaled carbon dioxide removed.
2 Water at depth exerts an immense pressure and a diver, supplied with air by a life-line to the surface, would suffer total collapse of the lungs unless wearing a helmet and suit.
3 As well as being airless, the moon is at the mercy of the sun's radiation. To keep cool the astronauts carry a special refrigeration unit in the packs on their backs.
4 By creating carefully controlled 'tropics' in a glass house at Kew Gardens in England, botanists grow the beautiful South African plant *Strelitzia reginae*.
5 Natural fibres become brittle and unusable when too dry. It is essential that during manufacture relatively high humidity is maintained in factories.

stale air passes immediately through them. This saturates the solids in the air so that their weight increases and they either fall into a sediment tank or are separated from the air by baffles.

After such treatment, the air still requires 'reviving'. This can be done by passing the air through carbon filters or, more efficiently, by treating it with an ozone generator. Ozone, which eliminates objectionable odours and is an antiseptic, is a condensed form of oxygen. When used in air-conditioning systems it reduces the amount of outside air required for re-circulation.

Ozone generators are simple to operate and resemble static capacitors with air as the dielectric. A capacitor, often miscalled a condenser, is an electrical device consisting of electrically conductive plates separated by a dielectric or insulating substance. In an ozone generator the capacitor plates are given an electrical charge, while the cleaned air passing through the conditioner acts as the dielectric. If, however, the charge on the plates is increased sufficiently, the insulating properties of the air break down and an electric spark passes through the air between the plates. The production of the spark ionizes the air and it is this that constitutes the source of the ozone. The ozone in fact derives from the oxygen in the air.

Threat of pollution

As a concentration of ozone in the atmosphere much in excess of 12 parts per million by volume would be harmful, only a fraction of the air handled by the conditioning plant passes through the ozone generator. The ozonized air is then injected into the main stream of conditioned air.

Industrial Man is so polluting the atmosphere of his environment that some health experts foresee the day when whole cities and industrial complexes will have to be enclosed in great plastic domes through which clean and conditioned air will be circulated to provide the inhabitants with a breathable atmosphere. They even go further and forecast farms covered by huge plastic domes in which plants will grow in an artificial environment independent of the natural, and often polluted,

atmosphere. Such farms will be free of the vagaries of weather and will be provided with carefully controlled ultra-violet and infra-red radiation to ensure healthy development of plant and animal life.

When Man ventures out of his natural environment to move under the sea or into space he must take with him an artificial environment which reproduces as nearly as possible his natural one. For astronauts and aquanauts, the artificial environment is not just a matter of providing a breathable atmosphere. The aquanaut must be able to survive pressures hundreds of times greater than the 14·72 lb to the square inch exerted on his body by atmospheric pressure at sea level on the Earth. The astronaut must take with him an artificial environment that enables him to survive fantastic extremes of heat and cold.

Since the earliest times men had been tantalized by the possibility of exploring the underwater world; but they first had to solve the problem of taking with them the breathable atmosphere. The earliest written reference to a device for breathing under the water is a passage in Aristotle (384–322 B C) which describes divers taking down with them weighted cylinders filled with air which they breathed through tubes.

Later Pliny (23–79 A D) tells of divers who drew air through a tube, one end of which they held in their mouths and the other made fast to a sphere floating on the surface of the water. Vegetius, a Roman author of the fourth century A D shows a drawing in one of his manuscripts of a diver wearing a tight-fitting helmet to which is attached a long leather tube leading to the surface of the water where its open end is kept afloat by a bladder. Throughout the succeeding centuries many other ingenious devices were invented for diving but none of them could have been used at depths much below 20 ft as they made no provision to counteract the pressure of the water which increases by approximately 4 lb per square inch for every ten feet below the surface. It was not until 1837 when Augustus Siebe introduced his closed diving dress and helmet which supplied the wearer with air pumped from the surface that really deep diving became possible. All diving suits now in use are based on the Siebe principle.

The pressure of the water on a diver working at, say, a depth of 100 ft would be 60 lb to the square inch and his muscles would not be strong enough to expand his chest to breathe in and out the air pumped to him from the surface. Therefore the diver is surrounded by compressed air pumped into his suit from the service ship on the surface. The compressed air is always delivered to the diving suit at the same pressure as the depth of water to which the diver has descended. Consequently, the pressure in the diver's body always equals that of the water outside his suit. By using special gas mixtures, including helium, suited divers can work for short periods at depths of 400 ft, where the water pressure is about 200 lb per square inch.

A new development in deep-diving is

independent diving or skin diving. In this type of diving the diver wears a skin-tight suit and a breathing mask. His air supply is contained in cylinders on his back and the pressure of the gases he breathes in can be adjusted according to the pressure of the water. The breathing equipment, called an *aqualung* is *self-regenerative*; that is, the exhaled air is purified of carbon dioxide by passing it through a suitable absorbent.

With the modern diving equipment, men can go down to depths of over 1,000 ft. Experiments have also been made with undersea houses provided with an artificial environment whereby divers can work and live far down in the sea for weeks at a time.

Survival in space

Astronauts voyaging into space require a much more elaborate artificial environment than aquanauts venturing into the depths of the ocean. A spacecraft's artificial environment or *life-support system* must be designed for an extended stay in completely airless outer space; as the craft clears the lower atmosphere in less than a minute after rocket blast-off, the artificial environment must come into immediate operation.

To survive in outer space the astronaut must have a pressurized cabin with means for replenishing oxygen, removing carbon dioxide and unpleasant odours, and maintaining within the cabin of his craft an ambient temperature and humidity approximating that which the crew would normally experience on Earth. Contour seats for the crew protect their bodies from the effects of high accelerations and decelerations during launching, mid-course manoeuvering and re-entry into the Earth's atmosphere. A heat shield on the outer surface of the spacecraft base prevents the craft and crew being incinerated by friction with the atmosphere during re-entry. A pressure suit for each crew member ensures his survival in the event of breakdown of the equipment maintaining cabin pressure and is worn when the astronaut leaves his craft during the voyage or when he lands on the moon or a planet.

Protection against radiation is also needed, according to the length of the mission and the flight path. A prolonged stay in the Van Allen Belts or a long interplanetary voyage, as from the Earth to Mars, requires greater radiation protection than does a low-altitude orbit flight. There also must be protection for the craft against the possibility of collision with meteor showers that could damage it.

Great as were the problems that had to be solved to enable astronauts to live in a spacecraft, the whole complex of equipment had to be so miniaturized that men who landed on the moon were able to carry their artificial environments on their backs. When manned observation posts are set up on the moon, the personnel will have to live in sealed buildings inside which will be an artificial environment similar to that provided for spacecraft, but on a much larger and more lavish scale.

1 The modern aeroplane flies at altitudes of 30,000 feet and more, where the air is far too rarefied to be breathed. The cabin must therefore be pressurized and the air conditioned.
2 Large modern buildings, such as airports and office blocks, are highly artificial environments.
The air is forced to circulate continually and is cleaned during the process.
3 The floor of this furniture factory has never to be swept clean of sawdust. Extractor fans linked to a system of ducts do the job more efficiently than a team of sweepers.

140

Storehouse of the sea

To meet the growing need for food, fuel and minerals, Man is turning to the sea. Through intensive study of the oceans, he is learning where this wealth is stored and the means to extract it.

THE OCEANS of the Earth – that is the actual water itself – contain more gold than all the land mines put together. In fact, sea water contains all the known elements. Some occur in high concentrations – sodium chloride (common salt), if totally removed from the water and spread out evenly, would cover the surface of the globe to a depth of some 450 ft. Others, in spite of their intrinsic worth, are diluted with such a vast quantity of sea water that extraction would be uneconomic. Still others, such as magnesium and bromine, are both useful and exist in large quantities.

The oceans have enormous potential as providers for mankind. Indeed, the elements dissolved in and extractable from the waters are just one aspect of the whole. The sea also provides food, energy and minerals from the sea bed – and the list is growing apace. The progress achieved in unlocking the door to the ocean treasure house rests to a great extent on the work of a group of scientists, called oceanographers. These scientists come from a wide range of fields: among their group are geologists, geophysicists, chemists and biologists.

Marine geophysicists and geologists are basically interested in elucidating the Earth's history. For this they need to know the topography of the ocean bed, so maps have to be made. They also examine the kinds of rock and sediment that occur in various places, and the ways in which these materials are arranged. Taken together, this may suggest ways in which the topography has changed during the Earth's history.

Mapping the sea floor accurately is generally carried out from a surface vessel. This presents a major problem; sea water is comparatively opaque to light and it is impossible to see the bed except in the shallowest of waters. The oceanographers, however, have overcome this by 'seeing' with sound – that is they employ the echo sounder. Equipment of a kind was in operation as long ago as 1922. Since then, primarily because of developments during the Second World War, equipment has improved. As a result the oceanographers have discovered many new underwater features – from vast underwater chasms to towering mountains.

Sounding the waters

The echo sounder basically consists of a noise source – nowadays an electric oscillator situated below the hull of the ship – and a receiver. When the oscillator is activated, a short ultrasonic signal is directed down to the sea bottom. There it is reflected and returns to the receiver as an echo. Since the speed of sound through water (about a mile a second) is well known, the depth of the sea bed can be

worked out from the time it takes the signal to make the two-way journey. The depths revealed by a continuous series of signals are automatically marked on paper to give a profile of the sea bed over which the ship is passing.

Echo sounding becomes less accurate in very deep waters. In a great thickness of sea water there are likely to be other recording surfaces like shoals of fish, and the beam of sound waves spreads out as they move away from the ship. This means that the further the reflecting surface is away from the emitting source, the greater

1 During seismic surveys, small surface explosions generate sound waves from which the number of layers on the sea bed and their depth can be identified. The geologist on a survey ship interprets the results from a continuous trace.
2 H.M.S. *Challenger* sailed around the world from 1872 to 1876, gathering information about the oceans, much of which is still relevant.

will be the area of it upon which the sound waves impinge. This area could be a mile across, and the returning echo could come from any part of it. Echo-sounding equipment mounted in submersibles, such as the all-aluminium *Aluminaut,* may provide the answer here, since the carrier can travel relatively close to the sea bed, and the crew can carry out visual checks.

In a great many areas of the ocean bed, the surface consists of sediment. To discover the depth of the underlying rock layers and their spatial relationships to each other, the oceanographers use a technique called seismic sounding. This is very similar to the echo kind, but relies for its sound source on the explosion of small charges on the surface of the sea. Thus a greater sound energy is emitted, part of which goes straight back to the receiver. But some of the explosive sound passes through the topmost rock layer before being reflected back to the receiver. A further proportion continues downwards until it reaches the next layer and some of it is reflected. By relating the time taken for the return journey by various parts of the signal to the known speeds of sound through various media, the scientists can work out the depths of the various layers.

Civil engineers also use such techniques for a multitude of purposes, such as to picture the kind of underwater terrain in which a communications cable must be laid, to monitor the build up of silt in harbour entrances and channels, and to reveal whether a particular geological structure is compact enough to allow some weighty construction like a bridge to stand upon it.

Tapping the oceans

The techniques amassed by the oceanographers have been used most spectacularly in the search for sea oil and offshore natural gas. Both of these valuable commodities tend to collect under humps of some impermeable material – it may be rock, clay or even salt – forced upwards in the sea bed by giant pressures from the interior of the Earth. The oceanographers' techniques can reveal such structures – as proved by the amount of oil which is being piped ashore from the sea bed around the United States and in the Persian Gulf, and the gas which comes ashore in Britain and Europe.

To establish the kinds of rock and sediments existing in various areas of ocean bed, the sea scientists have mostly had to rely on samples brought up by corer and dredge. But once again, the new submersibles come into the picture. Many are fitted with external manipulators which allow the scientists to gather samples at considerable depths in a much more accurate manner than before.

Nevertheless, surveys carried out by the old methods have revealed important deposits of valuable materials. Some have been exploited in a big way. Gravel extraction is a case in point, and even diamonds have been dredged up from the sea bed off the southwest coast of Africa. In South East Asia, tin comes from the same watery source.

Other important finds have yet to be

1 For centuries fishermen have used bright lights to attract fish into their nets. This method is being used on the Sea of Galilee, which, as in the time of Christ, still teems with fish.
2 In the search for oil off the west coast of Vancouver Island, a geologist takes core samples of the ocean bed. By taking regular samples he can trace the course of any oil-bearing rock.
3 Once they have matured sufficiently, artificially raised salmon and trout are transferred from their tanks into floating cages. The tides then ebb and flow over the fish.
4 When artificially rearing salmon and trout the breeder must accustom them to salt water. After the fry have hatched he transfers them to a tank into which he pumps salt water.
5 Mussels comprise one of the rich sources of food from the sea bed. They tend to collect on silt, and a dredger need not go far from shore to gather in its harvest.
6 Using an aqualung, the oceanographer can investigate the sea bed for himself. However, there are limits beyond which the diver cannot go in safety; he must then resort to other methods.

exploited. Oceanographers have located a phosphate of calcium called phosphorite in extensive deposits in comparatively shallow waters (averaging about 1,000 ft) off the coasts of the United States, Japan, South Africa, Australia and Spain. Phosphorite is vital to modern agriculture as a fertilizer and so will be in ever-increasing demand in the future.

Black lumps

There are also manganese nodules. These valuable black lumps, which also contain iron oxides, copper nickel and cobalt, were discovered on the ocean bed 100 years ago during what must be one of the most ambitious oceanographics expeditions ever to be mounted – that of the British corvette H.M.S. *Challenger.* The voyage lasted from 1872 to 1876 and ranged through the waters of the world in almost all latitudes, producing 50 volumes of information, much of which is still relevant. Later surveys have shown that

great areas of the ocean floor, particularly in the Pacific, are carpeted with these nodules. The Pacific's tally, according to the Institute of Marine Resources, University of California, stands at something like 1·5 million million tons.

But how to raise this wealth? Manganese is particularly vital in the making of many of the special steels used by industry. The trouble is that the nodules lie at depths around 14,000 ft and ordinary dredging methods are obviously unsuitable. One solution which has been suggested is that they should be sucked up by machines like giant underwater vacuum cleaners which are suspended beneath the mining vessels.

The biologists among the oceanographers are interested in the animal and plant life, particularly in establishing the links in the food chain and learning the

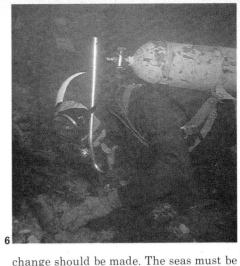

habits of the undersea creatures. For instance, how often and how does a species breed? Do they migrate? And if so, where? The commercial fisheries of the world need to know the answers to such questions.

The widespread use of sonar for fish hunting has helped to increase catches. Other methods – more novel – are also used. In the Caspian Sea, the Russians are operating boats which have electric lights, electrodes and a large-bore pipe hanging from the hull. The lights are switched on to attract the fish – mostly sardines – in the murky depths. An electric field is set up between the electrodes, and the current paralyses the lured fish. A shipboard pump then sucks up the massing fish in great quantities through the funnel-ended pipe.

Although the food resources of the oceans are very great, technical improvements like these may soon irreparably harm fish stocks. Indeed, some areas of the ocean are already barren, due to over-fishing even without the use of lights, pumps, or electric fields. Marine biologists have given frequent warnings about these dangers. But better still they have also come up with a possible solution, a way of reconciling conservation with the need for a rising food yield.

Thousands of years ago, the human being obtained his food in much the same way as other animals; he either hunted and killed it, or gathered it where it grew. Then he learnt to grow animal and vegetable foods for himself.

By contrast, fishing is still a hunting gathering process, in spite of the sophistication of modern methods. Now a number of scientists are urging that a radical change should be made. The seas must be farmed, just like the land. In essence, fertilizers should be added to the waters to promote plant growth, and since plants start the food chain, the size of fish populations would be boosted as well.

It is a pretty theory and appears to have sound practical backing at first sight. The Chinese proved that they could grow more, bigger and better carp by adding manure to the carp ponds. During the Second World War the fish yield of certain lochs in Scotland was improved by the addition of other fertilizers. The situation at sea, however, is very different. Currents would quickly disperse even the largest amounts of fertilizer until the concentration dropped to quite useless levels. But even if the fertilizers did work, they would also increase the pest population. In this context, pests mean the creatures which compete with edible fish species for food, yet are inedible themselves. The kind of inroads which such creatures can make into food resources is demonstrated by the discovery in Denmark that some 75 per cent of food material suitable for flatfish does not, in Danish waters, reach them. Instead it is eaten by such creatures as inedible starfish and sea snails.

The real answer may not be cultivating the sea, but fish farming. Here suitable adult fish are brought together in enclosed stretches of water for breeding to take place. Afterwards the eggs are collected in their thousands and put into hatcheries – large tanks with a steady flow of fresh sea water, no predators and no competitors. In carefully controlled conditions the hatched young are reared to a size at which they can be returned to the sea with a good chance of survival.

Some success and some failure has been reported from the, as yet, fairly small-scale attempts at seeding the sea, but the scientists involved are optimistic. One hopeful factor is the sheer quantity of young and sturdy fish which can be reared in this way. At the Marine Biological Station, Port Erin, Isle of Man, where experiments have been made for some years with young plaice, as many as a million have been successfully reared in a year.

The movement of ocean waters is of practical importance, and has been exhaustively studied by oceanographers.

1 Using an underwater camera lowered down from a ship, the oceanographer photographs the sea bed. Details can be seen of the terrain and underwater life as far down as a mile or more.
2 Seismic sounding in the North Sea from a survey vessel. Depth charges are fired about 200 yards astern of the ship at the rate of one a minute during tests.
3 Two divers check their exit and entry from a United States submarine workboat. They are preparing for when they will be diving in the deep ocean environment off the Californian coast.

The great ocean current systems, for example, have considerable effect upon the migratory habits of fish and other animals such as eels. To observe animal life within the Gulf Stream was one of the aims of the 30-day submerged drift northwards up the east coast of the United States by the research craft, *Ben Franklin*. The findings of Dr Jacques Piccard and his colleagues who crewed the vessel are likely to produce important new information.

Knowledge of the currents, their speed and direction is important to the mariner and on the surface they are fairly well charted. Below surface, the picture is not so clear. Even so, the oceanographers have established that great systems of submerged currents do exist.

The significance of this to submarine commanders is easy to see. One current complex in the Straits of Gibraltar was well exploited during the Second World War by U-boat commanders in the Atlantic who wished to slip out into the Mediterranean. Evaporation in the Mediterranean causes the water to become more saline and therefore more dense. It tends to sink and runs out into the Atlantic as an undercurrent, while less dense water comes into the Mediterranean as a surface current from the Atlantic. The U-boats were able to evade the Allied ships stationed at the Straits by switching off their engines and allowing the undercurrent to carry them through the opening.

Upwellings

Upwellings are also important movements of water for food yields. Caused by complex interactions of currents of various kinds, they bring to the surface mineral nutrients utilized by the plant life at the surface. The flourishing of plant life causes a population explosion among the fish. The discovery of such upwellings by the oceanographers is a matter of considerable interest to the world fishing industry. And some ocean scientists have seriously suggested that nuclear reactors could be sunk to the bed in barren areas of ocean where the heat they produce would cause up currents. In this way mineral nutrients would be brought to the surface artificially; the marine desert would bloom.

Oceanographers have now amassed a great deal of data on the wave behaviour of water under a great variety of wind conditions and in relation to different kinds of sea bed and beach. From this data it is possible to predict wave conditions, provided one or more of the variables involved is established. The Normandy landings in 1944 were postponed for 24 hours as a result of an adverse wave prediction – one which turned out to be correct.

These have been some of the practical benefits which oceanographic research has brought. And clearly the oceanographers and the men who have built upon their work have only just begun to understand how to tap the ocean's resources. Both the developing and the technically advanced nations are watching developments with interest as they turn to the oceans to meet their needs.

Keeping in step with time

To keep in step with time, Man has devised beautiful and ingenious instruments to measure the intangible. Today, he has clocks that will not lose or gain a second in three thousand years.

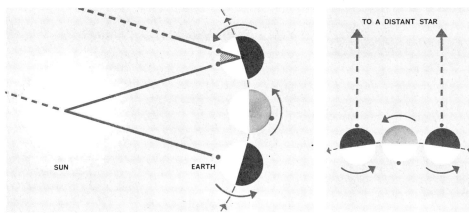

SUN   EARTH

TO A DISTANT STAR

WE ARE MADE conscious of the passage of time by noticeable events. Time elapses between two happenings of which we are made aware. For example, if we are sitting reading this article, we are aware of when we start reading a page, and we may notice when we turn over the page. Between these two events, all the while we were reading we have been made aware of no other happening, and an interval of time has passed. But if someone rang the doorbell when we had read only half a page, we would be aware of two time intervals: the time that passed from when we started the page and the doorbell rang, and the time that passed from then until we finished the page.

Early man did not have books to read or doorbells to interrupt him, but certain natural events made him aware of the passage of time. The existence of night and day, the succession of the seasons, the birth, life and death of his animals – all these events made him conscious of time. He observed the phases of the moon, the rise and fall of the tides, and the apparent rotation of constellations of stars in the night sky. Today scientists still use natural events to measure time precisely.

The first attempts to measure time were based on the motion of the Earth, moon, sun and stars. Originally, men thought that the Earth remained stationary and the moon, sun and stars moved round it in the heavens. We now know that this is not so; the moon orbits round the Earth, and the Earth-moon system orbits round the sun. And the sun, together with its attendant planets (including the Earth), is itself moving in the arms of the large spiral nebula that forms our galaxy – the Milky Way.

The fundamental astronomical units of time are the day (the time it takes the Earth to spin once on its axis) and the year (the time it takes the Earth to orbit once round the sun). Another unit, the month, is the time it takes for the moon to orbit once round the Earth. The lengths of the day and the year vary, however, depending on what reference point we take for timing the measurement of one complete rotation

Man measures time by observing the recurrence of natural events – chief among them the passage of day and night and the cycle of the seasons. There are two ways to calculate a complete revolution of the Earth. *Above left,* we calculate a revolution by reference to the sun. This gives us a *solar* day – the time taken for one place on Earth to make a complete revolution and return to the same position facing the sun. But because the Earth is moving round the sun, the solar day is four minutes longer than the time taken for a complete revolution. To measure the rotation of the Earth without reference to the sun, we can consider its position in relation to a distant star. This calculation, *above right,* gives us a *sidereal* day. The time taken for a fixed point on Earth to complete and face the star again is 23 hours 56 minutes 4 seconds. Other natural phenomena, like the vibrations of a quartz crystal, can be used in the clock, *right,* to keep time accurate to one second in three years. An alternating electric current causes the crystal to oscillate at the rate of 100,000 times a second.

of the Earth on its axis or one complete orbit round the sun.

For example, we may measure the time taken for one place on the Earth directly facing the sun to make a complete revolution and come back to the same position facing the sun. This time is called the *solar* day. But because the Earth moves round in its orbit during the time taken for it apparently to spin once on its axis, the solar day is a little longer than exactly one revolution. The difference is about four minutes.

The moving shadow

The speed of the Earth in its elliptical orbit round the sun also varies (it travels fastest when it is nearest the sun and slowest when it is furthest away). For this reason, the distance the Earth moves along its orbit during one revolution varies during the year. So the length of the solar day, measured in the way just described, also varies. The average value, taken over a whole year, is called the *mean* solar day (or mean time). This is the time which clocks are designed to keep, although clocks are in perfect agreement with solar time only four times a year. A mean solar day contains exactly 24 hours.

The errors of solar time can be avoided if we measure the rotation of the Earth without reference to the sun. Instead of timing how long it takes for the Earth's rotation to bring a point on Earth back into a position in which it exactly faces the sun, we can consider the position of a point on Earth directly facing a remote star. Because the star is so far away, there will be no error due to the movement of the Earth along its orbit during one revolution on its axis. This time interval is called the *sidereal* day, and it is equal to 23 hours 56 minutes and 4 seconds.

A year is the time taken for the Earth to make one complete orbit round the sun. It is equal to 365·2422 days, or 365 days 5 hours 48 minutes and 48 seconds (that is, mean solar days – days by the clock). In practice, we call a year 365 days and every four years have a leap year, which contains an extra day in February. In doing this, we have corrected too much, and have to omit leap years every hundred years, at the change of centuries. A final correction is made by retaining the leap year when the number of the century is an exact multiple of four. The year 1900, for example, was not a leap year, but the year 2000 will be.

The most accurate clock in the world until 1962, the atomic-powered device, *above,* was used to check the accuracy of the quartz crystal clocks used at Greenwich Observatory. This atomic clock

was accurate to one second in 300 years – but its successor is at least six times as accurate. Atomic clocks are based on the known rates of oscillation among the electrons of certain elements.

Water turned a paddle-wheel to operate a clock created by Chinese craftsmen in A D 1092. The model above reconstructs the device. Water clocks had one main disadvantage – they froze in winter.

The first instruments for telling time made use of the sun. In about 1000 B C, the Egyptians devised a shadow clock consisting of a horizontal bar mounted above and at right angles to a rod calibrated in hours. The shadow bar was faced towards the sun (eastwards in the morning and westwards in the afternoon) and the position of its shadow gave the time.

Various types of sundials were also constructed in ancient times. The simplest consisted merely of a stick pushed into the ground; the position and length of the shadow gave the time. More elaborate types have a *gnomon* (replacing the stick) and a calibrated dial. This might have been the function of some of the large vertical stones in monuments such as Stonehenge. Finally a triangular plate called a *style* replaced the gnomon. For accurate measurements, the angle of the style should be chosen to correspond with the latitude of the sundial's location, and it should be lined up exactly north–south, so that it casts no shadow at noon.

Sand, water and candle flame

Other early clocks made use of escaping water or sand. In the simplest water clocks, the rate at which water runs out of a hole in the bottom of a container is used to measure time. The container can be calibrated on the inside and the water level read off against it, or the level of the water can operate a float which controls the movement of a pointer – or, with the aid of cog wheels, a hand. The ancient Greeks built a large water clock called a *clepsydra* in Athens.

More elaborate water clocks have automatic means for refilling the chamber, or work paddle-wheels which drive hands round by means of cogs and pinions. A sort of water clock in reverse, invented more than a thousand years ago and still used in some parts of the world, has a bowl or cup with a hole in the bottom. The bowl is floated in water and the time

taken for it to fill up and sink is used as a measure.

Another natural process used by man for time-keeping is burning. In a candle clock, traditionally invented by Alfred the Great, a long candle of uniform thickness is calibrated by coloured bands on the outside. A wooden lantern round the outside protects the candle from draughts.

Swing of the pendulum

If the time taken for the candle to burn down between the bands is known, the device can be used to tell the time. In an extension of the same idea, the reservoir of an oil lamp is calibrated and the time found by reading off the oil level against the calibration. Sand-glasses use a similar principle to that of water clocks, but they are less messy and do not freeze solid in cold weather. They were often made in sets of four to record an hour in quarters.

The next great step forward in recording time came with the invention of mechanical clocks. The earliest mechanical clocks were powered by weights. In such a clock,

This simple Egyptian water clock allowed water to escape from a hole in the bottom of a vessel at a fixed rate. The passage of time could be read against the sinking water level in the bowl.

the weight is attached to one end of a cord, which is wound round an axle. As the weight falls, the cord unwinds and the axle turns. Although the rotation of the axle can be transmitted to other wheels by means of gears, some method of regulating the fall of the weight is needed if the clock is not to require rewinding every minute or so. The earliest regulator consisted of an *escape* wheel and a balance-governor or *foliot.* The whole arrangement is called an *escapement.*

The escape wheel with foliot balance came into use in the late 1200s. No further advance was made in escapements for weight-driven clocks until the Italian mathematician Galileo Galilei (1564–1642) made his famous study of pendulums. In 1581, Galileo discovered that the time taken for a pendulum to swing through small angles depends only on the length of the pendulum and is independent of its mass. According to tradition, Galileo's interest in pendulums was aroused when he saw the chandeliers swinging in Pisa cathedral. He probably thought of applying the constant swing of the pendulum to clock escapements and a drawing made by Galileo's son in 1641 (the year before Galileo died) shows such an escapement. It is doubtful whether a clock of this type was actually made by Galileo, but later clocksmiths were able to make clocks from his original design.

Christiaan Huygens, a Dutch scientist, is generally credited with making the first successful pendulum clock, in 1657. In his escapement, a pair of pallets alternatively engage and disengage in a crown (escape) wheel, as in the verge escapement, but the crown wheel is mounted with its axle vertical and the movement of the pallets controlled by a swinging pendulum.

About 13 years later, the British scientist Robert Hooke invented the anchor escapement for pendulum clocks, and his method is still in use today. In this

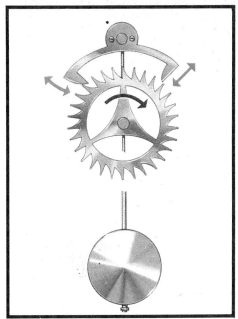

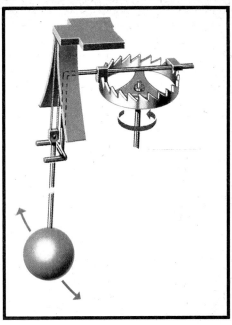

In a clock powered by weights, a device to regulate their fall is needed. In the anchor escapement, *above*, the swinging pendulum rocks a claw-shaped anchor to stop and release the wheel.

The hairspring (*A*), coiled on the same axle as a balance wheel (*B*) is the escapement device used in most watches. The spring turns the wheel back and forth to control a rocking lever.

Christiaan Huygens, the Dutch scientist credited as the inventor of the first pendulum clock, used an escapement in which a pair of pallets alternately engage and disengage a 'crown' escape wheel.

escapement, the swinging pendulum rocks a claw-shaped anchor which alternately stops and releases the escape wheel. The anchor escapement was improved by another Englishman, George Graham, who produced his 'dead-beat' escapement in 1715.

While these developments of weight-driven clocks were taking place, inventors were also turning their attention to clocks driven by springs. To turn an axle, the spring is attached to it and coiled tightly round it. Then, as the spring is allowed to unwind, it turns the axle round. The first problem which had to be overcome stems from the fact that a fully wound spring turns the axle faster than when it is nearly uncoiled – the turning force varies with the tension in the spring. The problem was solved by a device called a *fusee*. Neither the exact date of its invention nor its inventor is known with certainty. It may have been in use in the late 1400s, but some historians give the credit for inventing it to a man called Jacob the Czech in the 1500s.

Hairspring and balance wheel

The fusee compensates for the varying force from a coiled spring by making it exert less leverage on the driven axle when the spring is fully wound than when it is nearly unwound. To do this, the spring pulls in a cord or chain which is wrapped round a stepped cone-shaped pulley. The fully wound spring pulls on the narrow part of the pulley, and the nearly unwound spring pulls on the wide part.

Springs were also used to regulate a clock's escapement, in the form of a hairspring. It is also difficult definitely to credit one man with this invention, the two main claimants being Huygens (1674) and Hooke (1675). The hairspring replaces the function of the pendulum in controlling the stopping and starting of the escape wheel. The hairspring is coiled on the

same axle as a *balance* wheel, which turns first in one direction and then in the other. The oscillations of the balance wheel control a rocking lever with two teeth which alternately engage and disengage with the teeth of the escape wheel, in rather the same way as the anchor of an anchor escapement works. The hairspring and balance wheel are still used today in most watches.

All the inventions which we have just described resulted in more and more accurate clocks. The culmination of this progress was the development of the chronometer by two Englishmen, John Harrison (who worked from 1735 to 1773) and Thomas Earnshaw (1782). The important application of the chronometer is in

navigation. A ship's captain can find local time at the ship's position by using the sun or stars. If he compares that time with the time showing at the same instant on clocks at his port of departure, he can calculate from the difference in times how far east or west of his home port he has travelled. (Each 15 degrees of longitude he sails east or west corresponds to a time difference of 1 hour.) So by keeping on the ship an accurate chronometer, which always shows the time at his home port, he can easily calculate his longitude.

The next advance in time-keeping came with the invention of the electric clock. At first electricity, used to work electromagnets, was employed to drive the pendulum regulating the clock. This was the

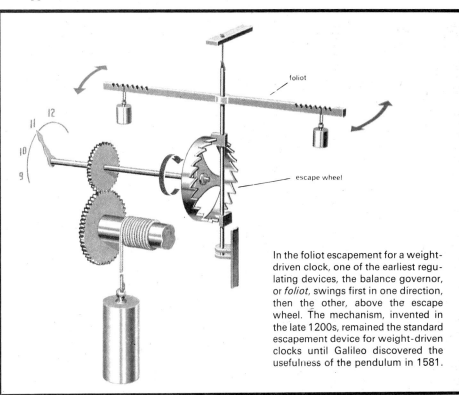

In the foliot escapement for a weight-driven clock, one of the earliest regulating devices, the balance governor, or *foliot*, swings first in one direction, then the other, above the escape wheel. The mechanism, invented in the late 1200s, remained the standard escapement device for weight-driven clocks until Galileo discovered the usefulness of the pendulum in 1581.

basis of an invention by Alexander Bain, a Scotsman who worked with Charles Wheatstone and who patented the first electric clock in 1840. Two years later, a Swiss clockmaker, Mathias Hipp, freed the pendulum somewhat, so that it was only driven by electromagnets when it swung less than a certain amount. Electromagnetism was replaced by electromagnetic induction, which was used to drive the pendulum in Fery's clock of 1900. Finally in 1921 W.H. Shortt made an electric clock in which the pendulum was virtually free.

After the 1920s, alternating current (AC) mains electricity became generally available and was used to drive motors to power clocks. These clocks keep good time by relying on the constancy of the alternating frequency from the generating station – 50 cycles a second in Britain and much of Europe, 60 cycles a second in North America. If the frequency of the AC supply varies, then the clocks also vary. But all AC electric clocks connected to the same supply keep perfectly in step with each other, and the electricity authorities keep a check on any variation in mains frequency, making sure that such variations are averaged out over a period.

Atomic clocks

Conventional electric clocks make use of current electricity to work magnets or motors. In the late 1920s, W.A. Morrison of the Bell Telephone Laboratories in the United States, developed a clock based on the electrical properties of a crystal of quartz. When a quartz crystal, carefully cut so that its crystal axes run in specified directions, is deformed by 'squeezing' it across its faces, an electric current is generated. This phenomenon is known as the *piezoelectric effect*. If an alternating electric current is applied across the faces of such a crystal, the crystal will change its dimensions by a microscopic amount in step with the applied current – the inverse piezoelectric effect. In a quartz clock, the crystal is made to oscillate at a rate of

The fusee, an elegant mechanical solution to a problem, stops a fully wound spring from turning an axle faster than a spring nearly unwound.

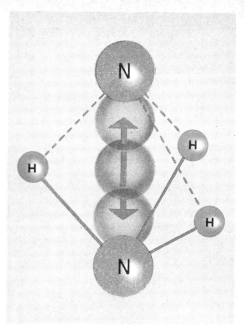

Devices old and new to measure time range from the charming hour-glass of the 1600s, *top left*, to the modern ammonia clock, in which the nitrogen atom in the ammonia molecule, *top right*,

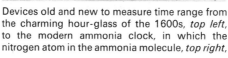

100,000 times a second. It keeps accurate time to within one second in three years.

More recently, scientists have used the natural frequencies of oscillations of molecules and atoms as time standards for clocks. The ammonia molecule contains one atom of nitrogen and three atoms of hydrogen, arranged in the form of a pyramid with the nitrogen at the apex. When stimulated by radar waves, the nitrogen atom flips through the plane of the hydrogen atoms, effectively turning the pyramid inside out. These oscillations of the nitrogen atoms in ammonia take place with absolute regularity 24,000,000,000 times a second. A clock based on this phenomenon – requiring a whole cupboard full of ancillary electronic equipment – was made in 1948 by the American scientist Harold Lyons. It keeps time to within one second in 1000 years.

Under certain conditions, similar oscillation takes place among the electrons of the atoms of some metallic elements.

oscillates backwards and forwards through the plane of the hydrogen atoms. *Above left*, an alarm clock for Italian monks of the 1400s; *above right,* clock by the clockmaker, Tompion.

These oscillations are responsible for the characteristic spectral lines used in identifying the metals. A clock has been made using the oscillation of caesium atoms, which takes place at a frequency of 9,192,000,000 cycles a second. It is claimed that the caesium clock will keep time accurately to within one second in several thousand years.

Apart from their phenomenal accuracy, molecular and atomic clocks are completely independent of external influences as well. Unlike even the best craftsmanship of the world's most famous clockmakers of past ages, today's instruments work unhampered by factors such as gravity, temperature and pressure. They can be used to calculate the timing of space-rocket launchings and manoeuvring, and are so reliable that they can detect the tiniest variations in the movement of the Earth, the motions of which probably gave Man his earliest ideas on time and its measurement.

Extensions of the human eye

Few branches of physical science are as useful in everyday life as optics. Not only is it the basis of spectacles, but it is a fundamental part of photography, television and the cinema.

NEARLY EVERYONE at one time or another has wished that the days were longer, especially when lolling on some sun-drenched beach during summer holidays. This is a rather selfish wish, however. The days already are longer, due to a physical phenomenon called *refraction of light*.

During most of its journey to the Earth, sunlight travels through the vacuum of space, and so travels in straight lines. But when it approaches the Earth, it is confronted with the Earth's atmosphere, which causes it to *refract* (bend). Since the air is denser near the ground, the sun's rays proceed from empty space through gradually denser layers of air to the ground. Particularly when the sun is low in the sky, the rays meet these layers at almost glancing incidence, and are then bent through substantial angles. The rays therefore arrive at the ground from a direction that differs from the true direction to the sun.

The sun is therefore not seen where it actually is, but where the direction of the arriving ray seems to indicate. In the morning, then, the sun is 'seen' breaking the horizon several minutes before it actually does, and in the evening it is 'seen' lingering on the horizon several minutes after it has actually set.

Another more familiar example of refraction can be had by placing a spoon into a drinking glass half-filled with water. The spoon will appear to be bent, but of course it isn't. What is bent is the light rays from the spoon as they travel from the water into the air and then into the eye of the viewer.

Light travels fast through the vacuum of space (low optical density), but is slightly impeded by the Earth's atmosphere, so it slows down a fraction and bends. At the surface of the Earth, light

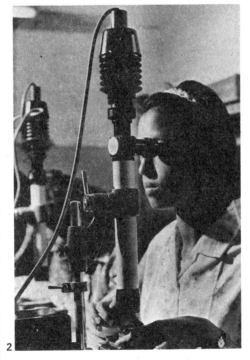

travels faster through air than, say, water. Thus, water is more optically dense than air, and light will refract in passing from one medium to the other. This accounts for the apparent bending of the spoon in the drinking glass.

It is quite easy to determine the direction a light ray will bend from the Fundamental Law of Refraction: a ray of light passing from a medium of low optical density to one of high optical density will bend *towards* the normal (perpendicular), and passing from a medium of high optical density to one of low optical density will bend away from the normal.

For instance, in the case of light passing through a glass prism, the imagi-

nary line perpendicular to the surface is called the normal (see diagrams page 1450). The angle between the incoming (*incident*) ray and the normal is the *angle of incidence*. Because glass is more optically dense than air, the light ray will refract towards the normal as it enters the prism, forming the *angle of refraction*, the angle between the refracted ray and the normal. As it passes out of the prism on the other side, the light ray goes from optically dense glass to less optically dense air, so it bends away from the normal.

In general, the larger the angle of incidence, the greater the degree of bending. A light ray entering the prism at an angle of incidence of 40 degrees will bend much more than a light ray entering at 20 degrees. At normal incidence (zero angle of incidence) there is no bending at all. But there is no obvious relationship between the size of the angle of incidence and the angle of refraction. Knowing the angle of incidence is 20 degrees implies nothing about the number of degrees in the angle of refraction. However, according to Snell's Law, the ratio of the *sine* of the angle of incidence and the sine of the angle of refraction is a constant, called the *index of refraction*.

For example, the index of refraction between air and water is 1·333. Suppose a light ray from the air should enter the water with an angle of incidence of 30 degrees. What is the angle of refraction?

From Snell's Law:

$$\text{Index} = \frac{\sin i}{\sin r} = 1\cdot333,$$

where i stands for angle of incidence and r stands for angle of refraction. In this example, i is 30 degrees. A table of trigonometric functions (see Vol 4, page 1410) gives sine $30° = 0\cdot500$, so:

$$\frac{\sin 30°}{\sin r} = \frac{0\cdot500}{\sin r} = 1\cdot333.$$

Solving the equations:

$$\sin r = \frac{0\cdot500}{1\cdot333} = 0\cdot375.$$

The table of trigonometric functions shows that the angle whose sine is $0\cdot375$ is 22 degrees.

The index of refraction may also be interpreted as the ratio of the velocity of light in a vacuum (or air) which differs little from vacuum to its velocity in the refracting substance. Thus, since light travels at 186,000 miles per second in a vacuum, its velocity in water may be found from the equation:

$$\text{Index} = \frac{c}{vw} = \frac{186,000}{vw} = 1\cdot333,$$

where c is the velocity of light in a vacuum and vw is the velocity of light in water. Solving the equation gives $vw = 139,548$ miles per second.

Total internal reflection

The fact that light bends away from the normal on passing from high optical density to low optical density leads to a rather interesting phenomenon called *total internal reflection*. As the angle of incidence of a light ray travelling from, say, water to air, increases, so does the angle of refraction. Eventually, the angle of refraction becomes so large that the ray just skims over the top of the water (angle $r = 90$ degrees). If the angle of incidence is increased still further, the light ray bounces directly back into the water by reflection at the surface, and does not enter the air at all.

Total internal reflection can be easily demonstrated. Fill a wide-mouth glass with water and wrap your fingers round the glass. Now look down through the top of the water. You will not be able to see your fingers, because all light rays coming from them are reflected back into the water. Now, look up into the water from the bottom of the glass. Your fingers will be seen clearly at the water's under surface, just as if they were being reflected in a mirror.

The phenomenon of total internal reflection finds ready application in optical instruments such as the periscope, prism binoculars and the single-lens reflex camera. In a periscope, a light ray at the top enters the tube into a right-angled prism. It is then reflected straight downwards to the bottom of the tube, where it enters a second prism and is reflected into the eye of the viewer. A similar sequence of events happens in prism binoculars. In the single-lens reflex camera, light enters through the lens and is reflected by a mirror straight up into a

pentaprism (five-sided prism) which in turn reflects the ray round until it enters the eye of the photographer. Thus, the photographer sees in the viewfinder precisely what passes through the lens and will register on the film. By this means, composing the picture is greatly facilitated. What he sees is exactly what he will get on the film.

However useful, the mirror and pentaprism in cameras are only convenient accessories. The real heart of the camera is the lens, because that is what forms the image the film records. A good camera lens, or any other good lens for that matter, is often quite expensive, because a really good lens is not easy to make. Ideally for a *converging* lens, every ray of light that emanates from a given point

on a distant object should be refracted towards each other just enough as they pass through the lens so that they all cross one another at precisely the same spot on the other side. This cross-over point lies in the so-called *focal plane* and is the place where a sharp, clear image is formed. This double meaning for image can cause trouble, so throughout this discussion it is important to recognize when 'image' means focal plane and when it simply means any light picture, clear or blurred.

Knowing where a sharp image is going to be produced is of obvious importance to the designers of cameras, as well as designers of other types of optical instruments. Since all rays from a given point cross at the same place, two rays are sufficient to 'find the image'.

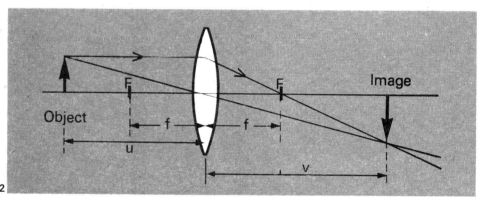

1

Double convex   Double concave   Plano convex   Plano concave   Concavo convex   Convexo concave

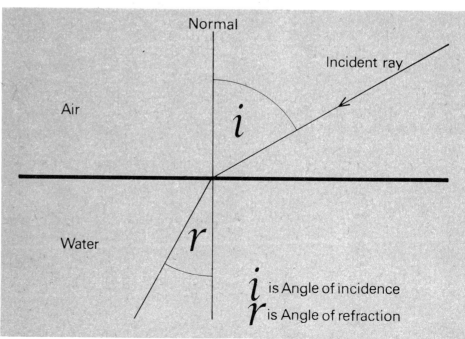

2

Object   Image

3

Normal

Air

Water

Incident ray

i

r

i is Angle of incidence
r is Angle of refraction

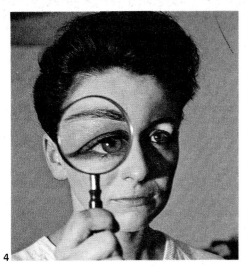

4

5

In the diagram, the point in the middle of the lens is the *optical centre* and has the special property that rays can pass through it undeviated (without bending). The *principal axis* is a line through the optical centre and perpendicular to the faces of the lens. The point on the other side of the lens marked *principal focus* is a special place on each side of the lens through which all light rays parallel to the principal axis will pass.

Suppose an object is placed 4 cm away from a lens with a *focal length* (distance from the lens to the focus) of 3 cm. Find the image. First, from any point on the object, draw a ray through the optical centre. It will pass straight through without bending. Next, from exactly the same point, draw a ray parallel to the

6

principal axis.

At the lens, bend the ray so that it passes through the principal focus, and continue until it crosses the first ray. Repeat the process with another point on the object until two cross-over points are obtained. The image (focal plane) is located on the line joining the two cross-over points, in this case 12 cm from the lens.

The focal plane may also be located mathematically from the lens maker's formula:

$$\frac{1}{f}=\frac{1}{u}+\frac{1}{v}$$

where f is the focal length, u is the distance of the object from the lens, and v is the distance of the image from the lens. In this example,

$$\frac{1}{3}=\frac{1}{4}+\frac{1}{v}.$$

Solving the equation gives $v=12$ cm, i.e. the image (focal plane) is 12 cm from the lens. If a piece of film inside a camera were placed 12 cm from the lens, one could get a photograph that is 'in focus'. Similarly, a screen placed 12 cm from the lens would show up a sharp image.

It will be noted from the diagram that the image is inverted (upside down) and magnified. The inversion is a direct result of the way the image is formed. Light rays coming from the top of the object are refracted downwards so they form the

1 Different types of lenses are used in optical equipment. Those shown are the most common simple types.
2 Image distance, object distance and the power of the lens are related mathematically. A diagram showing the path of a light ray through a lens is a useful aid to calculations.
3 When light goes from one medium to another (from air to water, for example) the rays are bent (refracted) as shown. It is this property which is the basis of all lenses.
4 A reading glass or 'magnifying glass' is the commonest lens in normal use. As can be seen, its function is to produce a large image of a close object.
5 Astronomical telescopes are extremely powerful instruments with large object lenses to collect as much light as possible from faint, distant heavenly bodies. This instrument is at the Royal Observatory, Hurstmonceaux, England.
6 Refraction of light makes a spoon standing in a glass of water appear to be bent.
7 At sunset, the sun appears flattened on the bottom edge due to refraction by the atmosphere.

7

bottom of the image. Conversely, light rays from the bottom of the object are refracted upwards so they form the top of the 'image'.

Magnification depends on the location of the focal planes. The further the image from the lens, the larger it is. More precisely, the magnification of the image is the same as the ratio of the image distance to the object distance. In our example the image is 12 cm from the lens and the object is 3 cm from the lens, so the image is $\frac{12}{3}=4$ times as large as the object. When the image distance and the object distance are equal, the image and the object are the same size, so the magnification is 1. Should the image distance be less than the object distance, then the image will be smaller than the object and the magnification will consequently be less than 1.

In general, the closer the object to the lens, the further away the image, so the greater the magnification. However, when the object is placed so that its distance from the lens is less than the focal length, i.e. when it is 'inside the focus', focal plane seems to disappear altogether. No matter where a screen is put, the image is always unclear and indistinct. This is because when the object is inside the focus, the ray through the optic centre and the ray through the focus *diverge* and never cross, so no focal plane can be formed.

The focal plane is not lost completely, however. Remember that the brain assumes that light always travels in straight lines, so if the rays do not cross on the side of the lens where the screen is, the brain assumes that they cross on the other

side of the lens where the object is. Since the rays do not really cross, this image is a figment of the imagination and is thus called a *virtual* image to distinguish it from a *real* image which can be projected on to a screen.

Like the converging lens, the diverging lens has an optical centre and principal axis. But since it bends rays away from the principal axis, its two principal foci are virtual, being the place where all rays parallel to the principal axis would cross if they were drawn back through the lens after refracting.

Correcting eye-sight

The fact that a concave lens forms only virtual images rather limits its value when used by itself. But in combination with other lenses, it has numerous applications, not the least of which is correcting the eye defect *myopia,* or short-sightedness. In this case, the second lens is the convex lens of the eye itself. Short-sightedness is often the result of an eye lens which refracts light rather more than it should, so the focal plane is formed in front of the light-sensitive *retina* at the back of the eye and the brain receives a fuzzy image (see Vol. 1, page 336). A properly prescribed concave lens can cause the incoming light rays to diverge just enough

1 Defective eyesight is very often due to malformation of the eye. An optician must measure the characteristics of the eye's light system before he can prescribe the necessary corrective lenses.
2 Microscopes are designed to produce an image of objects which are close to the objective lens, such as this shark's jaw.

so that when the lens of the eye over-refracts, the focal plane is formed directly on the retina, where it belongs.

In a somewhat similar manner, if light first passes through a convex (converging) lens and then a concave (diverging) lens, a real image can be obtained which is larger than it would have been using a convex lens alone. This is the principle of the telephoto lens of a camera.

Many other optical instruments also depend on a combination of lenses, though not always a convex plus a concave. The compound microscope uses two convex lenses arranged so that the image (focal plane) formed by the first lens falls 'inside the focus' of the second lens. The image of the first lens acts as the 'object' of the second lens, and produces a virtual image which is magnified. Of course, the image of the first lens is not really an 'object' for the second lens; it is only the place where the light rays coming through the first lens cross to form the focal plane. But mathematically and diagrammatically, the virtual image formed by the second lens is precisely where it would be were the image of the first lens a solid chunk of matter.

Really fine optical instruments seldom use just two lenses, because lenses are subject to numerous types of defects. One of the most common is *spherical aberration.* It is almost impossible to grind a single lens which will refract each and every ray passing through it the exact proper amount. In particular, the rays parallel to the principal axis do not all pass through the principal focus, as desired, but cut the principal axis slightly in front or behind the focus.

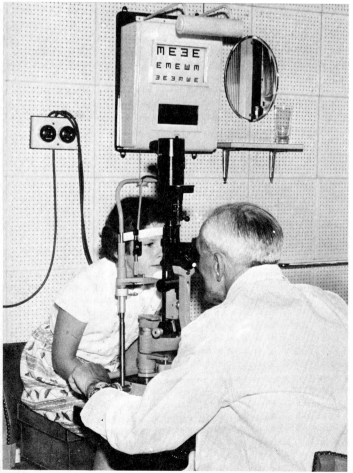

The latent image

A photographer can freeze a moment in time by using the energy of light to bring about photo-chemical reactions. These reactions must be processed before the original light pattern can be produced.

In his darkroom, a photographer of the 1870s develops a plate made of a glass coated with silver salt-gelatine emulsion, on which the light image was recorded.

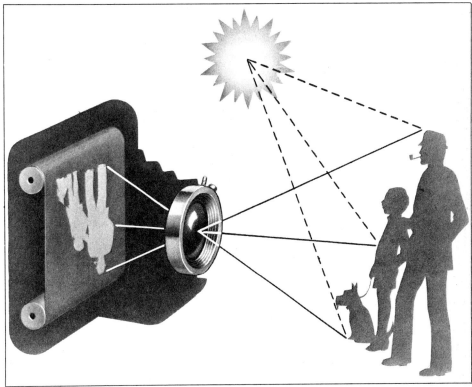

Light striking the man, boy and dog reflects into the lens of the camera. The lens focuses the light and produces an upside-down image of the group on the exposed area of film.

PHOTOGRAPHY AIMS to capture reality, to freeze light into permanance – indeed the word itself means writing with light. To record what he sees, the photographer relies on a thin layer of light-sensitive chemicals that can be processed to make the effects of the light visible and long-lasting. His camera is a light-proof box with a lens which throws an image on to a light-sensitive film. 'Pressing the button' starts a chain of chemical reactions and processes that end with a photograph.

The lens forms the image in the camera by bending the light rays striking it from the outside world. Normally, light rays travel in straight lines, but when they pass through glass they bend. The surfaces of the camera lens are curved so that they concentrate or *focus* all the light rays from the subject to a sharp point in the image. At the centre of the lens, the light passes straight through while rays from the top and bottom of the subject bend and cross over, producing an upside-down image at the back of the camera.

In the simplest cameras, the lenses are made from a single piece of glass and the image is unavoidably fuzzy because light rays near the edge of the lens have to bend so sharply that they cannot come to a clear focus. More expensive lenses contain several components that compensate both for this defect and for the effects of light of different colours. The lens's components also bear an anti-reflecting coating that stops stray light from *fogging* the film. Because a complex lens can be made wider, without affecting the quality of the image, it gathers more light, and the *exposure*, the time during which light passes through the lens to reach the film, can be made shorter.

F-numbers

To control the amount of light that passes through the lens, the photographer varies the lens's area or *aperture* by opening or closing a circular *iris* or *diaphragm* made of overlapping metal leaves. This changes the brightness of the image. The different apertures, called *f-numbers,* are calculated so that moving from one to the next doubles the aperture and so the brightness.

The photographer can also vary the speed of the *shutter.* This may be a diaphragm within the lens which flashes open when the button is pressed, or it may be a slit in a blind which travels across the camera as near the film as possible. By altering the combination of aperture and shutter speed, the amount of light reaching the film can be controlled. In bright light, the aperture can be reduced and an advantage gained because the lens gives a sharper focus; in dim light the time the shutter is open can be lengthened.

The film that records the image consists of a plastic base that is coated with a light-sensitive layer and backed with a dye that absorbs stray light. The light-sensitive layer, the *emulsion,* contains tiny crystals of *silver bromide* with some *silver iodide,* embedded in *gelatine.* A modern film contains many thousand million crystals to each square inch of film.

The emulsion is made by adding a solution of silver nitrate to a solution of potassium or sodium bromide in gelatine. This produces grains of silver bromide which cannot settle to the bottom because of the firm-setting gelatine. The warm emulsion is spread over the transparent celluloid base and, as it cools, hardens into a thin layer. The film can then be rolled in light-proof paper or a cassette so that the photographer can put it into the camera in daylight.

When the shutter clicks, light reaches the emulsion for a fraction of a second. The light energy causes free silver atoms in the emulsion to be released from the silver bromide grains. In the brighter parts of the image, enough free silver forms to make minute specks of metallic silver on the surface of the grains. In the dimmer areas, the light energy releases so few silver atoms that they cannot combine into specks. At this point, the film – bearing its *latent image* – must be developed.

To develop or process a film it must be

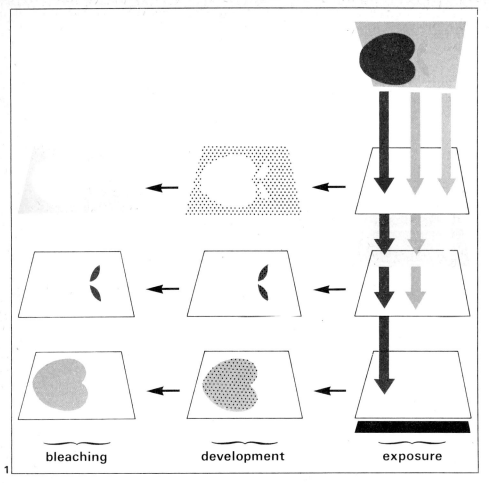

bleaching   development   exposure

1 A colour film has three layers of emulsion, the first records blue, a yellow filter then cuts out excess blue light, the second records green and the third, red. Mounted on a plastic base, a backing absorbs excess light.

2 A colour film after processing. When the film is developed, a yellow dye covers the image made by blue light, magenta dye that made by green light and a cyan dye that made by red light. Because each dye holds back light of its complementary colour, the final positive contains the original colours of the subject.

submerged in a solution containing a *reducing agent*. All reducing agents convert bromide to metallic silver but some, such as *hydroquinone* and *metol*, act very much more quickly on grains that already contain a small amount of silver: the silver speck speeds up or *catalyses* the reaction. As the reaction continues, the new silver formed increases the effect still further. So the developer converts to silver only those grains in which light energy has already released some metallic specks; the other, unexposed grains are unchanged. The developer solution also contains chemicals to increase and control the rate of the basic reaction.

All or nothing

Development is an all or nothing process which amplifies the minute effects of the light: each grain either turns completely to silver or it remains unaffected. The amount of light energy to trigger off a grain remains the same whether the grain is large or small. If the emulsion contains few but large grains, a smaller amount of light energy can affect a greater proportion of them, although the end result will be coarser.

On the other hand a slow emulsion, containing small grains, needs a long exposure to collect enough light to trigger sufficient numbers of grains to release silver. A fast film – to be used when the light is dim – therefore consists of large grains of crystals, and a slow film – needing more light – contains many more small grains. The slow film gives a finer end result.

To prevent changes when the developed film is taken into the light, the remaining silver bromide must be removed to leave only the metallic silver: in other words, the film must be *fixed*. Silver bromide is insoluble in water. But in a fixing solution of *sodium thiosulphate* (still known as *hypo* from the original name, *sodium hyposulphite*) it forms soluble silver thiosulphates that can be leached from the emulsion. Using an acid fixing solution also neutralizes the alkaline developer and stops further development. Processing the film, which is done in a darkroom, or a light-tight tank, at a temperature around 20 °C., usually takes about ten minutes in the developer, two or three minutes in a fast-acting fixer and up to half an hour washing in water. But by incorporating capsules of the chemicals into the film itself and running the stages into each other, Polaroid Land cameras can deliver a picture within seconds of taking it.

The negative is the half-way point. The finely divided silver formed during development is jet black and where the image was brightest and most silver had been formed, the negative is darkest; where the image was dark, the unchanged silver bromide is washed away leaving the negative transparent. White becomes black and the negative shows the original scene reversed. To produce a photograph, the negative must be printed.

By holding the negative against a sheet of paper coated with a light-sensitive emulsion, and exposing it to light, a *contact print* the same size as the negative

can be made. If the negative is too small to give a reasonably sized print, it can be enlarged. In the enlarger, a strong light is shone through the negative and a lens on to a sheet of printing paper. Because of their fine structure slow films give better enlargements.

For printing, as the exposing light is so bright, the emulsion can be less sensitive than that used in a camera: silver chloride may be used for contact printing and a mixture of chloride and bromide, or bromide alone, for enlarging. If these emulsions were used as film the exposure time would be far too long.

Washing

Exposing the paper produces a latent image in the same way as an image is produced on a film. The development process (reducing agent followed by fixing bath and washing) is the same, too; although the washing must last longer as the paper base soaks up more of the chemicals. Because the paper turns darkest where the negative is transparent and light shines through, the photograph reverses the negative and shows the original scene in black and white.

The black-and-white photograph matches the brightness of the original view; colour pictures, using a more complicated system which still depends on the light-sensitivity of silver bromide, match the colour as well. Virtually any colour

can be made out of a mixture of the three primary colours – red, green and blue. Between them, these wide bands of colour contain nearly all the colours of the visible spectrum. Colour photographs record the red, green and blue constituents of the original light separately and the viewer's eye recombines them.

Colour film contains three separate layers of emulsion, instead of the single layer of black-and-white: each records a different component of the light. The top layer, the layer the light reaches first, is made of ordinary silver bromide emulsion. This is sensitive to blue light and records *blue*. The light then passes through a layer of yellow gelatine which cuts out all the remaining blue light. Below the gelatine filter is an *orthochromatic* emulsion; dyes make the bromide sensitive to green as well as blue light. This layer records green. At the bottom, is a *panchromatic* emulsion, which is especially sensitive to red light and records red. After the picture has been taken, each layer contains a latent image corresponding to the distribution of the colour it records in the original view.

The latent image can be developed to give a colour negative, which can then be printed to give a colour photograph; or a *reversal* process can be used – this first forms a negative then converts the same emulsion to a positive to give a *transparency* or *slide* that can be projected.

To make the transparency, the film is

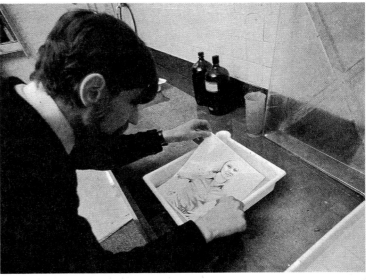

1 The enlarger enables the photographer to make a black-and-white print that is larger than the original negative. Light projected through the negative throws a magnified image on to light-sensitive printing paper.

2 Rolls of printing paper and developed colour negatives are fed into this machine which carries out the whole printing process automatically.

3 A photographer can vary what the final print looks like by exposing the printing paper to more or less light. As in developing a film he must fix and wash the print.

4 The negative shows everything in reverse – dark areas are light and light dark. During developing a negative is 'fixed' to prevent it reacting further to light when taken out of the darkroom.

5 The negative is the half-way point. To make it a positive it must be printed. This process entails using paper containing a light-sensitive emulsion.

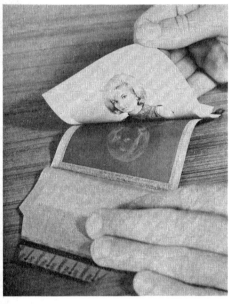

first developed normally: in the bright parts of the image complete grains of silver bromide are converted to silver. Then a flash of bright white light sensitizes all the remaining silver bromide in each layer – this gives the equivalent of a positive latent image. This image is developed with *paraphenylenediamine* or p.p.d. developer. In each layer, most silver is now formed where little light of the corresponding colour fell. In these areas large quantities of the p.p.d. developer are used, and the resulting chemicals react with *couplers,* compounds already dispersed in the emulsions, to give dyes – in the red layer, a *cyan* dye that absorbs red light and transmits blue and green; in the green layer, a *magenta* dye that absorbs green; and in the blue layer, a *yellow* dye. At this stage the film is completely black and all the silver, and the gelatine yellow-filter layer, must be dissolved away with a solution of *potassium ferricyanide* and hypo. Then all that visibly remains, in the red recording layer for example, is the cyan dye, and most has formed in the areas where the red light of the original image was weakest. When the slide is now projected, little red light is passed by these areas. The final picture on the screen, is made up of the red light, passed by the red layer, green light from the green layer and blue from the blue layer.

To develop a colour negative film, p.p.d. is again used and the products again react with couplers in the emulsion layers. The yellow-filter layer, silver and undeveloped silver bromide are then all removed at once, to leave a dye image which is negative and in complementary colours – a red wall appears green. Most colour negatives have an orange stain all over which comes from unused but coloured couplers. The colour compensates for imperfect dyes – cyan dye absorbs green and blue as well as red light – and after correction in the printing stage gives a better result.

'White light'

The negative is enlarged on to paper coated with a colour emulsion. The layers can be exposed individually through filters which pass red, green and blue light or all at once in the 'white light' method by filtering the enlarger light. The paper can then be developed in the same way as the negative to give a colour print, a full record of the original.

The light spectrum stretches beyond the colours the eye can see and specially treated emulsions detect radiation and record images in both longer and shorter wavelengths than visible light. The silver-bromide link is so delicately balanced and the development process such a strong amplifier of tiny chemical changes that an emulsion can even show the track of a tiny, energetic atomic particle or cosmic ray.

Infra-red 'heat' rays lie beyond the red end of the spectrum. They affect a film in just the same way as visible light – stripping silver from bromine to give a latent image which can be developed. But the long wavelengths are scattered less by dust in the atmosphere and the infra-red photograph shows better detail at greater distances and under conditions of mist and haze. Photographs can be taken in the 'dark', the subject being unaware that he has been photographed because the eye cannot see infra-red rays. A man hidden in bushes will show up on infra-red film because his warm body gives off heat rays.

Ultraviolet rays are at the other extreme. These rays of short wavelengths are very energetic and all films react to ultraviolet rays. Because of their penetration powers ultraviolet rays are often used in photography to detect forgeries: this they do by revealing traces of writing that are concealed from the naked eye as when cheques have been altered. X-rays are even shorter in wavelength than ultraviolet – and their penetration powers are even greater. X-ray photographs are shadow pictures: a beam of X-rays passes through the object, which absorbs varying amounts depending on its thickness and the material it is made from, to cast a shadow on the film. Developing the film shows the internal structure. Thus in X-rays of human beings, bones absorb more X-rays than flesh, and show up as deeper shadows.

Cosmic rays, with their still higher energy, can also be detected by photographic emulsion. The energetic particles leave a trail of silver behind them in the emulsion.

Photography relies on the effects light has on silver compounds. The silver plate daguerreotypes of the nineteenth century and the modern colour transparencies both depend on the minute change that light produces and development amplifies.

Used to extend and augment visual observations, photography has an enormous range of applications in all the branches of science and technology, including medicine, botany, astronomy, metallurgy, forensic science and aerial surveying. Events and reactions too fast or too slow for the naked eye to see can be permanently recorded. Objects too small or too distant can be photographed through microscopes or telescopes and the detailed results studied.

The cleaning revolution

Detergents, plastics, dust- and water-repellent substances, and labour-saving devices have transformed the housewife's work and the methods by which she now keeps her house clean and polished.

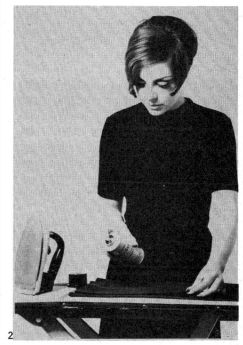

1 All manner of tests, including resistance to scratching and heating, are carried out on furniture finishes at the British Research Industry Association Centre at Stevenage.
2 Aerosol sprays have been a useful innovation in the home. Trousers sprayed with a thin layer of silicones after ironing become water-proof and they retain their creases.
3 Silicone polishes have many advantages over wax polishes; they give a brilliant shine without hard rubbing, they are durable, dust-repellent and water-resistant.

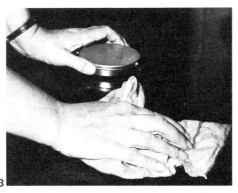

SINCE THE BEGINNING of the present century, and particularly since the 1950s, scientists and engineers have completely revolutionized the average home and changed out of all recognition the methods of keeping it clean and of performing a host of what were once laborious domestic chores. Yet the many labour-saving devices now available to the housewife were not specifically invented for her benefit but were simply adaptations of mechanical and chemical principles which had long been commonplace in industry and the laboratory.

Why did this sudden revolution come about in the household? The increasing shortage of domestic servants and the rise in the average family income accelerated demand for machines and chemical compounds to replace the labour of human hands. As a result, the washing-machine, the vacuum cleaner, the food mixer, the stainless-steel utensil, non-stick pots and pans, heat-resistant polishes, the impregnated duster and the high-speed cooker became commonplace in the home.

Machines and detergents have had an enormous impact on the housewife's quest for cleanliness. Doubtless one of the greatest revolutions was brought about by detergents. In this connection, however, the name detergent is not restricted to the cleansing powders and liquids sold under a variety of trade names. Ordinary soap is a detergent, so that any cleansing substance is a detergent. The word detergent comes from the Latin *detergere*, meaning 'to wash off'.

Soap was the first detergent. No one knows when or by whom it was discovered that a mixture of ashes and animal fat had a cleansing action. But since early times our ancestors had been making soap by mixing lye with hot grease or fat. They obtained the lye by letting hot water drip through wood ash. The making of soap was for centuries a major home task and until quite recently the lye hopper was a familiar sight in the backyards of rural communities.

Because the alkali used in soap-making was potash, the resulting soap never hardened, while the crudity of its manufacture was such that its alkali content was so highly variable that its efficiency as a dirt remover varied from household to household. When soap-making became an industry the result was a better and more uniform quality, while the substitution of soda for potash enabled the soap to be hardened into solid cakes.

It was a long time, however, before scientists discovered how soap performed its work of helping to keep things clean. Soap is basically a compound of an alkali with the fatty acid of an oil having a high emulsifying property. Its primary action is to allow water to wet greasy surfaces and thereby emulsify and remove grease and dirt. Because of its alkaline nature, soap is not always satisfactory for this purpose and there was a need for acid wetting agents.

With a better understanding of the action of soap on dirt, chemists were able to compound new synthetic detergents, or soapless soaps, which were to prove much more versatile and efficient than any conventional soap. The same cleansing principle, however, is involved in both soaps and synthetic detergents, in spite of the fact that soaps are made mainly from fats and vegetable oils, whereas synthetic detergents are compounded from the by-products of petroleum refining from coal tar and other sources.

The molecules, of which soaps and the majority of detergents are composed, have a dual action. One part of each molecule is attracted to water, while the other part is attracted to oil or grease and repelled by water. Thus when a conventional soap or detergent is used for washing clothes, the oil-seeking part of the molecule is attracted to the grease and dirt on the clothes, while the other part is attracted to the water in which the clothes are being washed. This induces a kind of chemical tug-of-war in which the particles of dirt are broken up and fall into the washing water. The detergent then coats the particles with a skin, so preventing them from forming clumps with other loosened bits of dirt. In this way, a detergent slides the dirt off the soiled surface and prevents it from settling on it again. Rubbing, wringing or agitating help to loosen the dirt so that it floats away.

To carry out its cleansing function, a detergent must also be a good wetting agent. This means that clusters of its molecules must crowd the surface of the water, so reducing surface tension and thereby making it easier for the water molecules to penetrate deep into the fibres of the fabric being washed. But it must be able to do this without damaging the fibres. A strong alkaline soap will deeply penetrate the fibres of a woollen garment but in doing so it will shrink the wool: if the alkaline concentration is strong enough, it will actually dissolve the wool fibres. An acid detergent has scarcely any detectable effect on wool fibres.

Soap detergents have many other serious disadvantages. It is almost impossible to obtain a lather in cold, salt or acid water, or in water that is very *hard*. Hard water is water that has absorbed an excessive amount of minerals, such as calcium and magnesium. When used with hard water, soap combines with the minerals to form a deposit or scum on the surface of the article being cleaned, which is very difficult to rinse out completely. The scum also forms on the sides of the vessel in which the clothes are being washed. This can be a particularly serious matter where the laundry is being done in a washing machine. Moreover, using soap in hard water is uneconomic, for the soap that combines with the minerals to form scum performs no cleansing action and is wasted.

Until comparatively recently, manufacturers were so anxious to provide detergents with high lather-making pro-

perties because housewives believed they were necessary, that they overdid it. Detergent suds became a menace, clogging drainage and sewage systems, and when water containing the suds was discharged into rivers they formed a blanket which deprived marine animals and plants of the oxygen on which their life depends. The danger was appreciated and new detergent formulas were evolved which kept sudding within reasonable bounds.

From these formulas developed special sudless detergents for cleansing solid surfaces such as floors and walls. There are also special detergents for the cleansing of stained or polished surfaces which otherwise would be damaged by washing.

'Digesting' dirt

One of the more recent developments of synthetic detergents is the so-called biological detergent. It is very effective for the removal of stains and other forms of deep-seated soiling against which the conventional detergent is often ineffective. Biological detergents react chemically with the dirt and 'digest' it out of the soiled surface. Some people consider that their action is very drastic and that fabrics left to soak in water containing biological detergents may be damaged. Some dermatologists are also critical of biological detergents on the grounds that they can be harmful to human skin and may be the cause of certain skin disorders.

There have been moves in the United States to ban the use of biological detergents pending an inquiry into their potentiality as a health hazard. In some other countries the strong biological detergents used in industrial processes are prohibited unless workers handling them are protected by gloves and clothing. Great care must be taken to avoid what could be a health hazard to workers in the factories producing biological detergents.

Synthetic cleansing detergents were first made in Germany and quickly found favour with textile manufacturers because of their effective cleansing of raw wool. The first of the many household deter-

gents now in use was put on sale in 1936. The effectiveness of any cleansing detergent depends upon, amongst other factors, the temperature of the water in which it is used, the mechanical or manual agitation of the water and the article being cleaned, and the length of time to which an article is exposed to the detergent's action.

It is not only in the kitchen and the washing-machine that detergents have a place in the home. They are found in shampoos, hand lotions, medicines, in cleaning vegetables such as cabbage and broccoli, and even in the milk bottle.

Many shampoos incorporate special detergents to increase foaming and froth effect. Most hand lotions contain talcum powder to make the lotion smooth and incorporate a detergent to break up the talcum particles into still tinier particles. In this manner the talcum particles are coated by the detergent in exactly the same way that detergents coat dirt particles in washing and prevent them from forming into clumps. Other detergents have a place in certain emulsions, such as solutions where oil and some other liquid, with which oil does not easily mix, have to be brought together. Tasteless detergents are used in place of eggs in cakemaking.

Amongst the most useful of detergents are those called *quats,* or quaternary ammonium compounds. They have the dual property of not only acting as cleansers but also as bactericides. Since they are particularly effective against the bacteria present in milk, they are finding increasing application in sterilizing milk bottles and other containers. In weak solution, 'quats' destroy any of the harmful bacteria found in drinking water.

One of the most remarkable substances which has gained an increasingly prominent place in the home is called silicones. This is the name given to a range of manmade chemical compounds the main component of which is silicon – one of the most abundant elements found in the Earth's crust. Some of these silicones are ex-

3

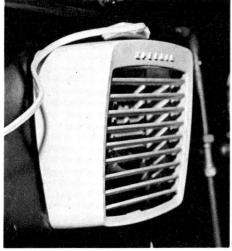

5

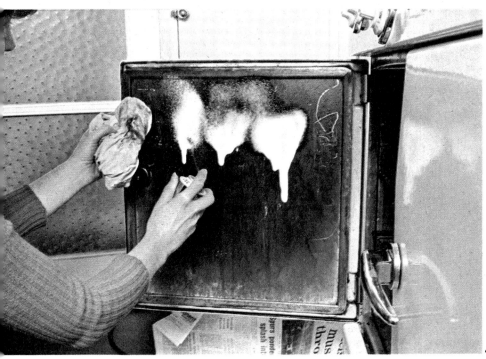

4

6

1 Synthetic materials, such as plastic, have proved a great boon to the housewife. Attractively printed, they can be used to cover any hard-worked surface, and they do not stain.

2 Clothes soaking in a biological detergent. These detergents, containing enzymes which 'digest' dirt, are very effective against certain types of stain.

3 Cooking on non-stick surfaces has made cleaning up much easier and no fat need be used. Scientists discovered the formula of a non-stick surface as an offshoot of space research into a water and heat-proof substance.

4 A powerful synthetic detergent, which is effective against ingrained and burned-on fat, is sprayed from a pressurized aerosol container on to an oven door.

5 Stale cooking smells and dust are removed by this small air-conditioner which draws out all the stale air from the kitchen and keeps the atmosphere fresh.

6 Detergents dissolve away dirt and grease by making them emulsify with water. Detergent foam in this carpet cleaner lifts the dirt from the pile and dries on the surface.

tremely useful because they repel water, do not react with other chemicals and do not easily decompose when heated.

Scientists had for long been tantalized by the possibility of so treating absorbent materials, such as fabrics and leather, so they would have the water-repellent and stain-resistant properties. The early experiments consisted in coating materials with a thin film of glass, but this only succeeded in making the materials far too brittle to be of any use.

Eventually, however, a team of British chemists obtained from silicon a very fine substance that could be sprayed, painted or otherwise applied to the surface of any material without altering its appearance, colour or texture. It is this fine substance that we call silicones, and its great advantage is that it does not stick to other substances and they do not stick to it.

The surfaces of frying-pans and cooking pots coated with a chemical compound prevent the food sticking, while baking pans and cake tins coated with it do not

need to be greased to prevent the dough from adhering. Car and furniture polishes containing silicones give a brilliant shine without hard rubbing; they are durable, dust-repellent and waterproof.

Silicones

Articles plated with chromium, silver and other metals can be given a silicone polish which will remain bright and tarnish-resistant in all weather. Adhesive tapes can be wound in rolls because one surface has a silicone coating. Paint containing silicones is sufficiently heat-resistant for it to be applied to the hot-plates of electric stoves and ovens. As such paints do not blister they can be used for fireplace surrounds and for application to hot-water pipes.

Silicones' resistance to water has been exploited in many ways. Fabrics treated with them can be of the finest possible texture, as each thread in the fabric is coated separately. Nylon stockings and the thinnest of dress materials treated with

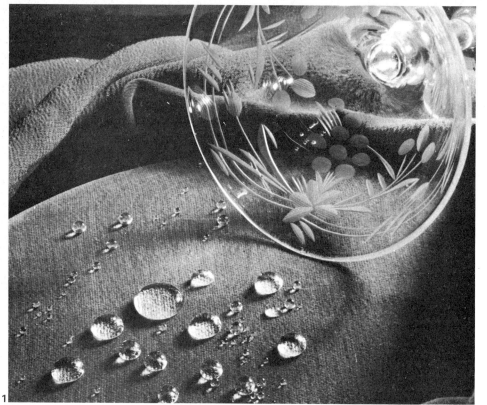

1 A fabric coated in silicones is effectively water-proofed and water runs off or can be shaken off. Because it cannot damp the material the water forms spherical drops.

2 The days of housemaids and 'dailies' are practically over and a housewife looks for labour-saving devices. This dish-washing machine washes and dries a full load in 35 minutes.

silicones withstand the heaviest rain, which simply rolls off the fabric. Garments made from nylon and other synthetic fibres continue to shed water even after they have been laundered or dry-cleaned.

Siliconized wallpaper can be used in bathrooms or kitchens without being damaged or dissolved by water or steam. The paper can have a rough or smooth surface or carry a coloured pattern and it does not have the shiny appearance of conventional papers rendered damp-proof by varnishing. Even the outer walls of a house can be made proof against damp by application of a silicone lotion. The lotion can be coloured or colourless; the latter is an important consideration when the lotion is applied to old and mellowed brick and stone work.

Silicone-treated articles are able to withstand extremes of heat and cold. Rubber articles, for example, normally melt at relatively low temperatures, but when treated with silicones they can withstand temperatures ranging up to 250 °C. and remain flexible at temperatures as low as −70 °C. Silicones have also exceptional electrical insulation properties. Voltages of up to 14,000 have been passed for periods as long as 12,000 hours through wiring sheathed in silicone rubber without the slightest leakage of current.

Probably the most striking development in the packaging of certain household materials is the aerosol bottle. The bottle is, in effect, a pressure vessel and depends for its action upon containing a substance which is liquid under high pressure, but immediately the pressure is released it turns into a gas. There are aerosol bottles containing sprays of starch, deodorizers, fly-killers, paint, furniture polish, hair lacquers and disinfectants.

Very fine particles of the substance to be sprayed are suspended in the container in a liquefied gas called the *propellant*. When the button on top of the bottle is pressed, the valve is opened and pressure forces the starch, paint or other substance out through the jet-nozzle at the top of the bottle in a very fine mist. When the button is released, the valve closes and the contents of the bottle return to a high pressure. The container is then effectively sealed off again.

Aerosol bottles are made from tin-plate or aluminium and have to be able to withstand a pressure of 20 lb or more to the square inch. The substance sprayed may be poisonous as, for example, in aerosol-sprayed fly-killers and other insecticides, and should not be allowed to come into contact with food.

The most usual propellant is dichloro-difluoromethane. This is the same liquid used in most refrigerators as it is a gas that easily liquefies. To a lesser extent, the hydrocarbon, butane, C_4H_{10}, is also used.

There seems no end to the applications of science and technology to the modern home. But for cleaning, in particular, technology has caused a revolution in both materials and in methods to take the drudgery out of the housewife's work.

Help for the housewife

Technology has brought vast changes to the average home. In the future, capsule kitchens, mobile furniture, computers and photo-electric cells will all be part of the housewife's domain.

IN THIS CENTURY, science and technology have brought about a revolution to the home. But what of the future? What kind of homes will people with average incomes live in by the end of the century? Will the changes be as great as they were between 1900 and 1970? The answer is undoubtedly 'yes'. The household of today will be developed and many devices which are now regarded as curiosities, or are in the experimental stage, will become part of everyday domestic life. The housewife will have more leisure and will spend less time on household chores.

One example of this is the amount of time taken to cook a meal on a gas or electric stove. Conventional gas and electric ovens and grills cook the food by convection or radiation. The ordinary electric grill is mainly a radiator of heat, the heating element radiating the energy that does the cooking in the form of electromagnetic waves. When the current is switched on, the elements in the conventional electric stove or grill glow and emit visible light. But more important than the visible light is the infra-red radiation from the element. Although invisible to the human eye, infra-red radiation can be detected because of the heat it carries.

Concentrated radiation

Infra-red radiation is induced by vibrations of electrons, atoms and molecules. When these are suitably excited, the radiation travels at the speed of light and heats objects in its path by causing vibration of the electrons, atoms and molecules constituting the object being heated. Much of the heat from the elements in a conventional electric stove or grill is lost because the heat tends to disperse and only a relatively small proportion of it reaches the food being cooked. The infra-red grill concentrates the infra-red radiation so that the maximum amount reaches the food and the heat loss due to radiation is reduced to a minimum.

Convection heat loss can be eliminated by enclosing the element in a glass tube or bulb and so creating an infra-red lamp. To direct the infra-red radiation in the required direction, part of the inner surface of the tube or bulb is coated with a substance which reflects infra-red radiation and helps to beam it in one direction. Infra-red rays are exceptionally effective in their heating property because their energy is absorbed by objects to a much greater extent than is the energy of shorter wavelength radiation of visible light.

One of the advantages of infra-red radiation is that the speed with which it heats up an object depends to a major extent on the temperature difference between the emitter of the infra-red and the object absorbing the heat. With an infra-red

1 Nuclear energy for the home. This prototype device converts heat produced by the radioactive decay of a small amount of polonium-210 into electrical energy.

2 Cooking by infra-red radiation – microwave cooking – is a very speedy process. Within minutes large pieces of meat can be cooked from the inside out.

heater the temperature difference may be as high as 2,000 °C; the object under the radiation, therefore, warms up very rapidly.

In the conventional grill or oven, the heat from the element is conducted and convected through the food to its centre. With an infra-red grill, however, the radiation is able to penetrate throughout the meat or other food. Instead of the centre of the meat taking the longest time to cook, the centre may be cooked more quickly than the outside. This is because heat can escape from the outside, but not from the centre.

Amongst other applications of infra-red radiation which will become increasingly commonplace in the future are infra-red cabinets for tenderizing meat, for the quick drying of clothes after washing, for the quick thawing of frozen packaged-foods, and for the rapid but controlled heating of greenhouses.

There is little doubt that the home of the future will make increasing use of ultra-violet radiation – the range of electromagnetic radiations extending from the violet (short-wave) end of the spectrum to the beginning of the X-ray spectrum. Ultra-violet radiators consist of a special glass tube or bulb filled with mercury vapour and argon gas. The radiations emitted are invisible as the vibrations they produce are so rapid and the wavelengths so short that the human eye cannot detect them. Ultra-violet lamps can be used to produce a cold radiation which preserves foodstuffs. A tube six in. long can protect a larder shelf with an area of 12 sq. ft. Another application would be as a barrier against bacteria, viruses and moulds.

Many homes of the future will have air-conditioning, and an ultra-violet lamp placed in the air ducts would protect the whole household against airborne disease. Tests have shown that 80 per cent of airborne viruses and bacteria can be destroyed by inserting a single ultra-violet lamp in the ducts of a heating or air-conditioning system.

Applying the principle of photochromism to glass-making will eventually provide houses with windows that shut out glare on sunny days. *Photochromism* means change in colour through exposure to light. During the manufacture of the glass, tiny, light-sensitive crystals of silver hidide (a compound of silver and either chlorine, fluorine, iodine or bromine) are added. When light strikes the window, the silver compound breaks up into the silver and the other constituent, so causing the glass to darken. According to the intensity of the light, the glass can darken until only 1 per cent of the light striking it penetrates. As the light intensity decreases, the silver and other elements rejoin, so clearing the glass and allowing more light through. The speed and intensity of the darkening and brightening of the light can be controlled from a fraction of a second to several minutes by varying the proportion of silver to the other element of the compound. Optical glass can be treated by the photochromism technique so enabling spectacles to become sunglasses in strong light.

What is claimed to be the greatest advance in room-lighting since the invention of the gas-filled electric bulb is now being developed and may eventually displace today's conventional methods of illuminating the house. The new lighting element consists of a flexible ribbon made up of a sandwich of a thin strip of aluminium foil, a layer of phosphorescent material, and a transparent coating of a substance able to conduct electricity. When current is applied to the aluminium foil and the coating, the material between them glows and emits a soft, clear light. The ribbon is one-sixteenth of an inch thick and has been made in widths of up to 12 in. and lengths of up to 150 ft. It can be bent, coiled, twisted and formed into any shape, and it does not generate any heat.

Lengths of the ribbon have been tested to give constant light for 12,000 hours before burning out. This means that a ribbon lamp used six hours a day would last for two years. One probable development of the ribbon lamp is to make it in sheet form for fixing to walls and ceilings.

As a large proportion of the energy going into an electric lamp is dissipated in the form of heat, scientists have been seeking ways to reduce this wastage. A major step towards this has been made by the development of a new type of gas-discharge lamp which will, in time, find its way into the home. This lamp consists

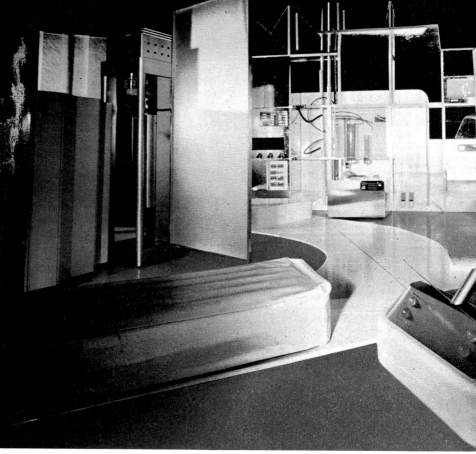

of a ceramic tube made from pure aluminium oxide pressed from a fine powder into crystalline solid. The tube is filled with sodium vapour through which a high-intensity electric current is discharged. Conventional sodium-vapour gas-discharge lamps emit a yellowish-orange light but the light of the new lamp is a clear white. This is because the sodium is heated to such a high temperature that it reverses its range in the light spectrum. In other words, the heat wasted in the ordinary electric lamp is utilized to heat the gas in the ceramic tube. As yet, the ceramic-tube lamp averages only 6,000 hours of lighting before burning out. This is considerably better than the life of 750–1,200 hours for the conventional incandescent filament lamp, but compares unfavourably with the mercury-vapour

1 An automated living area embodies many revolutionary ideas: a chair that moves on a cushion of air, inflatable furniture and a multi-purpose robot.
2 This kitchen of the future is designed to give maximum flexibility. The circular worktop with sink, cooking and storage units is motorized to revolve through 360°.
3 An innovation in central heating is a silicated carbon paint which, when connected to a low-voltage electricity supply, produces heat. The paint is sprayed on to the walls.
4 Computers in the home will take away many of the problems of running a house – preparing shopping lists, making orders from supermarkets and coping with household finance.
5 The glass in the windows of this London building has been treated during manufacture to screen 20 per cent of light and 60 per cent of heat from passing through.

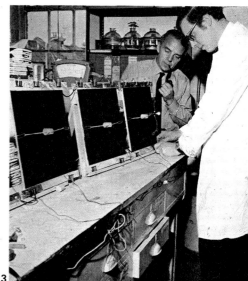

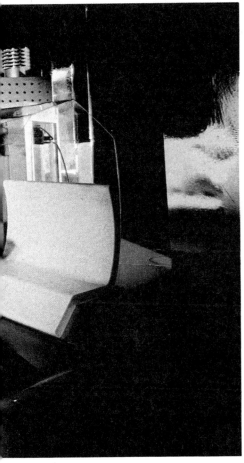

lamp's life of 16,000 hours.

At an International Television Symposium in 1969, electronic engineers delved into the future to forecast probable developments of domestic television, particularly the types of receivers that will be in use. According to the experts, the trend will be towards small and very compact receivers, made possible through the greater use of micro-circuitry, transistors and greatly improved screens.

Instead of looking at the present large and cumbersome tube, programmes will appear on a thin, electro-luminescent panel which can be cut to any desired size. This, in conjunction with miniaturized printed circuits, will make it possible to have viewing screens in several different rooms of the house which all take the programme from a single, central receiver. That missing a television programme will become a thing of the past is indicated by experiments now being made with a device for attaching to a television receiver. This will record on tape all the vision and sound of a programme. The tape with the sound and vision tracks is then put into a recorder which plays back the sound and projects the picture on to a screen.

Closed-circuit television, which is at present limited to large-scale industrial and hospital applications, will eventually be miniaturized for use in the home. This will enable a mother working in her kitchen or relaxing in her sitting room to keep a close watch on her children in the nursery or while they are playing in the garden.

The photo-electric cell, which comes into action when a beam of light shining on it is interrupted, promises to have many applications in the home. Linked to suitable relays, it will open doors; enable the driver of a car to open gates and the doors of his garage without leaving his seat; give instant warning of an intruder breaking into the house through a door or window; and ring a warning bell if a child falls out of bed.

In the United States experiments are being carried out which promise to revolutionize the whole concept of the home telephone. For example, a housewife out shopping will be able to telephone the kettle in her kitchen to boil water for a cup of tea when she gets back. Again, if a family is out visiting friends or at a theatre and a telephone call is put through to the empty house, the call will be automatically transferred to the nearest telephone wherever the family happens to be. This is done by electronic switchboards at the telephone exchange.

The instructions which an electronic switchboard needs to transfer calls and perform services, such as ordering a kettle to boil, are punched on thin aluminium sheets which are inserted in the switch controlling the subscriber's number. For example, one of the punched notes on a subscriber's card contains instructions for the kettle. The subscriber dials her home number followed by a code number. When the home telephone rings, even if no one answers it, the dialling of the code number operates a relay connected to the power switch on an electric kettle, so turning on the current. There is no risk of the water boiling away as a thermostat automatically cuts off the electric supply. In the same way, an electric oven can be connected to the telephone exchange, and by ringing the number followed by an appropriate code number the dinner starts cooking.

Even more remarkable results can be achieved by linking an electronic telephone exchange to a computer. A housewife, whose card at the exchange has a coded shopping list, can telephone a supermarket. The supermarket's telephone is linked to a computer which prints her order; an assistant collects the items she has ordered and parcels them for her to take away.

With electronic switching it will not even be necessary always to dial the number required for ordinary calls. Numbers frequently used can be punched on plastic cards, one card for each number. To telephone the number, the appropriate card is put in a slot on the telephone and the caller is instantly connected to the number required. An electronic switching and telephone exchange system is already

163

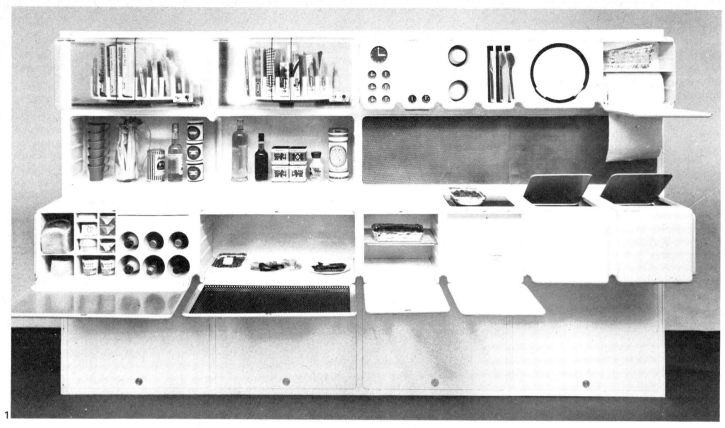

1

on trial at Syracuse, in the United States, and serves 200 private and business telephone subscribers.

Miniaturized computers will have their place in the home of tomorrow. Suitably programmed, the miniature computer will ease the task of the head of the household making out his income-tax return, while the housewife will use the computer's memory to store such information as cooking recipes and knitting patterns.

Miniature nuclear reactors

As yet atomic power has made little direct impact on the home except for the electric power supplied from nuclear generating stations. But the successful use of a miniature reactor in space satellites holds promise of an atomic power-plant in the house. Called SNAP, from the initials of its name, System for Auxiliary Nuclear Power, the pocket reactor used in satellites weighs $4\frac{1}{2}$ lb. It produces a continuous supply of power for five years on one load of fuel. The fuel consists of a small pellet of plutonium which, as it decays, releases heat. The heat is picked up by a thermo-couple which induces a direct electric current.

Although the current is very small it can be stepped up by a small transformer. The ultimate current obtained is equivalent to that from five tons of storage batteries used on motor-cars. At present, a SNAP generator costs £500,000, but it has been estimated that mass producing the midget power-plants could reduce the cost to £100. Nuclear engineers are now experimenting with a more sophisticated SNAP capable of producing 500 watts of power for three years on a single charge of fuel. Amongst the advantages of SNAP are that it has no moving parts, so reducing maintenance to a minimum, and the relative cheapness of the fuel, as the pluto-

1 The capsule kitchen is completely self-contained and can be put anywhere in the house. There is no need for a separate room or for the cook to be isolated from her guests.
2 'Intercom' systems in the home enable parents to keep a constant check on their children. They can also 'baby-sit' for other parents connected to the network.

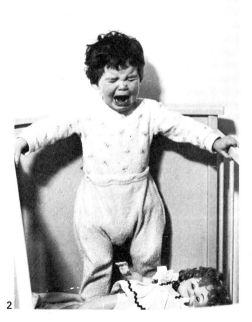

2

nium pellets are extracted from waste material left by conventional nuclear power stations.

By the end of the century, man-made materials such as plastic, stainless steel, glass and anodized aluminium will be more widely used in the structure of the home. Coloured plastic will replace many fixtures now made of wood. Doors, window-frames, floor skirting and picture rails will not require repainting; if a new colour scheme is wanted, plastic skins in any colour can be applied like a paint and will harden in a few minutes. Stainless steel and anodized aluminium fittings will not tarnish, while toughened-glass sheets will provide easily-cleaned work tables.

Although silverware has been prized for its elegance, strength and durability, most housewives regard their silver with mixed feelings because of the regular polishing it needs. But silver polishing will become a thing of the past. This will be achieved by rhodium-plating. Rhodium is one of the platinum group of precious metals and is exceptionally resistant to chemical action and to atmospheric corrosion. Silverware plated with rhodium has a hard, non-tarnish and permanent finish with all the appearance of silver plate. The only attention needed to retain the brilliant finish is occasional washing in warm, soapy water.

Oven-cleaning, the housewife's most unpopular chore, is now becoming a simple matter. A new type of oven on the market is coated inside with a special surface enamel. To clean the oven, the door is shut and the heat turned full on. In little more than a minute the grease and other dirt is reduced to a fine ash which can be brushed away. Experiments are also being made with an interior coating which reacts to oxygen and destroys grease splashes as they are made.

Problems of waste

Human communities create vast amounts of waste material which can contribute to air and water pollution and to disease. The smooth running of our cities demands a vast waste-disposal industry.

THERE ARE four fundamentals to the creation and maintenance of a hygienic environment in which Man can live with his fellows in reasonable good health. They are: clean surroundings, fresh air, pure water supply and the efficient disposal of domestic and industrial waste. The Greeks and Romans had the right ideas in these respects with their public baths, aqueducts and drainage systems. Unfortunately the fall of the Roman Empire not only ushered in the Dark Ages of learning and culture, it also saw the eclipse of hygienic living.

Matters became worse with the development of towns, when people were herded into verminous and rat-infested buildings where there was neither sanitation nor fresh running water and the very rudiments of hygiene were unknown. As a consequence millions of people fell victim to bubonic plague, smallpox, typhoid, cholera and other epidemic diseases which could have been held in check by the most elementary practice of hygiene. Windows were made small and rooms and beds heavily curtained to keep out fresh air which was thought to carry disease. Drinking water was taken from rivers into which human and household waste was emptied; in fact, the rivers that provided

2

1

1 Sewer workers inspect the junction between the main Fleet sewer and one of its tributaries. The junction is just below London's Ludgate Circus. The main sewer was once the Fleet River.
2 Bathers at Hoylake, Cheshire, swim in a pool of sea-water close to the end of a large sewage outfall pipe. Sewage needs careful treatment before it can safely be released.
3 An aerial view of a modern sewage-treatment plant at Colne Valley, Yorkshire. Primary sewage passes first through the settling tanks in the background and is purified in the round tanks.

3

towns and cities with their water supplies were also noisesome sewers. Personal cleanliness was practically non-existent: many people never had a bath in their lives and seldom troubled even to wash their faces and hands. Bathing was as unpopular with the wealthy as with the poor, and great mansions that boasted rooms hung with rare paintings and elaborate tapestries did not possess a single bathroom. No wonder both men and women drenched themselves in perfumes; they had to conceal the unpleasant smells of their unwashed bodies.

With the Industrial Revolution in the mid-eighteenth century, hygiene reached its nadir. More and more people were attracted away from the relatively hygienic conditions of the countryside to the squalor of the towns, which became more and more overcrowded. Fresh air, sanitation and pure water supplies were practically unknown, so that the general health of industrial nations rapidly deteriorated. Natural hazards from disease were magnified enormously by the concentration within small areas of ever expanding populations and industries drawing their water supplies from sources into which sewage of every description was emptied.

Matters had reached such a sorry pass that in the mid-eighteenth century the average length of life was only 35 years. By 1950 life expectancy had jumped to 67 years, and it is now moving towards the Biblical promise of three score years and ten. This remarkable achievement is due, at least in part, to the phenomenal advance in public hygiene, and to this the chemist has made the major contribution.

Because so many streams and rivers, particularly in thickly populated and highly industrialized areas, perform the dual function of water supply and sewage disposal, the hygiene scientist's first step to create a hygienic environment has been to dispose of sewage in such manner that it cannot pollute water supplies.

False theory

Sewage is mainly water and its most dangerous constituent is the human waste resulting from the chemical changes that food and drink undergo in the body. This represents a constant menace as it is the ideal breeding medium for germs and bacteria. This did not worry the authorities, who believed that the oxygen in stream and river water helped to decompose sewage and that the oxygen absorbed by the sewage during decomposition quickly replenished itself to keep the water clean.

It is quite true that oxygen in open water will induce bacterial action that will decompose sewage and render it relatively harmless, but the oxygen is not replenished at a rate sufficient to decompose constant additions to the sewage intake. In time the river or stream becomes little more than a drain. This is not only harmful to human health, but the lack of oxygen in the water leads to the asphyxiation of fish, plants and other organisms. Ultimately the sewage-laden water releases hydrogen sulphide and other evil-smelling gases.

166

1 Early detergents were difficult to destroy and caused foaming in rivers even after sewage treatment. Here, a weir near the Stratford Avon has stirred up a quantity of persistent foam.

2 Pure water is a luxury. In many parts of the world, as in this Formosan village, the same river serves the inhabitants for washing and drinking, and may serve other communities downstream.

It was not until the mid-nineteenth century that chemists were able to prove the utter fallacy of the self-purification theory. They proved that not only is domestic sewage dangerous, but certain industrial effluents are as well. Among these are the wastes from collieries, gas, chemical and dye works, food factories, iron and steel works and, more recently, oil refineries. This kind of waste is usually more direct in its action than is ordinary domestic sewage. Coal dust, ash, fine cinders and other solid particles form a blanket that destroys plants and other organisms on river beds, besides killing fish by clogging their gills.

Chemists have shown that sewage containing compounds of zinc, copper, lead and ammonium salts has toxic properties and destroys life by upsetting its biochemistry. Where there is a combination of low oxygen concentration and even a small percentage of toxic chemicals, pollution becomes particularly lethal. Although the oxygen content of a river may be relatively high, chemical pollution will kill practically all organisms living in the river.

The steadily increasing use of detergents in the home and in industry poses a new and serious problem for chemists concerned with sewage disposal. Many detergents contain the suds-producing agent tetrapropylene benzene sulphate. This chemical is structurally very stable so that it is not easily attacked and broken down by bacterial action. Besides lowering the rate at which open water can receive oxygen from the air, the foam created tends to clog sewage-treatment plants. Chemists have now made available substitute foaming-agents that can be broken down by bacterial action. Another serious source of pollution in sewage lies in the herbicides, insecticides and fungicides used in agriculture. These can be washed from the land to which they have been applied and find their way into drainage systems to retain their lethal properties.

Some idea of the major contribution that industry makes to sewage is indicated by the fact that processing a meat carcase at an abattoir produces waste equal to that produced in one day by 30 people. Laundering 100 pounds of soiled clothing deposits into sewage the amount of waste that would be produced in a day by 24 people. Processing 100 pounds of butter produces wastes equal to those from 34 people. Little wonder that in the days before chemists turned their attention to

hygiene, when sewage was dumped straight into the nearest river or stream, every centre of population was subject to periodic epidemics.

Nowadays, sewage is first piped to a disposal plant where chemists analyse its contents. It then has to be rendered harmless and, in some instances, even made useful. There are several methods of treatment, depending on the nature and quantity of the sewage solid content. First, the heavy inorganic material is removed, often by passing the sewage through a machine called a comminutor, which shreds the coarser materials. Sand and other heavy matter falls into a grit chamber from which it is removed by scrapers.

From the grit chamber the sewage is pumped to settling tanks, where some of the finer material is removed. The settling tanks hold the sewage for two or three hours, during which time a substantial portion settles to the bottom as sludge. These treatments remove about 60 per cent of the suspended solids and 35 per cent of the biochemically active material.

Further purification is carried out by adding to the sewage chemical coagulants such as iron salts or aluminium sulphate. This produces a light mass, called floc, which settles and takes with it a large proportion of the offensive material. Chemical coagulants remove between 80 and 90 per cent of suspended solids.

Science's greatest contribution to sewage treatment is probably the biological process which consists of introducing air into the sewage to encourage the growth of bacteria which attack the organic matter to decompose it quickly. Methods whereby this is achieved are: the intermittent sand-filter, the trickling filter, and activated sludge.

Intermittent sand-filtering requires the minimum of mechanical equipment and consists of a bed of sand below which are drains. The sewage flows over the sand and as it soaks into it, slimy jelly alive with bacteria forms on the surface and traps virtually all the harmful constituents of the sewage. An efficiently operated sand-filter will remove as much as 90 per

1 Huge volumes of water are needed for industrial and domestic use in large cities. These needs often conflict with local interests, as at the reservoir at Treweryn, North Wales.

2 Clear water, purified after passing through a sewage-treatment plant, flows over the sill of a final treatment tank. The water is now fit to be returned to a river or to the sea.

3 Preparation of activated sludge at a modern sewage-treatment plant. Partially purified sewage is agitated and aerated through compressed-air nozzles along the tank's sides.

cent of suspended solids. This type of plant is expensive to build and to maintain, besides occupying a great deal of ground. At least one acre of sand beds is required to handle a daily intake of 80,000 gallons of sewage – the average amount from 1,000 people.

Trickling filters are cheaper to operate than sand-filters and are just as effective. A trickling filter is a bed of coarse-crushed rock through which the sewage seeps. As it passes through the rock at a faster rate than it would through sand, much less ground area is required. Strictly speaking, the crushed rock does not perform any actual filtering. What it does is to provide a surface on which a bacteria-laden jelly can grow and attack the sewage bacteria. Trickling filters occupying an acre of ground can handle up to 30 million gallons of sewage a day. The continuous flow of sewage through the filter beds washes away excessive amounts of the slime or jelly, so ensuring that air has free access into the bed to encourage growth of the required bacteria. As the effective area of the clinker or crushed stone in the beds is enormous, the plant can handle vast quantities of sewage. Because the organisms need free oxygen to multiply and carry out their action on the sewage, they are said to be *aerobiotic*.

In both the intermittent sand-filter and the trickling filter, the biological slimes or jellies must gather on some collecting medium. With the activated-sludge process, the bacteria-laden slimes form within the sewage itself as air is blown into it. As the slimes float around in the sewage they pick up the dangerous organic matter and decompose it. Sludge then forms and with the sewage goes to a tank where the sludge settles out. Part of the sludge is returned to the sewage entering the aeration tank. In this way, the sewage is constantly seeded with living organisms and the growth of the purifying bacteria is accelerated.

Treating sewage by any of the activated-sludge methods described removes almost all the harmful solids, leaving a clear liquid, which is then sterilized with chlorine and can be pumped as harmless water into a stream or river.

Sludge disposal

Whatever treatment is used, there always remains a large volume of harmful sludge, the disposal of which posed a major problem until it was solved by chemists. The most efficient technique is *anaerobic decomposition*, that is, decomposition by bacteria that grow in the absence of oxygen.

Anaerobic decomposition is carried out in closed tanks which hold the sludge for about three weeks at a temperature of about 33 °C. until it is thoroughly decomposed or, as it is called, digested. At the same time, methane gas is produced and this is used to fire the boilers supplying heat to the digester tanks, and to fuel the motors driving pumps and other equipment.

After sludge has been digested, it contains a high percentage of water which is removed by vacuum drying. Suitably

In Los Angeles, California, air pollution has become such a problem that special patrols are constantly on the alert to check that smog does not exceed acceptable limits.

treated with chemicals, the residue can be sold as fertilizer. Where that is not economically feasible, the sludge residue is burned in incinerators and reduced to an inorganic ash.

The average household needs water for two purposes: drinking and washing, and in each case the requirements differ. Drinking water must be free of harmful bacteria, though its mineral content is not a matter of major concern. On the other hand, water for washing the person and clothes does not have to meet the stringent bacteriological standards of drinking water, but it must be relatively free of dissolved minerals.

Water can be partially purified by a

Water pollution is a serious hazard. In 1969 the accidental release of insecticide into the Rhine killed thousands of the river's fish. It may take years before the stock is fully replenished.

process called coagulation. This involves adding small quantities of calcium hydroxide and aluminium sulphate. These chemicals react to form a colloidal gel which surrounds and traps bacteria and suspended particles. The gel gradually falls through the water and carries the impurities with it to the settling tanks. From the coagulator the water goes to sand-filters to remove the traces of aluminium hydroxide and other suspensions. If necessary, the filtering is supplemented by passing the water through activated-charcoal filters to absorb gaseous impurities that would impart an unpleasant taste.

In most purification plants, the water flows from the filters to a chlorinator, where it is sterilized by dissolving in it chlorine gas. The amount of gas has to be carefully controlled and is determined by careful chemical analysis of the water. Often ammonia gas as well as chlorine are dissolved in the water to combine and form chloramines, which are very efficient sterilizers. In some reservoirs the water is constantly sprayed into the air, so that exposure to oxygen and sunshine will help to destroy harmful bacteria and eliminate unpleasant odours. A somewhat similar result is obtained by running the water in cascades over large surfaces called *aerating tables*.

Clean air is a third fundamental of food hygiene. In populous and industrial areas, the air we breathe can become seriously contaminated by dust, smoke and the carbon monoxide from the exhausts of motor vehicles. In large buildings such as shops and offices where many people congregate, the air becomes stale and very often germ-laden.

Chemistry plays a relatively minor role in ensuring pure air. The problem is either a mechanical one, as in the design of air-conditioning plant, or a legislative one to enforce the burning of smokeless fuels or to limit the emission of carbon monoxide by road transport.

Technology and sport

Developments in technology – photographic timing devices, improved equipment, all-weather arenas, synthetic tracks and mass audiences – have introduced profound changes to the world of sport.

The distances between runners are sometimes so slight as to be hardly discernible to the naked eye. By using a photographic timer the entire finish of the race can be recorded.

SPORT IS essentially an uncomplicated business. It provides the spectacle of men battling against men or against the elements without the trappings of modern civilization. But many people would argue with justification that the existence of modern sport as a mass entertainment for spectators would not have been possible without the technological advances made over the past 100 years.

The origins of many sports can be traced back through the centuries but it was not until the nineteenth century that sport began to be properly organized. And, significantly, this development coincided with technological advances. Newspapers, radio, television and photography are some of the factors responsible for the growth of sport. A hundred years ago it would not have been possible to stage the Olympic Games or the World Cup as truly international events since neither the aeroplane, the modern ship, television nor radio were available. In 1966, 100,000 spectators saw England win the World Cup final at Wembley Stadium near London but the world-wide television audience was an estimated 500 million. Until the twentieth century war seemed Man's great sport and it would not be unrealistic to claim that the sporting hero has taken the place of the war hero.

The development of timing is probably technology's most important single contribution to sport. As Lawrence Wright wrote in his highly entertaining book, *Clockwork Man*: 'Timing could not invade and mechanize sport until watches were accurate.' This applies chiefly to athletics – a sun dial or, later, the town clock were hardly the most satisfactory methods of timing races. But as the science of timing developed, so did athletics. Records began to be published with some regularity from around the 1850s and international records appeared for the first time from around 1880.

It was the stop-watch that provided the means of timing short-distance events such as the 100 metres. There is not much historical documentation about the stop-watch but in the 1830s reference was made to a watch with an independent seconds-hand. Benson's chronograph of 1860 was used to time the Derby horse race in 1866 – when the stop was pressed, the seconds-hand inked dots on a dial, enabling the timing of successive events. Around 1900 there was an electro-chronograph that could be operated by a finishing tape.

Importance of timing

Timing is a vitally important aspect of athletics. When a race is over, the spectators want to know the time. However thrilling a race may be, it loses all significance if the times are sub-standard. Timing has meant that the relative merits of athletes can be judged although they may be thousands of miles apart and may never meet.

Timing has now developed into such a fine art that hand-timing – a human being operating a stop-watch – is fast becoming unacceptable for short-distance events and electronic timing is used at the big meetings like the Olympic Games and the European Championships. When a man presses a stop-watch, he cannot anticipate the start and so the lag in the human nervous system means that there will be a fraction of a delay before he starts his watch. This delay gives the athlete a shorter time than he has actually achieved. The difference between electrical and hand-timing may be as much as a tenth of a second. As electrical timing tends to read

Pole vaulting was transformed with the introduction of the fibreglass pole in place of wood or steel. Because of its flexibility, the pole gives bend and whip to vaulters.

more slowly than hand-timing, records are becoming harder and harder to beat.

For the short-distance races at the Mexico Olympics in 1968, the electronic devices consisted of a synchronized starter's gun linked by cable to the photo-finish camera at the finish line. This type of camera is another example of technology taking over where human judgement is no longer considered accurate enough or sometimes even capable of deciding which runner finished first. The camera does not provide a photograph of six runners in their relative positions when the first athlete reaches the tape. What it does is provide a photograph of each athlete at the moment he reaches the line. This isolated recording of each runner is achieved by the continuous exposure of a film-strip rotating on a spindle exactly opposite the finish line. As well as recording the position of each runner crossing the line, it also records the time in minutes, seconds, tenths and hundredths of seconds that each athlete has taken to run the race.

A timekeeping apparatus used at the Olympic Games in Mexico in 1968 had its own developing tank that provided a negative in 30 seconds. A further half-minute and the camera provides the judges with an enlarged positive copy.

Nevertheless, hand-timing is very much a skilled art. In Britain, there are three grades of timekeeper and they have to pass examinations that include timing between 30 and 40 dummy races. A high standard is also expected of the stop-watches themselves and they are sent in for check-ups every two years. Mechanised devices are not confined to time-keeping in athletics. World records cannot be sent if the wind aiding the athlete exceeds two metres per second. Human judgement was used to decide on the strength of the wind but wind gauges now provide exact measurements.

While timekeeping in its most sophisticated forms revolves around athletics and swimming (at major events each individual swimmer touches a pad which is connected to a master clock), accurate timing is vital for many other sports. This is obvious in the case of show jumping against the clock but even in a game like football, the referee must have a means of adding on injury time to the 90 minutes of the game.

Technology has also played a major part in the development of equipment for sport generally. Rugby is a simple example of how vital high production standards are. When the English firm of James Gilbert Ltd began manufacturing rugby balls in the first half of the nineteenth century, they consisted of pigs' bladders inside a leather case. In 1870, lung power was replaced by a pump for inflation purposes and rubber was substituted for the pig's bladder. All in all, rugby balls have not changed much but by merely feeling a ball, a good rugby player can tell if it is up to standard. When the New Zealand full-back Don Clarke had to contend with the problem of balls being doctored in order to disrupt his kicking accuracy, he solved the problem by kicking inadequate balls over the grandstand.

Skilfully made footballs

Footballs can take more than four months to produce from the first stage of removing the skin from a slaughtered beast. The process is long and complicated and although mechanization plays a large part in the industry, much emphasis is still put on the skills of individual craftsmen. Animal skins are converted into semi-finished leather at a tannery before they arrive at sports factories. *Tanning* is the name given to the age-old discovery that if skins are immersed in water containing the bark of certain trees, they are transformed into very tough and long-wearing material. From the tannery, one British manufacturer uses about a million square feet of leather every year. About 16 per cent of the leather used for sports goods production ends up in the form of footballs. The work can be split into two stages. The first is leather-dressing, known as 'currying', involving, for example, re-tanning and stretch-removal. The second revolves around the manufacture of the case itself with the insertion of the bladder.

The work involved in producing a good-quality football is highlighted by the fact that the best balls have their panels completely stitched by hand – and a highly skilled stitcher can take as long as two and a half hours each case. One of the few changes in the finished product has been the post-war development of stem bladders instead of having the footballs laced up. The advent of floodlighting football matches has meant that footballs come in a variety of colours instead of the standard tan. Although the finished product has a high degree of toughness, waterproofing is not added during manu-

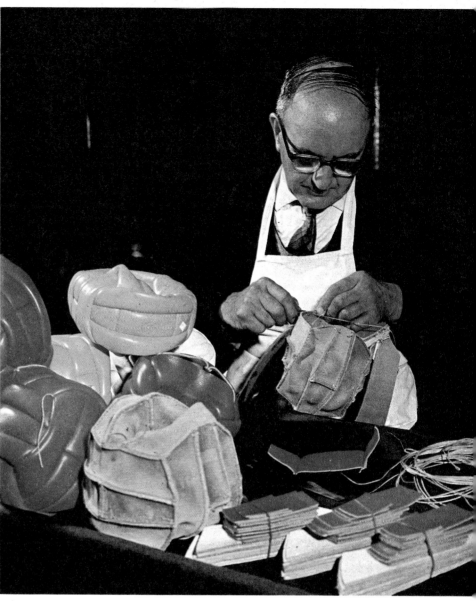

facture although experts are still working on the problem. Coloured soccer balls, however, are water resistant as the coating applied to them (either white, lemon or orange) is of polyurethane which is an excellent leather finish and which almost totally rejects dirt and moisture.

But technology plays a more dramatic role in the manufacture of golf and tennis balls. The production of tennis balls is a tremendously complicated and technical procedure. The slightest variation and it will fail to pass the necessary weight test. The first stage is the preparation of the rubber compound; a solid mass of rubber is then moulded into a hemisphere and two of these are joined. This assembly stage involves the introduction of gas pressure inside the ball – either air or nitrogen – to give it the correct bounce characteristics. The ball is then covered with Melton Cloth – the woven fabric that provides the furry surface to the ball. But the standards set make this whole process a complex one. The rules lay down that a tennis ball should be more than $2\frac{1}{2}$ in. and less than $2\frac{5}{8}$ in. in diameter and more than 2 oz. but less than $2\frac{1}{16}$ oz. in weight. The manufacturers have to ensure that when dropped from a height of 100 in. on to a concrete base, the ball bounces up again to a height of between 53 and 58 in.

1 The manufacture of footballs for international matches is a long, complicated process involving great skill. After tanning, the leather panels are stitched by hand. Coloured balls are produced for use at floodlit football matches.
2 Golf clubs have to be very finely balanced before use. Here a craftsman hand-finishes wooden heads for the steel shafts.

1 The kayak, originally an Eskimo canoe, has become very popular for competitive canoeing. Studies of the angles of the blades of paddles have increased their efficiency.

2 Racing cars have shown fundamental changes in recent years with the quest for a higher and better performance. Some designers have added fins to the cars to act as stabilizers.

The greatest development in the tennis world is the steel tennis racket. Extra power, compared to the conventional wooden racket, is the key to its success and the reason why it has had such a big impact on the market, despite the fact that it costs twice as much as the best wooden racket. Steel rackets were first manufactured around 1900 but were dropped as the wire strings proved too tough for the tennis ball.

In the 1960s, the famous French player, René Lacoste, produced his steel racket in France. The unique feature of his racket was the stringing system. Instead of being strung through the frame itself as in the conventional racket, the strings on the Lacoste racket were strung through a number of steel alloy loops on the inside of the frame. This provided the extra power – a type of trampoline effect – when the ball was hit. An American firm then obtained world patent rights from Lacoste to use his unique independent string suspension system. After extensive research, their steel racket was put on the market in 1968. Its impact was tremendous and many other firms attempted to take advantage of its popularity – but without being able to use the patented string suspension system. Other advantages of the patented steel racket included its aerodynamic design which cuts down air resistance and the fact that temperature changes do not affect steel as they do wood – in fact the metal racket does not need a press. Its disadvantages seem to be that it takes a player time to become accustomed to using it and a new stringing technique with a special adapter has to be taught to racket repairers.

Improved equipment

Athletics has seen many equipment changes. The advent of the spiked running shoe in the 1860s is probably the simplest example, while more complicated is the history of the pole vault. The pole used in this event has successively been made of spruce, ash or hickory, bamboo, tubular steel and finally fibreglass. The fibreglass pole provides a contrast to the days when vaulters were occasionally impaled on snapped poles. The great advantage of the fibreglass pole is its flexibility – the bend and whip it gives the vaulter. It has raised vaulting standards dramatically since it was first introduced in the 1950s. American Brian Sternberg thought its advantages were perhaps too great – after setting a new world record clearing a height of 16 ft 8 in. in 1963 with the fibreglass pole, he said: 'I don't attach much value to records made with the fibreglass pole.' Unlike other poles, the fibreglass pole is built with a stress directly related to the vaulter's weight, his take-off position and other factors.

In athletics, racing surfaces underwent a change with the advent of the 'Tartan' track. In good conditions, there is little to choose between a cinder and tartan track. But in bad weather, tartan surfacing has many advantages. It is an all-weather surface – it does not become waterlogged; it can be used in extreme weather conditions – it also requires little

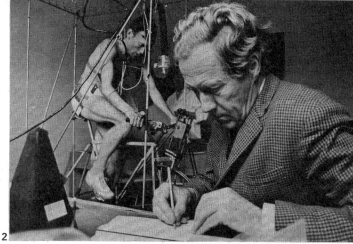

1 A 'tartan' international running track at a sports arena in Britain. Made of compounded synthetic resin, it has a hard-wearing, non-slip surface which can be used in all weathers.
2 To study the effects of high altitude on an athlete's performance preparatory to the Mexican Olympic Games, a doctor checks heart readings during a five-minute 'race'.
3 Starting blocks and spiked shoes are all precision equipment which help world record holders, such as Tommy Smith and John Carlos, to achieve their spectacular speeds on the track.

maintenance. Britain's first tartan track was laid at Crystal Palace in 1968 and it was provided for the Mexico Olympics and also at the new Meadowbank stadium in Edinburgh, the venue of the 1970 Commonwealth Games.

The major tartan surfacing is laid by a 'wet pore' machine, which looks like a macadam road layer. The finished product consists of $\frac{3}{8}$ in. or $\frac{1}{2}$ in. of tartan surfacing (a specially compounded synthetic resin). Underneath this are $2\frac{1}{2}$ in. of dense bituminous macadam in two layers laid at different angles. Underneath again are 8 in. of stabilized base clinker, then 3 in. of ash which is laid on the ground. Smaller surfaces, such as a long-jump run-up, are laid in carpet form with the surface already produced in a factory. The production and laying of all-weather synthetic turfs is increasing. Britain is testing all-weather football pitches and they are in use in America.

Frozen pitches

Underground heating is another scientific aid with increasing impact on the sporting scene. The underground heating system at Murrayfield, the headquarters of the Scottish Rugby Union in Edinburgh, was installed in 1959 to combat rugby's greatest weather hazard – frozen pitches which make it impossible for players to maintain their balance and avoid injuries. The system consists of 39 miles of cable buried about 6 in. below the playing surface. The system is controlled by a thermostat which is switched on when frost is forecast. When the temperature drops, the system operates automatically, ensuring that the ground does not become unplayable. Normally rugby authorities lay down bales of straw all over the field to keep the frost off – an elaborate but not always effective procedure.

Grass itself has been the subject of some extensive research. The Sports Turf Research Institute was started in 1929. It now has 2,000 experimental plots on a 12-acre site at Bingley in Yorkshire. Higher standards have meant that turf is more prone to disease and the centre provides invaluable research and advises the authorities at Britain's major sports grounds. In 1969, the first International Turf Research Conference with more than 70 delegates from all over the world was held in Harrogate, Yorkshire to discuss problems.

Finally a word about the most complex scientific development aiding sport – computers. They are now taking the drudgery out of compiling the most complex fixture list in the world – the English football league with its four divisions and 92 clubs.

Putting ink on paper

The purpose of all printing, from colour photographs in fine art books to cheap newspapers, is to put ink on paper. To achieve this, printing has developed into a highly technical industry.

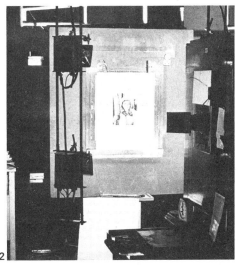

1 Copy typed on a Monotype keyboard is translated into punched tape instructions. These are then fed into a caster which moulds individual letters from molten metal.
2 The contrast of tone in a photograph is captured in printing by making a half-tone photo-engraving. Here a process camera is used to produce relief printing plates.
3 Chemically treated wood pulp is spread on a moving belt and drained of water. Heavy rollers then compress and dry the resulting paper which is wound into large rolls.

AN AUTHOR typing a novel or an artist making a drawing produces a single original, available only to a few, and easily lost or destroyed. Printing multiplies that original. Words, pictures, instructions, information and stories can be reproduced millions of times over.

All printing processes – of which there are three main methods – aim to put ink on to paper. In letterpress or *relief* printing – the first to be invented and still the most widely used – the ink is carried by a raised image; lithography or *planographic* printing uses a flat surface; while in the gravure or *intaglio* process the design is cut into the printing surface.

Letterpress printing uses metal *type* for words and photoengraved blocks for illustrations. The type carries reversed letters standing out from the surrounding metal: when coated with ink and pressed against the paper they print the right way round. Most type is now *set* (put together) by a *Linotype* or *Monotype* machine: only headlines, advertisements and other large letters are still assembled by hand. The operator has a keyboard like a large typewriter on which he types out the text or *copy* and the caster translates it into letters. When he comes to the end of a line, the machine automatically spaces the words so that all lines are the same length: the copy is *justified*. The Linotype machine moulds each line as a single piece of metal, a *slug*, while the Monotype produces lines of individual letters. Once set, the type is *proofed*; ink is rolled on to the type and a trial copy taken by hand. A proof-reader checks it for mistakes and writes instructions for any corrections that need to be made.

Blocks for photoengraving are usually made of zinc topped by a thin layer of copper and a light-sensitive coating. The coating is most acid-resistant in the areas which have received least light – in other words where the printed reproduction will be darkest. When the unprotected areas are etched away with nitric acid, a relief image forms, standing up to receive ink. *Line* blocks are the simplest, used when the drawing is pure black and white; *half-tone* blocks give the gradations of grey needed to print a black-and-white photograph.

The dots of a picture

The vital part in making a half-tone is the *screen*, a transparent plate ruled with two sets of opaque lines at right angles which the engraver places between the original and the plate. More or less light, depending on the brightness of the image, passes through the transparent spots of the screen. When the engraver etches the plate, only pinpoints of black are left in the brightest areas while in dark places almost all the plate bears ink. Thus the tone varies from black to white. A fine screen, used for high-quality work, may have up to 150 lines ruled to the inch; for coarse newsprint, between 55 and 75 lines are usual. By looking closely at a newspaper photograph one can make out the dots that make up a picture.

Blocks and type are then *made-up*; the compositors arrange them in their final positions on the *stone*, a metal-topped table, and lock them into a frame called a *chase*. In letterpress, the made-up type can be used to print directly, which is especially convenient when only a few thousand copies are wanted. But type metal is very soft and machines built for the long runs and high speeds of newspaper and magazine printing use harder duplicate printing plates – *electrotypes* or *stereotypes*.

Electrotypes, the better in quality, are formed by electrically plating with copper a wax mould taken from the type and strengthening the hard copper shell with a backing of type metal. The less expensive stereotypes, which are adequate for newspaper work, are made by casting metal in a papier-mâché mould. Heavy pressure forces the *flong*, a thick paper sheet, into the crevices of the type; when it has been dried by heating, the metal cast can be taken. More modern techniques substitute plastic for both flong and metal cast, but the result is the same: a single plate – flat or curved depending on the machine it is intended for – which bears all the words and pictures in relief.

All letterpress machines work on the same principle: rollers coat the raised type surface with ink and force paper against it to transfer the image. In the *flat-bed* machine, the type itself is flat, paper comes from a pile of sheets and a roller squeezes it against the inked type. Newspapers and magazines use *rotary* or *cylinder* presses which are faster and usually fed by a *web*, a continuous roll of paper. Because setting up the web wastes paper, the process is uneconomical if only a small number of copies are required.

The machine minder locks the *forme*, the complete set of stereotypes, to the curved printing cylinder and *makes-ready* the press by packing thin sheets of paper beneath parts of the forme until all of the

173

type surface touches the printing paper with just the right pressure. When he starts the press, inking rollers cover the type with ink while a pressure roller forces the paper against the cylinder.

By using two printing cylinders, each acting as pressure roller for the other, *perfecting* machines print on both sides of the paper at once. In other cases, the web may travel through several printing units before passing to cutting and folding machines that turn the printed roll into the finished magazine.

Lithography, the second kind of printing process, depends on the fact that grease and water do not mix. The printing plate bears an ink-attracting image while the background is water-holding and, when damped, repels the greasy ink.

The surface of the zinc or aluminium plate is treated to make it attract grease and then given a light-sensitive coating. After exposure to the print matter and development of the image, the plate is etched. Where there has been most light – that is in between the print matter – the plate becomes water-attracting. In modern, two-layer plates the print and non-print areas may even be of different metals – the top layer etches completely away. These plates are very durable and used for large printing runs.

Photographic process

The film used to expose the plate bears both text and pictures. The text can be a photograph of a carefully taken proof of metal type or it may be *film-set*. In the film-setting machine a keyboard produces a punched paper tape which controls the exposure of individual letter negatives on to the final film. Photographs are screened to give half-tones. Because a lithographic

1 The inks used in printing contain varnish to make them glossy and oil to make them flow. The pigment used in common black printing ink is carbon black which is fast and stable.

2 Line blocks are proofed on a small hand machine. Paper is applied under pressure to the inked blocks and the resulting impression checked for accuracy.

3 A letter heading is set by hand. The metal letters are picked out of the cases and placed in the composing stick. Great skill is needed to judge the spacing between the words.

plate results from a photographic process, this method of printing is very suitable for heavily illustrated work: it costs no more to print a page of pictures than a page of text.

Lithographic printing machines are nearly always *offset* (the method is often called *offset litho*). The plate cylinder, which rolls first against a water spreader and then an ink roller which coats only the sensitive image area, prints on to a rubber cylinder. This in turn 'offsets' the ink on to paper pressed against it by a third cylinder. Because of the flexibility of the rubber mat round the second cylinder, less time is needed to adjust the machine and

the offset process can easily print on rough materials, cardboard and even plastic. Offset lithography has the advantage that it is less trouble than letterpress (small machines are used in many offices) but it cannot reach the same quality.

In the gravure process, the third main printing technique, the print image is etched into the plate. During printing, the small holes fill with ink which is forced out again by pressure from the paper. The print material is prepared in the same way as for lithography but, in the final stage, all of it, type and pictures, is exposed on to the gravure cylinder through a very fine screen. During etching, the

final size of a particular pit depends on the brightness of the image. Because the pit size, and therefore the shading, can be finely controlled, gravure is very suitable for illustrations, but the all-over screen lessens the sharpness of letters.

For special purposes there are other printing techniques which supplement the three main processes. In *silk-screen* printing, a fine fabric stretched across a frame holds a stencil or photographic image. Forcing ink through the fabric gives a heavy printed layer suitable for a poster or carton. *Xerography,* a copying process, electrically shuffles fine powder to form the print image and fuses it in place by heat.

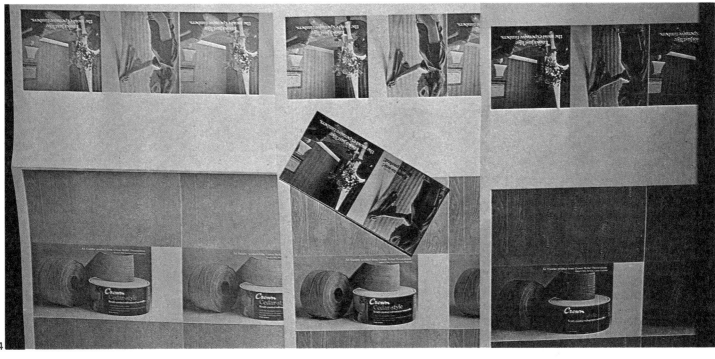

4 Sheets of a brochure printed by lithography. During the three stages, yellow is printed first, then red, followed by blue, which combines to form purple, and finally black is added.

5 Yellow cards on a small letterpress machine are picked up by suction, one at a time, and placed on the platen to be pressed against the inked type.

6 Using the original colour transparency and an enlargement on a light box as guides, an engraver removes excess metal from a half-tone colour block.

Any printing process can produce coloured pictures. In the simplest method, *flat-colour*, the printer uses coloured ink in place of black. He can pass the paper through the machine more than once (changing the ink each time) or runs the web through several printing units to give a number of different colours.

'Proper' colour, however, demands *process printing*. The final picture is a mixture of tiny coloured dots which the eye combines into lifelike tints. The first stage is *photographic separation*. The inks used for the final printing are usually three transparent colours – red, yellow and blue – and black. Using filters which pass only the complementary colours, the engraver makes first a photographic negative and then a half-tone corresponding to each of the colours. By holding the screens at different angles for each block, he ensures that the dots that form the picture jumble into an effective pattern.

Once the colours are separated the picture can be printed. In a sheet-fed machine, the paper may pass through the machine four times. On a web machine it will pass through four printing units each giving a different colour. These may vary in order, but usually the yellow is printed first, followed by red, blue and the black impression that completes the picture. For the printed illustration to be sharp, the four half-tones must fall exactly on top of each other: mechanical feelers and electronic eyes are used to keep the four units printing in *register*.

To get the effects he wants, the printer depends on his raw materials: the paper and ink. Some paper is made from cotton, cotton rags, wheat and rice straws, and grasses such as esparto, hemp and jute, but about 85 per cent is produced from wood

1 In a rotary machine, a continuous roll of paper is forced by a pressure cylinder against the impression cylinder which carries 20 inked stereo plates.
2 In this giant rotary press, the paper moves through at the rate of 1,500 feet per minute, is printed on both sides and is delivered folded into pages.
3 A printer prepares the rollers with ink before taking a 'pull' of half-tone blocks. He can then assess the quality before the blocks are put on a machine for mass printing.

pulp obtained from trees. From such pulp, it is possible to make hundreds of different types of paper – greaseproof, transparent, wrapping and high-grade papers with a hard, smooth finish. Cheap paper may also be made from repulped newsprint.

In the major process, the wood is first reduced to chips by machine and then treated with chemicals to produce the pulp. After washing, screening to remove waste material, and bleaching, the pulp is drained of water to form a thick porridge. At this stage, materials such as starch, alum, rosin size and china clay are mixed with the pulp according to the type of paper required. The pulp is then spread on to the first part of a machine which consists of a moving wire cloth belt. Suction boxes drain the water from the pulp and the remaining sheet is squeezed between heavy rollers, dried by heated cylinders and wound into large rolls.

No more need be done for the coarsest of papers – newsprint. But for higher-quality printing, the paper is coated. A mixture of clay and dyes spread over the paper fills small pits between the fibres and gives a smooth printing surface. The printer takes great care that the paper he uses is free from imperfections. He makes sure it stays dry and runs it through his machine at the best angle to prevent stretching: once the paper starts to stretch it is impossible to

keep the separate impressions of the plates in register.

Printing inks are more like paint than watery writing inks: a mixture of ground pigments and dyes for colour, varnish for glossiness and oil to make it flow. There are hundreds of colours but the most common are the three used for process colour – yellow, red and blue – and black. Virtually all black inks are made from carbon particles, the best use carbon formed when natural gas burns in too little air.

As well as being the right colour, the ink must suit both the printing process and the paper being printed. Lithographic ink must repel water, ink for gravure has to be thin so that the paper can suck it from the etch pits. Inks must also dry quickly to prevent smudging as the printed paper passes through other stages. In newsprint, the oil base soaks into the paper; on a higher-quality, coated paper the ink dries as fluid combines with oxygen in the atmosphere or evaporates. Many presses have heaters that speed drying.

Modern presses can print thousands of copies of books, magazines or newspapers in an hour; high-quality litho or gravure produces lifelike coloured pictures. Through such processes are derived the newspaper read by millions or the reference book, with its air of permanence and finely reproduced illustrations.

Science against crime

Many modern scientific developments can be applied to the detection of crime. The modern criminal faces a formidable array of experts backed by computers and sophisticated detection techniques.

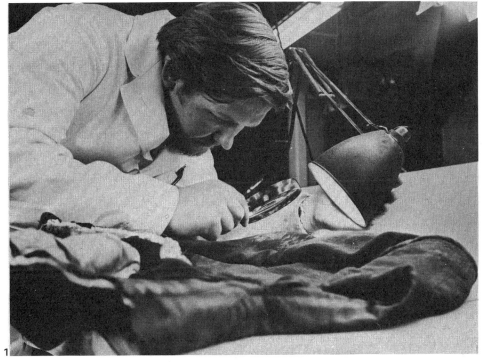

1

2

IT IS no accident that the most famous fictional detective of them all, Mr Sherlock Holmes, was provided by his creator, Sir Arthur Conan Doyle, with a knowledge of science which he used in his fight against crime. Conan Doyle had been trained as a doctor of medicine, and as such was aware of the power of science. The closing years of Queen Victoria's reign and the nine years during which Edward VII occupied the throne were notable both for rapid scientific advance on a number of fronts, and a general optimism that science would inevitably produce the answers to the problems which beset mankind, including that of crime.

Yet, when all is said and done, Conan Doyle's work was still only fiction, and Holmes's understanding of science was limited. In real life terms, the situation is very different. The professional police forces of the world have for many years been applying science to their work, and their understanding and techniques are highly sophisticated.

Science in the service of the law is called forensic science. The work of the different experts is complex and may overlap, but in general their methods may be divided into several distinct phases.

In the first phase, the forensic scientists must establish *how* and *when* the offence was committed. Then comes the collection of evidence from the scene of the crime and finally, its evaluation – which may point to the identity of the criminal.

The non-forensic policemen work closely with the experts. At this point in the investigation the former follow up

1 Using the traditional magnifying glass, a laboratory assistant at a police forensic centre begins an examination on the clothes of a man killed by a hit-and-run driver.
2 Further investigation in the same case. Part of the dead man's bicycle is being examined for significant marks. The rest of the bicycle can be seen in the foreground.

any leads provided by the forensic department and by any other sources. From the evidence they narrow the field to one or more suspects.

Once this has been done, the second phase of forensic work begins. The experts turn to the evidence again to see whether or not it is possible to link a suspect or suspects directly to the crime. If the investigation is successful, the police charge the suspect and take him to court. The final phase of forensic work takes place when the forensic scientist appears in court on behalf of the police, as an expert witness.

The chemist's work

The forensic worker may be a specialist in one particular field of science, like chemistry or biology, or he may be an expert in a field which is not truly a science at all, like photography or aspects of weaponry. But most will have this in common. Whatever their basic expertise, they are likely to have a working knowledge of a number of fields outside their own.

Among the truly scientific workers, it is the chemist who plays the widest role. As an example, take the all too common

hit-and-run accident. Very probably paint fragments will have been left behind at the scene of impact, and it falls to the chemist to analyse these, for a good deal of information about the vehicle involved can be gathered in this way.

Some of the analytical work is relatively simple. Only a microscope is necessary to count the number of paint layers that have been applied to the car and to note the colours. This may tell the police something of the history of the vehicle – that it has recently been resprayed, for instance, and that the old colour was bright orange while the new coat was a sober blue or black. Such a fact could help in tracking down the car and, more importantly, its driver.

When it comes to other matters – like identifying the pigments used in the paint, or the constituents of its base – more detailed methods are called for.

The chemist can get a good deal of accurate information about pigments by using a piece of apparatus called a spectrograph. To start with, he takes a small sample from the paint trace and vaporizes it in an electric arc. The vapour glows, emitting radiation consisting of a mixture of wavelengths. The actual wavelengths depend upon the elements present. Within the spectrograph the wavelengths are separated and the operator is provided with a visual indication of the elements involved.

However, the chemist may also wish to know how these elements are combined chemically. In such a case he would probably employ a technique called X-ray crystallography. Here the sample is exposed to X-rays which are then bent or diffracted by the lattice work of atoms which go to make up the various layers of the crystalline pigment. The angle through which the rays are bent depends upon the interatomic spacings within the crystal, spacings which vary from substance to substance in a known way. If the scientist works backwards from the angle of diffraction he can calculate the spacings and arrive at the identity of the compound or compounds concerned.

To discover the bonding agent or base used in the paint, the expert may turn to direct chemical investigation. A paint which is extremely insoluble is likely to be oil-based. The nitrocellulose paints will dissolve readily in amyl acetate or acetone.

It is important for the police to ascertain the chemical nature of paints in this way. Unusual constituents could, for instance, narrow the search down to a handful of spray shops which had taken delivery of such paint and in one of which the offender's car was resprayed. When a suspect's car *is* produced, the chemists will take a sample from it, submit it to the same tests as above and show whether the car was involved in the accident.

Murder

In shootings also there are many ways in which the chemist can lend a hand. Taking a hypothetical murder case by way of example, let us suppose that a bullet fired at the victim passes right through the body and out the other side. The murderer, aware that the firearms people can prove that the bullet came from his gun, prises the bullet from a wall in which it has lodged. Then he disposes of this and the gun separately.

A gun, even a hand gun, is a sizable object, so let us suppose again that the gun is recovered and is traced to the owner, the murderer. At first he will probably be unconcerned. How *can* the police prove that this particular weapon was used during the killings?

The answer could easily come from the forensic chemists. They simply take an outer garment through which the bullet has passed and subject it to an electron beam probe. This detects and analyses the minute traces of lead which have been deposited on the fibres surrounding the bullet hole. Any impurities in this metal are revealed, and if the same metallic mixture can be found inside the gun, its use in the murder is made probable.

The identification of poisons is another chore for the forensic chemist. The proper name for this is toxicology and it is a very wide field indeed.

Nearly all metals and metalloids (substances having some but not all of the properties of metals) are poisonous. Arsenic, one of the latter group, is no exception – in fact it is *the* classic poison. A test for the presence of arsenic in a body, particularly if it is thought that the fatal dose was administered all at once, is the Reinsch method. A piece of clean copper is boiled in a mixture consisting of hydrochloric acid and fragments

1 In this reconstruction of a crime scene, a detective dusts a glass for fingerprints with fine powder. Routine tests like this often give vital clues to the criminal's identity.

2 Forensic scientists test and try to identify samples of materials taken from the scene of the crime. Between the two researchers is a plaster cast of footprints from the area.

taken from the victim's entrails. If arsenic, or indeed any other poisons of this type, are present, they will be deposited on the copper as a black or grey stain. This can then be analysed spectrographically for final proof of the presence of arsenic.

If the chemist has reason to believe that small quantities of arsenic have been fed to the dead person over a considerable period, he will undoubtedly examine the victim's hair – for arsenic will certainly be deposited there.

Though it may appear otherwise, the chemist is by no means limited to crimes of violence. In short order he may be asked to determine whether forgery has been committed and therefore must investigate both papers and inks; he may be required to show what materials an arsonist used to start his fire; and most frequently of all perhaps, he will have to define with absolute accuracy the amount of alcohol in the blood or urine of a driver accused of drunkenness.

A recurring problem for the forensic biologist is the investigation of stains on objects used in crimes of violence, or on the clothes of the suspected attacker. Such stains may be visible, as on a shirt cuff or knife blade, or they may be invisible, as when blood has spattered on to a shoe and then been wiped away, leaving only the tiniest traces in stitching, cracks and so on. In either case, the biologists have the means of revealing the invisible stains, and showing whether or not these and the visible kind are blood.

A mixture of chemicals

For invisible stains, the peroxidase method is widely used. From experience the biologist will know that there are some areas of clothing or footwear which are more likely to be stained than others. To these areas he will apply a mixture of chemicals which contains among other things a compound which will react with the haemoglobin in the blood (the substance which is responsible for the red coloration) to give a highly coloured product. If benizidine is used along with the other ingredients, the product will be a very strong blue. Phenolphthaline produces a bright pink.

At the same time, the peroxidase test is not absolutely specific. Some plant materials and chemicals will cause a positive reaction so, having rendered the invisible stain visible, the biologist then tests exclusively for the presence of haemoglobin, or the substance into which it may have degenerated with time. A typical approach would be to apply Takayama's test which brings a stain sample into contact with pyridine, a substance present in coal tar and tobacco. Tell-tale pink crystals of pyridine haemochromogen form if the sample contains haem substances. Takayama's test and other similar methods can, of course, be used at once if the stain is visible.

But still the biologist must prove in an assault case that the blood is of the human kind. Most likely he will then turn to the preciptin test.

When the blood of one species of animal is injected into the blood-stream of

3 Frogmen play an increasing part in police investigations. Police divers are often called in to search for bodies, weapons and other objects that may be concealed under water.

4 Most police forces maintain registers of prints from known criminals. Unknown fingerprints can often be identified from the files, though much of this work is now done by computer.

another species the latter's system produces a substance (antibody) to cope with the invading blood proteins, which otherwise would be harmful to it. At such a time, the blood of the recipient is said to be immunized against the invading blood type, the defensive part of the fluid being called the anti-serum.

If a rabbit is injected with human blood, the animal produces a specific anti-serum as protection. The anti-serum can be removed from the rabbit's blood and is then ready for use in the preciptin test. An extract of the blood-stain found on clothing or elsewhere is brought into contact with the rabbit anti-serum. If it is human blood, a film (precipitate) of cloudy material forms where the two liquids meet.

The final step would be to take some blood from the victim and to discover its group. It will then be compared with the grouping of the blood found on the suspected assailant's clothing or perhaps on a weapon owned by him to see if they are the same. If they are, a possible connection has been established.

Similar techniques yield similar kinds of information from other kinds of stain such as saliva on a cigarette butt found at the scene of the crime or sweat on clothing which may have been left behind. The biologist will also seek to identify hair which may be associated with a crime and compare it meaningfully with hair from the head of a suspect.

Again, plant materials may provide vital clues. Clothing will pick up pollen, seeds or even foliage if the wearer brushes past or through vegetation. For such reasons, the biology section of the forensic department will also have experts in botany.

The final group of forensic experts are

1 Microphotograph of the butt of a murder pistol. Particles of hair and blood found in the circled dent on the butt proved that the weapon had been used to beat the victim to death.
2 C.I.D. officers in Yorkshire prepare to take a plaster cast of a footprint found close to the scene of a crime. The footprint is first sprayed to prevent the soil sticking to the wet plaster.

those who practise no particular science but are more concerned with techniques – like photography and gun identification.

The simplest use of the camera is to make a visual record of known criminals, to provide an aid in the tracking down of missing persons, and to make a permanent record of the scene of crime. But cameras of various kinds are invaluable in other more sophisticated ways. Hidden movie and television cameras have been used to record crimes as they actually happen.

Further, the camera brings out details of evidence which may be invisible to the human eye. Infra-red photography can reveal marks on an object which happen to have been obliterated by a medium transparent to infra-red. Powder traces from a close-proximity shooting normally do not show up on a dark cloth, but they, too, can be brought out in this way.

Direction of shot

The firearms expert also has a number of techniques to pinpoint evidence which for the untrained eye would be invisible. From the size and position of bullet holes, the forensic scientist can tell a great deal about the direction and distance from which the shot or shots were fired. From a bullet which is recovered in good condition, he can ascertain the calibre, type and perhaps the make of gun – and even its approximate serial number. This is achieved by making a detailed study of marks on the bullet. Some will be caused by the rifling, the spiral ridges or grooves (lands) on the inside of the barrel. They may vary in number, direction of twist, width and so on, according to the make of gun or year of manufacture.

At the same time, each individual gun has imperfections of machining which are unique to it and will be imprinted on the bullet. Thus, when a gun which generally meets the specification drawn up by the firearms expert is found in the possession of a suspect, test bullets will be fired. One of these is then placed under a comparison microscope along with the clue bullet. If the marks are the same, then clearly both were fired from the same weapon.

Shotguns – so beloved of the Chicago gangsters of the 1920s – are not rifled. Even so, some information can be gained by examination of the shot, gauging its weight and size. This information, added to a count of the pellets which may be found at the scene of a shooting, will sometimes indicate the size of cartridge used and therefore the size of gun.

This then is forensic science, or rather the flavour of it. The examples given here indicate only the tip of the forensic iceberg. Yet plainly, the police scientists have progressed a long way from the celebrated, but shaky methods of Sherlock Holmes. Just as plainly, science is increasingly at the forefront in the fascinating business of crime detection.

A ballistics expert, surrounded by reference weapons, uses a panoramic camera to record bullet marks. By comparing these with marks on the gun, bullet and weapon can be identified.

Detective chemistry

The chemical analyst is chemistry's detective – indeed, chemical analysis plays an important part in present-day police work. The analysts' skills also find wide application in other fields.

ALL OVER THE WORLD chemists with test tubes, Bunsen burners and weighing and recording instruments are at work finding out the composition of solids, liquids and gases, and determining the purity and standards of food and drugs and the materials from which are made the countless things we use every day. These chemists are the analysts. Although analytical chemistry may not be the most glamorous of the sciences, it concerns our well-being very directly. It is chemical analysis that gives us confidence in the branded products we buy, that ensures the purity of the milk left each morning on our doorsteps, prevents us from being poisoned by insecticides and herbicides, gives us an unpolluted water-supply, and even brings the criminal to justice or frees the suspect from suspicion.

Chemical analysis is concerned with identifying substances and establishing their composition. The analytical chemist may be given a liquid, solid, powder or gas sample, and asked to name the substance or substances it contains. At first glance, the sample to be analysed could be almost anything. So the analyst's first step is to make tests that will identify its main constituents. This he does by carrying out a *qualitative analysis*, which is essential both to save time and to prevent some constituent from being undetected.

Qualitative analysis is relatively simple and involves certain routine and simple tests. It merely tells the chemist what is in the substance, and does not tell him the amount of each of its constituents. This has to be established by series of tests called a *quantitative analysis* which measures, sometimes to within extremely fine limits, the quantity of each ingredient by weight.

Organic and inorganic

All chemical substances belong to one or other of two distinct groups. Group one embraces the *organic substance,* which are compounds of carbon and hydrogen; while group two, consists of *inorganic compounds,* which are of mineral origin. Many organic compounds derive from living things.

Organic and inorganic substances require different methods of analysis, but the analyst has one simple rule to distinguish them: most organic substances will burn but inorganic substances generally will not. In many instances, the appearance of a substance gives an indication of its ingredients.

Heating a sample gives much information about its composition, as the vapours given off by some metals impart characteristic colours to a colourless flame. Consequently, the *flame test* can be used to

An analyst in the nuclear laboratory at Riisoe, Denmark, uses a Bunsen burner to heat a crucible containing atmospheric dust before testing the sample for radioactive elements.

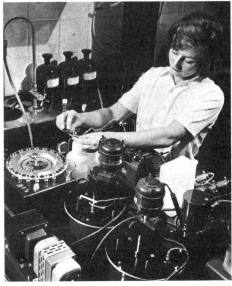

Testing for poison in blood samples. The analyst is using a machine which automatically carries out standard chemical tests on small samples and reduces total analysis time.

identify metals in compounds.

Another technique of analysing a solid by heating is called the *borax bead test*. A bead of molten borax is placed against the sample, causing a small quantity of the sample to collect on the bead. When the bead and the sample adhering to it are placed in a flame, the bead changes colour according to the constituent of the sample. Nickel gives the flame a brown colour; iron imparts a yellow colour, which turns to yellow-red when the bead has cooled, and so on.

Sometimes a solid can be analysed by heating it with a few drops of concentrated

sulphuric acid and then watching for visible indications of the constituent. A brown gas with oily drops collecting on the sides of the test tube signifies a nitrate, while a milkiness in the test tube suggests a chloride. A similar acidic test can be made by adding dilute hydrochloric acid to the sample in a test tube which is then heated in the flame of a Bunsen burner. This vaporizes the sample, and its constituent can be recognized by the appearance, behaviour, colour or smell of the resultant gas.

Analysing compounds to recognize certain metals can be done by heating them on a charcoal block. A small quantity of the sample to be analysed is put into a shallow hole scooped out of a block of carbon, and anhydrous sodium carbonate added. The sodium carbonate converts the specimen into its appropriate carbonate, while the carbon acts as a reducing agent to separate the metal from its carbonate.

The flame from a Bunsen burner is then directed on to the specimen in the charcoal block. The test gives one of two indications of the metal present in the samples: smell and appearance.

Analysts are frequently concerned to detect the presence of acids and alkalis in materials they test. Acids are often corrosive in action or sour to the taste, while alkalis are soluble hydroxides of a metal, particularly of one of the alkali metals such as caesium, rubidium, sodium or lithium. A simple test to establish acidic or alkaline constituents is that made with an indicator which itself either changes colour or changes the colour of a solution in the presence of an acid or an alkali. Probably the oldest indicator is litmus.

Litmus indicators are derived from lichens which impart red or blue colours and can be in the form of liquids, tablets or the litmus paper so familiar to schoolboys. Litmus paper is made from strips of a kind of blotting paper, soaked in the appropriate dyes to produce blue or red litmus paper.

If a drop of blue litmus solution is added to a strong acid such as nitric, hydrochloric or sulphuric acid it turns red. Weaker acids such as soda water or vinegar give a wine-red colour. In alkalis such as caustic soda or ammonia, red litmus turns blue. One the other hand, if hydrochloric acid is slowly added to caustic soda, which has a drop of litmus in it, a point is reached when the blue colour becomes purple; adding more acid turns the purple to red. When no colour change occurs with a litmus indicator the solution being analysed is said to be neutral because neither acid nor alkali are present.

Testing for sugar and starch

Agricultural scientists often analyse samples of soil to evaluate their acidity, while tests for acidity and alkalinity are vitally important in the work of pathologists and industrial chemists. One very important branch of analysis is concerned with tests to detect the presence of starch and sugar. Tincture of iodine turns starch blue.

There are several kinds of sugar. One of these is the glucose present in many fruits and vegetables, and into which all other sugars are converted by the saliva of the mouth or by the pancreatic juice of the small intestine. Apples and grapes are rich sources of glucose, the presence of which can be established by using Haines solution which turns red if glucose is present. This test is often used by doctors to test people's urine for diabetes.

Precipitation occurs when a substance that does not dissolve is formed in a solution and settles out. Often when chemical substances are mixed together in solution, the precipitates formed have characteristic colours which enable them to be identified. A chemist may be asked to analyse a perfectly clear solution which is thought to contain a silver compound. He will first pour some of the solution into a test tube and add water containing common salt. If silver is present this will at once induce the formation of a precipitate of a white curly substance, which on exposure to a strong light will begin to darken. As compounds of silver darken on exposure to light, the test proves the presence of silver beyond doubt.

With the development of man-made fibres, analysts are frequently required to test fabrics to establish whether, for example, they are made of a mixture of cotton and wool, wool and silk, all wool or all silk, or part silk and part rayon. One

Paint undergoing chemical tests to determine its exact composition. Quality control in many factories involves constant analysis of production samples to check consistency.

method of distinguishing silk from rayon is to burn a few strands of each separately and note any odour; rayon has no smell, but silk has a distinctive odour. If a piece of fabric is thought to be a mixture of cotton and wool it is put into a beaker of water containing sodium hydroxide and boiled for several minutes. At the end of the test, the piece of fabric will look like a piece of mesh, because the wool has dissolved out, leaving the cotton fibres intact.

An equally simple test reveals the difference between linen and cotton. A sample of each is first soaked in water and then put in a one per cent alcoholic solution of *fuchsin* (a red dye). After the samples have been thoroughly washed they are treated with ammonium hydroxide. This leaves the cotton fibres uncoloured while the linen fibres turn red.

By juggling with chemicals and watching their reactions under conditions of light, heat or cold, or even by odour, analysts can establish beyond doubt the constituents of practically any sample given to them. But this type of analysis consumes a great deal of time and effort, and is being replaced by quicker and, for many types of analysis, more positive methods. The chief of these are *spectroscopic* and *chromatographic analysis,* both of which are now the standard analysis techniques in industrial and other large laboratories.

Spectroscopic analysis is a development of the heat and flame tests already referred

to, and depends on the fact that every element has its own characteristic colour wavelength. This enables a spectrum of the substance to be analysed according to the wavelengths of the light emitted from it and thereby establish its composition.

The heat test for analysing the composition of a sample according to colours is

Biochemists have special pieces of apparatus for analysing the chemistry of living tissue. The Warburg respirometer, shown here, measures the tissues' oxygen uptake.

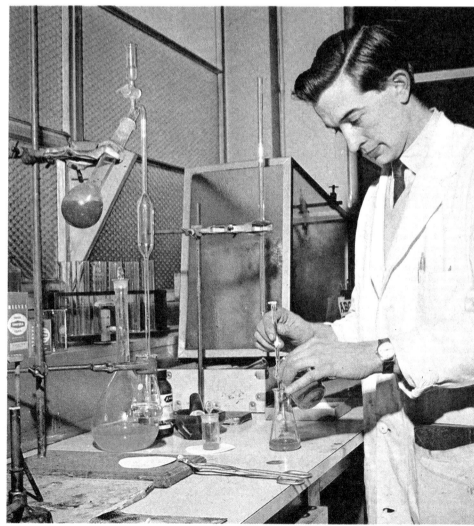

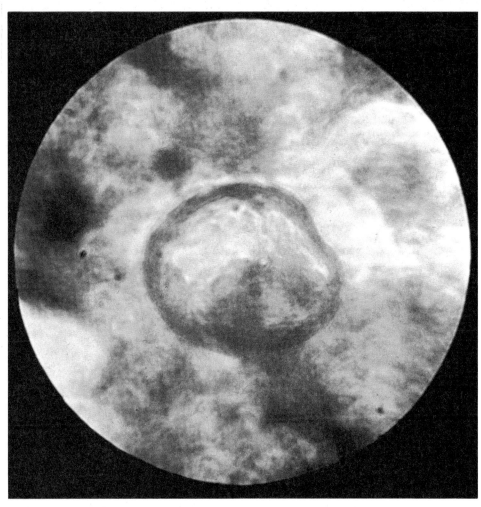

Chemical tests revealed that this speck of matter found in a meteorite had an organic origin. But the carbon compounds may be contaminants introduced as the meteorite landed.

sists of three main parts: a chamber in which the specimen is made to radiate energy; a complex of lens and prism to break up the light into its appropriate wavelengths; and a microscope or other instrument to observe the spectrum and identify the lines or wavelengths. The sample to be analysed is first heated so that it gives out light. The light from the sample is then focused on to the prism, causing it to fan out according to the various wavelengths.

Sodium, for example, gives a single yellow line on the spectrum, but when this line is magnified through the microscope, it is revealed as two yellow lines very close together. The spectrum of any particular element never varies. The only variation is in the intensity of the lines, and the degree of intensity of any particular line indicates the quantity of the element present in the sample.

In spectroscopic analysis, a *photomultiplier* is placed at each line of the spectrum. Each of the photomultipliers is placed behind a slit, through which the appropriate spectrum line passes, to shield it from unwanted light. By means of electronic relays, the current converted by the photomultiplier from the light energy moves a needle across a dial calibrated according to known quantities of the

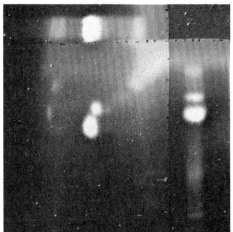

Chromatography makes use of the different rates at which compounds in solution move up wet paper. The various separate compounds here glow in ultra-violet light.

reliable enough when the sample contains only one element. But this kind of analysis is useless when the sample to be analysed contains a mixture of metals. The eye can neither analyse a mixture of colours, nor can it estimate the quantity of any constituent of the sample according to the intensity of the colour. It was to solve that problem that spectroscopic analysis was developed.

Spectroscopic analysing equipment con-

This complex arrangement of tubes and vessels is being used to test artificial fibres to determine their structure. The test sample itself is the brown fluid in the lowest bottle.

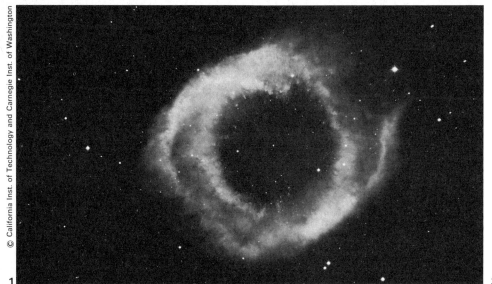

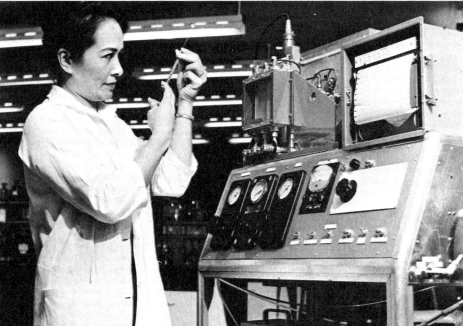

1 Spectroscopic analysis allows astronomers to study the chemistry of the stars. Helium was discovered on a star before chemists knew of its existence on Earth.

2 Using a spatula a scientist doles out chemical before grinding it to a powder with a mortar and pestle. The retort over the Bunsen burner carries a reflex condenser to prevent loss of water.

3 Automatic analysers are now widely used, particularly where large numbers of samples must be tested. This automated chromatograph is being used to analyse lung gases.

various elements. By means of a switch panel, the analyst can tell at a glance the quantity of each element in a sample.

Another form of spectroscopic analysis is *absorption spectroscopy* which, using the infra-red spectrum, is based on the phenomenon that matter absorbs radiation selectively according to source.

Conventional analysis by spectroscopy and absorption spectroscopy usually can be made in a matter of minutes, but a new development now makes possible what is, to all intents, instantaneous analysis. The instrument is called a *time-of-flight mass spectrometer* and is capable of analysing liquids and solids, and giving the precise composition and quantities of constituents in less than ten microseconds.

A time-of-flight mass spectrometer operates by ionizing the gases or vapours present in the sample and accelerating the ions along a field-free drift tube. The ions separate into bunches with velocities relative to the mass of the particular ion. Thus the low mass ions arrive at the end of the drift tube earlier than those of high mass, so producing a spectrum by way of an appropriate particle detector. The resultant ion-currents are amplified by an

electron multiplier. One important application of the instrument is to determine instantaneously the exact composition of the anaesthetic gas being administered to and exhaled by a patient undergoing long and complex surgery. It has been used successfully in heart transplant and similar organ operations.

If you examine closely a sheet of used blotting paper, you will noticed that each of the ink blots is not the same colour over its whole surface, and that the edges in particular are of a different colour from the centre. Now get a stick of white chalk of the kind used for writing on blackboards and dip it into a pot of ink. The ink not only rises up the stick of chalk because of what is called *capillary action,* but instead of the chalk being dyed with the colour of the ink, it has several distinct bands of colour.

This is the basis of the analytical technique called *chromatography,* which takes advantage of the phenomenon that certain liquids break up into their chemical constituents when brought into contact with absorbent materials such as chalk (calcium sulphate) or blotting paper. The constituents of the sample being analysed

can then be recognized by either their colour or the rate at which they are absorbed. For example, the different colours of the ink blots on the blotting paper and on the stick of chalk prove that ink is made from a number of different substances.

In *paper chromatography,* a drop of the solution to be analysed is placed near one end of a piece of absorbent filter paper. The edge or tip of the paper is then dipped into a suitable solvent. As capillary action raises the solvent up into the paper, the various constituents of the sample move behind the advancing solvent. The speeds of the movements of the various constituents of the sample depend upon their chemical compositions. The paper is then cut up according to the changes on it and the pieces are analysed to establish their exact composition.

With *column chromatography* a solvent and the sample for analysis are mixed together and allowed to flow down a column of powdered limestone enclosed in a glass tube. The constituents of the sample then collect as a coloured band at the top of the tube. The band of colour is then 'developed' by washing in pure solvent, which has the effect of breaking up the single-coloured band into a series of bands, each of which contains one or other of the various constituents of the sample. The column is then sliced according to the colours of the bands and each slice subjected to conventional analysis to establish its exact composition.

Mechanized and automatic analysis techniques have developed rapidly in the past decade and are taking much of the routine drudgery out of analysis, leaving the analyst to interpret the results.

Instruments for death

Since the dawn of time Man has devoted much of his effort and ingenuity to killing his fellow men. Starting with sticks and rocks he has now progressed to devices which threaten the entire planet.

This German Kolibri automatic pistol has a calibre of only 3 mm and fires one of the smallest cartridges ever designed to fit inside an automatic pistol. The coins indicate its actual size.

Built at the Krupp arms factory in Essen, Big Bertha was used to shell Paris from a distance of 40 miles during the First World War. It is one of the largest artillery pieces ever constructed.

THE PROGRESS OF CIVILIZATION runs alongside the sophistication of weaponry – the more civilized we become the better able we are to kill and maim our fellow men. This curious paradox lies at the root of many of the problems of the present day – though science can now bring great benefits to society through its peaceful application it also provides us with vastly improved means of destruction.

Anthropologists speculate about the origins of war and conflict between human beings, but one thing is certain: from very early times weapons have been used not only for hunting and killing game, but for attacking and killing human beings as well.

The frightening array of weaponry that confronts us today – nuclear, chemical and biological weapons, military aircraft, tanks, guns and small arms, together with their sometimes bizarre and ingenious variations – has evolved from small beginnings and become more devastating and sophisticated with the passage of time.

In the process, wars have been transformed from isolated events, in which most people participate only as spectators, to conflicts of world significance which may threaten the future of every one of us.

Present-day weapons can be divided into a number of categories according to the scientific principles which govern their operation. The simplest category involves those weapons that depend for their action on human muscle power. Swords, axes, maces, clubs and their various offspring until quite recent times played a predominant part in warfare. All depend on the delivery of some type of blow with a pointed or cutting edge or with some type of the traditional 'blunt instrument'.

Over the ages, many variations on this theme have been used. The Roman legionaries, for example, favoured short, broad-

The V2 rocket, shown here on its launching pad at Cuxhaven on the Elbe, marked a revolution in rocket warfare. Present-day ballistic missiles owe a great deal to the V2's advanced design.

bladed swords, which were highly effective in hand-to-hand conflict at ground level. Similar considerations dominated the evolution of the short dagger, popular during the battles of the Middle Ages, again for close fighting on the ground.

The horsemen of the Middle Ages, on the other hand, favoured another type of sword: the heavy two-handed variety which could be brought down from above on their victims. Part of the reason for the use of a heavy sword in that period, of course, was the fashion for heavy body armour which prevented lighter weapons from being effective.

Spears, pikes and lances represent another simple type of weapon with a long history. The most sophisticated spears were the halberds, used by foot soldiers in the fourteenth and fifteenth centuries. The halberd was an eight-foot spear which had a combined axe-head, hook and point attached to it. Halberdiers were frequently able to withstand cavalry charges with these weapons.

The projectile has some obvious advantages over the close-combat weapons. It can kill from far off without necessitating close combat. The simplest type of projectile is the sling-shot, which enables missiles to be catapulted further than they can be thrown by hand. The biblical story of David and Goliath indicates the antiquity of this type of weapon.

Much more advanced in principle is the bow, of which there are many thousands of varieties. The bow enables its user to store the energy of his muscles in the tensed bowstring and bow. A bow can store considerable amounts of energy and release it in a very short time, thus sending an arrow or bolt further with greater force than would otherwise be the case.

A later development of the original bow came with the crossbow, in which the

1 The Chieftain tank is one of the latest tanks developed by the British army. Tanks were first used in the First World War, where they marked a turning-point in hostilities.

2 A crossbow, of Spanish design, which once belonged to King Louis XII of France. By cranking the handles the bowman could gradually draw back the bowstring, thus tensing the steel bow. Although the rate of firing was slower than with the conventional bow, bolts could be shot over short distances with greater accuracy.

3 Acheulian hand axes give some idea of how the first weapons may have looked. These sharpened flint-stones were found in gravel sediments near the village of Swanscombe in Kent.

4 A print of 1845 showing soldiers of the Royal Artillery practising with an early version of the bazooka. Because of their unreliability these early rocket weapons were not a great success.

5 An early sixteenth-century painting by the Indian artist Paras shows bullocks dragging siege guns for an attack on the fort of Ranthambh, Rajastan, in 1568.

stored energy was accumulated and held mechanically. Though the crossbow could not fire as many shots in a given time as the longbow, its metal bolts were delivered with more accuracy and greater velocity.

The great revolution in weaponry came, of course, with the invention of gunpowder. This mixture of saltpetre (potassium nitrate), sulphur and charcoal was discovered in China, but its properties were first put to full use in the West. The Italian Wars of 1494–1525 saw the first large-scale use of weapons based on gunpowder – firearms. Gunpowder had been known for a number of years before that date – indeed Roger Bacon, the English scholar, wrote a treatise on 'black powder' in the first half of the thirteenth century. But it took time for weapons to be developed that could exploit the new discovery.

The first use of powder was in cannon, and the first cannon were extremely crude. Indeed, in many cases they were as much a danger to the user as to his intended victim. The original cannon were just iron buckets into which powder and stones were loaded and ignited through a hole at the bottom. Later the tubular form, imparting an accurate trajectory to the missile, developed. These weapons were used mainly in sieges and in defending fortifications. Accuracy was difficult to achieve, as it involved tedious calculations with the aid of the quadrant. Cannons were most useful from high on battlements where their accuracy was improved and their range lengthened.

It was in small arms rather than artillery, however, that the most significant changes were to take place. The bowmen who had dominated the battlefields of Europe since the days of Crécy and Agincourt were pushed off the stage of history by the new breed of musketeers.

The arquebus, the first type of small arm, was really a smaller version of the cannon. Though primitive, cumbersome and fairly dangerous to the user, it could kill at 100 yards. Arquebuses were ignited by applying a fuse to the priming powder. Through the succeeding centuries, the development of firearms was rapid. New

methods of igniting the powder – the wheel-lock and the flint-lock – were superseded by the development of the percussion cap. Finally, the modern breechloading cartridge has now almost entirely overtaken every other type of ignition, except in certain specialized uses. Guns, too, underwent very considerable changes. New methods of loading made possible advances in pistol and gun design, such as the invention of repeating pistols and rifles and machine-guns.

Firing without smoke

One of the most important developments that made possible many new weapons was the self-contained metallic cartridge. Bullet, propellant and primer were now supplied in one unit. The copper cartridge case expanded on firing to fill the breech of the gun and then contracted immediately to make easy extraction possible. This is the type of cartridge used in almost all modern firearms.

Gunpowder itself was superseded by the discovery of the new and more efficient smokeless propellants. Smokeless powder, discovered in 1884, was made of a gelatinized mixture of nitroglycerine and guncotton. Not only did it give off considerably less smoke than black powder, but it was a more stable and powerful mixture.

The usefulness of explosives in warfare

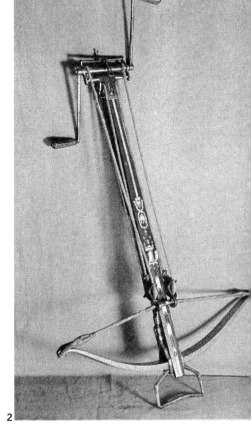

4

5

was not, of course, limited to firearms. In the late medieval period, gunpowder was sometimes used to blow up fortifications or to make explosive projectiles. Mines and grenades developed and formed the basis for a new branch of warfare. Grenades, originally crude pots filled with explosive and ignited through a fuse, have advanced enormously – though still in essence very simple. They found particular application in the static trench warfare of the First World War.

The modern grenade really begins with the further development of explosives to produce trinitrotoluene (T.N.T.). Because of its low sensitivity to percussion, its low melting point and its high explosive performance, the T.N.T. grenade was far more reliable than its predecessors. In a scored metal container, the explosive could be relied on to shower an enemy with sharp pieces of metal, thus vastly increasing its killing potential. Other types of grenade were designed to carry noxious gases, like tear gas, to harass the enemy, while others again could be used to lay down smoke-screens.

The mine or bomb – the two were originally almost indistinguishable – contained more explosive than the grenade and was originally used for attacking fortifications (hence 'undermining'). But, particularly in naval warfare, the word mine came to be used to described bombs which, released into the sea, would explode near enemy ships. During the two World Wars, vast areas of sea were mined to prevent enemy ships from venturing into them.

Dropping the bomb

The bomb, on the other hand, really came into its own with the advent of the military aircraft. The early attempts at aerial bombing were not strikingly successful, chiefly because of the difficulty of dropping the missiles sufficiently accurately on target. With the designing of accurate bomb-sights, however, and the building of aircraft capable of carrying larger bombs, air bombing became an extremely effective method of warfare. For the first time, civilians became exposed to the full horrors of war, though they might be hundreds of miles behind the lines. The impersonal character of this method of warfare gave it a potent terrorist value.

Bombs were designed for a wide variety of uses – incendiary, high explosive, armour-piercing, anti-personnel and so on. In some cases, as with the celebrated 'block-busters' used in the raids on the Ruhr Valley dams in 1943, the bombs were specifically tailored to achieve one particular mission.

But the most spectacular bomb of all was only to be developed right at the end of the Second World War. This was the atomic bomb, dropped by American bombers on Hiroshima and Nagasaki. The two cities were razed instantaneously with tens of thousands of deaths. Today, after the invention of the hydrogen bomb, the potential exists to destroy not just cities but whole continents and nations of people.

The hydrogen bomb has since been linked with new forms of rocket to deliver the weapons at great distances and speeds. The use of rockets to deliver explosive or incendiary weapons is nothing new in warfare: such means of delivery were used by the Chinese in very ancient times. But because of the difficulties of controlling the speed and direction of the primitive rockets of that period it was not until comparatively recently that rockets came to play more than a minor role in warfare. Improvements in propellants, and increased knowledge of the ballistics of rockets, made it possible to design weapons in which a grenade or small explosive charge could be delivered with acceptable accuracy. One weapon of this type, widely used in the Second World War, was the bazooka – a one-man rocket-launcher which delivered a powerful explosive charge for use against tanks. On the eastern front, the Soviet Army made considerable use of rocket-launchers as a substitute for artillery: batteries of rocket-launchers, resembling organ-pipes, were used with devastating effects.

German rocketry was rather more ambitious, and led directly to the design and use of the famous V1 and V2 weapons. The V1 was simply a pilotless plane which was allowed to run in on its target and then glide down when the motor cut out. The V2, its successor, was a far more ambitious project, anticipating in many ways the intercontinental ballistic missiles of today.

Modern rocketry, whether military or civil – and the dividing line between military and civil rocket programmes is often thin – draws on a vast number of sciences to achieve its remarkable feats. The physicist and the engineer, the chemist and the mathematician, are all required to contribute their special skills to the immensely expensive projects which give birth to these monster weapons.

Even the biologists are not left out of the development of modern weapons. Indeed, they may yet produce some of the most devastating weapons of all. Growing public concern has focused attention on the preparations for biological warfare, preparations which have been going ahead in almost all the major countries.

Germs that kill

The principle of biological warfare, of course, is nothing new, but it is only recently that it has been put on a firm scientific basis. In the Middle Ages the poisoning of wells, often by throwing in the bodies of plague victims, was an accepted tactic during siege warfare. Sometimes the bodies of plague victims were lobbed over the walls of a besieged town in an attempt to spread disease.

Such applications were of necessity rather limited in their application, but modern discoveries in biology have completely changed that situation. Now not only can the plague organism, and other organisms causing deadly diseases, be isolated and grown in culture, but their characteristics, their virulence, their power to withstand exposure to air, their temperature tolerance, can be adjusted almost to order by changing their genetic material. Thus microbes can be tailored to

fit particular military requirements.

Apart from the microbes themselves, there is also the possibility of using their poisonous toxins to destroy enemies. Such bacteria as *Clostridia botulina* give rise to poisons so virulent that a pound of botulinum toxin could, in theory, poison every human being on this planet. With weapons like these, polluting wells becomes child's play.

Like the biologist, the chemist is also drawn into the design of new and more bizarre and horrible weapons. During the First World War, large quantities of various disabling gases, like mustard gas,

chlorine and phosgene, were used against enemy troops. These gases killed relatively few of their victims, though many were permanently blinded or maimed. Though similar gases were not used generally in the Second World War, the search has continued for chemical weapons. Among new types developed are the nerve gases, minute quantities of which will paralyse a man completely, and the hallucinogens, with an action similar to the drug LSD.

These frightening new weapons underline the truth of the paradox that the nearer we get to 'civilization' the closer we come to killing the world.

1 An engraving showing naval gunners practising with a 100-pounder Armstrong gun in 1862. This type of gun was one of the first breech-loading artillery pieces introduced into the Navy.

2 An Amazonian indian fishing from his dug-out with bow and arrow. Despite his apparently primitive equipment, he is able to use the bow with remarkable accuracy.

A better life or utter chaos?

Through technology Man hoped to conquer the world but these hopes have not been realized. If he is to have a future, he must clear up the mess he has made and use his knowledge with greater care.

THE TWENTIETH CENTURY opened with glorious prospects. Great steamships were crossing the oceans. Motoring had arrived. Railways had reached an advanced stage of development. The Industrial Revolution had shown the way to cheap consumer goods for everyone. The electric telegraph was well established and the telephone was becoming commonplace.

In 1901, the extraordinary young man Guglielmo Marconi demonstrated that it was possible to send messages through space over vast distances without the use of cables. In 1903, Orville Wright made the first hesitant flight in a heavier-than-air flying machine.

It seemed then that nothing was impossible. Scientists, engineers and technologists had the world in their grasp. With patient development of all the new inventions and with parallel advances in the science of medicine to prolong human life, the prospects for mankind looked brighter than at any other time in history. The good life was already on its way.

Looking back from our vantage point we see that the dreamer at the turn of the century had little idea of future developments. Now there are scores of thousands of electronic computers in daily use, millions of cars and television receivers, nuclear power stations, laser beams, electronic microcircuits no bigger than a pinhead, processed foods, pest control, synthetic fibres, and space travel. The good life has arrived.

In November 1965 an area of 80,000 square miles of northeastern United States and Canada was plunged into darkness through a single failure on the electricity power grid system. The result was chaos. No one had realized quite how dependent on the electricity supply Man had become. People were trapped in lifts between floors, radio and television went off the air, traffic signals were out of action, meals were left half-cooked and there was not only chaos, but panic and fear.

The surprising thing about this episode was that the control system of the grid network had been designed to eliminate such a possibility. If one community supply becomes overloaded, then additional electric power is routed in from an area which is lightly loaded. At least, this was the theory. In this instance, a relay on one feeder line at one power station failed and put an unexpected surge of power on to the other feeders from the generating station. The shock wave rippled round the network triggering off safety switches in station after station until several cities, including

New York, had been completely blacked out. The elaborate automatic control system, so carefully designed to take care of every eventuality, had operated in a way quite contrary to the designers' intentions.

This single event raised the question of whether the engineers were being too clever. Had we reached the stage where the man-made machine could, in fact, turn on Man and destroy him? Was this a twentieth-century example of Man creating a monster which he was unable to control?

Danger to health

In 1953 United States scientists believed that radioactive fall-out from nuclear-weapon tests in the atmosphere would be uniform over the globe and that no single area would receive fall-out doses which would be a danger to health. In 1957 it was being said that the fall-out from the stratosphere would be quite slow, allowing plenty of time for the natural decay of radio-isotopes. We now know that fall-out is not evenly distributed and that it descends to the Earth much more quickly than was believed possible.

In 1957, when farmers in the Mississippi Valley started using a pesticide called endrin, a chemical relation of DDT, they could hardly have been expected to realize that a few years later the Mississippi River would be full of dead fish. In Europe a similar mishap came to light when, in June 1969, millions of dead fish were found in the Rhine, which has now been dubbed Europe's sewer.

Not only is the world population in-

creasing at a prodigious rate but each man, woman and child is consuming more of the world's resources. Paul Ehrlich of Stanford University has estimated that in 70 years of life an American citizen uses 26 million gallons of water and 21,000 gallons of petrol. Figures like this remind us that the natural resources of our world are not limitless. Energy reserves in coal and petroleum are being quickly used up. The same applies to other raw materials, both metallic and non-metallic.

In using up our natural resources we are creating new problems. When we burn a ton of coal, wood, petroleum or natural gas we contribute large amounts of carbon dioxide to the atmosphere. In 100 years, from 1860 to 1960, we added 14 per cent to the carbon-dioxide content of the air. Carbon dioxide tends to pass visible light but to absorb infra-red rays, just as glass does in a greenhouse. Scientists are now suggesting that further significant increases in the carbon-dioxide content of the atmosphere may produce a 'greenhouse effect' which could warm up the globe to a level which will melt the Arctic and Antarctic ice-caps and flood our major cities.

A counter-argument claims that the world might get colder. Smog pollution of the atmosphere might effectively act like an increase of low-cloud, shielding off the warming sun's rays and start a return to the Ice Age.

Naturally, there is scientific controversy over a number of points. But there is no controversy over the fact that we are beginning to suffer from ignorance of the long-term effects of our exploitation of

In June 1969, millions of fish in the Rhine were killed after a factory in Germany had accidentally released a poison into the river. Such disasters are on the increase.

nature. It may be arguable whether the world will still be habitable by the year 2000 A D but there is no argument that something should be done now to stop the unconsidered use of chemicals and fuels which are making our world a cess-pit and upsetting the natural balance of nature.

The situation is becoming so serious that even politicians have begun to take notice. President Nixon in his January 1970 State of the Union Message said, 'The great question of the 70s is shall we surrender to our surroundings or shall we make our peace with nature and begin to make reparation for the damage we have done to our air, to our land, and to our water?' The same question has been asked by Prime Minister Wilson in the United Kingdom and by other world leaders. Unquestionably, the key problem of modern governments is to employ science to check the drift to destruction. Within the main problem the physical scientists have their own subsidiary problems which can help in the solution of the whole. But central to the issue is how far the individual is prepared to go to make the solution possible. At a seminar on 'Man and the Future' staged to celebrate the centennial of the University of Kansas, the question of atmospheric pollution by the motor-car was forcibly raised and the delegates were unanimous in their condemnation of the motor-car as a menace to civilization. And yet, at the conclusion of their deliberations, they left the auditorium and climbed into their cars and drove away in the modern invention they had only a few minutes earlier condemned. The human motivation to use a convenient form of transport had already overcome their convictions.

The problem of carbon-monoxide production in exhaust gases from cars is already receiving attention. New cars emerging from the factories in the United States in 1971 belched out only 37 per cent as much carbon monoxide as 1960 cars did but the engine modifications, which will achieve the reduction, will be putting out more nitrogen compounds resulting in a

1 Nuclear power stations provide an answer to the eventual shortage of fossil fuels. Yet disposal of their radioactive waste presents a major problem for the future.

2 The demand for water for domestic and industrial use is increasing rapidly. To meet it, water containing effluent can be re-cycled in special plants and made fit for consumption.

3 In the refinery, oil is transformed into fuel that keeps industries running. But when oil is burnt, large amounts of carbon dioxide are released into the atmosphere which may change the climates.

substantial increase in nitrogen oxides. This, in the end, according to some pundits, could produce an even more devastating effect because nitrogen oxides in the air have already seriously increased in the past few years and they affect the quality of light which, in turn, affects the quality of crops.

The complete answer can lie in the electric car which produces no toxic fumes and creates little noise. The fuel cell, generating electricity directly from chemical reaction, is still thought to be the best solution, but development of the necessary lightweight batteries has been slow and uncertain. For short-range town use a number of schemes are possible, such as the use of conventional batteries with public 'filling stations' where the car can be parked and have its batteries quickly re-charged at the same time.

Another problem, that of energy resources, will probably be solved by the nuclear power station. This is the one big technological bonus which has been won from the atomic bomb. Mention has already been made of the squandering by Man of fossil fuels which took millions of years in the making by natural means. Atomic fusion, the form of energy used in the hydrogen bomb, taps the energy potential of heavy hydrogen which, in the oceans of the world, constitutes a reserve of energy many million times as great as that of our fossil fuel reserves. But the use of fusion for power production still seems

4 The advantage of electricity is that it is clean. If large cities are to be inhabitable in the future, not only trains but also cars will have to use electricity.

5 The River Mississippi has become a vast sewer, overloaded with all types of refuse. If Man is to survive, he must learn to save his fresh water from contamination.

6 Enshrouded in smog from chimneys and cars, New York is now an unhealthy environment. Such conditions shorten life spans in spite of tremendous advances in medical science.

1 An experimental steam generator is fitted into a car in America. Interest in steam-powered vehicles has revived because of the need to cut air pollution caused by petrol engines.
2 In Hungary a policeman tests the exhaust from a lorry to check that it does not exceed permitted levels. With engine modification, carbon-monoxide production can be reduced.
3 Passengers were stranded at railway stations in New York after a breakdown in the automatic control system led to a massive power failure causing chaos in northwestern United States.

very far away.

The nuclear power station, however, did not become a reality overnight. There were great engineering and safety problems to be overcome. And there was the question of economics. Only now are nuclear power stations beginning to compete seriously in cost-per-unit of electricity with the best coal or oil-fired stations. For the more modern types of nuclear plant there are still great engineering problems ahead.

The experimental Dragon high-temperature gas reactor, being developed by a consortium of 12 European nations, has been tested for ten years. The report issued by the European Nuclear Energy Agency in late 1969 stated that reactors of the Dragon type would be commercially viable in that generating costs would be lower than the British developed advanced gas-cooled or the United States light-water reactors. But there is still some doubt on the complete safety of the ceramic coated particle fuel elements.

Apart from being a useful substitute for fossil fuels, nuclear power has two other advantages. The economics of nuclear power are not nearly so dependent on geographical location as is a coal-fired power station which, ideally, should be sited at the coal field to save transport costs. Nuclear power stations can be sited in completely new areas which can be developed for industrial use, so relieving population and industrial congestion elsewhere. The second advantage is that they do not pollute the atmosphere with sulphur dioxide and carbon dioxide.

The huge power potential of nuclear energy can also be used in other ways. The water shortage in many parts of the world could be solved by large-scale desalination of sea water. Even in wet countries, like Britain, water supplies are becoming an increasing problem through increasing demand. It takes 18 pints of water to make a single pint of beer, about 100 tons of water to make a single ton of steel, and 15 tons of water are required for every half-pound of beef steak which is eaten.

The best water is rainwater collected in giant reservoirs. Calculations show that to meet anticipated demands for domestic use alone in Britain where, it is estimated, each person uses about 50 gallons of water a day, another 100 reservoirs would be needed by the year 2000 A.D. This would mean losing nearly as much land, most of it valuable valley-farming areas, as the present 117 square miles of reservoirs in England and Wales. It also means rehousing and compensating thousands of people.

Second-hand water

The solution this time might lie in using the rivers – if they were not so badly polluted by industrial waste and other effluents. Scientists have succeeded in re-cycling water to reduce effluents to a level low enough to make the water fit for human consumption; Londoners, although few of them realize it, are already drinking a proportion of purified effluent. But to be successful, the pollution level of the rivers must be rigorously controlled to a figure much less than the 40 per cent typical effluent content of, for example, Britain's River Trent.

A by-product of the nuclear power station, the waste heat discharged from its cooling towers, is being used experimentally for fish farming. For years bigger and better trawlers have been built and equipped with electronic fish-finding equipment but they catch fewer and fewer fish. The truth is that we have been robbing some parts of the oceans faster than the natural reproductive cycle of the fish. The problem is an international one.

But why not farm fish – as we farm animals or poultry – in captivity? The United Kingdom White Fish Authority and a commercial company have been experimenting with the idea. Flat-fish have been found the most suitable type and can be factory-farmed at densities over a thousand times that of their natural environment. In test tanks, warmed up by the hot effluent from Hunterston nuclear power station, plaice have grown to a size suitable for consumption in only 18 months instead of three years in the open sea. The warmer water stimulates growth and feeding rate. If the warm water discharged from all Britain's power stations were used to keep a whole series of fish farms warm, it has been calculated that a quarter of the home market could be met without a single trawler leaving port.

The turning point of scientific development may well come during the 1970s. The general public has been alerted to the dangers of ruining our atmosphere, our land and our oceans. It may well learn that travelling by electric train in urban areas, although less convenient, may be more beneficial in the end than travelling by a car which belches out poisonous fumes; that it may be better to pay a few pence more for food that has not been forced into growth through indiscriminate use of chemical fertilizers.

The scientists, together with their engineer and technologist assistants, are also becoming aware that all the key problems of today are connected, not with entirely new discoveries, but in learning how to use today's knowledge far more effectively and, above all, far more sensibly and with much greater care than we have done to date. But, finally, we may have to sacrifice some of the comforts of our technological age to survive in a world free of pollution.

Refining natural products

Petrol tanks and sugar basins the world over are filled with the products of refineries. Modern refineries are highly automated chemical factories, in which wastage is cut to the minimum.

FEW NATURAL SUBSTANCES are found in a pure state. Almost all are contaminated to some degree or another by other substances, some of which may not only be undesirable but actively harmful in the final product. The canes from which sugar is produced, for example, contain not only sugar but cellulose, proteins, chlorophyll and other colouring chemicals and salts, as well as water. The sugar we put into our tea is made from sugar cane by a complicated process in which the chemicals contaminating the sugar are removed by chemical and physical processes.

These processes come under the collective heading of refining, a word which is applied chiefly to the process of purifying crude oil. Refining originally meant the removal of impurities, but its meaning has been extended to cover the very complex operations which take place in a modern oil refinery.

Crude oil is rather like a conjurer's hat: if you are clever enough you can make it produce almost anything you want. In fact, the story of petrol refining is an excellent example of the economical pressures of demand causing a changing pattern in the supply of commodities produced by different refining techniques.

This comes as rather a surprise to people who have only a sketchy knowledge of the workings of a modern refinery. A common misconception is that crude oil is composed of the same materials always in the same proportions.

Constituents of crude

But oil varies enormously in composition, depending on its place of origin. The constitutents of crude can be divided roughly into three classes, together with a number of impurities present in small amounts, but the ranging proportions of the classes of compound give each crude a definite character.

All the main compounds found in crude oil are hydrocarbons, formed solely from carbon and hydrogen atoms. Of these, one of three main groups is the *paraffins*, or saturated hydrocarbons, which embrace products from methane, a very light gas, to heavy waxes. Paraffins have the special characteristic that, if the number of carbon atoms in the molecule is denoted by n, then the number of hydrogen atoms is $2n+2$. They are called 'saturated' hydrocarbons because each carbon atom is united with the maximum number of hydrogen atoms.

Containing fewer hydrogen atoms per atom of carbon, the *naphthenes* are distinguished by having the carbon atoms arranged in rings, giving a slightly closer packing of the atoms in the molecule, reflected in a higher density. In the *aromatics*, however, the carbon atoms arrange themselves in rings of six, and the molecule contains six fewer hydrogen atoms than the corresponding naphthene. From this indiscriminate mixture of so many different compounds, the refinery produces a large number of substances for varying purposes, and in amounts depending on the demands made at any one time in any place. In the early days of oil exploration the principal requirement was for kerosene (better known in Britain as paraffin) for heating and lighting. Natural

The oil refinery at Kirkuk, Iraq. The taps in the foreground regulate the flow of crude oil and oil fractions through the refinery's stages. In the background are stills.

gases and the lighter parts of the crude oil, which we now use as petrol or gasoline, were burnt as unusable waste products.

Early in the twentieth century the development of the petrol engine changed all that, however, and together with the use of gas for heating and lighting, led to an upsurge in the sales of petrol and, locally, of natural gas, while paraffin was regarded as an encumbrance at the refinery. But again, in the 1950s, jet and jet turbine engines began consuming vast quantities of kerosene, which is a much better fuel for these continuous-burning engines than the lighter and more volatile gasoline fractions. So the pendulum of refining swung back once again. Fortunately, refinery techniques had by this time reached a very advanced stage of development, so that subsequent unexpected demands, such as for the raw materials for the plastics industry, posed few problems to the refineries.

As with any item intended for mass consumption, the economics of oil products are particularly critical. Profit per gallon is low, and so the siting of a refinery, for example, is of the utmost importance. At first sight, since the volume of saleable products is only nine-tenths of the volume of the original crude, it would appear to be best to site the refinery near the well to save transport cost.

Since wage rates in the consuming countries are also generally higher than in the producing countries, there would

An engraving by Stradamus of the production of olive oil. In the foreground tyre-like baskets are filled with olives ready for the oil to be pressed. The oil is decanted into barrels.

appear to be a double saving. However, the risk of contamination of the end product and the problems of distribution more than offset these two factors, and so the refineries are almost always built near the markets.

In Europe, most crude oil arrives by tanker, and so refineries are usually on the coast or on an estuary which provides a deep-water berth for these vessels. But there is a second reason why a refinery should be built near the sea: vast quantities of water are needed for cooling and raising steam for the separation processes.

Modern refineries are operated on the stream system, in which the crude is processed continuously. This is distinct from the older batch method in which reaction vessels were filled with crude, the process run to completion, stopped, the vessel emptied and the process begun again. The high capital cost of modern refinery equipment, with its automatic control gear, makes it necessary for operation to be virtually non-stop.

Feedstock, the crude oil, must always be available, and each refinery has large storage tanks so that the refinery will continue to operate for a period of weeks even in the event of a breakdown in supply. Oil from the tankers is discharged directly into these tanks, which in turn feed the first refining stages.

Refining techniques

Refining processes can be divided naturally into two groups: physical separation, which depends on the physical characteristics of the constituents of the oil such as specific gravity and volatility (the best known of these processes is fractional distillation), and processes in which a chemical reaction is used to change the character of the constituents. Among the latter are cracking, reforming and polymerization.

The oldest of all techniques for reducing crude oil to usable compounds is distillation, a process similar to that used in producing fresh water from sea water.

In refineries these stills are known as fractionating columns, and they can be anything up to 50 ft in diameter and 180 ft high, as tall as the drilling rig at an oil well. Stills operate in banks, through which the raw material passes in sequence.

Normally, the first column operates at fairly high pressure, usually about 100 lb/ sq. in., to give the first separation of light and heavy fractions. Crude oil, previously heated to about 425 °C., is pumped into the bottom of the tower, which contains a number of catchment trays at various heights. As the crude enters the column, the lighter fractions, with their lower boiling points, ascend as vapour while the heaviest parts of the crude condense at the bottom of the column and are run off. As the vapours ascend the column, each liquefies out at its own boiling point, so that each can be extracted from the

The control room of a sugar refinery in Plaistow, London. Like most modern chemical plants, sugar and oil refineries are now highly automated, with large-scale production.

tower at the appropriate level. The fractions which are taken off at this stage are known as side-cuts, and they also contain a proportion of lighter fractions. These are further separated outside the column, and the light vapours are returned to the column by pumping them in from the top. Not only does this increase the purity of the side-cut, but it also improves the 'sharpness' of separation within the column.

Normally, only constituents which boil in the gasoline range, that is, the fractions which will eventually go to drive our cars, will be extracted in this first column. At least two other columns are necessary before the distillation is complete.

The second column in the bank is run at atmospheric pressure, and it is fed by the liquid run off from the bottom of the first column. In this second column, kerosene and the middle distillates are extracted and the 'bottoms' are run off to a third column. Because of the higher temperatures involved in the second column, it is fed by steam which is subsequently separated from oil products by an overhead condenser which is cooled by water. This explains why so much water is necessary for the operation of refineries, and why they are located near the sea.

When it has passed through a heater, the heavy fractions from the second column are fed into a third column, which is the vacuum column, operated at a pressure well below atmosphere. This partial vacuum is secured by injecting steam and rapidly condensing it. The third column gives separation of the heavy fractions in the crude oil, and completes the distillation process.

Besides the hydrocarbons in crude oil, there are certain impurities which can be either unpleasant or dangerous if included in the finished product, particularly if this is a fuel. Two of these impurities are sulphides and a class of compounds called mercaptans, which are rather like alcohols except that they have sulphur atoms replacing the oxygen atoms. The process

used for the extraction involves dissolving out the impurities and perhaps the most common is the Eldeanu process, which uses liquid sulphur dioxide at low temperatures as the solvent. An advantage of this method over chemical treating processes is that it yields valuable by-products.

Liquid sulphur dioxide is used to cool a kerosene fraction (known as the kerosene feed) and the kerosene is fed into the bottom of a chamber known as a contacting column while the much heavier liquid sulphur dioxide is allowed in through the top. The difference in density causes a mingling of the two liquids. The result is that a mixture containing 80 per cent purified oil and 20 per cent sulphur dioxide is extracted at the top, while

A water de-salinization plant on Grand Canary Island. Where water is scarce, sea water can also be refined to remove the salts and impurities and provide fresh water for drinking.

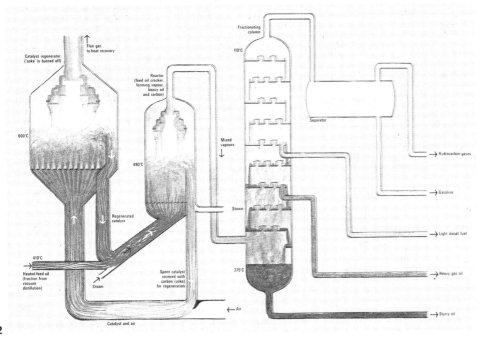

another mixture of sulphur dioxide and impurities is run off at the bottom. Depending on the fraction being treated, other solvents may be used. For example, with lubricating oils, the common solvent is furfural.

In extractive distillation, which is a related process, the solvents used act as catalysts which change the boiling point of some of the constituents, so simplifying separation.

One of the oldest methods of improving the yield from a crude oil is thermal cracking, which was first used with batch stills, but which has been developed into a process with continuous plant. In

Refinery products have to be checked constantly to ensure purity and consistency of the products. A scientist at a West German refinery tests the characteristics of oil samples.

thermal cracking, the heavier molecules are broken down by heat into simpler, lighter substances. The new substances produced by this method are of a type not found in the naturally occurring oil, called olefins. These olefins contain fewer hydrogen atoms than the corresponding paraffin, and they have the unusual property that they improve the anti-knock properties of petrols which contain them. Knocking is the detonation of the fuel/air mixture in the cylinder of an engine, before the spark has been applied. Apart from making the engine run roughly, it can also cause long-term damage. Compounds which reduce this tendency are added to all modern petrols, but they are particularly important in the high-compression engines used in high-powered cars.

For most purposes, the anti-knock quality of motor spirit is expressed as its octane rating, which is merely an expression of the resistance of the fuel to detonation relative to a standard fuel under specified conditions. As fuels of high octane numbers are in great demand, processes have been developed which are specifically aimed at yielding high-octane products.

One of these processes is thermal reforming; the feedstock material in this process is naphtha, which has a low octane number. This is reformed by heat to give naphtha of a much higher octane rating.

A catalytic cracker at Rotterdam, Holland. 'Cat cracking' makes it possible to obtain a higher yield of valuable motor and aircraft fuels than would otherwise be available.

Of all the many processes carried out in oil refining the one which is usually best known, at least by name, is catalytic cracking, or cat cracking. A catalyst is a material which alters the rate of a chemical change without itself undergoing any change, and various catalysts are used in oil refineries to reform and reduce crude fractions into usable and valuable products. Catalytic cracking is also used to remove sulphur from naphthas.

Sulphur removal, in the form of its naturally occurring products, sulphides

and mercaptans, is termed sweetening, and forms an important stage in the final preparation of commercial oils. Modern refining processes generally produce a fraction which is itself sweet, the impurities having been removed during the refining stages, but it is still sometimes necessary to carry out a final purification, especially in kerosene, where sulphur in the product causes an extremely unpleasant odour when it is used as a lamp fuel.

When the crude oil has at last been fully processed, it is almost ready for sale, but, particularly with motor spirit or petrol, it must be blended in the correct proportions to give the desired characteristics. Motor-spirit blending is mainly carried out to adjust the octane rating of the fuel. High-octane products, such as olefins, are mixed with natural light fractions with a lower octane number. As the olefins are comparatively expensive, oil chemists are always searching for ways of producing a high-octane fuel which uses less of these compounds.

This can be done by adding a little tetra-ethyl lead (TEL) to the fuel. This has the effect of increasing the octane number of the fuel at little extra cost, and TEL has in fact been the means by which low-cost high-octane fuels have been produced for high-performance cars.

During the blending stage, each product receives additives, which may vary from stabilizers to prevent decomposition of, say, the olefins, to simple dyes in lubricating oils. These dyes, apart from serving as a ready means of identification, are often a good sales point. Many users of motor lubricating oil equate a slightly blue fluorescent appearance with a high-quality oil, and so the manufacturer will often add this to the mix.

Finally, the various commercial products are shipped to the point of sale by pipeline or tanker. Some will go directly to garages or commercial users, and while the fuels and lubricating oils are end products, a large part of the bulk deliveries will be destined for the petrochemical industry, to be used as the feedstock in manufacturing plastics.

Refinery management

During the whole process of refining from crude to finished product, the refinery engineers must always be aware of the fluctuating demands of the users. Modern equipment and automatic control systems in today's refineries make it possible to change the balance of the finished range of products quickly in response to changing demands. This, in fact, is one of the main advantages of the modern, automated refinery.

For the better part of the twentieth century, oil has been a major source of power, overtaking coal even in the generation of electricity. Almost all commercial lubricants are derived from oil, and with the growth of plastics, many of the goods which we use are also products of the refinery. It is only modern refining techniques which have made these advances possible, and which keep the cost of the products at a steady level.

Metals in the service of Man

Simple tools gave primitive societies the means of cultivating the land. Sophisticated jet aircraft now span the globe at supersonic speed. The metals are the bright and enduring basis of both.

METALS ARE the most important structural materials in the world of Man. Many of them are beautiful and virtually indestructible, so that today we look with wonder at bronzes from Ur of the Chaldees and at exquisitely-wrought gold ornaments from ancient Egypt. Bronze gave its name to an age, as did the much stronger and keener iron. We are today still in this Iron Age, though the word 'steel' would be more appropriate.

Apart from gold and silver, the metals of the ancients were valued mainly for their utility. Bronzes could be beaten into shape to make weapons and tools and vessels not easily broken. It was a *manageable* material and probably its earliest form was almost pure copper. But very early on, Man began to smelt rocks and so make copper and tin from their ores. It was smelting that enabled Man to produce iron, which does not occur naturally as the metal.

This early iron of prehistoric times was a crude product, probably a sort of rough steel, and it varied from place to place according to the quality of the ore available and the closely guarded know-how of the artificers, some of whom came to have more than local fame, as the astonished Crusaders found millennia later when they faced the swords of Damascus.

For thousands of years the known metallic elements could be numbered on two hands. They were gold, silver, copper, iron, tin, lead (thought to be another form of tin), zinc and bismuth (both confused with lead and other metals). Mercury was known as an oddity as early as 300 B C.

The upsurge that gave us so many of our modern metals came in the great days of the experimental chemists, in the eighteenth and nineteenth centuries. Metallic elements were isolated and named, though only in the search for truth. They were not produced in bulk.

Metals and non-metals

Cobalt was isolated in 1735, platinum at about the same time, manganese in 1827, tungsten in 1783 and nickel in 1751. Caesium was isolated in 1861 and germanium in 1886. Aluminium came in 1827. Even a metal such as titanium, regarded as an exotic modern metal, was discovered in 1789. Today, out of the 92 natural elements of which everything in the Universe is made, some two-thirds are classed as metals.

Many of them were not recognized as metals; they were just elements to be named. Today it is difficult to make an exclusive definition of what is or is not a metal in a way that will satisfy the scientist. Half a century ago a bright schoolboy would have had a ready answer.

He would have said that a metal was a material that was malleable (i.e. workable, some needing to be hot for this property to be obvious), ductile (it could be drawn into rod or wire), had a metallic sheen and was a good conductor of heat and electricity.

This seems so obvious but it is not really satisfactory. The 60 or so elements classed as metals vary very much in their properties. Cast iron, and indeed many alloys, are not malleable; they are brittle. Some are not ductile and cannot be made into wire. Some are dull to look at. The metals vary tremendously in their properties. Some have great Ultimate Tensile Strength, frequently called just the 'Strength', which is the force that will make them give way finally under tension. Some are 'tough'. The melting points range from a mere 70 °C. for an alloy of bismuth called Wood's metal to 3,370 °C. for tungsten.

Their densities range from 0·53 for lithium to 22·4 for a platinum alloy. These properties are important in all

A number of metals were first used by the alchemists and doctors as remedies for various diseases, as this seventeenth-century engraving shows. Gold was often used in medicine, and it was widely believed that the metal transmitted some of its own properties to the patient.

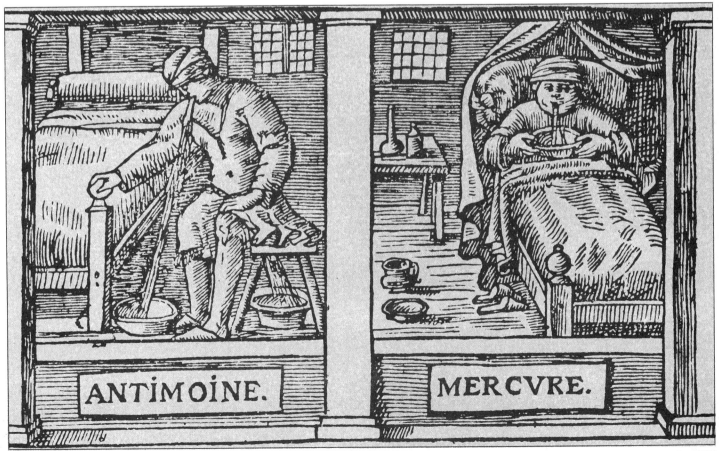

ANTIMOINE.

MERCVRE.

1 Copper ores are often extracted from open-cast mines such as this one in Zambia.
2 Electrolytic extraction of the metal from its ores involves the use of large electrodes. When an electric current is passed through a solution of the ore in water, copper is deposited in a highly pure state.
3 Because of its property of transmitting heat very readily (good thermal conductivity), copper is used in radiators of motor vehicles, and in industrial heat-exchange equipment such as these vast turbo-generator coolers. For the same reason, it is also used as a base for cooking utensils.

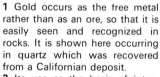

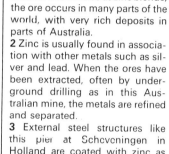

1 Zinc sulphide is the common ore from which metallic zinc is extracted. Known also as zinc blende, the ore occurs in many parts of the world, with very rich deposits in parts of Australia.
2 Zinc is usually found in association with other metals such as silver and lead. When the ores have been extracted, often by underground drilling as in this Australian mine, the metals are refined and separated.
3 External steel structures like this pier at Scheveningen in Holland are coated with zinc as protection against corrosion. This technique is more effective than painting.

1 Gold occurs as the free metal rather than as an ore, so that it is easily seen and recognized in rocks. It is shown here occurring in quartz which was recovered from a Californian deposit.
2 Its use as the basis of international currency means that gold must be available in an easily handled form. It is melted and cast into bars of a standard size and shape for storage by treasuries throughout the world.
3 The perfect state of this Peruvian gold mask after more than 700 years convincingly demonstrates the metal's resistance to corrosion. It was this property which first led to its use in currency.

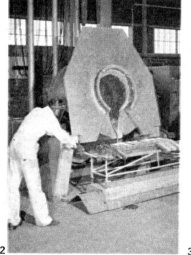

practical applications. Aluminium alloy is used for aircraft frames because of its strength combined with lightness. But it melts at just above 600 °C., so it would not do for supersonic aircraft travelling at 1,500 miles an hour or more. Titanium, melting at 1,800 °C. and with a relative density only about half as much again as aluminium alloy, here comes into its own. Nor would magnesium alloy do for canning the uranium in a nuclear reactor because it would melt. So stainless steel is used.

What about the metals' good conduction of electricity? A table of the values of the resistivity, which is the resistance in millionths of an ohm per cubic centi-

metre, shows some peculiarities. Silver has a value of 1·59 at room temperature, copper 1·72, gold 2·44 and aluminium 2·82 – all very low resistivities and therefore high conductivities. This shows why copper, which is so much cheaper than silver, is generally used for electrical conductors and power cables. Hard rubber, on the other hand, has a value of very many millions of millions and is thus a non-conductor, or insulator and it is a non-metal.

An electronic distinction

But what about hard carbon with a figure of 5,000? This is a non-metal and yet is a much better conductor than germanium,

which is classed as an element with more metallic properties than non-metallic. This has a resistivity of 46 million. It is in fact called a semi-conductor and was the earliest material to be used for transistors.

Attempts have been made to combine all the properties that are specifically metallic into a reasonable definition. One depends on the atomic structure of elements. Every one of the 92 natural elements consists of a nucleus with a positive electrical charge surrounded by moving negative electrons that exactly balance the nuclear charge.

Thus iron has a nuclear charge of +26 balanced by 'shells' or circular layers of 26 negative electrons. Each shell has its specific number of available places, like a

1 Aluminium is by far the most abundant metal on Earth. It normally occurs as bauxite, which is aluminium oxide. This ore is formed by the weathering of rocks such as mica or feldspar. Aluminium also occurs as cryolite.
2 Bauxite is easily mined, as it occurs in such large quantities on the Earth's surface. After the top layer of earth has been removed, the ore can be dug out and loaded by machine.
3 Its lightness, strength and attractive appearance make aluminium a common metal in households as well as in industry. It is easily rolled into thin foils and can be anodized in attractive colours.

1 Iron is second only to aluminium in abundance. But as well as occurring on the Earth, it is also a constituent of meteorites, as this fragment which was found in Australia indicates.
2 Extraction of iron from the ore is done by smelting, which reduces the oxide to the metal and separates out impurities such as silicates. Generally, this is only a first step, the iron then forming the basis of various steels.
3 Iron and steel have been used for armour and helmets throughout history. As this picture shows, stainless steel still has something to contribute to unusual types of clothing.

bus. When all the shells, from the nucleus outwards, are filled, the element is inert. It is therefore classed as a non-metal.

Elements with only one or two in the outermost shell are willing to give them up and so as a result become positively charged. Such an element, say the physicists, is a metal. But hydrogen has only one electron and can give it up very readily. So sometimes it acts as a metal and yet it is a gas and a non-metal.

This explanation agrees with another physical concept of the metallic state, one which conforms to the idea of 'true metals'. The identical atoms of the metal arrange themselves in an orderly way as closely as possible, rather like a lot of billiard balls, in rows and layers. The outer free electrons then act as if they are interchangeable between atoms, and their attractive force binds the atoms together.

Structure and strength

They act as a sort of cloud of glue. When an electrical pressure is applied, these free electrons are available to drift along. They constitute the electric current, and their movement also allows easy conduction of heat. This explanation shows the sharp distinction between metals and non-metals.

In non-metals either all the shells are filled completely, or almost completely filled, so that there is no tendency to provide free electrons; or the atoms may be held together by strong chemical bonds which maintain the electrons in the molecular pattern.

Sir Lawrence Bragg once gave an elegant demonstration of how such a system might work. He made a raft of identical tiny soap bubbles on the surface of water. With ingenious gadgets he showed how he could make one row of bubbles slither over another layer touching it. Very little force was needed. He then showed that if the raft was distorted so that the bubbles separated into groups with random lines of separation between the groups, then it was more difficult to make a row slide over the other because there were fewer

bubbles in a continuous row.

In addition, there was a sudden break at the separation of one group from another and this prevented further sliding. He also showed that if a larger or smaller bubble was inserted into the otherwise homogeneous raft this would also cause irregularities with the same effect as the distortions he had previously demonstrated.

This explanation can be transferred to real metals. Sir Lawrence was working with only one layer, whereas a real substance has many layers, so that the effects he showed operate in three dimensions instead of two. The creation of grains or crystals with separation boundaries strengthens the metal so that it is more difficult to stretch it; the smaller the grains or crystals and the more boundaries there are, the stronger the metal. On the other hand, a metal is very soft when there are very few grains. In addition, if foreign atoms are introduced into a metallic element its characteristics are changed. In some cases, such as the addition of the larger tin atoms into copper, the result is an increase in strength, so that bronze is stronger than copper.

These explanations, however, are not enough to provide a complete explanation of metallic properties. For example, selenium has spiral chains of atoms and can exist as a red amorphous (non-crystalline) material or as a grey metallic material. The first is a non-metal and the second more nearly a metal. Then again, bismuth and tin and lead can be alloyed to make a metal that melts several hundred degrees below the melting point of the separate elements. It is Wood's metal, which one can melt by the heat of a match. And everyone has used solder, which is an alloy of lead and tin which melts well below the melting point of either metal.

Thus the metallurgist is driven eventually to a classification that includes *true metals*, *pseudo-metals* (which are more like true metals than non-metals) and *hybrid metals* (which have the properties of both to about equal degrees). This discussion may seem academic and of

Iron gave its name to an age, and early iron workers used simple furnaces to refine and work the metal to make primitive tools, weapons and ornaments.

interest only to the pure scientist, but it is not.

Out of the detailed investigations has come understanding of what was for so long a rule-of-thumb branch of engineering. From inquiries into the solid state have come means of making all sorts of metals with special properties, such as magnetic materials not made of iron. One alloy of platinum and cobalt, for example, is the most powerful magnetic material, and is used for tiny devices such as hearing aids.

Shaping the properties

Skilful alloying can also produce metals that will withstand extremes of environment, metals that resist atmospheric corrosion (special stainless steels) and so on. There are more metallic materials available today than ever before and there is a more precise understanding of them as a result of scientific investigation of the metallic state. In this work the most advanced and sophisticated instruments are used.

The atoms-all-in-a-row explanation also clarifies some of the practices and phenomena of metals engineering. One of the commonest of these is *work-hardening*. If a man tries to break a piece of copper wire with his hands, as he would string, he fails. But if he bends it backwards and forwards a few times it breaks like a biscuit.

What he has done is to apply stresses that create more and more crystal boundaries until the metal becomes brittle and snaps. This is a simple example of work-hardening, a process which takes place when metal is forged or hammered or rolled, and allowance has to be made for this in the quality of the metal in the first place. It often occurs when a metal is being used in a moving device, and often leads to failure of component parts in metal structures and machinery.

Another useful method of altering the characteristics of a metal is heat-treatment. Heating does many things to a metal, one of them being to reduce the crystal boundaries and make the metal tend to flow. But if the hot metal – red hot perhaps – is suddenly quenched in water there is no time for the heat to diffuse out naturally and myriads of crystal boundaries are formed, so that the metal often becomes glass hard.

How would one make a file hard enough to cut other hard metals? Is there a tool hard enough to cut the ridges? The answer is easy. The ridges are cut when the steel is comparatively soft and then the file is hardened by heat treatment. Naturally, there are many other things to consider in an alloy, or a metal, such as the existence of true compounds (for example, iron carbide in some steels) but the grain-boundary explanation accounts for many of the phenomena.

Tough alloys of iron

By far the most important field of metallurgy is concerned with steel, or rather steels, for there are many. Steel is the cheapest structural metal in the world and the most widely used – 500 million tons of it every year. The basis of all steels is iron with the addition of other compounds to give the steels their particular properties. With the addition of a small percentage of carbon, iron becomes mild steel.

Increasing the amount of carbon gives medium steel, and the addition of chromium and nickel results in one form of stainless steel. Chromium, molybdenum, silicon, nickel, manganese among other metals are used to give properties of toughness, stainlessness, hardness and rollability to steels.

The steel industry throughout the world has replaced the skill of the old operators by computer control and advanced scientific testing techniques. Steel-making now uses oxygen instead of air to cause fierce combustion of the carbon and impurities in the raw material – scrap and pig iron and alloying materials. Above all there is the continuous casting of steel from furnaces into the billet form required by steel fabricators.

Electric-arc furnaces for the batch production of really large quantities of special steels are now in use. Analytical instruments of the most sophisticated sort are in continuous use to detect impurities present in only a few parts per million.

From their use in ornaments and jewellery, weapons and cooking pots, the metals have become the most useful and widespread materials known to twentieth-century Man. No office, home or city could serve its functions in the technological age without the metals in their many forms. The glitter and durability which attracted men so many thousands of years ago are among the properties which make the metals the most useful materials of the present day.

Continuous production of steels from the iron ore in one operation is now reducing both the capital cost of plant and the price of the end product.

Mixing metals

In their pure state, many metals are unsuitable for practical use. But by mixing two or more together, alloys can be produced with a huge range of special properties for particular applications.

APPROXIMATELY 75 per cent of the 92 natural elements found on Earth are classed as metals; of these only some two dozen are in common use as the basic materials from which are fabricated the countless everyday metal objects. The remaining metals are either too rare, too difficult to extract from their ores, or are too unstable for practical purposes. It is only by the process called alloying that Man has learned how to exploit to the full the wide range of metals at his disposal.

Even the commonest metals, such as iron, copper, aluminium, lead, have extremely limited applications in their pure state, because they are either too soft, too brittle, are too heavy, are too easily attacked by corrosion or are too liable to melt. However, most metals are capable of uniting with other metals to provide a composite mixture or alloy of metals possessing desired qualities that no component of the alloy possesses of itself in any marked degree.

Metallurgists define an alloy as an amalgam of two or more metals mixed together for such purposes as improving strength, hardness and heat-resistance. The properties of such an alloy are normally very different from those of its individual components. By varying the kinds and amounts of the metals incorporated in the mixture some 6,000 different alloys are now available and almost any desired qualities can be obtained.

Metals together

Nearly all alloys consist of mixtures or combinations of two or more of the following elements in various proportions: aluminium, antimony, arsenic, bismuth, cadmium, carbon, chromium, cobalt, copper, gold, iridum, iron, lead, magnesium, manganese, mercury, molybdenum, nickel, palladium, phosphorus, platinum, silicon, silver, thorium, tin, tungsten, vanadium, zinc. Most alloys are made by melting the metals together, but a few are compounded by electrochemical means or by pulverizing the component metals and then mixing and compressing them at a high temperature.

Sometimes when dissimilar metals are melted together to form an alloy they cool as a solid solution. In other words before solidifying, when the metals are still molten the atoms of each wander freely around in the solution. In an alloy of this nature, the metals remain in true solution even after they have cooled and solidified, and microscopic examination will reveal the same type of crystal throughout the alloy without trace of any crystals of either of the constituent metals. An alloy of this type is called a *one-phase* alloy.

There are two types of solid-solution alloys, dependent upon the relative sizes

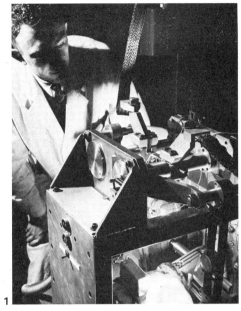

of the atoms of the metallic elements involved. These are called *substitutional* and *interstitial solid solutions*. In the former the two types of metal forming the alloy are of roughly the same size and an atom of one or other of the metals can take a place in a crystal-lattice structure without any great distortion of the lattice. With an interstitial solid solution the atoms of one of the metals are very much smaller and do not take up a place in the crystal-lattice structure. Instead, these atoms squeeze into interstices or gaps. Carbon with its small atoms can do this; steel, an alloy of iron and carbon, is an interstitial solid-solution alloy consisting of atoms of carbon filling in the gaps between the iron atoms.

In other types of alloys the constituent metals are only partially soluble in each other. The resultant alloy, of say two metals, consists of two different types of crystal. One consists largely of one metal with a little of the other metal dissolved in it, while the other type of crystal consists mainly of the second metal. This is what is called a *two-phase alloy* and most alloys are of this nature.

When two alloyed metals are insoluble in one another, crystals of one of the metals are embedded in a finely dispersed metallic mixture. Sometimes atoms of one metal in any alloy will creep into the crystals, stealing the place of atoms of another metal. Alloying two metals is relatively easy and the chemical or metallurgical structure of the alloy is comparatively simple. But when three or more metals are used to form an alloy the structure can become very complex. Despite the alloy looking like a single substance, microscope examination shows that it is made up of tiny crystals of one metal distributed in another.

Alloys that show minimum solubility often form what is technically called an *eutectic*. In such cases the two metals lower each other's melting points, although if the alloy contains specific portions of the two metals, the alloy solidifies as if it were a pure metal. This mutually instantaneous change from the liquid to the solid state is called the *eutectic point*. Another phenomenon of alloys is that

1 In a laboratory, nickel-chromium alloy is tested for resistance to heat fatigue. Specially developed alloys can resist the strain of rapid heating and cooling.
2 Copper alloys have been designed to have specific characteristics. The manganese-copper of this ship's propeller possesses special sound- and vibration-damping features.
3 Aluminium alloys have the great advantage of being exceptionally lightweight. These ridged sheets, produced on a roll-form corrugator, are used by the building industry.

sometimes two metals will combine to form an alloy only if the metals are melted together in certain proportions. Similarly some metals will only combine in certain proportions to form an alloy if they are melted together at a specific temperature; in such cases some of the metals may solidify separately when the alloy cools. In some alloys the metals may combine chemically to form a completely new substance or they may not dissolve into each other but separate into layers as the mixture cools. These layers do, however, solidify together to form a solid mass.

An alloy has different properties from its components because of the atomic structure of metals. Every natural metal is made up from layers of atoms arranged in a fixed pattern. Now imagine a metal with its atoms arranged in layers rather like a new pack of playing-cards. If you push the top cards of the pack, the cards slide over each other quite easily. But if the cards are old and sticky cards, you will have to push harder before the cards slip over each other. This is because the separate cards in the sticky pack are stuck together so that the grip between individual cards is greater and the combined strength of the pack has increased.

Slippery atoms

The layer of atoms in the metal are 'sticky' like the cards in the pack, the 'stickiness' being the electrical forces between the atoms. However, by pushing the atoms hard enough, they can be made to slip, just as the playing-cards were made to slip. That is what happens when an alloy is formed by melting together or otherwise combining two or more metals.

While the metals are molten, their atoms are all mixed up, but as the combined metals cool their various atoms start arranging themselves in layers. But the atoms are not in a regular pattern like those of an individual metal, because an alloy contains two or more metals, each of which has its own particular atomic pattern. Consequently when the metals in an alloy cool, the atom layers are rough and irregular, rather like the cutting edge of a file. Therefore it is much more difficult for mechanical or other conditions of stress to cause the layers of atomic patterns in an alloy to slip over each other. That is why an alloy is generally stronger and harder than the individual metals of which it is composed.

An alloy does not normally consist of equal parts of the metals forming it. The addition of a very small quantity of one metal can completely change the properties of the metal that is in the greater proportion; neither is it necessary that a hard metal be added to a soft metal to form a hard alloy. Aluminium and copper are both metals mechanically weak, but an alloy of 10 per cent aluminium and 90 per cent copper produces a metal three times stronger than pure copper and as strong as mild steel.

Another phenomenon of alloys is that increasing the amount of the strengthening metal does not produce a stronger alloy. Thus an alloy of 16 per cent aluminium and 84 per cent copper produces an

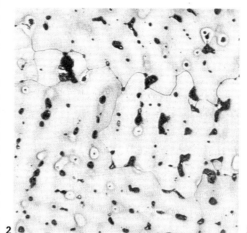

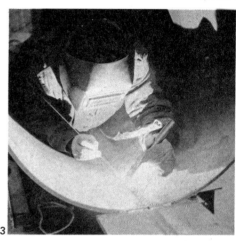

bronze some specially desired qualities. For example, plastic bronze, contains 73 per cent copper, 7 per cent tin, and 20 per cent lead; phosphor-bronze consists of 87·5 per cent copper, 7·5 per cent tin, 1 per cent of zinc, 3·5 per cent of lead, and 0·5 per cent of phosphorus; aluminium bronze contains in addition to tin and copper, 9·5 per cent of aluminium, 2·5 per cent of iron, and up to 2 per cent of nickel and manganese. Gunmetal, a bronze alloy which gets its name from having been first compounded for ship's cannons, consists of 86 per cent copper, 7 per cent tin, 5 per cent zinc and 2 per cent lead.

Bronze is only one of the thousands of different alloys now available to industry. Amongst the older alloys are: brass, a combination of copper and zinc; and pewter, an alloy of lead and tin. Another of the older alloys, and one of the first to take advantage of dissimilar melting and solidifying points of two metals, is the solder used by plumbers for making joints. The chief requirement of solder is that it must melt easily and remain molten long enough for the joint to be shaped by 'wiping' while it is still soft and malleable. This is achieved by alloying three parts of tin and seven parts of lead. Pure lead melts at 327 °C. and tin at 232 °C., but when the two metals are alloyed the solder-alloy stays malleable at 180 °C.

Changing properties

Some alloys are designed to have low re-melting points after solidification. One such is an alloy of tin (melting point 232 °C.), lead (melting point 327 °C.), bismuth (271 °C.) and cadmium (320 °C.). But when these metals are alloyed, the hardened alloy melts at only 66 °C. Because of this low melting point the alloy is used in safety devices such as plugs which melt at excessive rise in atmospheric temperature to set off automatic fire alarms and release fire extinguishers.

Calcium is a good example of a metal that has its natural properties radically changed by alloying. Pure calcium is little harder than wax. Yet an alloy of calcium and lead produces a metal as hard as mild steel. This is a particularly curious phenomenon as lead in its natural state is one of the soft metals.

Copper is one of the best electrical conductors, but power cables made of pure copper would break under their own weight when slung between pylons a reasonable distance apart. To make it strong but still possess high electrical conductivity copper is alloyed with aluminium, cadmium or with another good electrical conductor with poor mechanical strength. Many high-tension power cables are now made from aluminium-copper alloys.

Aluminium alloys are probably the most interesting of all metallurgical techniques. The great advantage of aluminium is its exceptionally light weight, but this is offset by its poor mechanical strength. Hence aluminium can for most purposes be used only when alloyed with a strengthening metal. All the various grades of aluminium used industrially and described as aluminium are, in fact alloys. Most of

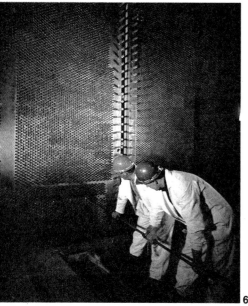

1 Aluminium alloy is rolled at a mill. Aluminium can be alloyed with many other metals to increase its hardness and tensile strength.
2 A photograph taken through a microscope shows the structure of gunmetal. This alloy of copper, tin, zinc and lead, gets its name from having been first compounded for ships' cannons.
3 It was at one time impossible to weld copper or any copper alloy. Inert arc gas welding, which prevents the joint from being oxidized, has overcome this problem.
4 Aluminium alloys are used for aircraft because of their light weight and strength. Duralumin, alloy of aluminium, iron, copper, silicon, magnesium and manganese, is nearly as strong as mild steel but only one-third the weight.
5 Stainless steel, an alloy of steel, nickel and chromium, is widely used for household articles and in the chemical industry because of its resistance to corrosion and rust.
6 Aluminium brass is used in the condensing unit of a nuclear reactor. Two per cent aluminium and 98 per cent brass (itself an alloy), it does not corrode in water.
7 Extremely thin sections of an extruded copper alloy are used for window-frames in modern buildings. Strong and durable, they require no protective treatment against weathering.

alloy which is as brittle as a dry twig and quite useless for any mechanical application.

History does not tell us when the first alloy was formed, but it was most certainly a mixture of copper and tin to form bronze. The first bronzes varied greatly in quality and their composition was entirely empirical: the tin content was small and it was long before it reached 5 per cent. But from the primitive copper-tin alloy of nearly 6,000 years ago metallurgists have developed scores of bronze alloys containing other metals to impart to the

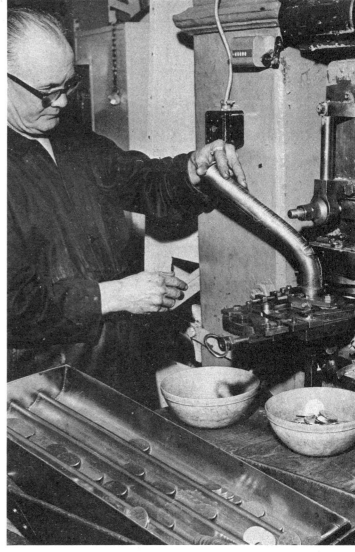

New steel alloys are being developed to meet competition from aluminium and plastics. Here they are being tested in a vacuum furnace which simulates atmospheric conditions of production.

'Silver' coins are minted at the Royal Mint in London. Most 'silver' coins are now made of copper and nickel alloy which is hard and resistant to tarnishing.

them contain iron and silicon to increase aluminium's hardness and tensile strength. Aluminium can be alloyed with nearly all other metals, and many aluminium alloys gain strength by *annealing* (controlled re-heating and cooling) or *age hardening*.

Age hardening of aluminium alloys begins at normal temperatures and, unless the process is controlled, the alloy ingots harden so quickly that they cannot be machined or otherwise fabricated. The age hardening of some aluminium alloys is so rapid that ingots have to be held in refrigerators until required. Scores of aluminium alloys have been developed to combine in one metal the light weight of aluminium with the strength of steels. One of these is duralumin, an alloy of alumium, copper, silicon, iron, magnesium and manganese. Duralumin – extensively used in aircraft – is nearly as strong as mild steel but only one-third as heavy.

Aircraft travelling at supersonic speeds build up high temperatures due to friction with the atmosphere on their fuselage and wing surfaces. Such temperatures would cause serious distortion of ordinary metals and could lead to metal fatigue and failure. This problem was solved by using alloys based on stainless steel and titanium which maintain their strength and do not deform at high temperature.

Iron is a metal which has benefited most from alloying techniques. Adding nickel to cast iron increases appreciably its strength and makes it more resistant to shock, while the mechanical strength of steel (made basically from iron and carbon) is increased fourfold by alloying it with nickel. One of the greatest contributions made by alloys to industry and the household is stainless steel. A commonly used stainless steel consists of 8 per cent nickel, 18 per cent chromium and the remainder steel. Monel, another metal resistant to rust and corrosion, is an alloy of copper and nickel. A form of monel, called cupronickel, which consists of 75 per cent copper and 25 per cent nickel, is used for 'silver' coins because it resists tarnishing.

In its natural state beryllium is a very brittle metal with poor tensile strength. Yet its alloy with steel is exceptionally resilient. In fact steel-beryllium alloys are used for heavy-duty springs subject to constant expansion and contraction. Beryllium alloys are also highly resistant to heat, and for that reason are used for making the fuel-cases in nuclear reactors.

Nichrome, an alloy of nickel, iron and chromium combines great strength with a high melting point and is used for the wire heating elements in electric fires. Another nickel-iron alloy called invar shows minimal expansion and contraction with changes in temperature and was specially compounded for making surveyor's measuring tapes. It is also used for parts in watches demanding a high standard of accuracy.

Pure gold is far too soft to be used in its natural state and for most purposes is alloyed with some other metal. Yellow gold is gold alloyed with copper, and white gold is an alloy of gold and silver.

Occasionally, the properties of one or other of the alloyed metals can be worsened. For example, alloying copper with even a small amount of bismuth renders the copper brittle and useless. The bismuth in the alloy creates around each grain of copper a thin and weak envelope, so that when any stress is applied to an alloy, the copper breaks between the grains.

Alloying is now a fundamental and exact metallurgical science; the designer of a metal object, machine or component, merely has to tell the metallurgist what a metal is to be used for, and the required alloy will be produced. The alloy will always be the same if exactly the same materials and methods are used, but the slightest change in the proportions may radically alter the alloy's properties.

The steelmakers

Man has surrounded himself with steel. Ranging from the stainless steel knife or can-opener in a kitchen to the stress-resistant rockets that probe space, it is the basis of modern civilization.

OF THE MANY crafts and skills developed by primitive Man, the exploitation of metal-working has outstripped all others in its contribution to the material basis of present-day society. An early reference to the craft is found in the Old Testament and archaeologists say that iron-ore has been reduced to forms of pig iron for nearly 4,000 years.

Ancient Man probably discovered iron-making by accident. By lighting a fire on or close to an outcrop of iron-ore he would have seen a shiny liquid form. From this initial discovery he developed the process for iron-making. Using the wind as a draught and a hole in the ground for a furnace he could make pig iron. By using charcoal in his simple furnace, the quality of the product was improved. This process of increasing the carbon content of wrought iron by heating it with carbon, with no air present, is the method known as *cementation*. By heating and quenching the iron, sharp-edged weapons could be produced.

The first successful use of bellows originated in Spain. Made of a skin bag, with a tube into the furnace, the bellows were used to increase the supply of wind to the furnace and so enable higher temperatures to be reached. Catalonia became an important centre for steelmaking in Spain and Toledo steel became world-famous. The furnace developed became known as the *Catalan forge*. Small lumps of ore were heated in a charcoal fire, with lime and marl binding them together and acting as a flux. The product, after repeated hammerings, gave a suitable metal that could

During processing, flat slabs of steel are fed into a heating furnace and passed through mills to produce this hot rolled strip which moves along a cooling bed.

Steel for special uses can be shaped with an accuracy equivalent to splitting a human hair 270 times. These mechanical seals have been made for space rockets at a Los Angeles factory.

be worked by the blacksmith.

Shortly before the close of the Middle Ages steel was first made by heating iron-ore together with charcoal in an air-free tube. This steel was known as *blister steel*. Further heating and hammering produced *shear* steel, which was a more homogeneous, uniform product. The steel produced was used by the blacksmith, armourer and cutler, for the production of small everyday items such as knives, locks, hinges, bolts, nails and weapons.

The great leap forward in steel production came in about 1340 with the development in Germany of the *Stückhofen*, an early form of the blast-furnace. This enabled the iron producer to control his process better, to reach a higher

temperature and made it possible to run the molten iron into big moulds.

With this single development iron and steel production raced ahead in size and quality. By the sixteenth century rolling-mills were being used in Germany and the Low Countries. The only factor which held back iron production at this time, the dependence upon timber as fuel, was overcome during the eighteenth century with the use of coke. After many decades of effort to develop an alternative to wood as fuel, Abraham Darby in 1709 first used coke successfully in smelting. The blast-furnaces worked at higher temperatures and were able to produce better, finer castings for more varied uses.

Modern blast-furnaces based on the same principles are used to produce pig iron for the steel industry. The ore, mixed with limestone and coke, is fed into the upper part of the furnace and is at once acted upon by the gases coming up from below. The principal gas is carbon monoxide and the temperature at the top of the furnace is between 200 °C. and 500 °C. Reduction continues with increasing speed as the charge of ore descends to the lower region of the furnace where the temperature is about 1,000 °C. The hot, spongy iron meets the rising carbon monoxide and decomposes. The iron dissolves and absorbs carbon as it passes down the furnace. It eventually trickles down and collects, below the level of the *tuyères* (openings) in a well. In addition to carbon, the molten iron absorbs phosphorus, silicon and manganese, which are also absorbed by the *slag* (the impurities which

In a shower of sparks, steel chain links are moulded by this semi-automatic machine. The strength and durability of the final product depends on the type of steel used.

1 The strength and flexibility of steel can be increased by repeated heating and cooling. Here ceremonial swords are reheated to produce a hard cutting edge.
2 A huge steel plant at Indiana in the United States. Situated on Lake Michigan, ore, coal and other materials are brought by rail and water to feed the blast-furnaces.
3 At an up-to-date mine in Sweden, television is used to watch and control the transportation of iron-ore to the surface.
4 A huge piece of red-hot steel is squeezed into shape between the jaws of an 8,000-ton press at Sheffield. This method of forging increases the strength of the steel.
5 In an electric-arc furnace, extremely high temperatures are reached when an electric charge jumps or *arcs* between the electrodes and the melting metal. Here the red-hot electrodes are raised above the roof of the furnace.

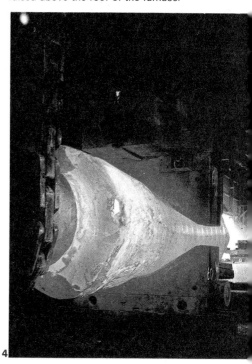

rise to the surface).

In the 1740s Benjamin Huntsman realized that by using the old cementation process and raising the cemented steel to melting-point, a better-quality steel could be produced. His idea was tried out in a large crucible and the slag impurities skimmed off the surface as they floated to the top. The metal was then poured into a mould and left to solidify into a mass which could be worked into the desired shapes. The steel was found to be homogeneous and free from slag and dirt. It was immediately recognized that for producing superior steels this process was the best and it was quickly adopted.

Developments in engineering helped the steel-maker and with the coming of the steam-engine larger blast-furnaces and mills were the order of the day. Pig-iron output rose in Britain from 20,000 tons a year in 1700 to 1,500,000 tons by 1850. At least half of this went to the railways.

The next step forward in steelmaking was in the 1840s and 1850s by two men working independently in different countries: Henry Bessemer (1813–98), an Englishman and William Kelly (1811–88) an American. Bessemer discovered that by blowing a current of air through molten pig iron, unwanted chemicals, such as carbon and silicon, were oxidized out of the melt. Bessemer used tuyères in the bottom of the refractory-lined crucible of molten pig iron to blow pressurized air through the melt. The product of the Bessemer process was *mild steel* which had

a low silicon and carbon content and which could not only be used for implements needing temper, such as springs, knives and tools but also for the railways, engineering and shipbuilding industries.

The process in the Bessemer converter receives energy in the form of heat from the endothermic oxidization of the impurities. About ten tons of molten pig iron are run into the large converter made of iron plates lined with siliceous bricks, and provided with holes at the bottom through which a powerful blast of air can be blown. The carbon monoxide which is formed burns at the mouth of the converter. By observing the flame, the correct moment to stop the blast can be determined. When the blast has been stopped the right amount of *spiegeleisen,* a ferro-manganese containing a known quantity of carbon, is added. Then the blast is turned on for a few moments and then metal poured into moulds. Unfortunately this process can only be used with phosphorus-free pig iron since, if phosphorus is present it is oxidized but not removed, and the steel is brittle and useless.

In 1877 Sidney Thomas and Percy Gilchrist showed that if the converter is lined with lime then, by blasting with air for a little longer, the oxides of phosphorus, sulphur and silicon which form remove themselves from the furnace by combining with the lime. Basic slag arises in this case, and is used as a fertilizer, due to its rich phosphorus content. If the lining of the Bessemer converter is siliceous, the

operation is called the *acid Bessemer process,* and if dolomite, the *basic Bessemer process.*

The melted iron from the blast-furnace is run into the Bessemer converter and the blast turned on. The silicon and carbon react with the iron oxide formed, then the carbon reacts, and large flames appear at the mouth of the converter. When the flame dies down, the molten metal is nearly pure iron with a small amount of dissolved oxide. The addition of spiegeleisen is made and the normal Bessemer procedure followed. This produces mild steel containing up to 0·25 per cent of carbon. Before the 1850s, axles, crankshafts, piston-rods, shafting, bars and plates were made of wrought iron. When Bessemer found how to make steel on a large scale, directly from blast-furnace pig iron, all these items were qualitatively improved. Gilchrist and Thomas improved on Bessemer's original converter for the handling of high-phosphorus ores 20 years later, by introducing a basic lining.

Open hearths

The next important development in steel technology came in 1864, when the Martin brothers in France first successfully worked the open-hearth process. This had been suggested initially in 1722 by René de Réaumur in France and by John Payne in 1728. The Martin brothers used an invention of Sir William Siemens to reduce heat losses from the furnace with the *regenerative gas furnace.* This utilized the waste heat in the burnt gases coming from a furnace to pre-heat the air needed for the burning of the fuel, and allowed for higher furnace temperatures.

The open hearth was able to save on costs and became widely popular since another advantage it had over the Bessemer converter was that large quantities of scrap metal could be used. Siemens's open hearth consists of a large flat hearth enclosed in a furnace heated by producer gas. The air and gas are supplied through different regenerators of chequered brickwork. The hearth is either *acid lined* with silica, or *basic lined* with dolomite or calcined magnesite, depending on which process is being used.

The charge used is pig iron, steel scrap and haematite, with limestone added for the basic process. Part of the carbon is burnt out of the cast iron by the action of haematite, and fluid steel remains. The subsequent operations in the hearth are the same as those in the Bessemer process. The furnace can be tilted and a portion of its contents discharged into a ladle. Usually eight to ten hours are needed for the full operation of the hearth, from start to finish.

The open hearth is more easily controlled than the Bessemer process and is used widely. Both processes, however, have certain limitations when the special high-quality steel is needed as the finished product. A high-quality steel is usually called an *alloy steel,* but the two processes described are incapable of producing alloy steel commercially, because of the whole process of oxidation, limited control of slag, and use of deoxidizers.

To overcome these difficulties, electricity is used for heating. All oxidizing gases are eliminated by the use of electrical energy and the character of the slag can be changed from oxidizing to reducing conditions, enabling the addition of alloys without loss in the slag. The principal type of electric arc-furnace was first used commercially in France in 1902 by Paul Héroult. In this process electric current is conducted into a covered furnace through three large electrodes made of carbon or graphite. Very high temperatures are obtained as the electricity *arcs* or jumps between an electrode, the metal and another electrode. These furnaces have a very large output of high-grade carbon or alloy steel.

In the *high-frequency* or *induction furnace* the charge of scrap metal is put into

Thousands of types of steel can be made by varying the ingredients. This piece of transparent steel — still a laboratory curiosity — was produced by research scientists.

a crucible of refractory material, surrounded by a coiled conductor. An alternating high-frequency current passing through the coil induces a secondary current in the charge of material and raises the temperature. The hearth of the arc-furnace may be acid or basic lined, according to necessity and is of the same design as the open-hearth furnace.

Basic-lined furnaces are used mainly for electric steel production, and acid-lined furnaces for the refining of semi-finished liquid steel. The latter is of greatest value to the steel manufacturers. The high-frequency furnace is used mostly for steel melting, not for refining, and the capacity of the furnace is less than the arc-furnace, being from a quarter of a ton to five tons. Carefully selected scrap and alloys are used and the steel produced made into articles like ball-bearings.

Duplexing and cascade casting

To combine the cheapness of the Bessemer process with the high-quality control of the open hearth or arc-furnace, steel is made sometimes by refining in the converter and finishing in one of the other furnaces. This method is known as *duplexing.* For some refined steels vacuum furnaces, first developed for non-ferrous metals, are used. Melting is carried out under high vacuum and an arc is used to heat the charge. The electrodes themselves are made of steel and they are eaten away as the current is passed. Titanium is one metal with a special application to this method.

A technique which has been developed since the 1930s is that of continuous or *cascade casting.* Initially developed for non-ferrous metals, by 1956 it was being used on an industrial scale in 12 countries. The continuous casting process starts when liquid steel from the furnace is poured into a water-cooled jacket of copper or brass, in the shape of a tube, with a round, rectangular or oval cross-section. The metal cools, solidifies, shrinks from the mould and is drawn out of the mould by rollers which grip the ingot at the lower end. It is cut or *sheared* as it emerges into the required lengths, and the ingots rolled or forged as needed. The metal is more homogeneous when

cast in this way, and ingot pits and moulds are eliminated from the foundry. This method is now used for the casting of large slabs and sheets.

At each stage of production of steel, many tests are made to control the contents and qualities, from the raw materials to the finished products. Altogether over 35 tests may be carried out on the molten steel in the furnace. In the past, the steelmakers had to depend entirely on their own experience and judgement. Now steel plants contain a huge array of instruments to control the furnaces, the temperatures and flow of fuels. Samples of steel are taken from the furnace for testing. When cool, they are examined and analysed in laboratories with such instruments as X-ray machines, electron microscopes and spectroscopes. They are also tested for strength, durability, resistance to wear and hardness.

Thousands of different kinds of steel are made by varying the chemical composition or the processing after the steel leaves the furnace. *Carbon steels,* the most widely used of all steels, contain up to 1·5 per cent of carbon with small amounts of manganese to make the steel less brittle. *Alloy steels* contain carbon and other chemicals, such as chromium, manganese, molybdenum, tungsten and vanadium, according to the properties of steel required. Nickel, for example, is added to steel to increase toughness and resistance to acids and heat. Nickel and chromium are used to make stainless steels which do not rust or corrode. *Tool* or *high-speed steels,* which usually contain tungsten and chromium, remain hard and sharp at high cutting speeds which produce temperatures sufficient to soften many other steels.

From the small, primitive beginnings, the production of steel has grown into a huge international industry with an output of over a million tons of steel a day of thousands of different types to be used in millions of manufactured products, ranging from sewing needles to space rockets.

Liquid steel from a furnace is poured from a continuous casting machine into water-cooled moulds. As the metal cools, it shrinks and can be drawn out of the moulds.

Putting chemistry to work

Switching on a battery sets off chemical reactions which are converted into electricity. The same kind of electro-chemical reactions are used for refining metal, electroplating and electrodialysis.

EVERY TIME you press the button on an electric torch and the bulb lights up you have a demonstration of electro-chemistry: for electro-chemistry is the science that relates chemical changes with the passage of electricity. There are scores of practical applications of electro-chemistry. Some, as in the torch battery, depend upon chemical changes to produce an electric current; others as in electro-deposition, depend on electrically charged particles of a substance depositing on a desired surface.

The *primary cell* of a torch battery is one of the simplest examples of electro-chemistry. Such cells are variously called *voltaic, galvanic* or *electromotive*. Devices in which the opposite occurs and electricity is used to induce chemical changes are called *electrolytic cells*.

There are various types of primary cell, but all depend on the principle that when chemicals react together they produce chemical energy which can be converted into electrical energy. If two metals, one positive and the other negative, are placed in an electrically conductive solution, called an *electrolyte*, the positive metal attracts electrons from the negative metal.

Gradually the negative metal is eaten away, while the movement of electrons to the positive metal produces a current, since an electric current is a movement of electrons. The two metals in the cell may be in actual contact, or they may be connected through a wire or through the filament of a lamp. The glowing filament of the torch bulb is visual evidence of electron movement in the cell.

A simple type of primary cell is the *dry cell*. One type consists of a zinc cup containing a carbon rod surrounded by ammonium chloride paste to form the electrolyte. A little manganese dioxide is added to act as an oxidizing agent. The zinc and the carbon are called the *electrodes*; the carbon being the positive electrode or *anode* and the zinc the negative electrode or *cathode*. The carbon anode or *positive pole* of the cell is a good electrical conductor and the zinc is the cathode or *negative pole*.

When the poles of the cell are connected, the zinc produces ions and releases electrons. As the zinc ions are formed they are dispersed in the electrolyte. The electrons flow through the external wires, and when they reach the carbon rod they combine with hydrogen (positive) ions to form hydrogen atoms. The function of the manganese dioxide is to oxidize the hydrogen to prevent the latter from forming a coating of insulating bubbles on the carbon rod, thereby reducing the efficiency of the cell.

Eventually so many zinc atoms are converted into ions that the zinc cup becomes thin and finally breaks down altogether. That is why a torch battery has a limited life. It cannot be recharged, although the action of a very moderate heat may temporarily revitalize it.

Because of its relatively short life the primary cell has many limitations as a practical source of current. These disadvantages are overcome by the secondary cell or, as it is often called, the *accumulator* or storage cell. The secondary cell can act in two ways: it can run down or discharge, or it can take up electricity and recharge. For that reason, secondary cells are used to provide current for the electrical system on motor vehicles. While the car or other motor vehicle is travelling, a dynamo driven by the crankshaft generates a supply of direct current which recharges the battery.

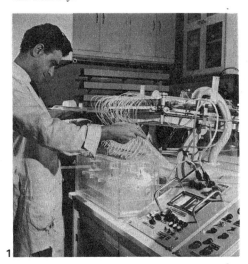

1 At a medical research institute, electrophoresis is used to sort proteins. When a voltage is passed across a solution of proteins, they are sorted according to their electrical charge.
2 Telephones run on electric batteries. In one of the telephone exchanges in London two of the staff check the specific gravity of the batteries by measuring their acid levels.

Many heavy-duty storage cells, such as those fitted in electrically propelled road vehicles, in submarines and in small, self-contained lighting and power plants, work on the principle that when a piece of lead is dipped in water a few atoms on the surface of the lead ionize and dissolve. Each ion leaves behind two electrons clinging to the surface of the lead. But there is a saturation point – or state of equilibrium – when the concentration of lead ions in solution remains constant, as does the negative charge left on the metal. The result is that the piece of lead has an overall negative charge, while the solution carries an overall positive charge. Although a potential difference now exists between the lead and the water, there is no current movement because there is nowhere for it to go.

Storage cells

It is this potential difference that is exploited to produce current in the storage cell. A lead storage or secondary cell consists of two plates: one, the negative plate, is a grid filled with spongy lead, and the other, the positive plate, is a grid filled with brown-lead dioxide. Both plates dip in a container filled with diluted sulphuric acid. When the cell is connected to an external circuit, electrons flow through the circuit to the positive plate in an effort to compensate for the deficiency there. But they cannot compensate because the electrons are taken up by certain chemicals immediately they arrive. Consequently more and more electrons flow and the result is a continuous current.

Lead atoms dissolve at the negative plate, leaving the plate negatively charged. The lead ions formed immediately react with the sulphate ions from the sulphuric acid to create lumps of lead sulphate and these stick to the lead plate. Electrons which have flowed round the circuit and arrive at the positive plate instantly combine with lead dioxide and the hydrogen ions from the sulphuric acid. Once again lead ions are formed, and as before they combine with the sulphate of sulphuric acid to produce lead sulphate which forms a coat on the lead dioxide plate.

Ultimately, because no more electrons can leave the lead electrode, the cell ceases to generate a current and becomes discharged. The cell can be recharged by connecting it to a source of direct current. The chemical action that then takes place is the reverse of that which occurred when the cell was discharging to produce a current. During discharge of a lead storage cell, removal of the sulphate ions tends to reduce the concentration of sulphuric acid in the solution, so that in time the solution or electrolyte contains less sulphuric acid. Water loss in the electrolyte is made good by adding distilled water.

No matter how big the plates of a single primary or secondary cell, the voltage produced by a single cell is constant. For a primary cell it is 1·5 volts and for a secondary cell it is 2 volts. Voltage can be increased only by joining several cells together to form a battery. The weight of batteries, particularly batteries of storage cells, is excessively high in relation to the duration and value of the voltage produced and it is this that hitherto has precluded their use for the propulsion of long-distance vehicles. At present electric traction dependent upon batteries is limited to milk floats, and other vehicles serving short routes.

Several types of light-weight storage batteries have recently been developed, but the metals used for the electrodes are, as yet, far too expensive and have too short a life between charges to be practical for long-distance road transport. Light-weight batteries using silver, cadmium and nickel have been used experimentally for the propulsion of cars, and as a power source in electric shavers, photographic equipment, rechargeable electric torches and in space craft.

Coating base metals

Electroplating is essentially a kind of *electrolysis*, whereby electrical energy causes a chemical change in a conducting medium. The medium may be either molten or a solution. The electrical energy enters and leaves the electrolytic medium through pieces of metal that act as electrodes. The electrons enter the solution at the cathode, and leave it at the anode. Positively charged ions, called *cations*, are attracted to the cathode, and negatively charged ions, called *anions,* are attracted to the anode.

Most electroplating is done to increase the value of an object made from a base metal, to give additional durability, or to render it resistant to rust and corrosion. To coat a base metal with silver, it is placed with a block of pure silver in a solution of either silver potassium cyanide or silver nitrate. The article to be plated is the cathode and the block of pure silver the anode. Passing an electric current through the electrolytic solution from one electrode to the other causes pure silver to dissolve and particles of the metal are deposited as a film on the object being plated.

Electroplating baser metals with copper is done in a similar manner. The article to be plated is connected to the negative terminal of an electric supply and becomes the cathode, while a block of pure copper forms the anode. Both are immersed in an electrolyte of copper sulphate. When current is switched on the copper from the copper-sulphate solution is deposited on the article being plated and is simultaneously replaced from the copper of the copper anode. In this way the strength of the electrolyte solution is maintained until the whole of the copper anode has fully dissolved.

Electroplating chromium on to steel in order to render the latter metal resistant to corrosion is somewhat more complex.

1 In 1868 a Frenchman, Georges Leclanché invented the prototype of the modern torch battery. The electrode is zinc, and the electrolyte is a special zinc chloride paste.
2 A battery-driven car like the Ford 'Comuta' may well be the answer to traffic exhaust pollution in the cities. The batteries are designed to be recharged from the mains.
3 Tinplate does not rust and is used for making tin cans. In one type of manufacture a pressed steel sheet is coated with a layer of tin as it passes through a special electrolyte.
4 When submerged, submarines cannot use fuels which use up oxygen and give out exhausts. Instead they run on batteries. The state of charge of these batteries must be checked constantly.
5 Special lightweight batteries using silver, cadmium and nickel have been developed for use in space craft. In space the problem of not using up oxygen is much the same as in submarines. 1

2

Although chromium gives an exceptionally efficient tarnish-free surface, it does not adhere well to steel when directly electroplated on to it. Moreover, minute crevices are left in the chromium film through which moisture can pass and make the metal below liable to corrosive action. Accordingly, good-quality chromium-plated steel is first electroplated with copper, which provides a good adhesive surface. This surface is then electroplated with a film of nickel to give protection against corrosion. Finally, the nickel surface is electroplated with chromium to produce the tarnish-free finish.

Electrotyping is a form of electroplating used in the production of the engraved copper plates for printing. An impression of the plate is taken in a plastic material which is then covered with a layer of graphite, silver or other substance that will readily conduct electricity. Next, the plastic mould is connected to the negative terminal of an electricity supply and

placed in a solution of copper sulphate in which there is a sheet of copper connected to the positive terminal of the current supply. When the electric supply is switched on, the current passes from the copper plate to the silver- or graphite-covered mould through the electrolyte and deposits a film of copper on the plastic. When the mould is removed a copper plate is left with the desired impression on it.

For successful electroplating, the objects to be plated must be absolutely clean, and the vat containing the electrolyte must be lined with glass or other material of good insulating qualities to prevent the current from leaking through it. The strength of the applied current must be carefully controlled: this is very critical as the thickness of the metal film deposited on the article being plated depends upon it. The time taken to electroplate varies between a few minutes to over an hour.

Large-scale electroplating is carried out in huge tanks of electrolytic solution with several anodes so that batches of a hundred or more articles can be plated simultaneously. By using suitable solutions, a wide range of metals can be electroplated.

Electro-chemistry can be used in the smelting and refining of metals. The extraction of aluminium from its bauxite ore is basically an electro-chemical process. Bauxite is first subjected to a series of chemical and heat treatments to extract the alumina or aluminium oxide. The alumina is then placed in the 'furnace' together with molten cryolite, which is an aluminium compound. Although alumina has a high melting point, over 2,000 °C., it will dissolve in molten cryolite at a temperature of about 1,000 °C. to form a solution which is electrically conductive. The furnace which is basically a type of electrical cell, consists of a steel bath lined with carbon. Dipping into the alumina-cryolite electrolyte are a number of carbon blocks or rods. The carbon lining of the furnace forms the cathode of the 'cell' and the carbon blocks or rods are the anodes.

When a strong electric current at a pressure of six volts is passed through the electrolyte from anode to cathode, molten aluminium from the solution is deposited on the bottom lining of the tank, the cathode. From there the molten aluminium is drawn off and poured into ingot moulds. The electro-chemical process consumes an enormous amount of electricity: 20,000 kilowatt-hours of current are needed to produce one ton of aluminium. That is enough electricity to keep a two-bar electric fire burning for 10,000 hours.

Electrodialysis is an electro-chemical process mainly used for the demineralization of water. It employs an electric current to induce migration of salt anions and cations in sea-water through an electrolytic solution and a barrier of membranes. The membranes, which contain permanent charges of ions are permeable to the water solvent and to either the anions or the cations, but not to both. By passing sea-water through successive tanks containing the membranes and using electric currents at each stage, the saline content of the water is completely extracted, rendering the water fresh.

Electroforming is an electro-chemical process similar to that of electrotyping. It consists of the electrolytic deposition of metal on forms or moulds made from graphite-coated wax, metal or plastic, and

is used in the production of medals and master gramophone records. Electroforming differs from electroplating in that the metal is not actually joined to the base on which it is deposited.

The *photoelectric cell* is an electro-chemical device which exploits the effect of light on certain elements. The cell consists of a glass tube from which the air has been evacuated, although a low-pressure gas is sometimes added to increase the current output of the cell. A curved metal plate coated with caesium is fitted inside the evacuated tube to form the anode. The atoms of caesium vibrate so violently under the influence of light that some of their electrons fly off. Close to the cathode is the anode, a thin metal rod. The anode is connected to the positive terminal of a battery or other source of electronic current and the cathode to the negative terminal of the current source.

When light falls on the cathode, electrons are knocked off the caesium and stream across to the anode, so providing a conductive path for the current from the battery and completing the circuit. The

photoelectric cell can be kept in operation continuously by keeping a light shining on it, or intermittently by shining a light on it at intervals.

Photoelectric cells are the basis of many burglar alarm systems. When the burglar approaches a door or safe so protected, his body interrupts a beam of invisible infra-red radiation, so cutting off the light shining on the cell. The interruption of the current through the cell operates relays which can be made to ring a bell, close a grill, or even operate a camera to photograph the intruder.

Photographers' exposure meters incorporate a photoelectric cell to move a pointer on a scale according to the brightness of the light in which the photograph is taken. Photoelectric cells are also used for counting mass-produced articles and components as they are carried on conveyor belts and interrupt a beam of light falling on the cell. Doors which automatically open when a person approaches are controlled by photoelectric cells, as are the garage doors which open automatically at the approach of a vehicle.

1 Electroplating base metals to make them more valuable, durable or rust-proof began in the last century. This scene is of a French electroplating factory in the 1870s.
2 Electrodialysis can be used for demineralizing water. At this plant in Italy sea-water passes through stacks of membranes and at each stage gradually loses more and more of its salt.
3 Alumina, the oxide of aluminium, is fed to an aluminium reduction furnace. The furnace works on an electro-chemical basis, with molten aluminium being drawn off as the end product.

Mass production test-tubes

Chemical manufacturing is a vast industry which plays a vital part in modern civilization. Many of the things we take for granted — synthetic fibres, petrol, fertilizers and drugs — are products of this industry.

THE DISCOVERY that fire could be produced by rubbing together two dry sticks was one of Man's first steps in the science of applied chemistry, because the wood had not only altered its chemical structure but had created new chemical compounds. The first firemaker did not know that he had given a demonstration of applied chemistry, he was only delighted to have found a way of keeping himself warm. Neither did he know as we do now that everything he saw, ate or used was the result of some chemical action.

Later, primitive Man discovered that leaving certain substances to ferment produced a chemical action resulting in alcohol, and that by heating clay objects he could turn a soft material into a hard one. Fire, fermentation and pottery-baking were the tentative and pioneering steps in harnessing chemistry in the service of Man.

The early civilizations of Egypt, Mesopotamia, India and China carried chemical progress forward and came, in some cases, to the modern concept of chemistry concerned with the composition of things. As a scientist, the chemist wants to know what things are made of and how Nature goes about making them. The industrial chemist takes matters another stage by

Mummification was one of the first large-scale industries with a chemical basis. This well-preserved mummy of a young girl, thought to be about 1,900 years old, was found near Rome.

trying himself to build things with chemicals and thus gains knowledge of how to produce new substances or make old ones in a new way.

The ancient civilizations knew how to make enamels, how to refine gold and how to use natural dyes. The ancient Egyptians were able to embalm and so preserve the bodies of their Pharaohs that the mummies resisted decay for thousands of years. Although they knew the art of smelting metals and the forming of alloys this did not mean they were aware of all the chemical processes involved. These arts may well have been the results of chance discovery, and those who applied them were artisans rather than scientists.

Glass-making

It was probably by accident that Man discovered that certain sands or flint or quartz turned into glass when melted with ashes. When he wanted to make glass himself, he had to look for the right kind of materials and then proceed by trial and error. There were no chemical formulae or text-books to help him. Glass-making also requires an alkali, but the pioneers of industry knew nothing of the chemical properties of lime or potash or soda. They did discover, however, that the materials used to make soap would also help in the making of glass. So the glass-makers used the soap-makers' lye, which happened to contain lime and potassium carbonate; but it never occurred to them to add

any calcium compound as a separate ingredient.

The tanning of leather, baking of bread, soap-making and hundreds more of the ancient crafts were all forms of applied chemistry, but the tanner, the baker and the soap-maker knew little of the chemistry their trades involved.

There was no system of chemical analysis whereby the product of a trade could be properly tested. It was impossible to agree on any chemical specification, and the purchaser had only his own rough and ready knowledge of what a product should look like and what it should do to assess its value.

Study of chemistry for chemistry's sake has been a science discipline for several centuries, whereas industrial or applied chemistry has been practised as a profession for less than 200 years. The conditions under which the pure chemist and the industrial chemist worked tended to maintain a sharp distinction between these two branches of chemistry.

Modern industrial chemistry has as its prime purpose the initiation of research programmes for the specific purpose of producing a chemical or a chemical result that either will fulfil some material need or become the mainspring of a commercial

An eighteenth-century engraving of Eskimos making fire with a fire-drill. Burning, among the first chemical processes mastered by Man, formed means for glass-making and other arts.

venture. The industrial chemist carries out his work for a business organization which pays his salary and provides his laboratory and other equipment. Much of his work is routine analysis required for the control and improvement of industrial processes and the development of new products. Sometimes his work results in new developments of chemical theory and in that way becomes linked with pure chemistry. In general, however, the industrial chemist is not encouraged to follow lines of research that do not offer prospect of profit to his employers. Conversely, the pure chemist working in the rarefied atmosphere of his university laboratory can become isolated from the industrial world and its needs.

This distinction between the industrial chemist and the pure chemist was particularly rigid until this century when there has been a tendency for it to break down, at least to a limited extent. Appropriately enough, the barrier has been breached by industrial chemistry. Commercial firms and organizations dependent on chemistry are steadily increasing in size and numbers and have come to realize that pure chemistry may have much to offer that will benefit their commercial expansion. So they encourage the pure chemist to work in their laboratories and carry out research work that appears to bear little relation to their commercial needs. In addition they support university laboratories for prestige reasons and thus maintain touch with lines of research which, although very remote from industry, may eventually have commercial value. All this has resulted in a phenomenal growth of industrial chemistry which has transformed the world.

Chemical reactions

Chemical reactions can be divided into four main groups: combination, decomposition, replacement and double replacement. These are the simple types of chemical change, but the industrial chemist often has to deal with far more complex processes. Indeed, certain reactions are so complex that they are not completely understood by the industrial chemist himself: hence the immense amount of research involved in running an industrial chemists' laboratory.

Apart from routine analysis of raw materials and the products obtained from them by chemical reactions, the industrial chemist's work has three main purposes. First the chemist endeavours to obtain simple substances from the more complex mixtures or compounds occurring in Nature. Examples of this are the distillation of petroleum or bituminous coal for the extraction of by-products; the separation of gases; and the extraction of metallic elements from their ores and the combining of the extracted metals to form alloys.

Conversion processes by which the chemist produces new substances by replacement and double replacement form a second category. In this type of work, the size of the molecules used does not differ very markedly from the size of the molecules of the substance produced. Amongst

the many examples of conversion processes are the production of soaps, fats and the heavy chemicals, including acids and bases, essential to the production of domestic and industrial materials. Third are synthetic processes, which are fundamentally aimed at building bigger and more complex molecules from smaller ones. In principle this procedure is the opposite of that used in extraction processes, and is the basis of synthetic chemistry, including man-made fibres, plastics and synthetic dyes. The production of synthetic materials is without doubt the greatest achievement of industrial chemistry.

Father of industrial chemistry

Nicholas Leblanc, a French physician, was the first to prove the commercial value of chemistry and he may be considered the father of industrial chemistry. In 1775, the Paris Academy of Sciences, concerned at the high price of soap and the consequent spread of dirt induced diseases in the Paris slums, offered a prize of 2,500 gold louis (about £5,000) to anyone who could find a cheap way of producing sodium carbonate. Better known as washing soda or soda ash, sodium carbonate is used in the manufacture of soap, glass and paper. The Paris Academy not only was anxious to cheapen soap, but also thought that more and cheaper glass would mean bigger windows to let extra health-giving sunlight into the houses of the poor, while cheaper paper would allow the printing of more books to reduce the illiteracy of the masses.

Leblanc, whose medical practice in a poor district of Paris had never been very profitable, was attracted not only to the money prize but also by the prospect of combating the disease so rife in the slums where he worked. Accordingly, he spent all his spare time trying to evolve some process to cheapen sodium carbonate. But although he had a good knowledge of chemistry, it required 14 years of hard work before he succeeded in perfecting a process using chalk, salt, charcoal and sulphuric acid.

When, however, Leblanc announced his formula to the Academy and claimed the prize, he was refused the money on the grounds that the academicians did not consider the process practicable. Undaunted, Leblanc approached some of his wealthy friends, who advanced him 200,000 francs to set up a sodium-carbonate plant in the Paris suburb of St Denis. By 1794 the Leblanc factory was producing 700 pounds of the chemical daily.

Leblanc's factory covered an area of nearly two acres and in order to keep down the cost of the new product, was laid out on lines which reduced handling of the materials to a minimum. In fact, it was not only the first real chemical factory, but it was the first to operate on the modern system of constant flow of the ingredients. The process began by heating common salt with sulphuric acid to produce sodium sulphate. This was then heated with carbon and chalk to form a mixture of sodium carbonate (soda) and calcium sulphide, to which water was added. As only the soda dissolved out of the solution it could be

separated and evaporated to yield crystals of sodium carbonate (washing soda).

Leblanc's sodium carbonate process is no longer used, but it was of great importance in his day and was the first example of factory methods being applied to the making of a chemical.

Another important step in the development of industrial chemistry was made in 1832 by Jean Dumas, professor of Chemistry at Paris University. One evening while working in his study he noticed that the candles were emitting irritating fumes and an unusually thick and pungent smoke. To find out the cause he subjected the candles to a series of chemical tests in his laboratory. He was able to identify the fumes as hydrochloric-acid gas created by the chlorine which the chandler had used to bleach the candle-wax. He further established that joining the chlorine and the wax had replaced some of its hydrogen atoms to form a new compound.

Combustion of the candle broke up the new compound and in doing so united the chlorine atoms in it with the remaining hydrogen atoms, so forming the pungent hydrochloric acid gas. Carrying his experiment a stage further, Dumas began a series of reactions of chlorine with other organic substances, and was able to show that the chlorine could replace hydrogen in some compounds, atom for atom. He obtained the same results with iodine and bromide. From all this he deduced that the elements in an organic compound can be successively displaced and replaced by others.

Dumas's experiments provide the basic knowledge of the substitution reacting

1 Oil forms the basis of many modern synthetic chemicals. Oil refineries, like this B.P. plant at Westernport, Australia, break down crude oils and provide raw material for chemical factories.
2 Another stage in oil treatment. Superheated steam passing through pipes at Esso's Fawley refinery reduces heavy oils into lighter ones for everyday use — a process known as 'cracking'.
3 Emptying a coke oven. Crushed coal is heated in a closed oven for about a day at a temperature of 1,000 °C. The tars and gases are driven off, and the coke is left behind.
4 Analysing chemical samples for traces of elements at the Amsterdam laboratories of Shell. Detailed analysis plays an essential part in modern industrial chemistry.
5 Testing a new synthetic dye and moth-proofing agent at an industrial laboratory. Small-scale pilot plants are frequently set up to test the feasibility of using new products.

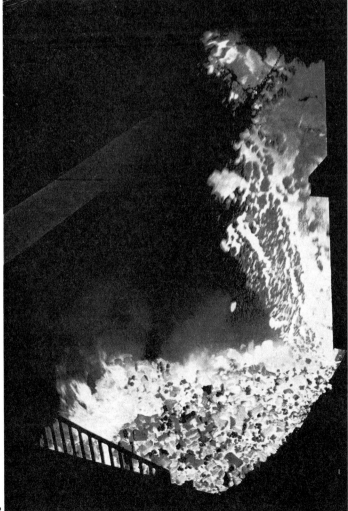

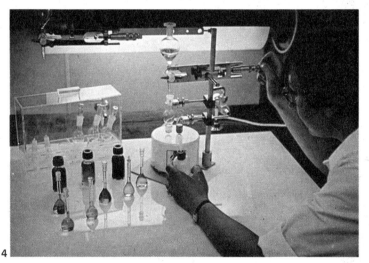

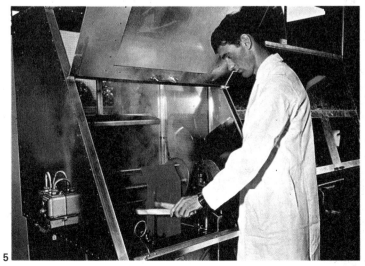

now so vital to industrial chemistry. But his experiments were never more than exercises in chemistry and it was left to industrial chemists to provide the means of turning them to commercial profit. Substitution can produce a vast number of carbon compounds which, despite their common origin, are very different from each other. Dumas's work was a striking example of pure chemistry pointing the way to a vast field of industrial chemistry.

Conversely, there are equally striking examples of a chemist deliberately experimenting to achieve some specific result. Herman Frasch, for example, had the commercial aspect before him when he evolved his process of mining sulphur by forcing super-heated steam into the deposit from the surface and then pumping out the melted sulphur. In this way the expensive digging out of deposits was avoided. Similarly, Alfred Nobel began experimenting with the deliberate intention of rendering nitro-glycerine safe as an explosive and so produced dynamite and blasting gelatine. Baekeland was concerned with the industrial problem of making a synthetic varnish when his experiments developed the first self-hardening plastic, called after him Bakelite. From that developed the vast modern industry of plastics, all of which are the result of industrial chemists juggling with molecules.

William Perkin can be considered the

1 A beaming machine at the Pontypool nylon fibre plant of ICI Fibres Ltd. Synthetic fibres — many of them produced from oil derivatives — now occupy a large part of the chemical industry.
2 Measuring the acidity of a solution during the manufacture of emetine at the Wellcome Chemical Works, Dartford. Emetine is used to treat amoebic dysentery in tropical countries.
3 A typical industrial chemists' laboratory, showing apparatus for distillation, controlled heating, drying and maintaining temperature. The scientist on the left is using a thermometer.

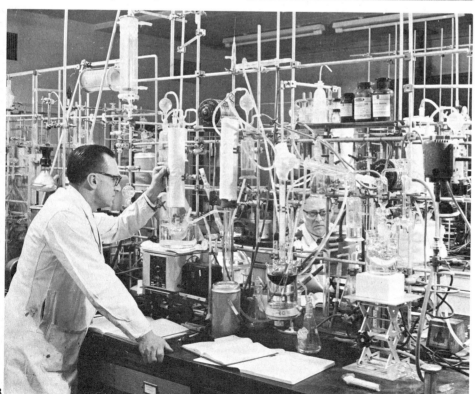

first of the great English industrial chemists, although the product that started him on his career was discovered by accident rather than by design. In 1849 Perkin was an 18-year-old laboratory assistant to August von Hofmann, the German director of the Royal College of Chemistry, London, who was then attempting to synthesize quinine. Hofmann was experimenting with coal-tar from which he had succeeded in obtaining toluidine, a benzene derivative which appeared to have a chemical structure similar to that of quinine. Hofmann was, however, far from satisfied that toluidine provided the solution to his problem and he abandoned it for another line of research. Perkin was not so sure and decided to continue the toluidine experiments in the modest laboratory he had set up in his home. He tried various reactions based on toluidine, but the only product was a reddish-brown sediment at the bottom of the flask.

Perkin was far from dejected and started a new series of reactions, this time with aniline, another, but more simple, derivative of coal-tar. The final state of his reaction was the addition of potassium dichromate, the oxidizing agent that precipitated in his flask a black powder. This was a most un-quinine-like product: but it roused the youthful chemist's curiosity and in order to see what would happen he dissolved the powder in alcohol. The result was a brilliant purple liquid. The liquid was not unfamiliar in laboratories, but chemists who had previously found it had always thrown it away as waste from unsuccessful experiments in other lines of research. Perkin did not do so. The sheer brilliance of the purple liquid suggested to him that it might have commercial possibilities as a dye. So he applied it to some strips of silk with results that surpassed everything he had expected. The dye stuck fast to the silk, it did not fade in strong sunlight, and repeated washing in soap and water failed to affect its colour. Repeated tests proved that Perkin's dye was far superior to any derived from vegetable sources. Perkin patented his process and founded the industrial chemistry that eventually evolved a whole variety of fast dyes obtained from coal.

Modern chemical industry

From this in turn developed the experiments which enabled industrial chemists to use coal as the basis of detergents, flavouring agents, explosives and plastics. Industrial chemistry has made gigantic strides on the basis of the work of the early pioneers. Today, vast chemical plants turn out thousands of tons of plastics, dyes, drugs, heavy chemicals and synthetics of all types. The chemical industry is now one of the largest sections of industry in the world. Scientific chemical theory is now applied to processes as varied as steel-making and the manufacture of stockings. Although the layman may not be aware of the full extent to which industrial chemistry has changed everyday life, he is still the recipient of countless benefits which flow from the chemists' activities. Without industrial chemistry our lives would be very different indeed.

Plastics revolution

Is the age of metals giving way to the age of plastics? More and more uses are being found for these very versatile materials, while new forms with useful properties are still being discovered.

UP TO the end of the Second World War, it would have been largely true to say that civilization rested upon a rubber cushion. Rubber had become a universal shock absorber; it not only protected mankind from many a physical jolt – as in the motor-car tyre, crash helmet and upholstery of all kinds– it also protected him from the elements – as in waterproof clothing, roofing and the like.

Since 1945, however, the role of natural rubber has dwindled considerably, in some cases almost to vanishing point. Its place has been taken to a great extent by a group of materials called plastics, which are now used everywhere in the machinery of our daily lives – from ball-point pens to domestic plumbing; table-tennis balls to aircraft construction.

Versatility is clearly the essence in plastics, and equally a number of manufacturing substances – not only rubber – have been displaced or reduced in importance by them. For plastics to be suitable for such a wide range of uses, they must individually possess very different properties. So first, how are plastics to be defined?

Very briefly, all have the following features in common. They are completely man-made and cannot be found in nature. Next, they consist of large molecules of organic compounds. Then at some point of their production they are liquid, during which time they can be moulded or otherwise shaped. And lastly, they are solid in final form.

This basic definition covers the wide variety of plastics as we know them. The variety of form depends on the skill with which the manufacturing chemists blend the constituent materials. The plastics story can therefore be regarded as one of the most important examples of 'putting science to work' in the twentieth century.

Carbon chemistry

The basic chemistry of plastics is carbon chemistry. It used to be thought that the chemical changes which take place in the development of living organisms were peculiar to such living organisms. So the study of these mysterious chemical happenings was at first called *organic chemistry*. But later it was realized that the reactions were no different in essence from those which take place in non-living materials; on the other hand, scientists found that most of the substances involved in the chemical changes of life contained carbon.

Organic chemistry therefore became carbon chemistry. It was research into an aspect of the latter that led to the discovery of nylon, a very widely used form of plastic. In the 1930s, an American chemist called Wallace Carothers was investigating the presence of large ring formations

1 Polyethylene is replacing traditional materials in a wide range of applications. Here barrels are in use at a Derby, England, fruit factory. The older wooden barrel is on the right.
2 Part of an all-plastic ship under construction. The hull, bulkheads, decks and bearers of the 600-ton design are all made from various types of plastic materials.

of carbon atoms in some natural substances (civet and musk) used in the perfumery industry. As a result, he began to wonder whether or not it was possible to take long carbon-containing chains of molecules constructed in the laboratory and cause them to join together so as to make similar rings.

He tried the experiment – only to discover that comparatively few rings were formed: the vast majority of the chains joined up to form even longer chains. Such superchains are called polymers, each chain being made up of hundreds of repeating molecular sub-units (monomers), and Carothers knew that what gives natural fibres like silk and cotton their fibrous properties, is the essence of giant polymers. It took him no time at all to realize that he had stumbled upon a way of making a new artificial fibre.

Even so, it was not all plain sailing. The fibres he first produced were weak and he set out to discover why. One reason he found was that water was produced during the mixing process, so he overcame this by carrying out polymerization at very low pressures. In consequence, the water vaporized and could be removed after condensation.

The second cause of the unwanted weakness was found to be that the polymers in the first fibres were laid down randomly – not smoothly, side by side. And to overcome this a process called cold drawing was found necessary. This means that the extruded nylon fibre is drawn out, while cold, to several times its own length and, as a result, the polymer chains rearrange themselves so as to lie side by side. The emergent fibre is now as bright and sheer

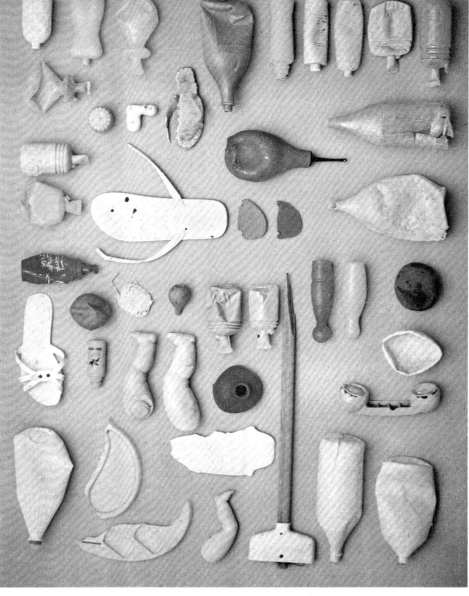

1 Rot-proof ropes and sails, water-proof clothing and boots and the yacht itself can be made with plastics. Plastics now have a wide range of uses in the sporting-goods field.
2 Relics of the age of plastics. A collection of plastic litter picked up on an Italian beach gives some idea of what our epoch may look like to archaeologists of the distant future.

as silk, and very much stronger.

Polymerization is the structural basis of the production of nylon and other plastics. But the constituents of the polymerizing materials are just as important. So, what are the basic materials which go to make nylon?

The nylon chain molecule consists of only four elements: carbon, nitrogen, hydrogen and oxygen. Carbon and nitrogen atoms form the central backbone of the chain, while the hydrogen and oxygen are attached on either side. This pattern is found in each of the sub-units, over 100 of which join to form the chain molecule.

These basic building bricks are relatively cheap and easy to come by. First, the nitrogen and hydrogen are taken from the air and turned into ammonia. Carbon and more hydrogen come from the inevitable by-products of the coal, oil and even natural gas industries. Oxygen comes from the atmosphere.

Nylon production

But to see just how all this works in practice, let us take a look at the production of one variety of the fibre, nylon 6:6. (The numbers denote the fact that there are six carbon molecules present in each molecular sub-unit or monomer.) This particular form of nylon is made by mixing two monomeric substances, hexa-methylene diamine and adipic acid. Both stem from synthetic phenol which is in turn made from benzene. And with benzene we find ourselves well and truly concerned with the coal or oil industries. For benzene is produced either when bituminous coal is destructively distilled to produce coal gas or coal tar, or when heavy oils are broken down ('cracked' is the technical term) to produce lighter oils.

The actual production of nylon 6:6 goes like this. Ammonia is built into hexamethylene diamine during its production and this latter substance is mixed with adipic acid to form nylon 6:6 salt. The salt is then mixed into a 60 per cent

aqueous solution and heated under pressure in a stainless steel container to a temperature of 280 °C. The water vapour which Carothers found such a nuisance is driven off as the reaction continues, and when all of this has been removed, the molten nylon is extruded under pressure by means of nitrogen.

It appears first as a ribbon and is sliced into chips and dried by tumbling in a stream of hot air. Finally, it is remelted and forced through small holes, or spinnerets, and the resultant fibre is cold drawn – in this case from four to seven times its original length.

This is only one form of nylon. Other varieties are made by using other constituents, but the general production method is the same. It can be produced both as fibre and in solid form for uses ranging from women's stockings, through parachutes to bearings of various kinds. The production process is also that used to manufacture all the other man-made fibres, and these, like nylon, show great resistance to dampness, to staining and to hard wear.

Like nylon, the raw materials for all other plastics – substances as different as Perspex, Bakelite, polyvinyl chloride

(PVC) and polythene – are the organic chemicals produced by the oil and coal industries. And here, the monomers join together to form polymers when subjected to heat, pressure or catalysis. (A catalyst is a substance which hastens a chemical reaction without itself taking part in that reaction.)

The properties of any particular plastic depend on three things. First, there is the actual length of the polymer chain involved. Second, there are the kinds of atoms employed and their arrangement in the chain. Finally, there is the way the chains are arranged in relation to one another. It is the variation of one or more of these factors by the chemist which gives rise to different properties in the eventual plastics.

Contrast, for example, the molecular chain structure of one of the oldest plastics, Bakelite (it was discovered in 1909 by the Belgian-born chemist, Baekeland), with that of another which came 20 odd years later, Perspex. The first is used widely for electric light fittings; the second for aircraft canopies. The constituents of each are very different but both emerge as tough and brittle plastics. Yet, Bakelite is the tougher, since its

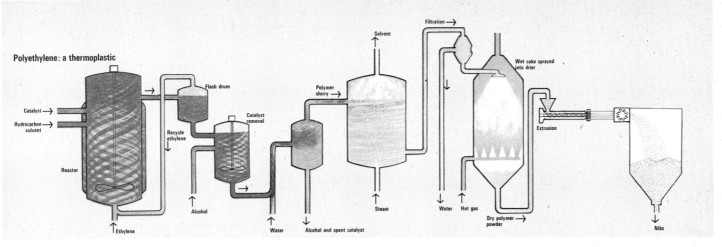

Polyethylene: a thermoplastic

Catalyst → Reactor
Hydrocarbon solvent →
Flash drum
Recycle ethylene
Catalyst removal
Polymer slurry
Solvent
Filtration →
Wet cake sprayed into drier
Extrusion

Ethylene
Alcohol
Water
Alcohol and spent catalyst
Steam
Water   Hot gas
Dry polymer powder →
Nibs

1 Stages in the production of polyethylene, one of the most versatile of today's plastics. Continuous production is normally carried out under automatic control.

2 Fun with plastics. This plastic dome, inflatable like a giant beach-ball, makes an ideal and unusual playground.

3 Plastics in the building industry. Their strength and versatility make them ideal materials for many functions in building. This portable bathroom unit, in plastic and fibreglass, can be added on or into an existing building.

molecular structure when set consists of a chain of rigid rings and it is also opaque. Perspex, on the other hand, possesses molecules with long side chains, which, while inherently a weaker combination, does allow light to pass through. Once the raw plastic of whatever kind has been manufactured, it still has to be turned into usable commodities. And in this respect, the methods used are very much the same as those employed in working metals.

First there is moulding, useful for mass producing articles of fixed shape and size like electrical fittings, washing-up bowls and toys. The mould is, of course, in the shape of the desired article, the molten plastic is injected into it and held there for something like 30 seconds. During this time the plastic sets hard enough to retain its shape and it is then automatically ejected from the mould for the process to begin again.

Polyethylene, or polythene for short, is much used in this field – look around any kitchen. It is also suitable for working with the second process, extrusion. Forced through a suitable *die* (former) in the extrusion machine, polythene can be used

to produce continuous tubing – anything from 1 in. to 40 in. in diameter – and this, cut into suitable lengths, is much used in the packaging industry. Other extruded plastics provide the tubular covering for electric cables and large-diameter pipes for sewage or drinking water.

Finally, there is the process known as rolling in the steel industry and calendering in plastics. Here sheet plastic is produced by squeezing the molten material between two rollers, both of which are hollow and heated. One of the rollers rotates a little faster than the other and the speed differential serves to smear the surface of the plastic as it passes through, imparting a very smooth finish to the

sheet. Inflatable beach toys, rainwear and curtaining are some of the goods in which calendered plastics are found.

The study of polymerization has also played a significant part in the production of synthetic rubbers and other substances with no chemical resemblance to natural rubber but with rubber-like qualities. (This last group are known as elastomers from 'elastic polymers'.) The search for these synthetics or alternatives was given great impetus by the two World Wars, during which the highly industrialized combatants were to a greater or lesser extent cut off from sources of natural rubber.

It has been understood for some time

Producing tubular Lupolen plastic film at a factory near Cologne, Germany. Raw plastic chips placed in the hopper at the top appear in front of the machine as a continuous transparent tube.

that the natural rubber molecule was in fact a natural polymer. Except in this case, the chain was not straight but twisted up, like tangled string. It only straightens on stretching, and in this lies rubber's natural elasticity.

The basic constituent of rubber is a substance called isoprene and to find a substitute for this in the manufacture of synthetics, the chemists had once again to turn to the oil industry. It was recognized that both butadiene (a direct product of petroleum cracking) and styrene (manufactured from two other petroleum products) were very similar to isoprene. German researchers thereupon experimented and found that they could get molecules of butadiene and styrene to polymerize. The result was called Buna S, and by 1943, the Germans were manufacturing over 100,000 tons per year without having to go near a rubber plantation.

But the synthetic rubber story does not end there by any means. For example, a substance called neoprene was developed in the United States during the 1940s. Here the basic molecule resembles natural isoprene, but chlorine atoms are substituted for certain parts of the natural molecule. The result is a synthetic rubber which is resistant to oils and petrol and does not soften or swell as much as the natural commodity. Then there are silicone rubbers in which the backbone of the chain consists of atoms of silicon and oxygen. These rubbers remain tough and flexible even in extremely high or low temperatures. And there is the plastic, polyethylene, which can be rubberized by adding chlorine and sulphur to the mix. These substances allow the polyethylene molecules to move more freely and hence impart rubber-like properties to it. Rubberized polyethylene is used for coating fabrics and in the manufacture of whitewall tyres for motor cars.

The list of artificial substances produced

Lightweight plastic pipes, resistant to chemical corrosion, are replacing lead, iron and copper tubes in many applications. Plastic is cheaper, lighter and easier to handle.

Plastics can be moulded into a huge variety of shapes. High-density polyethylene is being moulded here to form a strong, rigid plastic milk-bottle crate.

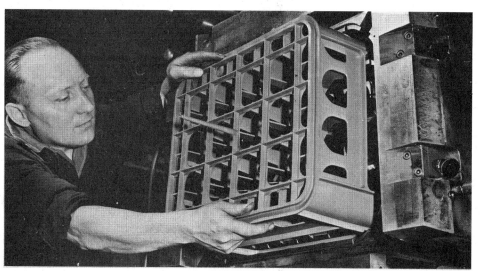

by the chemist continues to grow – not only in the field of synthetic rubbers, but in fibres and other plastics as well.

By applying his knowledge of the molecular structure of substances and his ability to manipulate that structure, the chemist is producing materials often far superior to those which nature can supply. In putting his science to work so effectively, he becomes truly a creative artist and as such is helping to change the quality of our lives by supplying a huge range of useful, durable and often, cheaper substitutes for natural materials.

From fibre to fabric

Since the Stone Age, Man has used the fibres from animals and plants to weave cloth. Science and technology and the invention of man-made fibres now provide a remarkable choice of fabrics.

THE FIRST CLOTHES were most probably made from animal skins but the availability of such clothing depended upon the availability of the right animals. Quite often, substitute materials would have been useful – and eventually Man found them in the shape of leaves and plant stems.

These it seems he interlaced to make clothing of a kind – but it could not have been very effective for comfort, protection or fit. But these unknown and primitive technologists of prehistory were experimenting in other directions. At some point, they discovered that bundles of long grass could be twisted together to make rope. The ropes could be made of varying thickness and from there it was a relatively short step to the weaving of crude cloth.

The small fibres contained in the structure of plants were the most suitable materials for such uses and it is upon fibres that the twentieth-century textile industry depends. Now, however, it is not only plant fibres that are involved, but animal and man-made fibres as well.

In the early days of textile production, the people involved were craftsmen rather than scientists or technologists. The producer knew that he could obtain certain effects by handling the fibres in certain ways but he often did not know why he got such results.

Since then science has lent a hand by elucidating the physical and chemical nature of the fibres. Such basic research was important in discovering new and improved manufacturing techniques and also in the quest for man-made fibres.

Fibres of cellulose and protein

But what do we know about fibres? Natural fibres come from two sources: plants (where they exist as a kind of skeleton binding together the fleshy parts of the plant) and animals (where they occur in the hair, skin and flesh). Plant fibres, such as cotton, linen and flax, are made of a substance called cellulose, the chemical components of which are carbon, hydrogen and oxygen. Animal fibres consist of various types of protein, mixtures of carbon, oxygen and nitrogen, sometimes with sulphur added.

These chemical facts lead to the most important consideration of fibrous matter – its molecular construction. The chemical substances in all fibres are arranged in units called *monomers,* which link together to form very long chain molecules called *polymers.* The polymers are laid down in roughly parallel lines, and the structure as a whole means that the fibres are strong and very flexible.

This is how fibres are built and the way they are put together. The result of this building process is a variety of outward

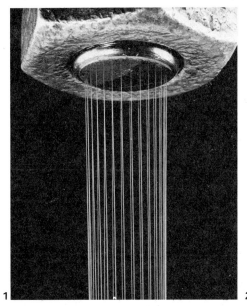

1

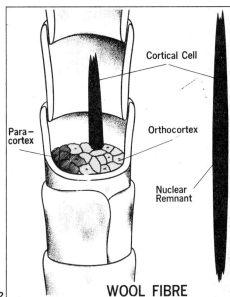

2

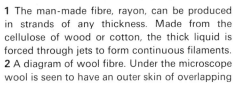

1 The man-made fibre, rayon, can be produced in strands of any thickness. Made from the cellulose of wood or cotton, the thick liquid is forced through jets to form continuous filaments.
2 A diagram of wool fibre. Under the microscope wool is seen to have an outer skin of overlapping scales. Because of this roughness, the fibres cling together during spinning into yarn.
3 A fully automatic cotton-spinning machine. The spun yarn is examined by a photo-electric cell, faults are cut out and the yarn re-tied as it is wound into packages for weaving.

3

forms, providing the qualities which the textile producer needs in different combinations. The cotton fibre is almost pure cellulose and is a single cell which in length varies from ½ to 2½ in.; it is many thousand times thinner than it is long. Under the microscope the fibre appears flattened like a hair ribbon, but it is also twisted. The twists occur when the cell walls collapse during ripening and there can be as many as 300 twists to the inch. It is these twists that makes the fibre such a good material for spinning, the roughness imparted by the twists causes the fibres to cling together.

Cotton fibres are strong, become even stronger when wetted, and they are absorbent. A natural resistance to boiling water, and bleaches, also makes cotton extremely washable. On the other hand cotton fibres have little stretch or elasticity so that the cloth creases and tears readily. Finally, cotton fibres are inflammable, weaken in strong sunlight and are prone to mildew.

Wool is a protein – in this case, the protein is keratin and contains sulphur. In length the wool fibre varies much more than cotton: fine wool may be anything from 1½ to 5 in. long; coarse varieties run from 5 to 15 in. in length (and the average thickness would be about 40 microns).

The structure of wool

There are two qualities of the wool fibre which make it a good spinning material and a warm cloth as well. First there may be as many as 30 natural waves or *crimps* to the inch and these ensure that the various fibres hang together well when the yarn is spun. Second, there is the surface of the individual fibre itself. Under the microscope, the wool is seen to be an outer skin or *cuticle*. The cuticle consists of overlapping scales (epithelial scales), the unattached ends of which point towards the tip of the fibre. The roughness implied by this means that the fibres cling together during spinning into yarn. Both crimp and scales tend to trap air in the yarn which acts as an insulator.

At the same time the crimp gives the fibre a natural spring, making it both stretchable and elastic, and although the weakest of the natural fibres, wool can be bent a great deal without breaking. It is also extremely resistant to creasing and crushing. Wool, however, has its disadvantages; for example, it shrinks. If the fibre is rubbed from tip to root, the rubbing surface catches on the projecting edges of the scales and tips them backwards. They then become jammed together and the fibre curls back towards its root. Shrinkage in woollen cloth is due to the fact that when rubbed – during washing, for example – some of the fibres curl or 'creep' towards the root end and the cloth becomes deformed. Wool is particularly susceptible to insect attack – hence the damage which the grubs of the clothes moth can do. And although it is not highly inflammable, it deteriorates in dry heat. Boiling and some bleaches also cause weakening.

These are two very common natural fibres, both of which have their drawbacks as well as advantages. And the same can be said for the other natural fibres. As a

222

1 A small loom can be used to produce a huge range of colourful weaves. By varying the thickness of the warps and wefts that make up the lattice work, different textures and patterns can be obtained.

2 When sheep's fleeces arrive at the factory they are sorted and passed through a series of wash bowls. This process of scouring removes the dirt, sweat and grease.

3 The highly magnified fibres of a nylon stocking. First produced in the 1930s, nylon is about twice as strong as cotton and is resistant to insect and bacterial attack.

4 A high-speed worsted cloth weaving machine. To produce worsted, fine wool yarns with the fibres lying as parallel as possible are used.

5 Silkworm cocoons being prepared for unwinding. Silk is an extremely strong, continuous filament that is smooth and elastic. Each cocoon may provide as much as 1,300 yards of silk which can be twisted directly into yarn.

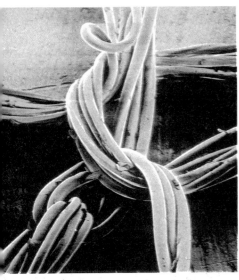

result scientists have looked round for a means of making fibres artificially, fibres into which all or most of the required qualities can be built. First came the viscose and cellulose acetate rayons. In the former, cellulose is obtained from spruce wood and poor-quality cotton. It is then treated with caustic soda and carbon bisulphide to form a thick treacly liquid, which is forced through tiny holes to form a thin filament or fibre and hardened in an acid bath.

Cellulose acetate rayons employ poor-quality cotton treated with acetic acid and acetic anhydride to form cellulose acetate. The acetate is then dissolved in acetic acid to form a thick liquid which is pushed through tiny holes into air where the filament hardens. Both types of rayon are lustrous and strong, and therefore were given the name 'artificial silks'. Both have ridged surfaces which improves the spinning capability, and the filaments can be manufactured into any length required. But the rayons also have one distinct drawback – although they will absorb water, they weaken when wetted.

In the 1930s an American chemist produced a fibre which was to be much more successful. The chemist was Dr Wallace Carothers and the fibre he produced was nylon. He took the chemical substances produced and involved in the oil and coal industries and found – during carefully planned experiments helped in the end by a fortunate accident – that they could be induced to form monomers (repeating sub-units) which in turn could be linked together to form long chain molecules – or polymers. In other words, he repeated in the laboratory a process used by Nature to impart the

fibrous quality to fibres. Nylon was found to be about twice as strong as cotton and water-repellent to a great extent. What water it did absorb had no effect on its strength. It was also resistant to insect and bacterial attack. There were, however, problems in weaving and dyeing.

Having once picked, caught or constructed a fibre, the next step is to spin it into yarn. Taking cotton as an example, there are a number of steps involved. After picking, the raw cotton is baled and sent to the spinning factory. Here the compressed fibres are loosened on a machine which also causes heavy impurities to fall out. It is spread out into a sheet (called a *lap*) and is now in a suitable state to be pressed on to the carding machine. This not only removes the remaining impurities and weeds out weak or otherwise imperfect fibres, but also combs the fibres so that they lie fairly parallel to each other.

The machine consists basically of a number of cylinders, the largest of which is covered with numbers of fine wire points. The cotton is fed to the larger cylinder and the points take up the fibres in a fine layer. This layer is then combed again by another device and passed on to a final cylinder called the *doffer,* where it is gathered together in a loose skein or *sliver* and finally coiled into tall cans. To provide a uniform quality of cotton yarn, several slivers are drawn out thinner and thinner – the loose-packed nature of the fibres allows this – until the required thickness is achieved. The drawn fibres are then twisted tightly together to make the yarn. If very fine yarn is required, the slivers are combed again before drawing.

The process for wool is rather more complicated and depends upon the kind of

5

yarn required. Sheep get very dirty and they also sweat. Two processes, scouring and carbonizing, are used to remove the impurities from the fleece when it arrives at the factory.

In the scouring phase, the wool is washed in a series of vats of soapy alkaline water, the mixture decreasing in strength as the wool moves through the series. This removes dirt, oils and sweat (called *suint*) and also the natural colour of the wool. Vegetable matter, like burrs and tough grasses, are the target of the carbonizing process. Here the wool is subjected to a very weak solution of acid. The excess liquid is extracted and the wool is then dried. While the wool is unharmed by its dousing in acid, the vegetable impurities begin to disintegrate. When the wool moves on to a crushing machine the burrs become powdered and can be shaken clear. At this point the preparation of wool yarn becomes a forked path. One branch leads to a type of yarn called *worsted*, employing the finer wool fibres and intended to make fine cloths; the other branch leads to a type called simply *woollens*, which utilizes coarser fibres and ends as coarser cloth. The two types of yarn also differ in that the fibres in worsted yarns must be as parallel as possible, in woollens the parallelism is much reduced.

Both cotton and wool are what is known as short staple fibres (that is, the actual fibre is relatively short). Silk and man-made fibres, however, have continuous filament yarns. For example, the two threads spun by a silkworm can be as long as 1,300 yards, while the man-made fibres can be produced to any length required. Both are therefore twisted directly into yarn. With man-made fibres, the exact process employed differs according to the material employed, and there may here be some further complications. If, for example, a 'stretch' artificial yarn is required for garments like socks or stockings, the yarn itself must be twisted even further and the twist is heat set. It is then unwound and as a result has a spring-

When wool is rubbed during washing, it shrinks and felts. This is caused by the scales of the fibre interlocking. Here wool is experimentally treated for shrink resistance.

like form which gives it 'stretch'.

Cloth consists of a lattice-work of threads at right angles to each other. Those running the length of the piece are called the *warps,* while the crosswise ones are called the *wefts.* The warps are stretched in parallel lines (perhaps 60 warps to the inch) from one roller called the *weaver's beam* to another called the *cloth beam.* On the way each warp passes through an individual eyelet on one of two wire frames called *heddles.* The odd-numbered warps (one, three, five and so on) pass through the eyelets on the first heddle; the even numbers pass through those on the second and both heddles are movable in the vertical plane.

Heddles, shuttles and reeds

To weave, one heddle is raised and the other lowered, and the weft (carried by a *shuttle*) is passed through the gap between them. The weft, therefore, passes over half the warps and under the rest. After each pass, the weft is pressed back against its forerunners with another wire frame called a *reed,* to make the texture of the material tight. The position of the heddles is then reversed, and the process repeated. This produces the simplest kind of weave; different textures may be achieved by varying the number of warps.

The second major fabric-making process is knitting, and here again the basics are simple – although modern technology has provided some very complicated machines to do the job quickly and efficiently. Basically knitting depends upon forming the yarn into a series of loops; the free end is then passed back through these loops so that it not only stops the first line from pulling straight but also forms a second row of loops. The manoeuvre is then repeated over and over again.

What of colour? This is imparted by either dyeing or printing. Dyeing can be carried out during any of the stages of fabric production. Loose fibres are evenly packed into a perforated drum and the dye is injected. Yarn is hung in a vat in which the dye is circulated by a propellor. Woven fabrics may be *jig dyed,* which means that the material is opened out and drawn back and forth through a dye trough; knitted fabrics are put on to a

winch dyer which gently dunks them in the liquor (the jig dyer would stretch them).

Multi-coloured fabrics, like carpeting, may be made by weaving together yarns which have previously been dyed. Otherwise, printing can be employed and, for large runs – that is, extensive lengths of material – roller printing is used. The material is passed between a series of rollers each of which is engraved with part of the pattern and each of which carries one of the colours in the form of a paste of pigment and gum. The component parts of the pattern are printed on contact with the cloth, the colour is heat set, and the gum washed out.

The finishing processes, of which there are a great many, are designed to improve one or more of the qualities of the cloth. If some non-shiny cloth, like cotton, is to be given a shiny finish, the material may be *calendared* – passed through heavy rollers which both flatten and polish the yarn. There is also shrink resistance. In the case of cottons it may be done mechanically – the weft threads being closed up together with a high degree of compression, so that shrinkage can cause them to close up no further. But with wools such a process is less effective, for here the shrinkage comes about through *felting* (the scales on the fibre interlock). The trick in this case is to cause the edges of the scales to disintegrate slightly so that the surface of the fibre is smoothed. The wool is, therefore, treated with any one of a number of chemical agents – chlorine gas is often employed – to carry out this work of controlled destruction. Boosted crease resistance can be brought about by impregnating the fibres of the yarn with resin so that they become stiffer. Fabrics can also be treated with chemicals to make them resistant to fire.

It is just one of the 'tricks' which science and technology have brought to the job of providing and improving materials which also bring comfort, protection and colour into our lives.

A skilled operator ties a broken thread on a weaving machine that can weave two or more cloths at the same time. Such machines can be adapted to produce a variety of textiles.

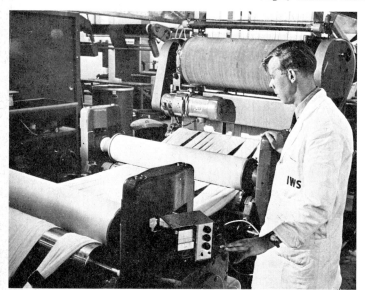

Glass and ceramics

Revolutionary breakthroughs in the development of glass and ceramics have transformed these basically fragile materials into a specialized range with important applications in science and industry.

WINDOW-PANES AND TUMBLERS, crockery, roofing tiles and countless other articles made of glass or ceramics are all visible links with our distant ancestors' tentative ventures into the arts of manufacture, or the crafts of making things from naturally occurring raw materials.

The term ceramics comes from a Greek word meaning 'potter's clay', and a ceramic product is anything made by shaping a mixture of clay and other materials into a desired form, drying it and then baking it hard by firing in a kiln. Bricks, cups or priceless porcelain vases are all basically the same.

Over a period of thousands of years pottery developed into the clay bricks used by the ancient civilizations of the Euphrates for building their temples and palaces. It was realized that a design impressed on soft clay became hard and permanent after the clay had dried. Men were soon to write their records on clay tablets and from these the history of ancient civilizations can be pieced together.

The first clay pots and bowls were dried hard in the sun but they became soft again when filled with water. Then it was discovered that this could be remedied by drying the clay pot or bowls and firing them at red heat. That marked the turning-point of craftsmanship in pottery: ceramics had been made durable.

When clay is hardened by firing, the tiny particles of clay lose water and in doing so change their structure. There is also a certain amount of melting, particularly of the felspars and micas present in the clay. On cooling, the silicates in the clay *vitrify,* that is, they become glass-like, and act as a binder to cement the clay particles together so that the clay becomes hard and strong.

The first ceramics were earthenware. In the earthenware process, ordinary clay is moulded to the required shape and fired to approximately 800 °C. Because only a small percentage of vitreous material is present in the clays used for earthenware, there is very little recrystallization and, unlike other ceramics, it tends to be porous. Earthenware can be made waterproof by covering it with a substance, or mixture of substances, which melt during firing to form a glazed surface. One of the first substances used for this purpose was salt, and articles were said to be salt-glazed. Wash-basins and other cheap chinaware are made in this way.

Bricks and tiles

Clays used for bricks and other outdoor building-components require carefully controlled drying. This is to prevent too rapid an escape of moisture during firing which would cause excessive shrinking and cracking. Clays used for bricks and tiles contain iron compounds and the final colour of the fired articles depends upon the atmosphere in the kiln during firing. A plentiful supply of oxygen oxidizes the iron compounds to give a red colour, less oxygen gives a blue colour, and further adjustments a brown or mottled appearance.

Ceramic products designed to resist melting at temperatures in excess of 1,000 °C. are called *refractories* and include the heat-resistant bricks used for lining furnaces. Many types of bricks and other industrial ceramics must, in addition, be able to withstand the corrosive action of chemicals. They are made from sands and clays having a high proportion of silica and are mixed with lime to produce a binding medium. Firing at a temperature of 1,400 °C. converts the normal silica crystal formation into one that remains stable when subjected to high temperatures.

For certain special applications, refractories are made from dolomite, a double carbonate of magnesium and calcium. Fireclay, one of the most common of heat-resistant ceramics, is derived from carboniferous rock and obtains its heat-resistant property from its alumina content.

Porcelain, which is the highest quality of all ceramics and is used for electrical insulators, vases and other decorative articles, is made from kaolin, or white china clay. It is composed almost entirely of the mineral kaolinite, a hydrated silicate of aluminium, and is formed by the decomposition of granite felspars. In the making of porcelain the kaolin has added to it quartz, felspar and, sometimes, ball clay. Ball clay also derives from granite felspar, but during its formation the kaolinite grains leave the parent rock. It is finer grained and more plastic than china clay and contains quartz and mica.

Porcelain was first made about 200 BC by the Chinese. Kaolin is a Chinese word meaning 'high ridge' and the clay was originally dug from the sides of hills. The Chinese also discovered another material called petunce which, when added to kaolin enabled porcelain vases and other objects to be fired at relatively low temperatures and they become hard and glass-like. For centuries the Chinese were able

At this plant in Tennesee, a continuous sheet of glass is drawn out of the furnace and rolled on to a grinding and polishing line. After cleaning and inspection, it is cut to size.

A large porcelain electrical weather-shield is turned vertically at a factory in Britain. Its basic material is kaolin which is fired at extremely high temperatures.

to keep the ingredients of their porcelain secret. Then, in 1718, a traveller returned to England with samples of kaolin and details of how to make the pottery. European potters attempted to make porcelain from the coarse clays then available but were unsuccessful until 1758, when the Cornwall china-clay deposits were found in England. Chinese porcelain reached its greatest perfection during the Ming dynasty (1368–1644), when wonderful colour effects were achieved. Other notable periods of Chinese porcelain are the Tang and Sung dynasties.

Porcelain is fired at temperatures ranging from 1,200 °C. to 1,400 °C. These temperatures ensure maximum vitrification and, therefore, great impermeability, making porcelain invaluable for insulators and chemical equipment.

Bone china, used for high-quality household crockery, consists of china clay mixed with fluxes and calcium phosphate, or calcined animal bone; hence the name bone china. The addition of the calcium phosphate gives bone china its characteristic translucence.

Before shaping and firing, most clays have various non-clay ingredients, chiefly white mica and felspars added to them. These melt easily and lower the firing temperature of the clay. On recooling, a glass-like substance forms to give the ceramic extra strength and make it waterproof. Excessive shrinking of ceramics after drying and during firing is prevented by the addition of a quartz filler.

Certain industrial and scientific applications of ceramics demand hardness, strength, heat resistance and an ability

1

2

3

4

5

1 An inspector examines plates made on moulds by a fully-automatic machine at a pottery in Staffordshire. Glazed and dried, the plates are then fired in kilns.

2 Molten glass, which resembles thick, sticky toffee, flows between patterned rollers to produce flat glass with a textured surface. It is then slowly cooled to avoid cracking.

3 His eyes protected from the glare, this glass-worker checks the glass mixture in a furnace.

Any impurities in the ingredients can discolour and spoil all the glass in the melt.

4 Ceramics are packed into a kiln, lined with heat-resistant bricks, before firing. Kiln temperatures ensure maximum vitrification and great impermeability of the porcelain.

5 Red-hot molten glass is extruded from an automatic machine to form soft-drink bottles. The glass is made from carefully measured quantities of sand, soda ash, lime and other materials.

to withstand sudden changes of extreme temperatures, which ordinary clays cannot meet. Accordingly, an entirely new range of ceramic materials has been developed, amongst them oxides of beryllium, aluminium, thorium, zirconium and magnesium, and certain synthetic nitrides and carbides. Beryllium oxide ceramics are employed in the casing for the rods of nuclear fuels in reactors. Aluminium oxide ceramics, which can resist temperatures up to 2,100 °C are used as insulators for sparking plugs and heat shields on space rockets. Zirconium-oxide ceramics are essential in metallurgy and chemistry where temperatures up to 3,000 °C are encountered. Non-organic binders are added to non-plastic ceramics materials in order to hold the shaped article together while it is soft. During the firing process, the binder is destroyed, while the grains of the non-plastic material are *sintered* (bound together by the heat).

The chief tool in ceramics used to be the potter's wheel. Although still used for the shaping of high-quality articles, it has been largely replaced by automatic moulding machines for crockery and similar ware, and extrusion-moulding for pipes. Ceramics for certain industrial uses are shaped by putting semi-plastic clay mixtures on a lathe and turning the material like soft metal. The article is then fired in the usual way.

After ceramics, glass was Man's major

step towards the development of industrial crafts. There are no reliable records as to when or where it was discovered that a transparent material could be produced by fusing together sand, soda and potash, but the art appears to have been established in Syria some 7,500 years ago. From there it was introduced into Egypt, and by the seventh century BC glass was being made in Europe. The Egyptians initiated many technical advances; they were the first to make glass vessels, they invented glass-blowing, and they produced coloured glass by adding copper to the molten materials to obtain a red tint.

Much of the glass used now is made from the same materials. Sodium or window glass, which is the cheapest and most extensively manufactured, is produced by heating a mixture of sand, soda ash and limestone at a temperature of 1,500 °C. The intense heat causes sand to replace carbon dioxide in the soda ash and limestone and so form silicates. The molten glass is then a mixture of the silicates of calcium and soda. If molten glass cools too quickly it sets up internal stresses which result in cracks and bubbles. To prevent this, the articles being moulded or blown are passed through annealing ovens to bring them gradually down to an atmospheric temperature.

Glass does not crystallize on cooling; nor does it appear to have any definite temperature at which it may be said to solidify. Consequently glass is classed as an *amorphous solid* which retains some of the properties, particularly transparency, of a highly viscous fluid. Chemists describe glass as a *super-cooled liquid*, thereby emphasizing that it is not actually a solid, but a fluid of almost infinite viscosity.

Modern glass-works melt the ingredients in tanks built up from fireclay slabs. Before the ingredients are added a proportion of broken glass, called *cullet,* is put in to hasten the fusing process. As the mixture melts and fuses, impurities rise to the surface from which they are mechanically skimmed. The molten glass is allowed to cool until it resembles a thin, sticky toffee. It is then ready for drawing off to go to the mechanical moulding and blowing machines or for rolling into plate glass.

One of the most difficult tasks in glass-making is to ensure that the ingredients are free of impurites and that they are mixed in the correct quantities. A tiny piece of iron in a mixture for making plate glass will discolour every particle of glass in the melt. Cheap glass frequently develops a greenish tinge due to ferrous compounds in the sand. This can be overcome by adding manganese dioxide. Alternatively, small quantities of compounds are added to give a colour which offsets the green.

Glass can be coloured to any desired shade by adding to the melt appropriate metal oxides. Copper or gold produce ruby glass, cobalt gives blue glass. Manganese colours glass in a variety of shades from pink to purple according to the amount added; chromium gives shades of green; uranium gives green and yellow shades and copper colours glass red or black, depending on the quantities.

Cut glass contains a considerable amount of lead silicate, but an excess of lead in the melt destroys its characteristic brilliance and sparkle. It is this care in the mixing of ingredients of the right quality and the careful addition of colouring agents that has made the techniques of quality control so essential in the glass industry.

Hundreds of varieties of glass have been developed by technologists to meet the ever-expanding demands of industry

Chemists have produced many special types of glass for particular uses. The glass of this tank has been tempered to have the strength and durability of steel.

and science. There is heat-resistant glass for smelters and convertors; glass which shields against nuclear radiation; glass to allow the passage of the ultra-violet rays in sunlight, optical glass ranging from spectacle and microscope lenses to the huge mirrors for telescopes; glass bricks for the walls of buildings; splinter-proof glass for windscreens and bullet-proof glass strong enough to resist machine-gun fire.

Ribbons of glass

Grinding and polishing processes to produce plate glass began in 1688, when the glass had to be cast in sheets at least 50 per cent thicker than the final product required. Later the molten glass was poured into shallow moulds on a rotating table and ground with metal discs working in a mixture of fine sand, emery and water before being polished with rouge and water. An improved method was the Bicheroux process, in which molten glass was fed through rollers on to a flat surface and then annealed before polishing, but the area of the glass remained limited. Then, in 1920 the Ford Motor Company and the English glass-making firm of Pilkington Brothers invented a method of rolling plate glass in the form of a continuous ribbon as it left the furnace. Five years later Pilkington Brothers developed a machine that ground and polished sheets of plate glass continuously, first on the top surface and then on the bottom surface.

In order to avoid having to turn the glass over, in 1937 they introduced a machine in which the ribbon of glass passed between grinding heads so that its two sides are worked on simultaneously. In this way, a sheet of glass 1,000 ft long and 100 in. wide could be ground and polished at the rate of 200 ft a minute. Even so, they still had to discover how to support the hot, fluid glass without strain, so that a truly flat, distortion-free sheet could emerge of any desired length. The problem was finally solved in 1952, when

Alastair Pilkington invented the float glass system, whereby the continuous ribbon of glass passes from the furnace to float on the surface of a molten metal at a controlled temperature. It emerges as sheet or plate glass with a brilliant lustrous finish on both sides.

There is also glass that can be drawn into fine thread, and woven into a fibre-glass cloth, and glass that can be combined with resins to make fibreglass, for car and aircraft bodies. Many plastics tend to elongate under tension, crack under bending or impact, or turn soft under heat. Reinforcing them with fibreglass increases their strength, much as concrete strength is reinforced with metal rods. Fibreglass plastics enable large structures to be made of plastics without risk of collapse or other failure.

Another type of glass is low-expansion glass designed to withstand sudden changes of extreme temperatures. One glass of this type even resists fracture when placed on a block of ice and molten iron is poured on it at a temperature of 2,600 °C.

Applications of glass seem endless. There is glass that can be folded or crumpled; glass that bounces like rubber; glass that can be cut with a saw or have nails driven into it; glass sutures for surgery; and glass fishing-rods and lines. Transparent cooking utensils are made from glass mixtures to which boric and aluminium oxide have been added. They can withstand great changes of temperature without cracking.

Glass is a bad conductor of heat, but it has a good compression and tensile strength, and is unaffected by most acids. Finally, glass cannot be corroded by the impurities in the atmosphere: an all-glass building would never need painting and would probably last indefinitely.

Glass is blown and shaped to make scientific instruments. Resistant to acids and other corrosive chemicals, it is widely used for laboratory apparatus and storage containers.

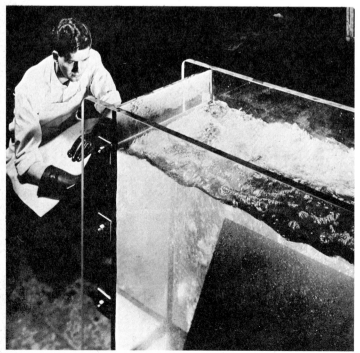

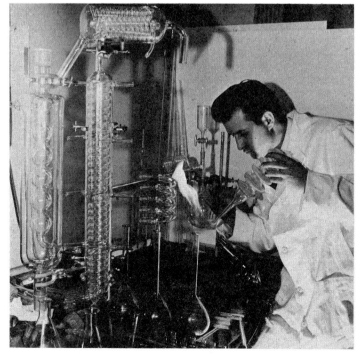

Carbon's shapely compounds

Plastics, penicillin and paints — all products of organic chemistry. This is the chemistry of a million compounds, complex, diverse, and holding the prospect of tomorrow's health and wealth.

IN 1828 a German chemist named Friedrich Wohler discovered by chance that a simple laboratory chemical, ammonium cyanate, could be converted into urea by evaporating a solution in water to dryness. Urea is an organic chemical present in the urine of many animals and is the form in which unwanted nitrogen is removed from their bodies. Before 1828 most scientists thought it would be impossible to prepare in the laboratory any substance made by a living organism because, they argued, there was a 'vital life force' that could be provided only by a living organism. Wohler's experiment was the beginning of organic chemistry as we know it today. Once the old idea of a vital life force had been discarded, scientists set about trying to prepare even more organic compounds in the laboratory.

On this planet, at any rate, living things are composed mainly of substances built up almost entirely from two chemical elements, carbon and hydrogen, although, of course, other elements such as oxygen, nitrogen and phosphorus are also present. Carbon is ideally suited to this 'building brick' role, as it has the property of being able to combine with itself to form either long chains or rings of atoms. This enables the very complicated types of molecules necessary for life processes to be formed. Silicon also possesses this property to some extent and it is possible that the life on a planet of some distant star might be based on silicon compounds (silanes) instead of carbon.

Oil as a source of chemicals

As our bodies are made of organic compounds they are naturally of great interest and importance to us and a lot of time and money is devoted to their study. Most of those which are used in the laboratory are derived from plants or from crude petroleum oils which are, of course, formed from the remains of prehistoric animals and plants. In a sense we have gone back to the days before the 'vital force' theory was exploded, in that we get most of our organic chemicals from what were originally living sources.

The starting materials for the chemical industry are obtained from crude oil by the process of *fractional distillation*. This separates the light substances, such as ether and petrol, from the heavy ones, such as motor oil and road tar, by boiling off increasingly heavy fractions as the temperature is raised. The fractionating columns in which the distillation is done are a familiar scene at any oil refinery. If the crude oil contains too many of the heavier chemicals they can be broken down into lighter ones by a process known as *catalytic cracking*. The newly formed light chemicals can then be redistilled. If,

Oil refineries reduce crude oil to its various components, which then form the basic 'building bricks' for the synthesis of many organic compounds, including plastics.

on the other hand, there are too many of the light chemicals present in the crude oil, then some heavy ones can be generated from these by a process known as *plat-forming* using a platinum catalyst. The light and heavy fractions from fractional distillation can be repurified until there are many fractions, each containing only one substance.

Then the real chemistry starts. Each of these simple substances can be converted into a variety of others, and these raw materials will be used to make the various products that we need. Practically every industry is dependent to some extent on these starting materials. The pharmaceutical, dyeing, fibre, plastics, engin-

eering and agricultural industries all need petroleum products at some time.

Nowadays, many clothes are made from artificial fibres such as nylon and terylene. These are both made from products of the petroleum industry. Nylon was the first of the two to be produced, although it was by no means the first artificial fibre to be developed. All fibres, whether artificial or natural, are made up from long, chain-like molecules which make it possible to spin the short filaments into strong, continuous threads. The long-chain molecules of artificial fibres are made up from many identical parts and are called *polymers*. They are often made in *autoclaves* which are large, heated pressure vessels rather similar to a domestic pressure cooker, but of course very much bigger. When these polymeric fibres were first being made, the small laboratory autoclaves sometimes used to burst, with

229

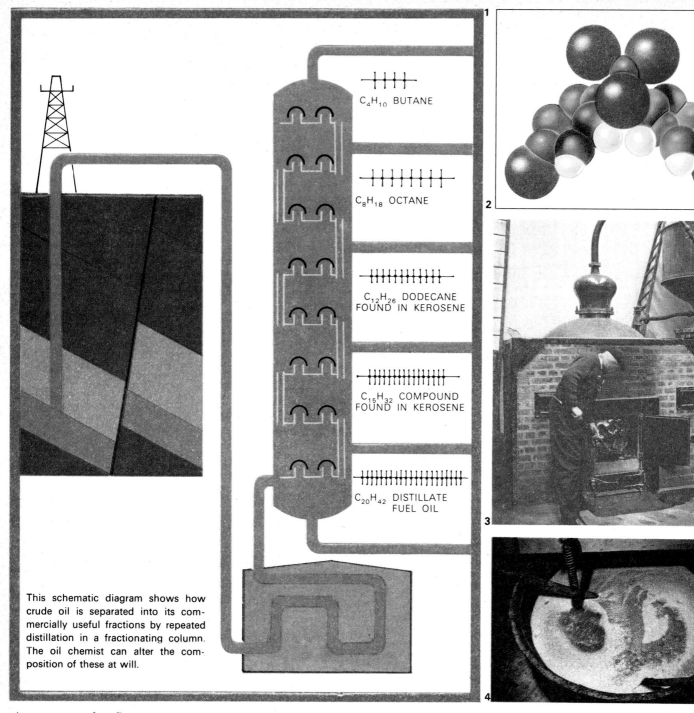

This schematic diagram shows how crude oil is separated into its commercially useful fractions by repeated distillation in a fractionating column. The oil chemist can alter the composition of these at will.

C₄H₁₀ BUTANE

C₈H₁₈ OCTANE

C₁₂H₂₆ DODECANE FOUND IN KEROSENE

C₁₅H₃₂ COMPOUND FOUND IN KEROSENE

C₂₀H₄₂ DISTILLATE FUEL OIL

disastrous results. Great care is taken to ensure that this does not happen on the large scale.

Nylon is what is known as a *polyamide* fibre; that is, it is an amide polymer. An *amide* is a chemical compound formed when an amine combines with a carboxylic acid. An example of an amine is ammonia and an example of a carboxylic acid is acetic acid, which occurs in vinegar. The substance formed when these two compounds combine is an amide known as *acetamide*. In this process a molecule of water is eliminated.

To make a polyamide fibre, a substance with an *amino group* at each end of the molecule – a di-amine – is reacted with a di-acid, which has a carboxylic group at each end. In this way a very long chain in which the molecules alternate can be built up. In nylon the di-amine is a substance known as *hexamethylenediamine*, which is a chain of six carbon atoms with an amino group at each end. The di-acid

1 Light components of crude oil can be boiled off at comparatively low temperatures, while heavy fractions, including waxes and tars, require much higher temperatures.
2 The geometric distribution of the atoms in an organic molecule can be found by chemical techniques. 'Billiard ball' reconstructions are widely used in chemistry teaching.

used is known as *adipic acid* and also contains six carbon atoms.

A complete molecule of nylon is composed of a large number of both of these units, each alternating in the chain rather like a long line of boys and girls in which each boy holds hands with two girls and vice versa.

It is convenient that both the di-amine and the di-acid parts of nylon each contain six carbon atoms, as this means that they can both be made from *phenol* (popularly known as carbolic acid) which is available cheaply in large amounts from the petroleum industry. There is now another kind

3 Production of alcoholic beverages by fermentation is one of Man's most ancient skills. Stronger liquors are then produced by distillation, in this case of wine.
4 Grapes are fermented in vats. The action of yeast on the natural grape sugars produces alcohol. This reaction is self-regulating, production of alcohol ceasing automatically.

of nylon called *nylon-12* in which the di-amine part of the molecule contains 12 carbon atoms.

Terylene is another widely used artificial fibre. It is a polyester fibre, made from a chain composed of alternating di-alcohol and di-acid groups. In this case the di-acid is *terephthalic acid*; hence the name terylene. The di-alcohol used is *ethylene glycol*, another very common chemical which, by the way, is the main constituent of anti-freeze.

Once a fibre has been made there is the problem of developing a series of dyes which can be used on it. Modern dyes

1 Whisky, the traditional drink of Scotland, is a distillate of a barley mash. Malt whisky, favoured by connoisseurs, is made by double distillation in a traditional pot still.

2 Careful selection of the distillates produced is vital in the manufacture of whisky. This highly skilled process is controlled from the 'spirit safe'.

must be colour-fast and must not wash out. The artificial fibres were not problem-free at first because many of the dyes traditionally used for colouring wool and cotton did not suit the new fibres, which are chemically different from the natural fibres. Dyes stick to a fibre either by combining with it chemically or by means of parts of the molecule which are simply attracted to the fibre. Terylene is a very stable fibre and does not easily form chemical compounds with dyes.

This means that many of the older generations of 'combining' dyes do not stick to terylene very well. This sort of problem was overcome by synthesizing a whole new range of dyes and colouring specially for use with the new fibres.

Discovering dyes by accident

One of these new groups of dyes, the *phthalocyanines,* were discovered when some dye-workers were preparing a substance called *phthalimide.* They made it by heating *phthalic anhydride* with ammonia in an open vessel made of enamel-coated iron. On one occasion a dark blue pigment was formed as an impurity, and when this was examined it was found to contain iron. The enamel lining of the reaction vessel had become chipped, allowing some of the iron to dissolve and form this impurity. As this happened in a dye works there was naturally some interest in this new blue substance.

It was discovered that in the presence of copper a similar reaction took place which gave a beautiful greenish-blue pigment. This was found to have a rather complicated ring structure, composed of carbon and nitrogen atoms, which was wrapped round an atom of copper. The substance, named Monastral Blue, is extremely stable, but is almost completely insoluble in most solvents.

By making small changes in the struc-

ture of the molecule it is possible to alter the colour of these dyes. This can be done simply by putting a different metal atom into the middle; for example, lead phthalocyanine is a yellowish-green colour, while the phthalocyanines containing nickel and cobalt are a similar shade of blue. Other modifications to this type of dye include ones to make the dyes soluble in water so that they can be used as direct dyes. The very insoluble ones can be used only as pigments which are dispersed on to the fibre, or other surface, in the form of extremely fine particles.

Long-chain polymeric molecules similar to synthetic fibres, but more complicated, occur in our bodies, mainly as proteins and nucleic acids. Proteins comprise muscle fibres and, in the form of enzymes, are responsible for most of the chemical reactions which take place inside us. They are composed of long chains made up of amino acids. The links in the chains are amide bonds, the same as those which hold the molecules of nylon together. However, proteins are far more complicated than nylon for several reasons.

For one thing, the individual amino acids are sometimes quite complicated in themselves. Also there are about 20 different ones and they are not arranged in a regular fashion along the chains. Instead, they are in an apparently random order. However, this order is not really random, as it is always the same for a given protein. The absence of a regular order of amino acids allows an infinite number of variations in protein structure, and so any number of different proteins is possible.

In addition to the above complications, the protein chains can be coiled in many ways, but in only one particular spatial arrangement will the molecule possess all the properties of the true protein. The molecule is usually held in this shape by very weak attractive forces and also by

rather weak bonds known as *hydrogen bonds.* These are usually broken if the molecule is subjected to any kind of rough treatment such as being heated. When the hydrogen bonds are broken or disturbed, the protein loses its characteristic properties and becomes denatured. This is what happens to egg white as it gradually goes hard and opaque when the egg is boiled.

The nucleic acids are another important type of long-chain polymer which occurs in the cells of all living things. These substances contain one or two sugars, present as a phosphate. The sugar is either *ribose,* which is a molecule slightly smaller than *glucose,* or the related *desoxy-ribose.* It alternates along the chain of the nucleic acid with four different organic 'bases'. These are very weakly alkaline substances containing nitrogen. The usual bases which occur in nucleic acids are called *adenine, guanine, cytosine* and *uracil,* usually abbreviated to A, G, C, and U. Much of the work on the chemical nature of the nucleic acids was done at Cambridge by Sir Alexander Todd (now Lord Todd) and his collaborators.

The chemistry of inheritance

One of the two classes of nucleic acids, the desoxyribonucleic (DNA), are responsible for passing on the information about the make-up of the body from one generation to the next by means of the 'genetic code'. DNA is probably the factor responsible for all our inherited characteristics. In the past decade the fine structure of DNA has been worked out by James Watson and Francis Crick. Now this is known, it is possible to solve the genetic code to some extent. For example, it has been found that DNA is capable of specifying the order in which amino acid units are built into a protein molecule. The bases in the DNA chain are arranged in groups of three called *codons.* Each of these codons tells the cell which amino acid to attach next to the growing protein chain. The reaction is actually performed in cell components called *ribosomes* which move along a

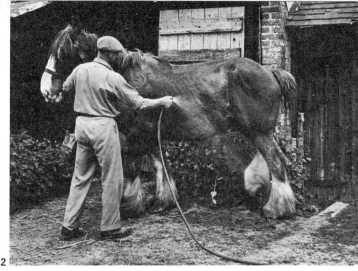

1 Carbon tetrachloride, a simple organic chemical, is extremely useful in fighting petrol fires. Water would merely float the blazing petrol, so spreading the fire.

2 Insecticides and pesticides are a major industry based on petroleum products. Many of these are applied directly to the coats of infected animals.

molecule of 'messenger RNA', formed from the DNA. This messenger RNA is another nucleic acid, which contains ribose instead of desoxyribose, and it too contains the codons. The process is rather like an assembly line: the ribosomes move along the RNA adding another amino acid to the protein they are making as they come to each codon. It is similar to the way in which a car is made, a new bit being added at each step in the assembly line until the structure is complete.

As the groups of three bases forming codons can consist of any selection of the four bases in DNA there are 64 possible combinations ($4 \times 4 \times 4$). Each of these codons specifies an amino acid, although most of the amino acids correspond to

The efficacy of chloroform as an anaesthetic was first established by Sir James Young Simpson, who pioneered its use in surgery and childbirth.

more than one combination. There are also codons corresponding to 'start' and 'stop' so the sequence of bases along the length of a DNA molecule is a sort of computer programme for building up proteins. As proteins are responsible for the synthesis of all the other compounds present in the cells of living organisms the DNA is effectively the ultimate information store.

There is one more type of polymer which occurs in the body which should be mentioned. This is glycogen. It occurs mainly in the liver and is one of the body's ways of storing energy. It is a polymer made up of many thousands of glucose molecules. When these glucose molecules are required to supply energy to the body, they are split off and transported by the blood-stream to their site of action. This is why there is always some glucose in the blood. When the body is obtaining glucose faster than it is using it, more glycogen

is deposited. The structure of glycogen differs from the other substances described here in that it possesses many cross-links between the chains, and therefore occurs as more of a solid mass.

Not all long-chain chemicals are polymers. The soaps and synthetic detergents are also long, thin molecules; their backbone is composed simply of a chain of carbon atoms each carrying two hydrogen atoms. These substances also owe their typical properties to the shape of their molecules. One of the main functions of detergents is to remove greases which get on to clothes. Oily things are hydrophobic; that is, they tend to avoid water and stick to other surfaces. The principal action of a detergent is to render the greases water-soluble so that they can be rinsed away.

Carbon for cleanliness

The carbon and hydrogen (or hydrocarbon) end of the detergent molecule sticks to the grease because oily things are also made of hydrocarbon chains. However, the other end of the detergent molecule is a hydrophilic (water-liking) group which has an affinity for water. The result is that the detergent covers the surface of the grease particle with the hydrophobic groups on the inside and the hydrophilic ones sticking out. The grease-detergent complex, known as a *micelle,* is then free to float off into the water.

Soaps are really a special type of detergent which can be made by boiling natural fats with an alkali. In the soaps the hydrophilic group is the sodium salt of an organic acid. Soaps have the disadvantage that they do not work very well in hard water because the calcium and magnesium salts present in this water react to form the calcium and magnesium salts of the soaps. As these are not soluble in water, they form an unpleasant scum and use up much of the soap which is wanted for washing.

These are only a few of the many hundreds of kinds of organic compounds which have been manufactured by organic chemists. The skill of these chemists lies in making new substances, and determining compositions of new and unknown substances.

Farming with machinery

Agriculture depends on tilling and cultivating the soil and collecting the harvest. Modern machines, which can perform highly specialized operations, are causing a revolution in farming.

1

2

3

1 In many parts of the world traditional methods of agriculture are still used. Too poor to buy machinery, this Asian farmer uses water buffalo to drag a plough through the rice fields.

2 The Russians have developed a tea-harvester, which does the work of countless labourers. This harvester not only cuts the leaves on the bushes but also 'selects' the tender ones.

3 Picking machines, which strip the ripe bolls from rows of cotton plants, move slowly across a large plantation on a collective farm in the Pushkin District of the U.S.S.R.

WHEN OUR DISTANT ANCESTORS ceased to be nomads and began to settle down in agricultural communities to grow their food instead of hunting for it, they tilled the ground with a pointed stick which was pushed through the soil to cut furrows two or three inches deep. The pointed stick was the first farm implement and from it stemmed the host of ingenious and complicated machines which now serve the highly mechanized industry of farming.

Machinery in a factory does its work more efficiently, quickly and cheaply than a human worker, but mechanizing a farm poses many more problems than installing factory machines. A machine in constant use is always much more economical than are human hands, so explaining why many highly mechanized factories work shifts to

keep the machinery operating as long as possible. On the other hand, few farm machines, except tractors, can be found tasks that keep them in action for more than a week or two every year.

Yet the variety of tasks that could be done by machinery on the farm is far greater than in a factory. On a farm each of the scores of different tasks suitable for machinery needs its own specific machine designed for a specific job. Thus a mowing machine may be used for not more than ten days in the year on the average farm, while a trailer binder may work for only a fortnight every 12 months. This means that a mechanized farm has a variety of expensive machines which lie idle for most of the year and the conditions under which they must work change from season to

season, from hour to hour and even from field to field. Changes in weather and soil conditions are always liable to interrupt their smooth working.

It was the modern tendency towards larger farms that inspired much of the agricultural machinery now in use. Although so many agricultural machines are in operation for comparatively so little time, the farmer finds them more economical than employing large numbers of labourers. A farm machine works hour after hour tirelessly and efficiently so long as it is supplied with motive power and has someone to operate it. During harvesting, for example, one machine with a crew of two or three men will complete in a day the amount of work that would occupy ten men for several days; the time saved is worth far more than the price of a machine and the cost of operating it.

One of the most revolutionary agricultural machines was the self-propelled combine harvester. As the machine moves forward, revolving arms in front pull the growing grain towards a platform, where a row of scissor-like clippers cuts the crop about three inches from the ground. The cut stalks are then carried by a conveyor and elevator to a spiked cylinder in which the grain is threshed. The grain then falls on to a vibrating pan across which blasts of air from a fan blow away the chaff. Next the cleaned grain falls through a sieve into a chute and on to an endless screw to a storage bin. In some machines the bin delivers the grain to a device that pours it into sacks, or the grain may be fed into a tractor-drawn waggon for delivery to a silo. The straw is carried on racks to the rear of the harvester where it is baled and dropped on the field.

Combine harvesters developed from a machine called the crop stripper invented in Australia in 1845. At that time Australia was embarking upon large-scale wheat-growing for export, but the labour needed for traditional harvesting was both scarce and expensive. The stripper was the answer to cheap harvesting. As the machine moved forward, drawn by a team of horses, revolving blades geared to the transport wheels stripped the wheat from the ears, which were then winnowed mechanically and the grain shovelled into waggons for carriage to the bagging sheds. As the grain was the only part of the crop considered worth harvesting, the straw and chaff were left on the field and later ploughed in. Australian strippers were exported to the United States where they were greatly improved and developed into the combine harvesters, which were in general use by about 1917.

The first combine harvesters were towed by teams of as many as 30 or 40 horses or mules. Later, steam tractors were used until the internal-combustion engines enabled the combine to be completely self-contained and self-propelled.

Steam tractors

Until the invention of the steam engine, ploughs had for thousands of years been drawn by horses one furrow at a time. The first attempt at mechanization was a steam engine at both ends of the field which hauled the plough by a steel cable. The engine moved across the ends of the field as each furrow was cut. Later, steam traction-engines were used to pull a battery of two or three ploughs. But the engines were so heavy that they rolled the ground and made it difficult for the following plough-shares to cut into.

The introduction of the internal-combustion-engined tractor made possible efficient and economical mechanical ploughing. The tractors now in use can pull a plough having six or more shares, so enabling one man to plough a field in a fraction of the time that would be needed by a horse-drawn plough.

Without the tractor, much of modern mechanized farming would be impossible. Bigger and more effective reapers and mowers, harrows and rollers, drilling and

1

2

had a rake at the rear which covered the seed with soil as it was planted.

From the horse-drawn seeding machines developed the tractor-hauled, multi-purpose planters now in use. Seed and fertilizer are contained in hoppers from which tubes lead to the soil. In front of each tube is a steel drill. As the machine moves forward, each drill punches a hole into which the seed falls through the tube. Behind the tubes are devices that cover the seed with soil. The flow of seed and fertilizer is controlled by the opening and closing of shutters which are mechanically adjusted so that the right amount of seed and fertilizer are put into the ground according to the crop and type of soil. The drills are also adjusted to ensure that the seed is planted in the correct quantity at the best depth to ensure germination and growth. Some of the more sophisticated seeding machines also deposit herbicides and pesticides and have meters that register the amount of seed sown per acre and the number of acres sown from each filling of the hoppers.

Somewhat similar to the seeding machine is that used for planting seedlings and small and tender plants. The machine opens a broad furrow of even depth and width wherein the roots of the plants are deposited by a continuous chain of rubber fingers. An automatic device then presses the soil around the roots. One seeding or planting machine can do in one day the amount of work that formerly required the labour of 20 skilled men.

One of the most ingenious seeders now coming into use on large vegetable-growing farms is the tape-planter. The seeds, together with appropriate fertilizer, are enclosed in long gelatine, plastic or petroleum-based tape. The tapes are wound on to drums carried on a machine that cuts a furrow. At the same time drums

1 Before the advent of modern machinery, land clearing was laborious and slow work. Now scrub land and young saplings can be felled and pulped in one single operation.

2 On small farms where a combine harvester is too cumbersome, the ripe corn is still cut with a 'binder'. The sheaves are collected and stacked by hand and threshed at a later stage.

3 Some processes on farms are still only semi-automated. Young kale plants are fragile and they must be fed individually into the machine which plants them in the ground.

4 Until relatively recently sheep were sheared by hand. Power-operated clippers are now widely used with the result that a single labourer can shear several hundred animals a day.

5 A combine harvester cuts the corn and threshes it in one single operation. The grain, free of the straw, is either put in sacks or, as here, blown into a separate trailer.

sowing machines, and manure and fertilizer distributors can all be towed by a tractor. And as two or more of any one type of machine can be hauled by a single tractor, acres of ground can be treated in a working day.

Sowing seed by hand is inevitably a wasteful process, as some parts of the soil receive too much seed and some none at all. One of the first attempts to mechanize sowing was made in the early eighteenth century by the Englishman Jethro Tull, a barrister turned farmer, who did much to encourage a scientific approach to agriculture. Unfortunately, Tull's machine was not only very costly but it was far too complicated for use by unskilled labour.

It was not until the mid-nineteenth century that a really efficient machine was designed for sowing seed. It consisted of a long hopper mounted on two wheels and drawn by a horse. Projecting downwards from the hopper containing the seed were a number of evenly spaced tubes each ending in a hollow spike. As the machine was drawn across the field, the spikes dug ridges into which the seed fell through the tube. Sometimes the machine

unwind the tape, laying it in the furrow, which a scraper at the rear of the planter covers with soil. The moisture in the soil then dissolves the tape, leaving the seed free to germinate. The machine is capable of laying a dozen or more tapes of seed simultaneously.

Devising a machine for lifting potatoes efficiently was a problem that for long defied solution by agricultural engineers. The trouble was that machines could lift the potatoes but they also lifted stones and clods of earth. Various devices were tried to separate the potatoes from unwanted material, but none was really successful and entailed a great deal of hand-picking.

The problem was eventually solved by the electronic potato-harvester which became available to farmers in 1969. As the potatoes, stones and clods are lifted they fall on to a belt where they are spread out by mechanical fingers and carried past a battery of 16 X-ray beams each shining on to a form of photo-electric detector cell. The detector cells can recognize the differences in the densities of objects passing between them and the X-ray source. Stones and clods are identified by the detector cells as being of greater densities than potatoes. Through electronic relays, the cells signal to mechanical finger-units which then push the stones, clods or other material of greater density than the potatoes off the belt.

By using the electronic potato-lifter, one man can do the work that formerly employed six men in sorting. Equally ingenious machines are available for harvesting carrot, beet and other root crops. There are also machines for harvesting fruit in orchards and for picking tomatoes and peas.

If fruit- and vegetable-picking machines are to operate efficiently, the objects they gather must be of approximately the same size and shape. This has led to the development of, for example, rounder and smaller tomatoes and potatoes.

The raising of fruit and vegetables under glass has made tremendous strides of recent years through the use of electronic and mechanical devices. Glasshouses can be equipped with photo-electric cells that switch on infra-red and other beneficial illumination when natural light fails through overclouding; thermostats turn on artificial heating when the temperature drops below a certain reading; and time-controlled sprays provide artificial rain exactly when it is needed. By these means

1 The first machines on farms were steam driven. The steam engine itself, like the modern tractor, was multi-purpose. Here, by means of a belt-drive it is working a threshing machine.
2 This potato picker can harvest 17 acres per day. Electronic detector cells in the machine distinguish between clods of earth and potatoes, which are then separated.
3 Intensive farming calls for more and more technology. In this modern feeding and dairy unit in East Germany, a herd of cows can be milked simultaneously by machine.

many fruits and vegetables, once considered strictly seasonal, are available nearly all the year round at economic prices. This availability is increasing due to new methods of controlled ripening which irons out the seasonal glut which follows the harvest, and the fruit can be marketed out of season. Better storage methods and pest control also benefit the year-round sale of some vegetables.

Contented cows

On dairy farms the traditional milkmaid with her bucket and stool has been replaced by milking machines which deliver the milk direct into tanks for storage until pumped into road or rail tankers for transport to the pasteurization or other processing plants. On many farms the cattle are kept in heated byres and fed on a carefully balanced diet brought to them on conveyors. Contented cows mean a rich and plentiful milk yield and to keep their cows contented many dairy farmers provide their herds with soft lights and soothing music.

One of the most highly mechanized branches of agriculture is poultry farming, as exemplified in the battery system. The fowls are automatically fed at fixed intervals and the eggs they lay are stamped with the date and carried directly to the packing sheds. Automatic counters record the individual laying of each hen.

What will farming be like in the future? Judging by the tremendous strides that have been made in mechanization during the past 50 years, farms of the future will bear little resemblance to those of today. According to the survey carried out by a panel of agricultural scientists and engineers, much farming will become completely independent of the weather by erecting huge glass or plastic domes to cover areas of ten or more acres. The moisture of the soil within the domes and the amount of heat and light it receives will be automatically controlled merely by turning dials. In this manner the best possible environment will be created for the growing of crops.

Electronic-eyed machines will plant seeds by pneumatic injection and the seeds will be coated with chemical fertilizers, herbicides and insecticides. Machines fitted with electronic devices and computerized fingers will decide when a crop is ripe for harvesting.

On wheat fields and other areas too big for covering with glass or plastic domes, machines will be pulled by driverless tractors controlled by computer tape, buried wires or sensing devices. Hovercraft will be used for spraying, and there will be machines able to harvest one crop and simultaneously plant another.

Techniques for breeding plants designed for mechanical harvesting will make tremendous advances. Tall wheat stalks will have given way to new, squat plants like miniature fir trees. In this way they will absorb more energy from the sun and the ears will be concentrated at the top for easier harvesting.

Livestock farms of the future will bear little resemblance to those of today. Instead of grazing land, the landscape will be dotted with many-storeyed buildings, like blocks of flats, occupied by cattle, sheep, pigs and poultry. The temperature, air, light and humidity within the buildings will be precisely regulated to provide the stock with the best possible environment. Waste products from the animals will be pumped directly to plants for conversion into solid and liquid fertilizers.

According to the agriculture futurist, farmers will have to have an expert knowledge of big-business management, electronics, computers, botany, biochemistry and biophysics while farm labourers will have to be technicians with the professional skills needed to operate the sophisticated equipment.

Farming with chemicals

Farming, traditionally the most backward industry of all, is undergoing its own 'Industrial Revolution'. New chemicals — insecticides, fungicides and plant hormones — are changing the face of the farm.

FARMERS WERE THE FIRST manufacturing chemists, although the modern farmer would be very surprised indeed if he were told so. When a farmer sows a field he plants thousands of tiny chemical compounds and the soil acts as a laboratory in which mass chemical reactions take place to produce the crop that will be harvested. For thousands of years farmers knew nothing of the actual chemistry of agriculture and were content to accept that something went on in the soil to give them a crop: they let nature do the actual chemistry, their only contribution to the actual processes being the application of manure. Insects were laboriously removed by hand, while weed pests were suffered unmolested, as were most of the plant diseases.

In order to achieve healthy growth, plants need in varying degrees some 22 of the 92 natural elements. The most important of these are hydrogen and oxygen (present in water) and sulphur, chlorine, potassium, phosphorus, silicon, magnesium, iron, sodium, nitrogen, calcium. Most of these occur in the soil in the form of soluble compounds. About ten more elements, including zinc, copper, boron and iodine have a marked influence on plant growth. These are called *trace elements,* because only very small quantities or traces of them are needed for plant development and in general they are always present in the soil in sufficient amounts. Many of what might be called the agricultural elements are normally present in sufficient quantities in most soils that are well watered by the rain and given sufficient fresh air by periodical ploughing.

Essential elements

Nitrogen, potassium and phosphorus are the most essential of all the agricultural elements as they supply plants with the food that makes them grow. Although these elements are naturally present in the soil, they are soon depleted by plant growth. By the time a ton of wheat is ready for harvesting, it has taken from the soil in which it grew 47 pounds of nitrates, 18 pounds of phosphates and 12 pounds of potash, with a consequent reduction in the soil's fertility. Each of these elements has its own particular function in ensuring the growth of a healthy plant. Potassium is essential to the production of seed, and also inhibits many of the fungoid diseases. Phosphorus is mainly a root food, while nitrogen is necessary for the development of root, stem and leaves. Yet any one of these elements is useless without the other two. Thus a soil exceptionally rich in nitrogen but with a low potassium or phosphorus content would not produce healthy plants.

1 Fleecing without shears. After treatment with a growth-prevention drug, the sheep's wool can easily be removed by hand.
2 Scientists at a plant pathology laboratory examine wheat seedlings to test the results of treatments for leaf rust disease.

On wild and uncultivated land, the elements taken from the soil by growing plants are replaced when the plants die and fall to the ground. This is because phosphorus, for example, forms part of the living substance of plants and returns to the soil when they decay. Similarly, soils consisting of clays and feldspar normally contain an adequate supply of potassium which is restored when the plants wither. On farmland, however, plants are grown to be removed when they ripen. Consequently, the elements taken from the soil during their growth are not replaced, which is why agricultural land has to be re-fertilized artificially.

When Man first began to cultivate the soil, he found that crops would not grow in the same soil year after year. He realized that something was wrong with the soil, but he did not know what or why. So he solved his problem by abandoning the land and cultivating a new piece. Then he discovered that if ground that had grown crops was left for a couple of seasons the soil again became fertile. So he learned about letting ground lie fallow.

covery of the large deposits of guano or seabird droppings on the shores and islands of the South American coasts.

But agricultural scientists soon realized that the deposits of natural fertilizers were not unexhaustible, and that if farming was to keep pace with increasing population something must be done to manufacture fertilizers. To meet the demand, the now gigantic fertilizer industry was established as a result of research by chemists who devoted their energies to solving the problem.

Although farm manure is still the best enricher of agricultural land, it plays a steadily decreasing part in modern farming, particularly since horses have been largely replaced by tractors. By far the greater part of the fertilizers now applied to farmland are manufactured, and the annual production runs into hundreds of millions of tons. One of the great advan-

It was the farmers of ancient Rome who found that their land produced bigger and richer crops if farm waste was spread on the ground and ploughed in. That was the beginning of artificial fertilization and the start of agricultural chemistry. Among the fertilizers which have been used since Roman times are sewage, farm manure, wood-ash, mussel and lobster shell, powdered limestone and marble. The latter is a form of soil consisting of clay and carbonate of lime. For centuries the chief source of applied phosphates was raw bones, which were ground into powder and then spread over the soil. Wood-ash provided the soil with the essential potash. But the most valuable of all the early applied fertilizers was farmyard manure. A ton of farm manure contains on average 20 per cent potassium, 15 per cent nitrogen and 10 per cent phosphorus. In addition to its fertilizing properties, farm manure improves soil by retaining moisture.

Although the need for fertilizing farmland was, therefore, being slowly appreciated, very little was understood about the actual chemistry involved. Even by the mid-eighteenth century virtually all that was known was that certain salts, especially potassium nitrate (saltpetre) promoted growth. It was wrongly thought that plants obtained their carbon from the humus content of the soil in which they grew.

It was fortunate that science turned its attention to agriculture when it did, for world population has steadily increased since the mid-nineteenth century. Had not science shown the way to grow bigger and better crops, there would have been worldwide starvation by the beginning of the present century. Long before that, the supply of farmyard manure and the production of potash from wood-ash would have supplied only a fraction of the increasing need for fertilizers.

Some alleviation of the shortage of fertilizers, that was steadily becoming more alarming, was provided by the dis-

1 A modern version of the old sheep-dip. Sheep channelled into the metal trough are sprayed with insecticides and fungicides developed experimentally by agricultural chemists.
2 Spraying vines in Champagne, France. Growing grapes require careful attention to ensure that they do not fall victims to a variety of fungus and insect-borne infections.
3 One side-effect of over-use of fertilizer is to encourage the growth of algae in nearby ponds and streams. These 'blooms' consist of millions of tiny green organisms.

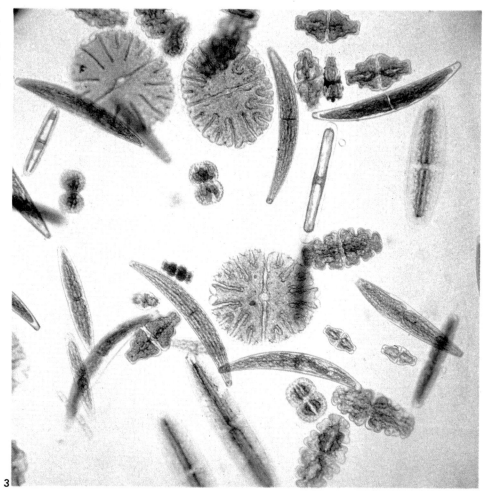

tages of synthetic fertilizers is that they are generally easier to apply to the soil than are natural fertilizers, especially when mechanical spreaders are used. Moreover, synthetic fertilizers can be tailor-made to specific types of soil or crops.

But the most efficient of natural or synthetic fertilizers would be useless to the farmer if his crops were to be weed-ridden, devoured by insects and stricken by disease before they could be harvested. The chemist has now provided agriculture with increasingly effective weapons in the farmer's constant war on these pests.

Practically every plant disease can now be prevented or limited by chemical means. An example is wheat, one of the world's most important food crops. Not so very long ago, one or other of these fungoid diseases, rust, smut and bunt, were present to a greater or lesser extent in every wheatfield. All three diseases cause greatest damage on well-fertilized land. This is because the richer the soil the more the wheat growing on it can provide nourishment for the fungi, which multiply very rapidly.

Various fungicides were compounded to combat rust, smut and bunt, but they all proved ineffective. The problem of defeating the depredations of these fungi seemed insoluble until scientists hit on the idea of treating the wheat seed with chemicals that destroy the spores before the wheat is sown.

Once upon a time the only way to keep weeds in check, and prevent them from either overcrowding the growing crops or taking nourishment from the soil and depriving the crop of wanted nutrients, was to remove the weeds by hand. The development of efficient herbicides was a particularly difficult problem, because weeds are themselves plants and any spray applied to a crop is just as likely to kill the crop plants as the weed plants. One solution to the problem is to spray the field with a weed-killer before the crop is sown. By the time the field is ready for sowing, the herbicide has destroyed the weeds and become mixed with the soil so that it is harmless.

Selective herbicides

Another type of weed-killer depends upon the fact that certain chemical compounds destroy plants at a specific stage of their growth. Fortunately, most weeds grow faster than food plants, so the field is sprayed with a herbicide that kills the more advanced weeds without seriously harming the young crop. The herbicide is then dispersed throughout the soil and becomes innocuous long before it could damage the crop. Considerable success has also been achieved in the development of selective herbicides that destroy weed plants and leave plants unharmed.

The development of insecticides has also been successful. Some selectively kill pests, while others render the males or

1 On a modern Texas ranch, a high-pressure jet of an anti-parasitic fluid is wielded by a cow-hand. Modern chemicals greatly assist the rancher and cut cattle losses.
2 An entomologist weighs a locust using a specially sensitive insect balance. Careful studies of insects assist farmers in their constant war against destructive insect pests.

1 An electronic meter in use to test the amount of lean meat on a pig. Scientific aids like these are developed by agricultural scientists on experimental farms throughout the world.

2 Testing an insecticide for use on tobacco plants. The tiny Perspex and nylon gauze cage prevents aphids and other insects escaping from the chemically treated plants.

females sterile and so prevent the pests from breeding. Some insecticides destroy the eggs or grubs. Even more remarkable are the systemic insecticides, such as *octamethyl pyrophosphoramide,* which render plant juices poisonous to insects but are non-toxic to the plants or to the mammals that feed on them. These types of insecticides hold considerable promise of solving the problem of the serious effects which many of the insecticides now used have on wild life, particularly birds.

Rodents destroy a considerable amount of crops, and various poisons have been evolved to keep them in check, but most are unselective and prove just as fatal to farm stock as to rodents. Attempts have been made to introduce selective and contagious disease among rodents. Myxomatosis was an example of this against rabbit pests, but it had the disadvantage of driving foxes, which normally hunt rabbits, into chicken runs in search of food.

Besides providing farmers with an unlimited supply of fertilizers and efficient pesticides, scientists have been working on plant hormones to provide bigger and better crops in a shorter time and to grow larger crops on smaller areas of land. It has been found that certain relatively simple organic substances, which can be synthesized cheaply and in quantity, have considerable effect on plant growth. Some of these synthetics promote root formation and are revolutionizing the propagation of plants from cuttings. But the application of scientific knowledge to farming has not been wholly beneficial. Many of the chemicals now being used are extremely powerful, and are not always applied with sufficient caution. Nitrate fertilizers, for example, can, if over-used, drain into rivers and lakes, where they encourage the growth of algae. The algae in turn can form a dense, thick mat of vegetation, hindering navigation and lowering vital oxygen levels of the water. If this process is allowed to go too far the lake or river can be rapidly exhausted and unable to absorb sewage and waste.

Again, some insecticides and weed-killers are known to be long-lasting in the soil and poison animals much higher up the food-chains.

Some agricultural scientists foresee a day when the farmer will be free of the soil and independent of the vagaries of the weather. This Utopia will be brought about by growing plants without soil. The seeds are sown in beds of fibre or gravel through which circulates a solution containing all the fertilizing and nutrient elements essential to plant growth. The plants can be sown in beds or trays several tiers high in air-conditioned buildings which can be maintained at the correct temperature for any particular crop. In this way crops can be raised in any kind of climate from the torrid heat of the tropics to the zero conditions of the Arctic or Antarctic.

Composition of the nutrient fluid varies according to the type of plants under cultivation. Moreover, ripening can be accelerated by adding to the fluid high levels of appropriate nutrients. After the nutrient fluid has passed through the fibre or gravel beds, it drains into tanks and is pumped back on to the crops.

Amongst the many advantages of *hydroponic* cultivation, intensive application of the principle enables normally annual crops to be harvested two or more times a year; the properties of the bedding material being constant, the constituents of the nutrient fluid can be standardized to within fine limits for any particular type of plant; there is greater control over weeds, disease and insect pests; greater plant yields are obtained than with plants cultivated in conventional conditions; and much larger crops can be raised in a smaller space.

In some parts of the world, tomatoes, cucumbers, and even wheat have been grown by hydroponic culture, and large-scale production of other plants has been undertaken in India, America and the

At a research station, the grass yield of a field is measured after fertilizer treatment. In this experiment grass from a treated area is compared with that from a similar non-treated area.

Middle East. As yet such crops tend to cost more than those grown in the normal way in soil, but many agricultural chemists are convinced that eventually the cost can be lowered below that of conventional farming.

Such a method of farming would have far-reaching social effects. For one thing, it might well be possible to grow more food in less space than is used at present, while the full resources of mechanized harvesting could be used to reap the hydroponic crops. Again, if the cost of hydroponic and similar artificial crop-growing methods can be brought down, the benefits in terms of feeding the Earth's potential population increase would also be considerable. For the first time, farming would cease to be dependent on the vagaries of the weather, and could be dealt with in the same way as any other industrial process. Whether or not hydroponic farming can be made sufficiently cheap to be practicable on a mass scale, we can be certain that science will have an increasing impact on agriculture.

Index

Figures in *italics* indicate an illustration of that subject. The letters a, b and c indicate the first, second and third columns of the page respectively.

A

Abacus 49a
Absorption spectroscopy 183a
Accumulator (secondary cell, storage cell) 209b-210a
Acetic acid 122
Activated sludge 167c, 168a
Adenine 231c
Adipic acid 218a, 230b
Aerosol bottle 160c
Air 137a-139c
  carbon dioxide in 189c
  pollution of 137a-139c, 168c, 189c
Air conditioning 137c-139b, *137*
Aldebaran 80a
Alexandria, Greek science at 60b-c
Algae 240a, *238*
Alloys, alloying 201a-204c
Alloy steels 208a-c
Alpha Centauri 73a, 80a-b
Alternating current 16a
  and electric clocks 148a
Alum Bay (Isle of Wight) 37b
Aluminium 197b, *199*
  alloys of 203c-204a, *202*
  as conductor of electricity 198b
  extraction of 211c-212a
Aluminium bronze 203c
Aluminium-oxide ceramics 227b
Amides 230a
Amino acids 231b
Ammonia atomic clock 30a, 148b
Ammonium cyanate 229a
Anaerobic decomposition 168a
Analytical chemistry 181a-183c
Analytical engine (Babbage) 49c-50a
Anaximander 84b
Anchor escapement 146c-147a *147*
Anderson Boves trepanner 119c
Andromeda, nebula in (Messier 31) 81b, 84b-c, *79, 80*
Androsterone 248b
Angle of incidence (light) 149c
Angle of refraction (light) 149c
Aniline dye 216c
Anion 210a
Anode 209a
Antares 80a
Anthracite 121c
Anti-knock ingredients for petrol 196a
Apollo lunar module *103*
Aqualung 140a, *143*
Aquanauts, 139c-140a
Aqueduct, Roman 107c
  Pont du Gard 107c, *106*
Arc furnace, electric 11c, 208a-b, *207*
Arch, in engineering 106c, 107c, bridges 107c, 108a
Archaeology, radioactive dating in 100a-c
Archimedes (ship) 136b
Arc lamp 11c
Arcturus 80a
Arecibo (Puerto Rico), radio telescope at *61*
Aristarchus of Samos 60a-b
Aristotle 59c, 140c
Aromatics (crude oil) 193b
Arquebus 186a
Arsenic 178c-179c
Artificial fibres, *see* Fibres, artificial
Ascorbic acid, *see* Vitamins, Vitamin C
Asimov, Isaac 79c-80a, 80b
Asphalt, *see* Bitumen
Asteroids 76c

Astrology 58a-59a
Astronauts 139c, 146a, *139*
  clothing of 140a
  on moon 29a, *139*
  space walk by *35*
Astronomical clock *84*
Astronomy 57a-84c
  ancient Greek 59a-60c
  astrology and 58a-59a
  Chinese 57a
  computers in 64c
  history of 57a-60c
  instruments used in 61a-64c
  radio 64b-c, 82a, 84c
  see also Radio telescopes, *see also* Moon ; Solar system ; Stars ; Sun ; Universe
Athletics 169b-170a
  first records of 169b
  spiked running shoes introduced in 171c
  Tartan track for 171c-172a, *172*
  timing devices for 169b-170a
Atlantic Ocean, first bridged by wireless 37a-c
Atmosphere, *see* Air
Atomic bomb 93b, 94a, 187c, energy source of 90a
Atomic clock, *see* Clock, atomic
Atomic energy, 93a-96c
Atomic power station, *see* Power station, nuclear
Aurora Borealis 89a
Autoclaves 229c-230a
Automation 53a-56c
Aviation, civil
  radar used in 26b-27c, *27, 28*
Axe, prehistoric *186*
Aztecs
  calendar of *59*
  observatory of *57*

B

Baade, W. 82a
Babbage, Charles 20b-c, 49b-50a
Babylonians 57b-c
Bach, Johann Sebastian *44*
Bain, Alexander 148a
Baird, John Logie 39b-c, *33*
Bakelite 216a, 218b-c, 219a, *147*
Balance wheel (in watches) 147b, *147*
Ball bearing 103c
Ballistic Missile Early Warning Station (Fylingdales) 26b, *25*
Balloons
  in astronomy 62a-c
  in meteorology 28c
Bardeen, J. 16a
Barnard's Star 80b-c
Base two (binary) number system computer use of 51a
Bat, echo-sounding used by, *26*
Battery 210a
  for electric vehicles 210a
  torch 209a-b
Bauxite 211c, *199*
Bayeaux tapestry, comet in *59*
Bazooka 188a, *187*
Beam bridge 107c-108a
Bearing (engineering) 103c-104a
Bell, Alexander Graham 33a
  his telephone 33a, *36*
Bell pit (coal-mining) 118a
Benbecula, radio beacon on *98*
Ben Franklin (research ship) 144c
Benz, Otto 113a, *113*
Benzene 218a
Beriberi 242a-b
Bertone, Nuccio *102*
Beryllium, alloyed with steel 204b
Beryllium-oxide ceramics 227b
Bessemer, Henry 206a
  Bessemer process 206a-207c, 208a

Beta rays 17b
Betelgeuse 80a
Betel nut 246c
Bicheroux process 228b
Bifid bow (ship) 134a
Big bang theory 83c
Big Bertha (gun) *185*
Bile acids 247c, 248a
Binary number system, *see* Base two number system
Binoculars, prism 150a
Biological warfare 188a-b
Bireme 134a
Bismuth 197b
Bitumen (asphalt)
  in road surfacing 109a, 110c-111b, c
  Trinidad asphalt lake 111b, *110*
Blast furnace 205b-206a
Blister steel 205b
Block (printing), *see* Photoengraving
Bloembergen, Nicolaas 30a
Blood, in forensic science 179c-180a
Bolometer, *see* Germanium bolometer
Bomb 187c
  see also Atomic bomb, Hydrogen bomb
Bondi, Hermann 82a
Bone china 226a
Boot, H.A.H. 26a
Borax bead test 181b
Boulton, Matthew 130a
Bow (weapon) 185c-186a
Bragg, Sir Lawrence 21c-22a, 23a, 24a, 199c-200a
Bragg, Sir William Henry 21b, c-22a 23a-b
Bragg's Law 22a
Brake, hydraulic, *see* Hydraulic brake
Brass 203c
Brass musical instruments 48a-49a
  brass band *42*
Bridge 106c, 107c-108c
  arch 107c, 108a
  beam 107c-108a
  cantilever 107c, 108a-b, *105*
  suspension 107c, 108a, b
  Sydney Harbour bridge 108a
  Tower Bridge *107*
Britannia (paddle-steamer) *125*
British Broadcasting Corporation, 39b, c
  Crystal Palace aerial of *39*
Broadcasting (radio) 38a-39b
Bronze 203b-c, 197a
Brunel, Marc Isambard, 108c
Bullet, in forensic science 178a, 180c
Buna S 220a
Bunt 239b
Burgular alarm, photo-electric 212c
Butadiene 220c

C

Cable, electric 203c
  first transatlantic 33a, 37a, c
Cadmium, in nuclear reactor 94a
Caesium 197b
  atomic clock 148c
Calcium, alloying of 203c
Calculating machine 49a-50a
  see also Computer
Calder Hall atomic power station 96c
Calendar, Aztec *59*
Camera 153a-b
  f-number on 153b
  focal length of 151b
  fuzziness, cause of, in simple cameras 153a-b
  lens of 150a-152a, 153a-b, *153*
  telephoto 152c
  shutter of 153b
  upside-down image in 153a, *153*

Candle clock 146b
Canes Venatici, nebula in *78*
Cannon 186a, *185*
Canopus 80a
Cantilever bridge 107c, 108a-b, *105*
Capacitor (condenser), in air conditioning 139b
Capella 80a
Car, *see* Motor Car
Carbolic acid, *see* Phenol
Carbon,
  basis of living things 229a, 217a
  carbon 100a-c
  in coal 121b-c
  in nylon 218a
  in oil 121c, 193a-b
  resistivity of 198b
Carbon dioxide, in the atmosphere 189c
Carboniferous period, coal formed in 121b
Carbon steels 208c
Carbon tetrachloride, petrol fires fought with *232*
Cardan shaft 114a
Carothers, Wallace 217a-c, 223b
Cartridge 186b
Caruso, Enrico 45a
Carvel construction (ships) 134b
Cascade casting (steel) 208b
Catalan forge 205a
Catalytic cracking 124b, 196b, 229a, *195, 196*
Catenary 108b
Cathedral
  arch used in building of 107c
  Liverpool *108*
  Wells *107*
Cathode 209a
Cathode rays 21a-b
  cathode-ray tube 11c-12a, 18c-19a
Cation 210a
Cell, electric 209a-210a
  photo-electric cell 212b-c
Cellulose 221a, 223b
Cementation of iron 205a
Cepheid variables 80c, 81c-82a
Ceramics 225a-227b
  bone china 226a
  firing of 225a-b, 226a, *227*
  glazing of 225b
  oxides in 227b
  porcelain 225c-226a
  pottery 225a-b
  refractories 225b-c
Ceres (asteroid) 76c
Chadwick, James *95*
Chain reaction, nuclear 93b-94a, 95c
Challenger, H.M.S. 142b, *141*
Chase (printing) 173b
Chemistry, analytical 181a-183c
  and electricity, *see* Electrochemistry
  industrial 213a-216c
  in farming 237a-240c
  inorganic 181a
  organic 181a, 217a
Chieftain tank *186*
China, the Chinese
  astronomy 57a
  porcelain 225c-226a
China clay (kaolin) 225c-226a
Chlorine, Dumas and 214c
  in water purification 168c
Chromatography 181b, 183b-c, *183*
Chromium plating 210a-c
Chronograph 169b
Chronometer 147b-c
Civil (construction) engineering 101c-102a, 105a-c
Clarinet 43a
Clay
  china clay 225c-226a
  in pottery 225a-b
Clegg, Samuel 122a
Clinker construction (ships) 134b
Clock 146a-148c
  astronomical *84*
  atomic 148b-c, *146*
    ammonia 30a, 148b
    caesium 148c
  candle 146b
  electric 147c-148a
  mechanical 146b-147c
    pendulum in 146c-147c
    spring in 147a-b, *147*

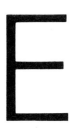

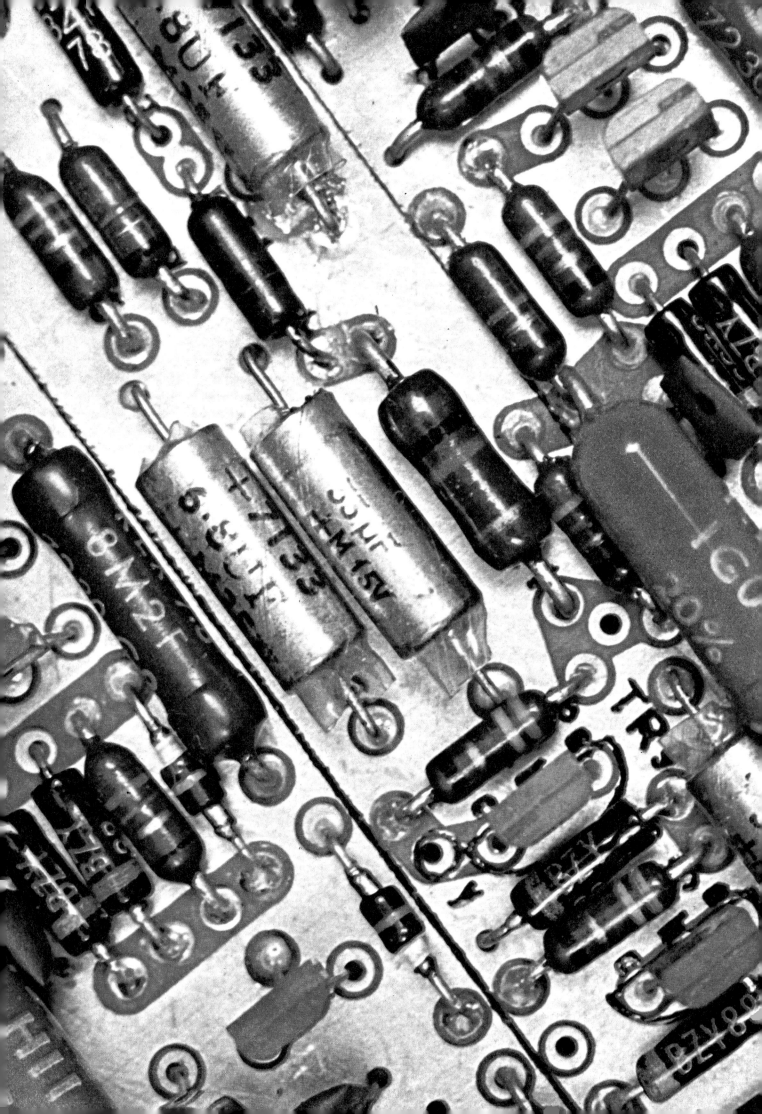